LIFE BETWEEN INNINGS

"a Memoir"
Blessed Beyond Deserving

LEO MOONEY

Copyright © 2012 Leo Mooney
All rights reserved.

ISBN: 1475220863
ISBN 13: 9781475220865

Dedication

I dedicate this book to my three children, **Dionne Reshea Toliusis, Marcus Vaughn Mooney** and **Whitney Renea Allen.** It is my prayer that as they read the pages of this book they will catch a glimpse of the eternal significance a personal relationship with Jesus Christ has on those, imperfect as any of us may be, who yield to the knocking on our heart's door by the Savior, the Risen Lord Himself, and welcome him in. Life generally offers many second chances, as my life so vividly demonstrates, but eternity's doors do not. Once the doors of eternity have slammed shut, there is no second chance to open the door and to "redeem the time."

Acknowledgements

A project of this size doesn't happen in isolation. There are a couple people beyond my wife, Tina Lynn, who I want to thank for their assistance in putting this memoir together.

My sister-in-law, Vicki Herbel, did the first edit and provided invaluable help and insights with regard to my overall writing approach!

Dear friends, Bob and Donna Middendorf, allowed me the use of their lake home on three separate occasions where I could get away and concentrate on finishing the writing. The use of their home was a huge, huge blessing!

Also, my good friend, Mrs. Betty Porter, did the final edit and helped me to tighten up the language and the story lines. Betty was so kind to this novice writer, but she challenged me on several points, which were helpful in developing the final product! Betty is a gem and greatly to be loved and appreciated!

Table of Contents

Dedication — iii
Acknowledgements — v

Spring Training: Introduction — ix
Dugout Interview: Prelude — xiii
Inning #1: The Childhood Years (1947-1959) — 1
Inning #2: The Teenage Years (1959-1965) — 43
Inning #3: The Bible College Years (1965-1968) — 89
Inning #4: The U.S. Air Force Years (1969-1973) — 137
Inning #5: The Liberating Years (1973-1978) — 231
Inning #6: The Searching Years (1978-1984) — 275
Inning #7: The Union Years (1984-2002) — 351
Inning #8: The Retired Years (2002-?) — 449
Inning #9: Epilogue — 511
Star of the Game — 521
Scoreboard Show — 523

About the Author — 537

Spring Training

INTRODUCTION

Every February, professional, college, and even some high school baseball teams head to Florida or Arizona to begin Spring Training. In Spring Training hope springs eternal. Everything is new. Everyone has a chance. No one has lost a real game. When I started writing this book it was like experiencing my own Spring Training and the long season that is baseball. I knew it would take a while to complete, would be somewhat easy and fun in the early going, but would probably be hard to press through those "dog days" of late July and August when it seemed the project would never come to fruition. But, like some baseball seasons, it has ended in triumph with a completed project and one that I am proud of. I have no idea how this project will be received by those who read it, especially my family. But, I am hoping that in some way the stories and anecdotes that I share will reveal a little about me to them, and especially my three children, so that they can know me just a little bit better. I want them to know a little about what has made me tick and a lot about the blessings that God has so graciously bestowed upon me.

I started writing this book in August of 2003 and I am putting the finishing touches on it in March of 2012. Every time I thought I had an "Inning" done I would think of something else that I wanted to include, so I would go back and edit again. Consequently, it was a slow process, a very slow process.

However, in the grand scheme of things, this has been one of the more "fun" things that I have done. At the same time the introspection has been hard, because as you will see I have not always made the best decisions. Revealing some of my faults and failures were not easy to put on paper. But, what I do think you will see is how God has chosen to bless me, not because of good things I have done or good decisions that I have made, but in spite of my sinfulness and failures.

It might be interesting to know that I rarely reveal intimate details about myself to others; I am most definitely a very private person. For years, while working in the power plants of Union Electric (now AmerenUE), it was not uncommon for us guys (and gals) to sit around during our idle time and talk. It was also not uncommon that as we talked some of the guys would share very personal, very intimate details of their lives. It was unbelievable the graphic detail that some of the guys would go into. But, when the conversation would inevitably come around to me, it became somewhat of an inside joke that, *"Oh, we forgot, you don't talk about your personal life."* And, I didn't. It was kind of funny that when Shirley and I were going through our divorce in 1978, none of my friends and co-workers knew, at least initially. It was only when Bill Dorner, who later became one of my better friends, saw my clothes and a few belongings piled into the back seat of my car that my deep secret came out. Bill put two and two together, having recently been "there" himself, and confronted me as to whether I was having marital problems? I finally confessed to him, and eventually to the work crew, that my personal life was going through some very bumpy times.

Keeping personal things hidden was something I developed very early in life. I also learned to cover my tracks pretty well as that was part of the process. Being raised in small Pentecostal churches and spending much of my time in the church and

Introduction

with church people, I realized very quickly, like age 5 or 6, that if you didn't want anything told, then don't invite others to participate with you in your "sin." Rumors and gossip, unfortunately, run rampantly in churches, which is why I suppose the Apostle Paul spent considerable time addressing how we should tame our tongues. But, this should not be surprising, I suppose, as sinners like me frequent the place. So, unlike most kids, if I decided to do something "worldly," something that I shouldn't be doing, I most always did it alone.

My wife, Tina, occasionally jokes that I probably lead a second life that no one else knows about. I never set out for it to be that way, really, but it's probably true to some extent. As an example, I often go out to a movie or to dinner (breakfast/lunch) alone and my doing so will never work its way into the fabric of that day's conversation. And, no, I don't have another family in another town and, "Yes," I have been true-blue and faithful to my bride of 29 years. But, I do things alone; and I enjoy doing things alone. As my exception to that rule, if we were to go out, given the choice, I will/would always take an evening out with Tina, and when she lived with us, our daughter Whitney, rather than going out with another couple or with the crowd. Yet, oddly, I enjoy the large crowds and I enjoy the spotlight. It is just that when the crowds have gone home and the spotlight has been turned off, let me return to seclusion. And, it is there that I find peace and tranquility. It is all so uncluttered.

When I started this book I was not sure how many private or personal stories I would tell. I had hoped that a few would leak out just so that my family would see that I really wasn't this perfect kid or perfect man, not that perfection would be bad, it is just that they will never understand how deeply grateful I am for my Lord and Savior, Jesus Christ, who has shown me great love, great patience, even greater mercy

Life Between Innings

and abundant grace in providing for me, " . . . *oh, such a great salvation! (Hebrews 2:3)."* I so desperately want my children to understand this truth and claim it for themselves! I have truly been blessed beyond deserving and I do not know why except because of His *Grace.* May His grace leak all over each page as I relate to you my *life between innings.*

The Dugout Interview

PRELUDE

I am not sure who introduced me to the *St. Louis Baseball Cardinals* at the ripe old age of six. I seriously doubt that it was my mother, Janie Edith, as she did not became a big fan of the Cardinals until much later in life, in fact sometime after we moved to St. Louis from Salem (Missouri) in 1959. I am quite sure that it was not my sister, Bonnie Jean, who is four years my senior, as she, like mom, was not a true baseball fan until probably late in her high school years. My brother, Douglas Gale, who is six years older than me, was busy with his much older friends during this time of my introduction to sports in general and baseball in particular and we just simply did not do much together until our adult years. However, I guess I would credit him for introducing me to baseball, as he was the one who taught me to hit left-handed when I started playing the game around age four, a trait that followed this right-handed kid into manhood.

Regardless of how or by whom I was introduced to the St. Louis Cardinals, somehow I was, and so my baseball life, as I know it, began around age four or five and by age six I had already developed a growing, driving passion for baseball in general and the *St. Louis Cardinals* specifically. Regardless of what activity I might be involved in, as soon as the Cardinal game came on the air (Salem's radio station *KSMO*), I would be found lying in front of the radio listening to the likes of Harry

Life Between Innings

Caray, Jack Buck and Joe Garagiola give a colorful, often dramatic description of the game. As I listened intently, I would keep score of the game while maintaining the batting order with my baseball cards, flipping over the individual card of each Cardinal or opposing player as they came to bat, then changing out a card when a player was substituted by the manager.

Unfortunately for me the Cardinals were not very good in 1953, 1954, 1955, and so on. In fact, they were not really good until my senior year in high school, that miraculous year of 1964, when they came from so far back that final month of September to overcome the Philadelphia Phillies and the Cincinnati Redlegs on the last day of the season. I can still hear Harry Caray yelling out over the airwaves, *"The Cardinals win the pennant, the Cardinals win the pennant, the Cardinals win the pennant!"* The poor Phillies endured one of the great choke jobs in the history of baseball that season under their manager, Gene Mauch, as they had it all but won, and then didn't, coming into September's stretch drive with a 9 game lead only to lose it. And, as we now know, the Cardinals went on to win the World Series that year dramatically in seven games behind the great, gutsy pitching of Bob Gibson, who faced the likes of Mantle and Maris and those hated *New York Yankees*. But that is a story for another day.

The family still likes to remind me of how in my early years I would be moved to tears (literally) and would kick and stomp at the floor after the frequent Cardinal losses and proclaim, *"I could play better than those stupid Cardinals!"* There was only one person in those years that I could talk to of those dreadful Cardinals and feel that my frustration was understood. My confidant was an older (by my youthful standards) gentleman from *Revival Tabernacle*, our local church. His name was Mr. Rainy Bryant, a postman in the nearby rural community

Prelude

of Sligo. He would from time to time take me with him on his route, which gave us plenty time to talk. Ironically, I discovered professional basketball while visiting at his home one Saturday afternoon as we watched the *St. Louis Hawks* play the *New York Knickerbockers* on his television. We didn't have a TV until we moved to St. Louis in 1959, so being able to watch his TV was a real treat. While the Cardinals remained my passion for years, and still are to a large degree, the *St. Louis Hawks* of the NBA (National Basketball Association) and the *St. Louis University Billikens* would play a large role later in my life as I grew to be a fan, player and coach of "the Great Game" of basketball.

Perhaps my youthful years were no different than most boys raised in a small rural town like Salem, Missouri (population 3000) who lived for nothing more than baseball and basketball. But, it's hard to imagine any boy having a greater passion than I did for either game. Baseball was king, but baseball and basketball together were life. And, while the games were great fun, the real fun and the lasting stories were the ones that developed between innings while we sat on the bench cheering and heckling and trash-talking each other. And, it's because of the great impact of those games on my life and the repartee with the many special guys (and gals) that I have played competitive games with that I have divided the chapters of this book into the same format that became so familiar to me as a kid with my ear glued to the big family radio in the living room, in the car or my new fangled transistor:

- *Spring Training*
- the *Dugout Interview*
- the 9 Innings of the Game
- the *Star of the Game Show*
- the *Scoreboard Show*

just as Harry Caray and Jack Buck did it for me for so many, many years.

xv

Life Between Innings

As the Cardinals have had over the years, I too have had plenty of good innings and a few bad ones. But, I have been blessed, in fact blessed beyond deserving, as God has given to me a great life with great memories, with only two significant regrets. Should I die due to some unforeseen reason here at age 64, I could not complain. God, for reasons only He can know, has been very good to a very undeserving, sinful man. As I detail my life in this book, it will become painfully clear what those two exceptions are, exceptions that still trouble me even today. But, because I kept my nose clean as a kid growing up and because of the many blessings I have enjoyed then and since, coupled with the fact that I have lived a fairly conservative lifestyle over the years, I have avoided facing too many personal issues. That said, unfortunately, I have lived far from perfection, it's just that my skeletons have stayed hidden for the most part. Thank goodness for a loving and forgiving God!!

Some have asked why I would want to write such a memoir as this. The reason for writing this book is very simple. It is not that I have some important message to tell or some exciting stories to relate. I have been and still am much too conservative to have too many exciting stories to tell. You generally need to be a risk taker to have great stories. Now my two older children from my first marriage, Dionne Reshea and Marcus Vaughn, they have some stories to tell, but it is really for them and our youngest daughter, Whitney Renea *(who has lived her youth much like I did under the watchful grace of our Lord)*, that I am writing this book. I never knew my Dad, as he was accidentally killed on the job when I was only four months old. Even today, though I have asked a lot of questions regarding him, I still know very little about who he really was or what he was really like. So, the reason for writing this memoir is simple; I would like for my children to know me better, much better than I knew or know of my father. And, I think I also have a

xvi

Prelude

few memories and a couple important thoughts that I would like to leave them, especially regarding my personal faith and relationship with Jesus Christ. As my season of life rounds the bend of fall and is now rushing headlong into winter, I cannot leave my children any greater gift than for them to know that a right relationship with Jesus Christ truly trumps all else, and my life is the perfect representation of that fact.

Lastly, in an attempt to write a fairly honest accounting of my life, it is not my intent or desire to hurt anyone or to write anything that would be an embarrassment to those that may be mentioned. Consequently, every story I would like to tell cannot be told and every detail that I would like to share cannot be shared. This accounting is obviously my version, my recollection, of what I have seen and what I have done and what I have experienced. As with most stories, there is another version to be told, I am sure, by those who saw or experienced it differently, and I respect their right to have a different view or perspective.

The 1ˢᵗ Inning

THE CHILDHOOD YEARS
1947-1959

In 1947, Harry S. Truman, a Missouri Democrat, was President of the United States having succeeded President Franklin D. Roosevelt on April 12, 1945, upon his death. Under President Truman, Germany surrendered on May 8, 1945, ending World War II in the European Theatre. On August 15, 1945, Japan surrendered on the Asian side of the world bringing a final end to World War II. The St. Louis Baseball Cardinals were closing a very successful era having won the World Series in 1946. However, the Cardinals would not win a pennant or a World Series again until 18 years later. In 1947, Jackie Robinson, playing for the Brooklyn Dodgers, became the first black player to play baseball in the modern era of the major leagues. In June of 1950, the Korean War began and the United States entered into a new era of fighting wars with no plans on how to win them. This was also the debut year for the comic strip "Peanuts." In 1954, Dwight D. Eisenhower, a Republican and a great military figure and Army General during World War II, became President, serving two full terms. In 1955, Ray Kroc opened the first McDonald's Restaurant. President Eisenhower made history again in 1956 when he signed the Federal Aid Highway Act authorizing the construction of the interstate highway system that is so important to our national commerce and personal travel today. In 1958, the face of baseball was changed forever as the New York Giants moved to San Francisco and the

Life Between Innings

Brooklyn Dodgers to Los Angeles. *The face of our nation also began to change that year as armed federal troops were ordered into Little Rock, Arkansas, to ensure the safe entry of nine black students, which became known as the "the Little Rock Nine," into Central High School. In 1959, the Soviet Union jumped ahead of the U.S. in space exploration by launching Sputnik, a space satellite that circled the earth every hour and thirty-five minutes. It was also in 1959 that Fidel Castro and his Cuban Revolution movement took over the country of Cuba and announced that it would be a communist state. This same year the pop music world mourned the loss of Buddy Holly, Ritchie Valens and the Big Bopper, all who died in a plane crash in Iowa. However, Elvis Presley was well on his way to establishing himself as the King of Rock-and-Roll while Alaska became the 49th state of the Union and Hawaii became the 50th.*

My dad, Jewell Lee Mooney, was born on May 1, 1921, in the very rural town of Gang, Missouri, the son of Thomas Lee and Lillie Mae (White) Mooney. My mother, Janie Edith, was born on February 11, 1922, in West Fork, Missouri, an equally rural location, the daughter of William Henry and Marquettia Elvia (Dodd) Anderson. Mom and dad were married in Centerville, Missouri, on the courthouse steps on May 18, 1940.

On Friday, May 2, 1947, at 11:13 A.M., my mother arrived at Bethesda General Hospital in St. Louis, Missouri, to give birth to a 7 pound, 02 ounce, baby boy. And, thus begins my story. Why my dad and mom decided to crown me with the name of Norman Leo, I do not know. I asked Mom that question once and she just simply smiled and stated it was a name she liked. Nevertheless, upon my arrival, my older brother by six years, Douglas Gale (born in Rector, Missouri, September 22, 1941), was there to greet me along with Bonnie Jean (born in St. Louis, Missouri, on July 12, 1943), my older sister by four years.

The Childhood Years 1947-1959

After my birth, I was escorted to our home at 1745 Missouri Avenue near Lafayette Park in St. Louis. Mom and dad had moved there following dad's release from the Army. While serving in the U.S. Army (1942-44), mom was able to join dad in New Orleans for a portion of his service time. Doug and Bonnie were already born at that time and had accompanied her to New Orleans, traveling by train. Previous to this, dad had been transferred to Japan during the height of World War II. While the family has been reluctant to tell us kids the whole story, it seems that dad had become shell-shocked during Japan's shelling of Pearl Harbor. Due to his emotional condition, he was sent back to the USA. He was honorably released from active duty sometime in 1944. Consequently, I was conceived in August of 1946 and became one of the great number of Baby Boomers that arrived upon the scene following World War II.

After arriving home, dad had taken a job as an Insulator-Electrician. So, as the story goes, dad would go away to work and mom stayed at home to care for us three kids in the apartment in St. Louis, Missouri. From a newspaper article I have read, and personal accountings given to me from family members, my dad was away working in LaPlatta, Missouri, a small town near Kirksville, Missouri, when he was killed on September 5, 1947, at the age of 26. I was barely four months old at the time of his death. It appears that he was working in the attic of a small grocery store doing some insulation work coupled with electrical duties. The storeowner did not want to cut the electricity while dad, along with some other men, did their work, as he was afraid that his foodstuff might spoil. It was a very hot day and dad had gone up into the attic off and on all day, and even complained once about being "bit" by some stray electrical wires lying loose in the area where he

Life Between Innings

was working; evidently he had kind of shrugged and laughed it off.

As the day was drawing to a close, it came time for dad to come down from the attic but he had not rung the bell indicating to those below that he was ready to come out. After some time, and becoming a little concerned, one of the men climbed up to check on him and found him unconscious from electrical shock. He was dead on arrival at the hospital. My mother was later told that the electrical current that had struck him was of such low voltage that had it "bit" him earlier in the day it probably would not have killed him. But, since he had made contact with the wire late in the day when he was most likely dehydrated, the low voltage had probably killed him instantly.

Had dad been a member of a strong Labor Union, with concerns for workplace health and safety, or had OSHA (*Occupational Safety and Health Act*) been in place as it is currently, there is every possibility that dad could be alive today. Unfortunately, such was not the case and he died unnecessarily and much too early, leaving a somewhat timid woman with a grade school education to raise three young children.

From all accountings I favor my dad more than Doug and Bonnie. Most of the family, when they describe him, mention that he was a handsome man (*did I mention that it is said that I favor him.*) with a pretty good sense of humor, perhaps even a mischievous side. Although not discussed by the extended family, ever, Dad may have had a way with the ladies that was an irritant to my mom; however, for the most part she tried to put the best face on their relationship and only related some of the negative side of Dad in the years just before her death, and even then, only when questioned rather specifically.

To my knowledge, only my Uncle Leland Mooney, my dad's younger brother, has ever mentioned that he thought he may have been a Christian, based on some observances he had

The Childhood Years 1947-1959

made of dad in a worship service at a local church just a week or two before his death. No one else has ever indicated that Dad had a serious, or even a casual, relationship with our Lord and Savior Jesus Christ, an issue that is obviously very haunting to me personally. The thought of anyone, especially those of our immediate family or those we love intensely, spending an eternity apart from the warmth and fellowship of Jesus Christ our Lord, is painful to consider. This thought helps to keep me on my knees in prayer for my own children, especially Dionne and Marc, my children from my first marriage with Shirley (Redman). Their lives have been marred by bad decision upon bad decision and have given little evidence of God's saving grace, until just recent months. Dionne, with the help of God's angels, has gradually restored her testimony over the past couple of years, renewing her faith in Christ and living in the fellowship of a good church, but it has been a tough battle for her. Marc continues to be plagued by bad decisions and acquaintances and at the time this book was going to print remains incarcerated in an Oklahoma prison and giving no indication of a personal faith in Christ. Whitney, my daughter from my marriage with Tina, has been a joy to watch as she has matured in God and her Christian faith through her teen years and into early adulthood. For this we praise God daily!

Dad was buried in Knuckles Cemetery on Blair's Creek, a graveyard located about 150 or so miles southeast of St. Louis near his parents home at that time in Midridge, Missouri, a very remote and difficult place to get to. The road leading up to the graveyard was a narrow one-lane dirt path, which took us up and over a number of rolling hills and then back down into the valleys. It was necessary to cross several gravel bottom creeks in the process, which were much more suited for horse and buggy traffic than an automobile. It was a source of some chuckles as mom would rarely get stuck driving across these

Life Between Innings

creeks as we would travel to the graveyard on Memorial Day, but many of the men were not so fortunate. When we would visit the graveyard, all the families would meet up together at a designated spot and travel in a convoy. This way, as the cars would be stuck crossing the creeks, there would be plenty of manpower to help push out. Once there, and after some extensive decorating of the graves, we would always enjoy a big dinner on the grounds as the families would jointly spread out their food for all to partake. Here, I would enjoy some of the best variety of homemade, country style foods and the best eating a man, or boy, could possibly hope for. I usually focused on the fresh chicken and dumplings and cornbread dressing, topped off with a huge slice or two of coconut cream pie.

In 1957, mom had dad's body moved to Ellington Memorial Cemetery, a gravesite located on Missouri State Highway 21, just south of Ellington, Missouri, where his parents had moved. The old Blair's Creek site was becoming less and less visited as people moved out of this rural area or died off and the graveyard was not well cared for. The new site was obviously more accessible and later became the gravesite of my Grandpa and Granny Mooney, my dad's parents. Philip, the oldest son of my brother Doug and his wife June, is also buried there, having passed away in November of 1961, within three months of his birth with a heart defect.

Shortly after Dad's untimely death in 1947, Mom decided to move to Salem, Missouri, so that we could be closer to family and to her mom and dad. Evidently, mom received a settlement from the store's insurance company where dad was killed and she used it to purchase a home at 705 West B. Street. This small, two-bedroom, shingle and frame house remained our home, becoming the cornerstone for most of our Salem memories, until moving back to St. Louis in the early summer

The Childhood Years 1947-1959

of 1959. It was here that our family possessed the infamous telephone number of 322-J. If you wanted to call us, you picked up the receiver and the operator would come on and ask, *"Number Please?"* The caller would then say, *"322-J, please,"* and the operator would ring it up, that is unless someone else was already talking on our party line.

Obviously, memories of life in Salem, especially in those early years, are very sketchy. I do not recall my Grandpa (William) Anderson, my mom's dad, as he passed away on October 3, 1949, at age 66, almost two years after our move to Salem. But her mother, Marquettia, lived with us with just two short exceptions, till shortly before the time we moved back to St. Louis. I do not recall grandma, even rarely, doing anything with the family away from the house, although I think my sister Bonnie remembers it differently. I do not recall her helping Mom with the laundry, cleaning house or cooking meals as a general rule. I am told that she had some serious health issues that prevented her from doing too much. I do recall her helping Mom with quilting and with canning, but that is about all. When I think of grandma I think of an old lady with very defined wrinkles lining her face, sitting in her red chair in our living room, a chair from which she rarely moved. She regularly smoked a pipe while sitting in that chair, but would quickly hide it in the recesses of the cushions if a visitor dropped by unexpectedly. No one was to know that she was smoking, but I am quite confident that every visitor to our home had to know that she did since the smoke residue in the air was certainly not the result of anything mom or us kids were doing. My biggest dream, however, was that the chair would catch on fire and expose her for the smoker she was. I know that is evil thinking but she seemed hypocritical to my small and childish mind and I would have thought it justified if it had ever happened.

Life Between Innings

Grandma was also my babysitter in my preschool years. Doug and Bonnie were in school so I spent the day playing soldier or cowboys and Indians while grandma would listen to the Soaps coming in loud and clear on the 50,000 red hot watts of St. Louis radio station, KMOX. The program that seemed to be of most interest to her was *The Many Loves of Helen Trent*, which would be followed by the booming voice of Rex Davis reading the news. If I was not playing soldier or cowboy and Indians, you could likely find me lying before our combination radio-record player pretending to be a disc jockey, playing my brother's stack of 45s, which seemed to feature Elvis Presley above all other artists.

For whatever reason I never felt close to Grandma Anderson. It wasn't that she was mean or hateful or anything like that; it just seemed we never had much of a relationship. Perhaps one of the reasons is that she was always diagnosing my ills; like the belly aches I developed quite often as a 7- or 8-year old. Her diagnosis was that I had "worms" and that the only cure was a healthy dose of cod liver oil. Now cod liver oil has got to be the most disgusting thing that I have ever ingested, even unto this day. I can close my eyes, here some 50 years later, and I can still taste that gawdawful stuff. It only took a few doses of this "snake-oil" and my "worms" disappeared, or at least the acknowledgment of the pain. The fact is, I could have had any disease, and if cod liver oil was prescribed as my cure, I would have rather died than to ever acknowledge to her that I was in pain. The stuff should have been outlawed by some childcare agency as cruel and unusual punishment.

To compound things, I can never remember her giving me a hug or asking all those grandma type questions about girls or sports or school. It just seemed she was there; and more often than not, she was a deterrent to the things I wanted to do, like go to the show (the movies). You see, grandma never really

The Childhood Years 1947-1959

struck me as being much of a spiritual person; she did smoke you know, although Bonnie says grandma could really "get in the spirit" when she would occasionally attend a church service. But, she never went to our church with us, which we did at least three times a week, that being twice on Sunday and again on Wednesday night. There were also Saturday night services from time to time and revivals that lasted all week and sometimes two weeks. On occasion, she would go with us to a Fifth-Sunday Meeting somewhere, usually in Bunker, Missouri. And it was here, according to my sister, that she could shout and holler and wave her hanky with the best of them; I never saw it.

Yet, grandma must have had strong opinions on what we Christians and proper people should do and not do as mom would occasionally tell us we could not do something because, *it might offend grandma,* or that *grandma doesn't believe in that.* One of the things we could not do as "Christians," according to grandma, was go to the movies, and evidently grandma was not silent about this evil. Once, while I was in the 4th grade, mom allowed me to go to the Salem Theater with my cousin Ivan to watch the *Harlem Globetrotter Story.* Of course I was allowed to go on this one occasion on the threat of life should grandma find out. Being at the show was so cool. The smell of the popcorn that permeated throughout the entire theater and the excitement of just being there, was one of those experiences as a kid that has stuck with me for a lifetime. From that time on I would carefully watch the movie listings in the local *Salem News* to see if anything might be showing that was sports related, or better yet, had "God," or something sounding biblical in the title. I knew my chances of getting back in were intrinsically tied to religion in some way.

However, I was growing impatient as a suitable movie title did not seem to come up very often. I do remember one that

Life Between Innings

I thought would be my ticket back in, entitled *God's Little Acre*. However, when I saw the billing photo showing a woman in a provocative strapless dress, I had my doubts that this was the movie I had been holding out for. Finally, I could wait no longer, as rumors had started to surface that my girl friend, the beautiful and blonde, Anna Lee McCarter, had been spotted sitting with Paul Hogan at the theater the Saturday prior. To make matters worse, it was reported that he had sat with his arm around her. So, in desperation, and probably hyperventilating in some fashion, I gathered up the nerve to approach mom and ask her if I could go that next Saturday.

Well, the answer was not what I had hoped for as Mom stated emphatically, *No, you cannot go; grandma doesn't believe in them!* My quick and immediate response was, *Well, I wish grandma was dead!* It was one of those times, even as a kid, when the words were barely off my lips that I realized that I had said the wrong thing. I do not think I have ever seen my mother any angrier, prior to or since, that most unfortunate moment. I am convinced that the beating that I took that day, which I am sure brought me within an inch of my life, changed my life forever, as I have been one to weigh my words carefully in tense moments, even until today.

Other than the whole family sneaking off to the drive-in theater to watch the inspiring film, *A Man Called Peter,* a story about the Rev. Peter Marshall, former Presbyterian Chaplain of the U.S. Senate, who died in his 50s at the height of his ministry, I never asked nor did I attend any other movies while living in Salem. And, I lost Anna Lee McCarter to Paul Hogan; I will always blame my bad luck on grandma's religious beliefs and the fact that I could not be at the theater to buy her popcorn and to put my arm around her like Paul could and did. It couldn't have been any thing other than that because Paul was a sissy boy who couldn't play baseball or basketball very well.

The Childhood Years 1947-1959

He even wore funny-looking jeans without pockets in the back and elastic in the waste line, the kind fat boys wear.

Anna Lee was probably the first girl that had returned my "love," regardless of the shortness of our romance. Anna Lee had even brought a *May Day Basket* to my door on a sunny May 1 loaded down with candy and gum. I saved the gum (Wrigley's Juicy Fruit) and only chewed it on the day of my baseball games to bring me good luck. However, my first love was Billy Jean Key, my first grade classmate. I remember coming home one Friday and going straight to the closet in my mom's bedroom, closing the door, and crying for some time because it would be Monday before I would see her again. To compound things, she became seriously ill in the spring of that semester and missed a lot of school. Upon her return, a friend and I chased her around the schoolyard slipping candy into her sweater pocket. Finally, she reported us to Mrs. Johnson, our teacher; we were quite embarrassed! It was humiliating enough just to hear Mrs. Johnson explain to her that the reason we were doing that was probably because "we liked her," even though we did.

From the second grade through the sixth grade I maintained a deep crush on a beautiful blonde, Sue Moffitt, who was not only a classmate but also lived right across the street from my Uncle Roy and Aunt Marie Anderson and then later my Uncle Bill and Aunt Arlene Anderson. Nevertheless, while I was struck hard, Sue rarely gave me the time of day and eventually married one of my best friends, Ronnie Torbitt. Man, did Ronnie ever "marry up!" I have seen pictures of her in the *Salem News* once or twice in the past and if I thought she looked good back then, well, she looks even greater today as a mature women.

Of course Anna Lee McCarter was my girl until I lost her to Paul Hogan early on in the fifth grade. Anna Lee lived right

Life Between Innings

across the street from one of my best friends from church, Billy Wayne Lunn, but that never helped my plight much either. Then, in the sixth grade, I fell madly in love with Sharon Eudy, whose big brother played on my baseball team. I even carried her books once, so you know it had to be the real thing. Well, it was the real thing until I woke up one morning and discovered she was really ugly, and that ended that romance. But Sue Moffitt, she was there all those years and none could beat her beauty; Sue with that flowing blonde hair and a smile that made a young man's heart melt! Such was my love life in Salem.

While Grandma Anderson moved out sometime shortly after my "wish of death" and subsequent beating, she only moved two doors down, so things did not change much as to what we could or could not do based on what grandma believed in. Grandma moved one more time while I was in the sixth grade to a small home in south Salem, closer to two of my mom's older brothers, Roy and Bill. Shortly after that move, mom moved us back to St. Louis. It was only a short time after moving to St. Louis that grandma died. Mom always felt that grandma just kind of gave up after she left and blamed herself unnecessarily for grandma's passing.

While I did not have much of a relationship with Grandma Anderson, my relationship with Grandpa and Granny Mooney, my dad's parents, was totally different. Granny Mooney just couldn't hug you enough and could never do enough for you. She was one wonderful, beautiful lady.

My first memory of visiting them is still pretty vivid. I would guess that I was five, maybe six, when one summer day mom packed us three kids into a cab for a ride to Midridge, Missouri. You do not accidentally arrive at Midridge, you have to purposely be going there, with a map, to find this town. To get to Midridge we traveled from Salem and on through Bunker, Missouri, the town with the widest main street in the state. It was not uncommon to see cattle, pigs and chickens running free on Main Street, which always fascinated me. My Uncle Bill Anderson, the third oldest of my mom's four brothers, pastored a small Pentecostal Church on Bunker's main street for a number of years.

Midridge was nothing more than a few houses, an old mill and a store that doubled as a post office and gas station. The old gas pump had glass at the top, and you could see the gasoline swirling around inside as it was pumped. The EPA would probably not allow such pumps today as those were kind of outdated, even in the early 1950s. Midridge at one time was the home of a large logging company and logging camps. In fact, it was in such a logging camp that mom and dad first met and began the relationship that led to their eventual marriage. However, I doubt today that Midridge is even on the map.

Upon arriving at Midridge and the general store, we hooked up with the rural postman who gave us a lift in his Jeep, up and down the rolling hills along the narrow dirt road that was more rut than road. Before going up a hill or down a hill we would stop and sound the horn. If anyone was already going up or down the hill that we were approaching, they would sound their horn and we would wait till they reached us before moving on up or down the hill.

Upon reaching Grandpa and Granny Mooney's home, I was immediately impressed with the simplicity of their lives, even from the perspective of a small child from a relatively poor family. The two-bedroom wooden frame house was covered in black tar paper and was not well insulated. Off to the side of the house was a barn with a few cows and horses, plus chickens that could be seen scurrying around pecking at the ground.

There was no electricity or indoor plumbing. All around the house were kerosene lamps that grandpa or Granny would

Life Between Innings

carefully trim and then light by striking a match, as darkness would creep in around us. In Granny's kitchen was a hand water pump, which she would prime with a cup of water, if the pump had not been used in the last half hour or so. Out back was the outhouse with a nice Sears and Roebuck catalog to use for wiping after you finished your business. Those Sears and Roebuck catalogs also served for educational purposes as a young man such as myself might linger at the bra and lingerie sections longer than I should have. You could be sure that they were not the first pages that would be used up.

However, the most fascinating item for me was Granny's cooler. Since they did not have any electricity, they did not have a refrigerator or icebox in the house. Instead, grandpa had built a wooden box over the ever cool and flowing spring that ran just a few feet from the house. It was there that Granny stored her butter, milk, eggs and other items that she did not want to spoil. It seemed to serve her well.

On Sunday, grandpa hooked up the horses to the wagon and off to church we went. It didn't seem that the ride was too awful long. I do not remember anything about the service, as I probably slept through it, but I do remember it was quite dark on the way back to the farm, but the horses seemed to easily find their way.

Sometime around the fifth grade, grandpa and Granny retired from farming and moved on to the small town of Ellington, Missouri. Somehow they were able to obtain a nice white wooden three-bedroom frame home in the heart of town that backed up to a small stream. Here, they had a few modern conveniences such as electricity, a gas kitchen stove and refrigerator. Even though they lived in town, there was still no running water except for the hand water pump in the kitchen. And, yes, the outhouse was still out back. We visited a little more often in Ellington as mom was now driving and

The Childhood Years 1947-1959

it was much easier to get to their home, perhaps an hour and a half or two away from Salem. Granny always met us kids at the door with great hugs and a pinch of the cheek and she made over us like we were the Rockefellers.

Meals at Granny's were nothing short of a feast each and every time we sat down. I can close my eyes and still recall those great breakfast odors waffling through the house, as I would awaken. No one, and I mean no one, could fix white rice like she could, smothered in butter and whole milk and just the right amount of sugar. That was served along side as many eggs as you could possibly eat, coupled with ample portions of sausage and thick country bacon. The climax to the whole meal came, however, with the serving of the best hot milk gravy that would ever grace your lips, poured out over the world's best homemade fluffy biscuits that have ever melted in your mouth. And just in case you still were not full, there were the fruit jellies and fresh sorghum molasses that were available to smear on the remaining biscuits. And, that was just breakfast. Everyday.

The home in Ellington became home to many more memories. Sleeping at grandpa and Granny's house was like sleeping at no one else's home. Grandpa would turn down the wood-stove for the night and the house would get quite cold during the winter months. But, you would never know it was cold, except for the chill on the point of your nose, as Granny would tuck you into the softest, thickest, feather mattress that you could ever imagine and cover you with so many home stitched blankets that you could hardly move. Man, it was great! It was also neat to lie there in the still of the night and hear grandpa's pendulum clock chime away at each passing hour.

A year or two after grandpa passed away on April 9, 1959, at age 63 (heart attack followed by a stroke), my cousin Dennis and I visited Granny during our summer vacation and had one

Life Between Innings

of the best, most memorable vacations of our lives. Oh, it was nothing that we did that was so exciting; it was just simply one of those Norman Rockwell kind of vacations that was fun. Besides eating, our day would usually consist of playing some type of baseball or whiffle ball game in the front yard, do some crawdad fishing in the stream and take a walk into town to the local Drug Store to buy some new Lone Ranger, Superman or Archie Comics. Of course I just had to have a genuine fountain cherry coke from the soda counter or the visit to the Drug Store would not be complete. At the conclusion of our visit, Granny placed us on the Trailways Bus for our trip back home. We were big stuff!

Grandpa and Granny Mooney were both God-fearing people who were just simply the best. They could not have been more proud of their grandkids, whether it was Doug, Bonnie or me or the children of their other two sons, Leland and Bill. Each Sunday that we would visit we would, without fail, march off and up the hill to the Assembly of God Church. The church had a bell that rang every Sunday morning announcing that it was the Lord's Day. Granny would be sure to introduce us to everyone that she could; we always felt so very special. My wife Tina is as close to the type of person that Granny was of anyone I know. Granny would give and give and never thought much about herself; she was always putting others first. People like Granny and Tina are in store for some great rewards when our Lord finally comes to take his children home.

We were still living in Salem at the time grandpa died. The family all met at grandpa and Granny's home in Ellington for the deathwatch as grandpa lay in his own bed slowly dying. I remember clearly hearing the wheezing sounds coming from the bedroom as he gasped for his final breaths, and then slipped into the arms of his Lord and Savior. Granny

The Childhood Years 1947-1959

eventually had to move to St. Louis (Berkeley) and live with her son Leland. Granny later came down with kidney cancer but no one ever heard her complain. When she died on June 6, 1963, at age 61, those that were with her said that there was no doubt where this lady of faith was headed as the Holy Spirit was obviously in the room at her passing. In fact, it was reported that at her passing, those in the room burst out into praise and worship, the power of the Holy Spirit was so prevalent. Grandpa and Granny had lived the Christian life in front of us kids and they died with their "faith on." They were shining examples of what grandparents should be. I regret that I will never be able to attain their stature in that regard as they truly broke the mold.

In those early years at Salem we would occasionally see my dad's two brothers, Bill and Leland. After moving to St. Louis, Leland would become a very important figure in the lives of all three of us kids. Dennis and Darlene, Leland and Louise's two youngest children, became two of my closest cousins after our move to St. Louis in 1959. In fact, Dennis became more like a brother than a cousin to me as we grew older. We did visit Uncle Bill in Eminence, Missouri, occasionally, and we always had fun when we visited, but for a number of reasons we never developed the same relationship with them as we did with the Anderson family or with the Leland Mooney family.

However, the Anderson side of the family visited us often and we likewise visited them. The family was pretty much scattered from St. Louis to Salem and parts south and east of Salem in rural Missouri. It seemed that Easter, Memorial Day and Christmas were key holidays for us all to get together. On the Sunday of the Memorial Day weekend, we would drive down to West Fork-Sutterfield Cemetery to visit the Anderson family gravesites, primarily those of Grandpa Anderson and then later Grandma Anderson. Just as it was at my dad's first

Life Between Innings

gravesite, only on a more grander scale, after a morning of decorating the graves and long-winded preaching by the various ministers, plus skipping a few rocks across the West Fork River, we would all put our food together on the longest cement table I have ever seen, and then eat and eat and eat. I think this might be what heaven will be like, especially at mealtime. The Anderson family continues to meet annually for a reunion at the Maramec State Park near St. James, Missouri. The reunions started as a way to celebrate the 50th birthday of each of my seven Anderson Aunts and Uncles. As those birthdays came and went, the annual tradition of the reunion became entrenched and has continued to this day. It never takes long for everyone to get reacquainted and conversations seem to pick up right where they left off the year before.

With the exception of Ivan, Roy and Marie Anderson's youngest son, my closest cousins on the Anderson side of the family were girls. While I wasn't all that comfortable around girls until much later in life, for some reason I was comfortable with and close to Sue *(Floyd and Enzie Sullivan's daughter)*, Kathy *(Henry and Sada Anderson's daughter)*, Pamela *(Bill and Elaine Anderson's daughter)*, Connie *(Bill and Arlene Anderson's daughter)* and Nancy and Carol *(daughters of Bob and Magdalene White)*. Pamela was probably my closest cousin for a number of years as she lived in the same 6-family flat in St. Louis that we did from 1959-63. Perhaps the biggest reason was that she was a tomboy who loved to play ball with us boys. And, she was good, usually better in fact than many of the boys we played with.

While Sue was not an athlete, I probably share some of my best memories with her, whether it was daring each other to drink the gawdawful concoctions that we would mix together from everything we could find in the kitchen pantry to throwing rocks at each other (primarily me at her) down on the

The Childhood Years 1947-1959

creek bed that ran near their farm. Once while visiting Sue at their home in Corridon, Missouri, I threw a rock that hit her squarely in the middle of her forehead. David and his sling-shot have nothing on me. She didn't start crying, however, until she discovered that it was bleeding. Of course I tried to console her at that point, knowing that I was probably in serious trouble, but as she said, *I have to cry, it's bleeding.*

But best of all, all these girls were beautiful, they really were. Not wanting to slight any of them, I withhold my thoughts as to who was the most beautiful!

When the families would get together for the holidays, you slept wherever you could be stacked. I remember once sleeping in a large box, which was great by me, as I did not end up sleeping with the bigger boys. You would find kids sleeping everywhere, often two at the top of the bed and two others sleeping at the foot of the bed. With families that ate a lot of pinto beans, this was not always the most comfortable of situations. But it seemed no one ever complained; well, at least not most of the time.

Our good times as a family are easily recalled as we sit around and talk at the Anderson Family Reunions. There is the story about the largest snowman that any of us have ever seen, built one white Christmas by all the cousins, with the help of Uncle Henry, in our front yard. I don't think Frosty completely melted until sometime the following March. There were the nighttime games of hide-and-go-seek and the kick-the-can games that would seemingly go on for hours. Once, while we played our games, the Wisdom Family, our next-door neighbors, were robbed. Several of the cousins saw the thieves going in and out of the Wisdom house but none thought anything of it until much later when we found out what had happened. There is also the famous story of my older cousin, Lindell Anderson, who about decapitated himself on a low hanging clothesline in our back yard one night while trying to run to home base during one of our games. There were also evenings when we would all sit around and tell ghost stories and try hard to scare each other. It was not uncommon to get a little help with the scaring part from my Uncle Henry and my mom.

And board games, like *Monopoly*, *Chinese Checkers* and *Sorry*, got a lot of play along with the traditional card games like *Old Maid*, *Crazy 8s* and *Snap*. Us kids would literally play for hours, usually off to ourselves, much unlike today, when kids and parents seem to spend more time together. However, in the era of the 1950s, kids were still to be seen and not heard, and we did our part to honor that code. It was not uncommon, in fact it was common, to arise in the morning, eat breakfast and never see a parent again until they would call us in for supper.

However, there was one exception to that rule and that was with our own mom. Mom was always in the midst of things, especially when Doug and Bonnie's friends came over. I used to tease them that I did not believe that they were really popular, that the only reason that so many of their friends liked to come over was because mom was so much fun. When we kids grew older, things never changed; mom was always in the midst of our orneriness, laughing and enjoying her family like no one else did.

During the summer, I would on occasion spend a couple weeks with one of my cousins, namely Sue Sullivan on their family farm down on Big Creek (*a river stream in Missouri near Bunker*), swimming and splashing around in the creek on the "Slippery Rock," and then later at their farm outside of Corridon, Missouri. I also spent time with Connie and Stanley Anderson, two other cousins, likewise on Big Creek, on their family farm swimming and running from blue racers (snakes). I remember one summer, it was in 1956, I spent a few weeks with my cousin Judy Anderson in St. Louis watching a lot of television and enjoying the city sites and sounds found on Jefferson Avenue, about a half block away from their home. My greatest fascination was the streetcars that would go clanging by. It was while visiting her that summer that I viewed my first National Presidential Convention on television. The Republicans were in the process of nominating President Eisenhower for a second term. I remember that I was frustrated because the gavel-to-gavel coverage kept interrupting the shows that I wanted to see; yet even at the age of nine, I found the speeches and the politically charged atmosphere surrounding the convention fascinating.

I spent a lot of my Friday nights with my cousin Ivan who lived a short walk from our home in Salem. There were a lot of good reasons for staying over with him as I just might get a glimpse of Sue Moffitt out in her backyard. He also had a great wooded area for playing cowboys or army and smoking some kind of reed that we easily found in the open fields. He was one of the cousin's closer to my age, but more importantly, it was his family that was one of the first to have a television. I would try to weasel an invitation into their home as much as possible in the hopes of catching a live Cardinal baseball game, somewhat of a rarity in comparison to the amount of games on television today, or just to watch television in general.

When invited, if I was able to get to his house early, I might even catch my favorite non-cowboy or detective show, the *Howdy Doody Show* with Buffalo Bob, Howdy and Clarabell the Clown. At worst, there would be the *Gillette Cavalcade of Sports* presentation of *Friday Night Boxing*. We always stayed up late and caught a movie after the fights on the *CBS Late Show* and then another on the *Late, Late Show*. This was often followed by two of my favorite programs, *Highway Patrol* and *I Led Three Lives*. Of course, you had to stare through the black and white "snowy" picture as cable and satellite TV had not yet been invented. From time to time it would be necessary for one of us to go out in the yard and rotate the antenna to improve the reception while the other would stay in the house and yell when it was time to stop turning. But who cared, or better yet, who knew better; man, it was great just to watch TV.

Should I get to stay over on Saturday morning, there were all my favorite Westerns, one right after another, like *The Lone Ranger, Wild Bill Hickock, Roy Rogers, Sky King, Sergeant Preston of the Yukon, the Cisco Kid, Captain Midnight, Hopalong Cassidy* and *Annie Oakley.* Saturday night was equally as good as we would watch professional wrestling with some of the top pros like Gorgeous George, Johnny Valentine and Killer Kowalski, with his famous iron claw-hold.

While we never had a television while living in Salem, I probably knew more about what was on, and what time it was showing, than most of those who had a television. One of the things I collected as a kid was the *TV Guide* that came out each Sunday in the *St. Louis Post-Dispatch.* There is a *Seinfeld* episode where George Castandza's father collected issues of *TV Guide* and now I laugh, as that is obviously rather nerdy, but it was the closest thing to having a television that I had at the time.

Now I was a *St. Louis Globe-Democrat* reader from about the 4th grade until its demise sometime in the 80s, as I became a great fan and reader of the daily Bob Burnes' *Benchwarmer* column. Many years later while in Bible College, and then again while in the military, my mom would send me the clippings of the Bob Burnes column. But Sunday meant the *TV Guide* and I had to have it and it was in the Post. I would walk to the grocery store each Sunday, unless I could finagle a ride, probably a good three or four mile round trip, to secure my copy. And, I would study it and read through the listings thoroughly, right after devouring the sports pages and the latest news on the St.

The Childhood Years 1947-1959

Louis Cardinals or the *St. Louis Hawks*. Then, during the week, I would take out the current copy of the *TV Guide* and read it again just so that I would know what I would be watching if only mom would buy a TV.

Although us kids did not realize it, we were a pretty poor family. However, I never recall us ever lacking clothes or missing a meal, ever. Our diet was pretty simple with pinto beans, cornbread and fried potatoes as our staple. On occasion, supplies might be a little slim and our meals would of necessity be supplemented with cornbread crumbled in milk, but that was rare. We were more fortunate than other members of mom's family as certain families had milk and cornbread as their supper meal on a fairly regular basis. But we were never hungry, never.

Uncle Roy, my mom's oldest brother, would come by from time to time and drop off fish that he had caught or some squirrel and rabbits he had hunted. Occasionally, he, or one of the other brothers, would bring by some fresh deer meat that tasted so good. It seemed we always had a garden of sorts so we had plenty of fresh vegetables. One of the things I do remember Grandma Anderson helping mom with was canning. Mom and grandma would can some of the green beans, tomatoes, apples, and blackberries and such that we would grow or would be given to us by mom's family; we just didn't lack for good food. God truly had His hand on this little family from the beginning.

Following meals it was the responsibility of us kids to wash, dry and clean up the dishes. Usually, Doug and Bonnie would switch off on the washing, the other would put the cleaned and dried dishes away and I, as the baby in the family, would climb up on a chair to reach the dishes that were draining, and would dry them. This particular daily chore actually could be fun on occasion, as it was not rare that someone would

Life Between Innings

get wet. There were other chores that we all were assigned to do, although I do not remember having any specific ongoing chores, except the dishes. There were two chores that I had to perform from time to time that I did not like to do and that was stacking the firewood in the backyard upon delivery and then bringing in the firewood during the winter months for heating our home. In the heart of winter the wood would often be covered with snow, or even worse, the pieces would be frozen together and hard to separate. For an eight, nine or 10-year-old kid, bringing in the wood was not fun.

I was not a great fan of school during my Salem years and my grades kind of reflected that. I was pretty much a C student (called an "M" in that day) with a few Bs scattered throughout my report card. I attended William H. Lynch Grade School, which was located right in the heart of Salem and the downtown area. While, in reality, the walk to school was only about 6 or 7 blocks, in the heart of winter that walk could get pretty long. I arrived at school many a winter morning with frozen hair as this was the era of the slick look, made popular by Elvis Presley, complemented by a healthy dab of Byrlcream or Vitalis.

None of my grade school teachers stand out much in my memory except my sixth grade teacher, "Old Lady" (Irene) Langworthy. My first grade teacher was Dorleska Johns; second grade teacher was Marcia Kinder; I cannot recall my third grade teacher unless it was a Ms. Cox; fourth grade was Lillian Stevens; fifth grade was Esther Masters and of course Ms. Langworthy in the sixth grade. Most of the students didn't like her and dreaded the thought of being assigned to her class. However, I recall her as the one who greatly encouraged me, especially in reading, which I did plenty of. I am sure that is one of the basic reasons why my grades started to gradually improve from that point forward.

The Childhood Years 1947-1959

My love for reading had already been germinated by reading the sports pages of the daily newspapers, and especially Bob Burnes' daily columns. But, that love increased even more dramatically in Ms. Langworthy's class, reading over 30 some books during my sixth-grade year. We were required to read and provide a report on about six books, but I had discovered the children's *Blue Books Biography Series* and had become quite challenged by the lives of George Washington, Abraham Lincoln, Benjamin Franklin, George Washington Carver and others. Embodied in these books were stories of men and women who made a difference and dared to dream big, and I was captivated. Over my fourth- and fifth-grade summers I had also signed up for the summer *Weekly Reader Book Club* and would read dozens more books during the summertime. My favorites were the infamous *Trolley Car Family, No Room for Pets* and any bio on a baseball or basketball sports figure.

Life in Salem had a nice routine about it. We kids had developed very good lives for ourselves and our little family unit was pretty solid. Mom ruled with a firm, but gentle hand. I can rarely remember harsh words being spoken; certainly there was no yelling and screaming at us kids that is so common in many homes. Believe me, we got our share of paddlings, but all in all it was very effective discipline. My only issue with her discipline was that she had me, on a couple occasions, go out to the peach tree in the backyard to select my own "switch." Fortunately, I kept my paddlings to a minimum.

The only threat to our routine as a family were those occasions when someone would come in and try to stir mom's love interest. As a young woman, mother was a very beautiful lady and easy on the eye. She maintained her beauty well into her years and it was easy to see why the suitors would come around. However, mom was very careful about who she allowed in, which suited us kids just fine. I don't think any of

Life Between Innings

us were against mom finding us a dad or getting remarried, but none of the gentlemen callers that came around, at least while we lived in Salem, were acceptable to us. I think Mom sensed our strong apprehensions. One particular suitor was Rev. Richard "Dick" Eldridge, a smallish man with a noticeable limp, who came around often for a couple years, trying hard to get mom to marry him. However, none of us kids liked him; in fact we probably disdained him. It was a great day in the Mooney household when Mom finally convinced him that they had no future and that he should not come around anymore. I don't think Mom cared that much for him either, but I think the real reason that her suitors were sent packing was that mom didn't find any man amongst the group that she wanted raising her family. And, from the slim pickings that came through Salem, we thanked God that she maintained her strong principles!

Without a husband around, mom obviously had to work. For many years she worked at the Brown Shoe Company, which didn't pay a lot, but evidently provided us with enough to get by. Consequently, we kids had to learn to do a lot for ourselves like fix our own breakfast, make our own beds, clean up our rooms and iron a few of our own clothes. Mom taught me the fine art of ironing, starting me off with handkerchiefs and pillowcases, and I gradually moved on to pants and shirts. These skills became very useful as we kids grew older. Mom did most of the washing out on the back porch with the use of the old wringer washer. Of course we did not have dryers in those days so all the laundry had to be hung in the backyard on the clotheslines, winter or summer made no difference. Bonnie seemed to get that chore quite a bit; at worst, I rarely did any more than bring the laundry back in once it had dried. One thing we all did was make our beds every morning and pick up our clothes. For the most part we just lived comfortably

The Childhood Years 1947-1959

and Mom seemed content to have the house picked up, but certainly not spic and span, a trait that she maintained all though life. Her home was always clean and fairly organized, but you knew people lived there. And, that made for a fairly contentious-free home to grow up in.

In the summer, Doug and I would cut the grass with our hand pushed lawnmower. If the grass was not too high, the task was not too difficult. At other times, lawn mowing could become a real chore and cut into more important things like my baseball or basketball playing and practice time. All in all, Mom didn't seem to burden us kids with too many chores and I made it my business to be up early and out of the house, usually playing ball somewhere, until forced in for food, due to darkness, or the start of the Cardinal game on radio. Except for school and church, baseball, basketball, the Cardinals and the Hawks were my life. And it was a very good life!!

Mom made it an even better life for us kids after she learned to drive and bought her first car, a 1947 Pontiac. I can't remember much about the car except for what it looked like. But, for some reason we kids were always fascinated with its radio and the excellent reception that we got with it. Maybe it was because it was our first car, but whenever the talk gets around to that car, it's always the radio we talk about.

Mom's learning to drive was quite interesting and at times quite embarrassing. One of the first times she ever drove a traditional stick shift, Bonnie and I hid in the back floorboard in the hopes that no one that we knew would see us "hopping" along the street. However inauspicious her beginning driving experience was, she became a very good driver. She came out of her timidity pretty fast as a single mom and she became known in the family as the adventurous one. Mom thought nothing of packing us kids into the car and taking a trip to the

Life Between Innings

Lake of the Ozarks or detouring to Arkansas on the way home from visiting Grandpa and Granny Mooney in Ellington.

One of our trips was down through Oklahoma and on to Galveston, Texas, to get our first ever view of the ocean. Of course this was before the advent of the Interstate Highway system, so traveling along Route 66 into Oklahoma City took awhile. There we visited the state capital building and some distant relatives that Mom knew and then we were back on the road to Texas and the Gulf of Mexico. It was along this road that one of Doug and Bonnie's favorite stories regarding Mom occurred; I was too young to understand. As we were running low on fuel, Mom pulled into the gas station to get the tank refilled. In those days, an attendant would come out and ask you what you needed and he would fill the tank, clean the windows and check the oil. Evidently, when the attendant approached, mom fumbled a bit with her words when he asked her what she wanted and she excitedly stated, *"Feel it up."* Doug and Bonnie "went off" hysterically. Mom never denied saying it, she would only laugh, so evidently she said it.

Alas, we reached our destination, the beautiful beaches of Padre Island at Galveston, Texas. Swimming in the ocean and playing on the beautiful sandy beach was such a treat for a kid seven or eight years old. My love affair with the ocean never left and I have spent many great vacations sitting on its shores. After swimming just off Padre Island, we headed back into town. I was sitting in the front seat on my legs in order to see out through the windows. Of course seat belts were unheard of in those day so I was not wearing one. As mom was rounding a corner, I kind of rose up and my back pocket hooked onto the door handle, opening the door. There for just a brief moment, I found myself swinging out over the pavement as we were speeding along. Fortunately, I was able to

The Childhood Years 1947-1959

grab back onto the doorframe and pull myself back in quickly. No one seemed to panic; they only laughed!

We finally pulled out of Galveston and headed out of Texas toward Louisiana. Mom kept looking for a convenient, but not too costly restaurant for us to eat in. Finally, after a search of many, many miles Mom pulled into a little Italian Restaurant. We were not only hungry, but by now we were parched as the salt water from the ocean and the long drive had left us "dry." Glasses of water were brought out to us and we gulped them down before the waiter could leave our table. He brought another round with the same results. He finally just brought us a pitcher, and then another, and I think another. We also wore funny bibs for the first time in public as the waiter brought them to us and tied them around our necks. This kept all of us in stitches as we hungrily ate our spaghetti and meatballs.

Mom's next car was a light green 1953 Chevrolet followed by a very stylish burnt red 1957 Chevrolet. With a car, our lives had changed quite a bit, especially when it came to getting to church.

For as long as I can remember we were a family that attended church. Maybe it was just the times, following shortly after the war, but both the Anderson family and the Mooney family had its share of Christians and preachers. From the Anderson side, three of my five uncles were preachers. Uncle Elmer and Uncle Lowell became Baptist ministers while my Uncle Bill was Pentecostal. From the Mooney side, my Uncle Leland founded and pastored a Full Gospel Pentecostal Church in St. Louis County and later pastored another in Oklahoma City. Mom seemed to favor the Pentecostal churches, although I do not recall her ever becoming demonstrative, translated "shouting, dancing or speaking in tongues (in a public fashion)," such as was the custom in our services.

Life Between Innings

The first church that I remember was a little Assembly of God church in Salem over toward the middle of town just off Highway 19 setting underneath the city water tower; in fact that little church is still there, only it is some other denomination. Mom did not drive in those days so we always walked to church, which meant two trips on Sunday. In actuality, the walk probably took about 20 minutes or so but for a little kid like me it seemed it took forever. It was on these walks that our family would often engage in very interesting conversations, like where did little babies come from. I was convinced, and would proudly announce, that mom had made me on the sewing machine. I remember Doug and Bonnie trying to convince me that this theory was not true, although they would never provide any details. They would only laugh and giggle like they knew something, but I would have no part in it. Later, in fact, about the third grade, after persisting with my questioning, mom gave me "the talk." Wow!! She related the process so gently and so naturally; it was not embarrassing at all. I was glad she told me in the darkness of my bedroom, however, as I do not know how I would have reacted in the light of day. I quickly lost interest in the part about "birthing babies," but my overall interest in how that process got started, grew quickly, very quickly!

I am not sure why we left the Assembly of God church, although I have heard my brother say he thought it had to do with the married pastor, Rev. Clyde L. Parsons, having a severe crush on mom, which became a little bit uncomfortable for her, so we left.

Later, we started attending a church in an old clothing factory in downtown Salem pastored by Rev. Gander. His family remains friends with our family to this day. It was there that I performed in my first Christmas play with a speaking part. I was probably all of six or seven years old at the time.

The Childhood Years 1947-1959

I remember being rewarded with a large chocolate Hershey candy bar for my great performance. Our last church in Salem was the one that we attended the longest, *Revival Tabernacle.* We were part of the "Latter Rain" movement, which was a little different than the traditional Pentecostal, Assembly of God churches. Our services were much more expressive in worship than our past two churches with open, corporate speaking in tongues and personal and corporate prophecy. Here we were pastored by Rev. Roy (wife Bonnie) Graham and then later Rev. A.M. (wife Gracie) Boatman. Rev. Boatman evidently was a noted preacher of the Word and was highly respected by Mom, Doug and Bonnie. Bonnie became the organist at the church and was quite good, playing at all the services and a number of funerals and weddings. My best memories of Pastor Boatman were not his messages, but the fact that he had no qualms in calling out my name, along with a few other boys, right in the middle of the service and tell us, "you boys, settle down back there." And, we did!!

While I stayed in Pentecostal and Charismatic churches until about 1981 (34 years of age), I never really felt comfortable with it at all and certainly was not comfortable in inviting my friends to come to services, although I did on occasion. There were always so many things to explain about our services, other than just the simple gospel story of grace, and I found that distracting and frustrating. However, it was following one of our more evangelistic Sunday evening services at Revival Tabernacle that I accepted Jesus Christ as my Lord and Savior. It was one of those summer evenings when several members of the Anderson family were in town visiting and so they attended church with us that night. For whatever reason, the adults did not come home immediately, but all of us kids and older teenagers did. Lindell Anderson, oldest son of Henry and Sada and one of my oldest cousins, began to encourage

Life Between Innings

me to give my heart to God; it did not take much convincing. He, along with a few of the older kids, knelt with me in our home at the old red couch. It was there that I tearfully confessed my sins and need of a Savior and asked Christ to come into my heart. I do not have any real explanation for what happened immediately after that, as I was not coerced in any fashion, but I broke out in a dance while speaking in tongues for some five, six, seven or so minutes. Much like my mother, who professed to have been filled with the Spirit, evidenced by speaking in tongues, I occasioned to speak in tongues during the prayer and praise time of our services for many years thereafter, but never such as the night I encountered Christ for the first time and was saved (born again). Something very important happened to me that night, something that no one can take away from me. It was a real, genuine experience that changed the course of my life. While I cannot remember my age or the exact date, although I believe I was in the third grade, I certainly remember the experience, an experience that has brought me into a life long, solid relationship with my Lord and Savior, Jesus Christ. There were times that I stumbled and my relationship became strained with Him during this long journey, but God in His grace has never let me get far from Him; and thankfully so.

Out of it all, when people think of "Little Leo," most think of his relationship to the bouncing (basketball) or batted (baseball) ball. I actually remember getting my first hit at about age four. By "hit" I mean feeling the sweetness of the bat hitting solidly against the pitched ball. I have no idea how far the ball went, all I remember was how great it felt, that almost indescribable rush that occurs when ball and bat collide solidly. I also remember the first basket I ever made. I was five years old and playing with Doug's basketball in the backyard. The only way that I could reach the rim with the ball was to use the two-handed, underhand (granny style) shot. After a few shots one of them went in and I was forever hooked. The fact that Doug had told me not to play with his basketball while he was at school was beside the point until the day it hit a nail in a board laying behind the goal. I can't remember him yelling at me too much so he must have gotten over it.

Beginning at age six, baseball became pretty much my life for seven months of each year. And, at age seven, I was already developing a passion for basketball that would occupy the other five months. In Salem, both the *St. Louis Cardinals* and the *St. Louis Hawks* could be heard over the local radio station, KSMO, and usually I was tuned in, regardless of the time of day or the lateness of the hour. As Harry Caray and Jack Buck broadcast the Cardinal radio games, I would be found spread out on the floor in front of the radio. Here I kept the score while maintaining the batting order for both teams with my large collection of baseball cards.

When the Hawks were playing, Buddy Blattner, one of my all-time favorite announcers, would describe the game while I would roll up a large ball of socks and hang a clothes hanger, formed into the shape of a basketball hoop, over the closet door. I would then reenact the side-line jumpers of "Big Blue" Bob Pettit, the hook shot of "Lil Abner" Cliff Hagen, the long-range bombs of "Boom Boom" Clyde Lovellette and the precision passing of Slater Martin. Victories were always sweet, but victories over Elgin Baylor and Jerry West of the *Minneapolis Lakers*, later the *Los Angles Lakers*, and Oscar Robertson and Jack Twyman of the *Cincinnati Royals* were extra sweet. But wins over Bob Cousy, K.C Jones and Bill Russell of those hated *Boston Celtics*, were sweeter still. The Hawks won the Championship in the spring of 1959, beating out the *Boston Celtics* in game seven, with Pettit scoring an unbelievable 50 points. Pettit was the man but Cliff Hagan was my favorite Hawk.

Life Between Innings

In Salem the big winter sport for the high school was basketball, as it did not field a football team during the '50s. Salem High had some pretty good basketball teams in those days and even better cheerleaders. My favorite was the very blond Ella Mae Leonard. I may have been only ten or eleven years old, but I knew a good-looking, full-figured woman when I saw one and she was it. WOW. Even by today's standards, I would put Ella Mae up against anyone.

The city of Salem fielded its own baseball team during the summer and they too played some good baseball in those days. My favorite player was second baseman Jimmy Edwards, a scrappy player who could both hit and field. On the mound was a lefty they called "Old Crow," as he pitched better when he was a little inebriated than he did when he was sober. And there was Bill Wynn, a left-handed hitter and our primary slugger, who had played a little minor league ball somewhere. When Bill got a hold of one it would rocket out of the small Salem Fairgrounds ballpark like a rocket.

It was while watching the Salem baseball team that I had my first exposure to black people. All-black traveling teams, like the St. Louis Monarchs, St. Louis Stars and the Kansas City Royals would come to town occasionally; these teams could play some serious baseball. The rule, unwritten of course, in Salem was that all black folk had to be out of town before sunset. So, when these black teams played night games at Fairgrounds Park, the police would have to escort them out of town when the game was over. It was not until my teenage years in St. Louis that I began to realize how disgraceful and shameful that practice was.

In those days the Cardinals had a few black players coming on the scene. I could have cared less what color they were as long as they could field, hit or pitch. Being a baseball fan, the game had already been integrated by the time I started

The Childhood Years 1947-1959

following it and had no reasons for racial prejudice. For me, when the black teams came to town, it was just a novelty since we did not see any blacks living in or driving through our area. But, being an infielder and usually playing second base for my little league teams, Don Blasingame became my first favorite player and favorite Cardinal. My nephew, Steve Mooney, one of my brother Doug's sons, gave me a Don Basingame baseball card a few years ago that I treasure.

The first Cardinal that I "almost" ever met face to face was left-handed pitcher Vinegar Bend Mizell. Adams Grocery in Salem had brought him in to town for a Saturday appearance one winter to sign autographs and meet the fans. However, I showed up just a wee bit late and missed this "opportunity of a lifetime." Nevertheless, he still became one of my favorite Cardinals after that. Many years later (about 1981), Vinegar Bend, then a former U.S. Senator, spoke at our church *(Hope Congregational* in St. Louis County). However, something came up and I left the church service early and missed him again by mere minutes.

While I say that baseball occupied my time seven months of the year, it really occupied my time for the entire year. I would read every newspaper article I could get my hands on regarding my beloved Cardinals. As noted earlier, my favorite baseball writer was Bob Burnes and I read his daily sports column regularly. Unlike most kids in the third or fourth grade, I would take my extra nickel and walk the next block over from our school to an uptown restaurant that had a rack of newspapers outside their door. I would purchase the paper and turn directly to Burnes' column. I credit Bob Burnes for teaching me to read and developing my love for the newspaper, a love that I still have today. I then would regularly snuggle up to the radio for the nightly 15 minutes of Sports News at 6:15 PM. This routine kept me up to date on all the latest trade rumors

Life Between Innings

and the "hot stove league" talk during those cold winter days. February, and the start of Spring Training, could never quite get here soon enough.

Once the baseball season was in full bloom, all was well. During the day I would play out in front of the house throwing the ball on the roof to practice catching fly balls or would toss a ball against a cement slab to practice fielding grounders. I was pretty much in my own little world as I would play for hours on end, inventing my own games and game situation to work through. Eventually, some of the other boys in the neighborhood would come out or my cousins would come over and we would play catch or practice pitching to each other. We also played a lot of Indian Ball as you could play this game with as little as two players, but was much more fun if you had four or six. The game was played by the batter tossing the ball in the air and hitting it hopefully past the first player, who represented the infield, to get a runner on, or hit it over the second players head, who represented the outfield, for a home run. Again, this was a game we would play for hours and generally only stopped due to darkness or the call for dinner.

Our tools were simple, to say the least. Our bat was usually one that had been broken (splintered) in a little league game or by one of the Salem players and then nailed back together. Our baseballs did not last long as we literally tore the covers off with our constant play. We would tape them up with black electrical tape until we had finally worn the ball completely out. Of course the glove was the key. I had a Wilson that served me well and lasted until we moved to St. Louis. That glove just might have been the most valuable possession that I owned.

I began to play Little League Baseball in 1956 when I finally reached the fourth grade. Unlike today where kids play 40, 50, 60 games a year, we played 8. The director of the league, Charlie

The Childhood Years 1947-1959

Garrett, and a few dads would get together and try to evenly balance out the 4 or 5 teams. We did not have uniforms. In fact, we did not even have team shirts. But, I could have cared less. This was the big leagues for me and our weekly game came much too slowly and was over much too quickly. Even with all the practice that I put in daily, my fielding never became my strong suit. Hitting was the thing. And, it wasn't until I approached my high school years that I finally developed into a pretty good hitter. However, as I approached the fifth grade, my second year in the league, I developed an uncanny ability to bunt the ball. Unbelievably, my skill at bunting the ball became my ticket to recognition. As I would approach the batter's box, the opposing players and coaches would call out, *Move in, it's Mooney; be ready for the bunt.* Although armed with such knowledge, more often than not, I could still find the hole in the field where I needed to lay down my bunt and reach first base. It was a little bit weird, maybe even a little bit unorthodox, but it was effective. It was truly "in their face" and I loved to do it. The opposition hated it.

Despite my obvious lack of skill, except for bunting, my tremendous desire to play was just as obvious. During my sixth grade season I somehow caught the eye of Charlie Garrett, the League Director. Charlie saw something in this thin, freckled faced, crew cut kid that he liked and he named me to the *Salem Little League All-Star Team.* Unbelievable! I was in heaven. We were given pro like uniforms with cotton pants and shirts with SALEM boldly printed across the front and a big number 6, the great Cardinal, Stan Musial's number, on my back. We wore real baseball socks and tennis shoes and were no doubt the best-uniformed team in the *Route 66 League.* After each game, the uniform had to be dry-cleaned, not washed. Picking up that uniform at the cleaners each week prior to the next game and putting it on was one of the greatest thrills of my young life. I'll say it again; it was simply unbelievable!

Life Between Innings

Playing in the *Route 66 League* took us to "exciting places" like Fort Leonard Wood, Rolla, Belle, St. James and Bourbon. While I was not a starter and did not play regularly, I was probably the happiest kid on the team. Wearing that uniform and just participating in the pre-game warm-ups were enough to keep me excited and practicing. Probably my greatest game highlight was catching the final out in a victory against St. James on their home field. So, you know what kind of career I had!

Being named to the *Salem All-Star Team* had other benefits. One was being selected by Mr. Garrett to ride in the back of a truck in the *Salem Fall Festival Parade* with my best buddy and our best pitcher, left-hander Billy Hastings. We were decked out in our SALEM uniform and were obviously the envy of every kid, and probably some dads, along the route.

Another benefit was being selected to ride the bus to St. Louis to attend a Cardinal baseball game. This was the culmination of years of dreaming; I was actually going to Busch Stadium (previously Sportsman's Park till renamed in 1953) where Harry Caray and Jack Buck would be sitting as they broadcast the game. It was probably considered a boring game to most of those in attendance. It was late in August of 1958, and the Cardinals, destined for fifth place that year, were not in contention. The game itself turned into a pitcher's duel between the Cardinal's ace, Larry Jackson, and the Cincinnati Redleg's (now called the "Reds") ace, Joe Nuxhall. There was no score going into the bottom of the seventh inning when Ken Boyer, the Cardinal third baseman, launched a home run into the left field stands for the only tally of the game. Cardinals win 1-0.

However, in August of 1957, just the year prior, came one of my biggest disappointments ever as I missed out on what would have been my first major league baseball game. We were

The Childhood Years 1947-1959

in St. Louis at the time visiting with my Uncle Henry Anderson, who was a casual baseball fan at best, and most certainly not a huge fan like I was. I guess mom had talked him into taking me to a Cardinal game and I was beyond excited as I thought about finally getting inside the holy grounds of Busch Stadium. And, to add to the excitement, young rookie sensation, 18-year old Von McDaniel, was to be pitching that night. McDaniel had already won five games in a row knocking off some of the National League's top teams like the Brooklyn Dodgers and the Pittsburgh Pirates. In fact, McDaniel had pitched a one-hitter against the Pirates just a few days before allowing only that one hitter to reach base. As a fan, I knew we needed to go early because when McDaniel pitched, the stadium was selling out. However, I could not convince my uncle that we needed to go early. I am sure he thought, *What does he know, he is only a kid?* So, we did not leave early, despite my warning because, as he said, *They always have seats.* As we approached the ballpark the lines outside the stadium were long and winding around the corner away from the ticket office down Grand Avenue. My heart sank, as I intuitively knew that our chances of getting a seat were slim. Gradually the line carried us to within just 15 or 20 feet of the window when they announced, "*Standing Room Only.*" Uncle Henry quickly announced that we did not want to stand to watch the game and we made our way back to the car. There was no way for him to know how disappointed I was. The fact was I would have stood on my head, if that were what it would have taken, to get into the park and see the game. I didn't cry, at least not outwardly.

One of my greatest memories in Cardinal baseball lore occurred on May 13, 1958. I was 11 years old and just finishing the fifth grade. Cardinal great, Stan "the Man" Musial, was on the verge of getting his 3000th Major League hit and the Cardinals were in Chicago playing the Cubs in a day game.

Life Between Innings

Cardinal manager, Fred Hutchinson, had announced that he would be holding Musial out of the game in the hopes of allowing him to get his historic blow in front of the St. Louis crowd during the next home stand. However, it was known that should the game be on the line, for the integrity of baseball, Hutchinson would have Musial pinch-hitting. There was no way that I could chance that happening and not be able to hear Harry Caray make the call live. As any avid baseball fan, it suddenly came to me how sick I was feeling and notified mom, as she prepared to leave for work, that I better stay home from school. Without much time to check me over, she thought it best that I stay home and in bed, which I gladly was willing to do.

As I recall the Cardinals were trailing 2-1 in the top of the sixth inning and Manager Hutchinson decided to send in Musial to hit for the pitcher, "Sad" Sam Jones. Batting against Moe Drabowsky, Musial laced a double into left field for his 3000th hit, chasing home Gene Green for the tying run. Harry Caray, with even more enthusiasm in his voice than usual, gave the memorable call, *Swing, and there it is . . .* At the time, Musial was only the eighth player in Major League history to get 3000 hits. The Cardinals went on to win the game 5-3. The next night in St. Louis, Musial received a standing ovation; and then, in his first at bat, he launched a home run for hit 3001 and the fans went wild.

In the spring of 1959 the future of *Brown Shoe Company* in Salem was obviously in jeopardy and layoffs were looming. Mom decided to take a trip into St. Louis to check out the job market. Doug was graduating from high school that spring and would be moving to St. Louis to work, so a projected move did not concern him all that much. For Bonnie, it would be a rather significant move as she would be leaving Salem at the conclusion of her sophomore year and would be attending a strange high school her last two years, obviously not a desired situation for any teenager. However, for me, I was elated at the thought of moving. When mom finally made the announcement to the family that we were in fact moving to St. Louis, I can't speak for anyone but myself, but I was thrilled. Starting in a new school in the seventh grade was not a problem. I was going home. I was going to the Holy Land of the Cardinals and the Hawks. I was going to a city that seemed to have a small grocery or confectionary on every block, and that meant easier access to buying baseball cards. I was going where parks and baseball diamonds dotted the St. Louis landscape in goodly numbers. What else could a 12-year-old boy want? For me, this was like going to heaven; this was a dream come true, and there were absolutely no regrets! None!!

The 2ⁿᵈ Inning

THE TEENAGE YEARS
1959-1965

In 1959, Republican President Dwight D. Eisenhower was late into his second term in office. In 1960, the Chicago Cardinals of the National Football League moved to St. Louis giving St. Louis both a football and baseball team named the Cardinals. In 1960, Jack F. Kennedy, a Democrat and the first Roman Catholic ever to hold the office of President, was elected. In 1961, Russian Astronaut Yuri Gagarin was the first person in space and to orbit the earth. Two months later, U.S. Astronaut Alan Shepard became the first American in space. In 1962, John Glenn became the first American to orbit the earth. It was also in 1962 that the United States came face to face with Communist Russia over missiles located in Cuba; the world stood at the brink of nuclear war but the Russian Premier, Nikita Khrushchev, backed off at the last possible moment and war was averted. Also that year, Jackie Robinson, became the first black player ever to be inducted into the Baseball Hall of Fame. Cardinal great and future Hall of Famer, Stan Musial, retired at the end of the 1963 baseball season. On November 22 of 1963, President Kennedy was assassinated in Dallas, Texas, and Vice-President Lyndon B. Johnson succeeded him. In November of 1964, President Johnson was elected in his own right while the United States' controversial and divisive involvement in the Viet Nam War escalated. The Civil Rights Act of 1964 was established outlawing major forms of discrimination against blacks and women,

Life Between Innings

legally ending segregation in the United States. Earlier that year, the Beatles arrived to a throng of screaming fans at a New York airport and Beatle mania was born. Future Hall of Famer, Lou Brock, joined the Cardinals in 1964, coming to St. Louis in a trade with the Chicago Cubs. September of this year began my senior year in high school. It was in this month that the Cardinals came back from 9 games out and overtook the Philadelphia Phillies and Cincinnati Redlegs on the last day of the season to win the National League Pennant. The Cardinals went on to beat the hated New York Yankees to win the World Series in seven games behind the great clutch pitching of fireballer Bob Gibson. The 1965 baseball season was the last season for the Cardinals at the old Busch Stadium (formerly Sportsman's Park) on Grand Avenue, as St. Louis would open a new Busch Stadium downtown the following year.

It was not long after mom had made the announcement early in 1959 of our pending move to St. Louis that we began to make preparations for the move. Mom was having some anxiety, as she was a little fearful that her mother would not get the kind of attention and care she had given her while we lived in Salem. However, as for me, I was excited. No, I was ecstatic! On May 2, I celebrated my 12th birthday. Later that month I successfully completed the 6th grade and we were on our way to St. Louis. The day arrived and we loaded up our personal effects and were on our way. I am not sure what happened to the furniture as we did not take it with us. When we moved into our first St. Louis apartment later in the summer, we had different furniture.

Upon arriving in St. Louis we moved in with my mother's youngest sister, Magdelene. Aunt Magdelene and Uncle Bob White were into buying flats and apartments and refurbishing them. They were involved in such a project upon our arrival at their home on Waterman Boulevard near the now famous Central West End and Forest Park. My brother Douglas had moved in with our aunt and uncle, Louise and Leland Mooney, in Berkeley, Missouri, a suburb of St. Louis. He had found a job at the *Dog and Suds Restaurant* in Carsonville, Missouri, that was likewise owned by our uncle Bob. It was here that my 18-year-old brother Doug met June Belyew and they would be married within the year.

Living with the Whites proved to be a pretty nice experience for me. Three of my cousins, Carol, Nancy and Robby were there and we all got along well. They also had a television which helped highlight the stay, as I was able to see many of the shows that I had been missing living in Salem. It was during that summer that a new adult cartoon was being promoted entitled *The Flintstones*. The only aggravation that I had was that the Whites were not avid Cardinal fans. On the occasion that KSD-TV, Channel 5 would broadcast a Cardinal road game, my cousins were generally interested in watching something else. However, I managed to get a peek or two now and then.

My cousin Carol also introduced me to a boy about my age named Whitey and we fast became good buddies. We spent a good amount of time throwing the baseball or playing basketball on the grounds of the nearby Hamilton Elementary School, located just off of Delmar Boulevard. Another regular activity was to ride one of my cousin's bikes around the area. Just one block from their home was the famous DeBalievere Strip, a hotspot for upscale nightclubs. One of the clubs featured *Evelyn West* and her $50,000 *Treasure Chest*, as insured by Lord's of London. I had seen her advertisement while reading the sports pages of the *St. Louis Globe-Democrat* many times while living in Salem. I found it somewhat intriguing to know that she was "working" a mere block from where I was staying. It was not uncommon for me to ride by the club during the day when it was closed with the hopes of getting a glimpse of

Life Between Innings

Ms.West. Obviously I never did see her but her provocative picture was prominently displayed in the window of the club making those frequent trips around the block still worthwhile.

While I was watching TV, playing ball and chasing Evelyn West, mom was out looking for a job and a home for us to live in. It wasn't long before mom found employment with the Rawlings Company. Her primary task was to lace up the famous baseball gloves that they produced. This was exciting stuff and somewhat prestigious to have a mom working in such a hallowed place.

Before we could hardly get settled in St. Louis, mom's greatest fear in leaving her mother was realized. On July 11, 1959, we received word that Grandma Anderson had passed away at age 73 at her home in Salem. I think mom felt very guilty over grandma's death, feeling that grandma had just simply given up after our move. Following the services, grandma was buried at the West Fork-Sutterfield Cemetery. Mom never said much about grandma's death to me but she confided in my sister, Bonnie, that she blamed herself, somewhat, for grandma's death believing that none of the family living in Salem could or would take care of her the way that she had.

As summer reached full bloom and the heat and humidity, for which St. Louis is famous, became more and more intense, mom purchased a four-family flat in south St. Louis. It was actually a six-family flat but only four of the apartments were for sale. It was located just two blocks from the world-famous Anheuser-Busch Brewery and four blocks from the banks of the mighty Mississippi River. To say that it was a beautiful building would be a huge stretch. In fact, it was without a doubt the least attractive flat in a several block area; well OK, a several mile area. It was situated right at the edge of the cobblestone sidewalk. In fact, those who lived on the lower level would walk out of their front doors and directly onto the sidewalk.

The Teenage Years 1959-1965

Yet, somehow, as I look back at this very humble flat, I realize that some of my best moments as a teen were captured here.

Mom decided to take one of the upper apartments for us. I thought our address was rather interesting: 1920½-A Arsenal Street. To get to our three-room apartment we had to walk around to the back through a narrow, unlit cobblestone walkway between our complex and the next and up a series of wooden, gray-painted steps. It was kind of a scary walk on those dark nights when we would get home late, especially if the moon was not in full bloom. However, the area was actually pretty safe and we never had any problems. Since we only had one bedroom, mom and Bonnie shared it and I would roll out the couch in the living room each evening. The couch easily folded out into a nice full size bed that just happened to be in front of our first TV, a black-and-white" model, which we obtained shortly after moving in.

My mom's youngest brother and her sister-in-law, Uncle Lowell and Aunt Elaine Anderson, decided to rent one of the lower apartments from mom, which proved to be a real blessing. Lowell was a very reliable man who could provide some help to mom around the complex as well as give valuable advice on certain maintenance issues. It also meant that one of my favorite cousins, Pamela, would be living just below us. Pamela was a tomboy, but a cute one, who enjoyed playing ball; she actually was pretty good and continued to develop into a decent ballplayer. It was to Pam that I turned over my rather large baseball card collection a couple years later, a decision I have regretted over and again. Not that she wasn't worthy; it was just one darn good collection of just about every major league player who was playing at the time.

One of my great memories occurred here in front of our old black-and-white TV. On that first Tuesday in November of 1960, mom and I stayed up till the wee hours of Wednesday morning

Life Between Innings

watching the presidential election returns come in between Richard Nixon and John Kennedy. For all our perseverance, the election was so close that it was not till much later in the morning that Nixon finally conceded the election to Kennedy. At the time, it was the closest election in our history.

Another great memory occurred one Saturday morning when Bonnie and I contrived the idea of tying a billfold on a string and placing the billfold out on the sidewalk in front of the apartment and in full view of the second floor window. Here, mom and Bonnie could observe the reaction of our victim. I was to hold the string tied to the billfold and hide in the gangway between our home and the neighbor. When someone passing by attempted to pick up the billfold, I was to slightly pull the string and watch the reaction of our victim. As our first victim approached, he spotted the billfold and bent down to pick it up. Just as he was about to pick it up I pulled the string, first with just a quick jerk, and then I took off running with great haste to safety, pulling the billfold behind me. Our victim never saw me. I ran up the stairs and back into the apartment to find mom and Bonnie lying on the couch, kicking their feet up and down in the air and laughing as hard as I have ever seen them laugh. Evidently, the reaction of the man trying to pick up the billfold was quite entertaining and they could not control their laughter. It was great!

Just outside our door was the stairway to the attic. The attic was a very interesting place. One of the tenants had stored away a number of rather explicit magazines, even by today's standards, which provided some early *educational* material. I tried not to linger over them too long or too often as I struggled mightily with my Christian convictions versus my desire to "be informed." But the greatest part about the attic was being able to crawl out onto the roof, which would be the 3rd story, and lie there in the cool of the evening, looking at the stars

The Teenage Years 1959-1965

and the moon, hearing the distinctive sounds of the city such as the horn of the Admiral excursion boat as it floated along the Mississippi River, the hot tamale man yelling, *"Red Hots, get them here,"* the clanging of the old cart pushed by the knife and lawnmower blade sharpener, the rush of cars, trucks and buses along Arsenal Street, the newsboy hawking his papers, the faint sounds of pedestrians talking as they went shuffling along the cobblestone sidewalk down below, the smell of the brewery and the hot sultry summer air, and do all this while listening to the Cardinals' game on my transistor. There just wasn't anything like it. For me, this was quite the life.

While the apartment was crowded and certainly not beautiful, for a kid like me the location was perfect. We lived in the middle of the block. Up the block to the east, Arsenal Street intersected with Lemp Avenue. On one corner was the famous landmark, the St. Louis Pretzel Company, the home of the best soft pretzels in the world. On the other corner was a small café with great hamburgers and a pinball machine that I could actually beat. On the other corners were a gas station and a drug store that sold baseball cards. This corner also became the home of my first job, selling the afternoon edition of the *St. Louis Post-Dispatch*. I purchased the corner for 50 cents from one of my seventh grade classmates making a penny and a half on each paper sold. I usually made about 35 cents a day. I worked this corner through the fall of 1959 and into the winter. After about seven months I sold the corner for a profit and retired from the newspaper business. A block down the street from that corner on Lemp was the Lemp Park and Pool where I spent a lot of hours swimming and playing baseball. In fact, it was at the Lemp Park that I pitched my one and only no-hitter. The fact that it was only a three-inning pick-up game is beside the point. It was also probably the last game I ever pitched as I was much more interested in hitting the ball than pitching it.

Life Between Innings

Heading west on Arsenal Street within a block of our apartment were two confectionaries where I could also conveniently purchase baseball cards. Two blocks down was Benton Park where I played basketball and whiffleball with my friends. We developed one of the finest whiffleball diamonds that you could find anywhere, spending hours playing the game. In doing so, I developed a pretty good knack for pitching both left-handed and right-handed with decent control. We would usually mimic our favorite Cardinal pitchers when we played; mine was the crafty left-hander Curt Simmons. However, whiffleball probably led to my demise as a serious baseball player as I am confident it led to the arm troubles I later developed in high school.

It was also at Benton Park that I played a lot of basketball in the summer and winter. Unlike Salem, in St. Louis, basketball was never truly "out of season." During the winter, it became necessary on occasion to shovel the snow off the court so that we could play, as we could not wait on Mother Nature to get the job done. It was also here that I first met several members of the St. Louis Hawks professional team. During the summers of 1960 and '61, the Hawks, working in conjunction with the St. Louis City Parks Department, held a series of basketball clinics. Assigned to participate were 6'10" Clyde "Boom Boom" Lovellette, the biggest man that I had ever met up till that time, and 6'9" Charlie Share, a strong rebounder and defensive forward. Lovellette, whom I had emulated playing while listening to the Hawks games in my Salem bedroom, was also one of the best pure long-range shooting big men that I ever saw play the game. He had a tremendously soft touch, unusual for anyone, but especially for a big man. For whatever reason these clinics were not that well attended, which was fine with me, as I received more individual attention from the players. St. Louis was proving to be Heaven.

The Teenage Years 1959-1965

When September of 1959 rolled around I entered the seventh grade at Fremont Elementary School, located about five blocks from the house. While my grades did not jump off the chart, they did seem to improve, building on my sixth grade experience with Ms. Langworthy back in Salem. My teacher that year was Ms. Irene Mayer who had been dubbed the "Old Gray Mare."

My eighth grade year marked a major challenge for me, which proved to be a blessing in disguise. Because I was younger than most of my classmates, the St. Louis Public School system had determined that I was too young to promote into High School unless I could reach Track I status. Track I students were considered superior students and were eligible to promote even though they may not have reached the required age that the school system had set. By this time, my grades and achievement tests were coming along well except, oddly enough, in Reading Comprehension Skills, an area that I would have assumed some excellence based on my love for reading.

For whatever reason, my eighth grade teacher, Ms. Mary Brassil, decided to invest some extra time in me giving me extra reading assignments to improve my comprehension. When it came time to take my final achievement tests, I scored well in all areas, including Reading and Reading Comprehension, and I attained Track I status. Consequently, after just reaching my 14th birthday on May 2, 1961, I graduated from grade school and was successfully promoted to high school. Ms. Brassil was the first of many people who I recognized as making a significant contribution to my life, outside of family, and I have never forgotten her. From this point on I began to be a pretty good student and would go on to finish in the upper third of my high school class, being inducted into the O'Fallon Technical High School Honorama Society, and much later graduate with Magna Cum Laude honors from St. Louis University.

Life Between Innings

It was during that first year at Fremont that I met Ray Huskey, a tall, stocky boy that became a longtime friend and one of the funniest guys that I have ever known. Just like any friend, Ray would occasionally do things that would irritate me and cause a momentary breach in the friendship. However, when buried deep in one of those occasions, he would work so hard, intentionally, to make me laugh that it was impossible to stay mad at him and our friendship continued to grow.

One of the most memorable, funniest incidents in my life, one of those brief but lasting "Polaroid moments," occurred one Saturday evening while he and I were at our neighborhood theater, the *Gravois*, at the corner of Jefferson and Gravois Avenues. Almost immediately after arriving in St. Louis, Mom had lifted the ban on movies, so I began to go quite frequently. After a full day of basketball, Ray and I took off to the theater. For us, the worse the movie, the better, as we liked to exchange with each other our own dialogue. This meant that we talked constantly during the movies, making our funny quips, which were not always popular with others in the theater. I am surprised that we were never thrown out.

On this given day the movie was so bad that Ray and I had dialogued throughout the movie, providing some irritation to an older man sitting a few seats down from us at the end of the row. Suddenly, and without warning, Ray developed a tremendously painful cramp in one of his legs. As he struggled to massage his leg and relieve the pain I could only laugh. Not obtaining any relief, Ray decided to try to get up from his seat and get out to the aisle where he could walk it off. After struggling to get to his feet, stumbling past me and still obviously in much pain, he attempted to get by the older gentleman at the end of the row. Just as he passed in front of the seated man Ray accidentally stepped on the man's foot. The gentleman immediately began to cry out, unfortunately at that precise moment,

The Teenage Years 1959-1965

the cramp in Ray's leg intensified causing him to bare down even harder on the man's foot, being further immobilized and unable to move off. With that the older man grabbed his hat and from his seated position began to swing wildly at Ray trying to hit him, or at a minimum, move him while screaming loudly in the darkened theater, *Get off my foot! Get off my foot!* I was no help as by this time I am absolutely and hopelessly laughing hysterically. Finally, Ray was able to stumble into the aisle where he made a quick get-away dragging his leg like the Frankenstein monster up the aisle as fast as he could go. At that point, our older friend either moved elsewhere in the theatre or left the building.

I enjoyed my two years at Fremont. I had become a better student and had made a number of friends. The avenue to most of my friendships came from my involvement in sports. Even though I was only in the seventh or eighth grade, most of my classmates knew that I was a professing Christian, yet they accepted me into their lives. I think that my acceptance was primarily based on the fact that my friends and I seemed to always have fun, plus I was trustworthy. And, except for being a Christian, I seemed normal.

At school we played pickup games of basketball almost daily during our recess time or at the end of our lunch hour. Since I was one of the better players I was usually named a captain, which meant I would be one of the "pickers." And, since my teams rarely lost, most of the guys wanted me to pick them. While our neighborhood gangs and school gangs were not as malicious as those of today, there were still some pretty tough characters in our school and neighborhood. These tough guys did not like losing either so they would solicit my selection for these pick-up games even though most of them were not very good. However, I saw two values in selecting them. One, they were willing to fight and scrap for rebounds,

Life Between Innings

which were essential to winning, and I was buying a certain amount of protection at the same time. In all the years I lived in this so-called tough area, I never had a problem with any of the "bullies" as I made them winners along with me.

There are a number of memorable playground incidents but one kind of stands out in that I was a little out of character in this one. We were involved in one of our pickup games of basketball when I took exception to the rough play of Ronnie Tidwell, one of the smaller bullies at Fremont that I really didn't like, and had not selected to play on my team that day. After a little bumping, we entered into a little verbal exchange, where I stated emphatically, "OK, you little bastard, cut it out." Even I was surprised at the words that proceeded from my mouth. Oddly enough, after that, Ronnie and I became friendlier with each other and we never had another problem that I can recall; go figure. However, if I were to guess where Ronnie is today, but for the grace of God, I would have to say he is probably serving a long sentence in someone's jail.

A number of my Fremont classmates were decent people from decent, hard-working families. But, as I mentioned, we had some that were already developing a life style very foreign to me. Some of these guys were good friends, although I learned quickly you never trust thieves. For example, in the eighth grade, the powers that be decided that twice a week our class would walk about 10-12 blocks over to another school for Shop Class. Along the way we would pass a number of confectionaries. The plan was always to have four or five of the guys to go into the store together, and while the owner was busy with a customer, they would take the opportunity to help themselves to candy displayed along the shelves. Some would steal just a few items but others would be a little more brazen and stuff their pockets pretty full. Of course the guys knew that, *Leo won't eat any if it's stolen.* The trick was to convince

The Teenage Years 1959-1965

me that the piece that they were giving to me was one that was actually purchased; sometimes it was and sometimes it wasn't. Their fun was to get me eating some of their stolen loot and then tell me that it was actually stolen, just to see me spit it out. They thought this was very funny and it would always get a great laugh, yet in a strange way, this created a bond between them and me as the one guy they could trust.

While at Fremont, Fred McGill was probably my next closest friend, other than Ray, yet he was conceivably the best thief of the whole group. In retrospect, Fred resembled, unbelievably, my own son Marc, at that age, who became a pretty "good" thief in his own right. Fred was a good-looking, athletic blonde guy that even at our age of 13 or 14 was a "chick magnet." But Fred was uncanny when it would come to stealing stuff and it was a fact, he just loved the thrill of stealing. Stealing for need was secondary to his love of just stealing. One of Fred's favorite places to "shop" was Western Auto on Cherokee Street, just a few blocks over from Benton Park. Stealing candy was chicken feed to him; he liked the more challenging things. He would walk into Western Auto and come out with all sorts of things. If we didn't have a good ball to play with, he would go "shopping" and bring back the needed equipment. Once, while trying to steal some baseballs, he couldn't figure out how to get them out of the store. So he decided the best route was to hide the balls in a new, but stolen glove, and walk out, which he did. He once stole a radio, listened to it until time to go home, and then just threw it into the pond at Benton Park. It was not uncommon for the park crews to find radios, bicycles, baseball bats, etc. in that pond and I am quite confident that Fred contributed a large collection of those items.

A souvenir Stan Musial (stamped) autographed baseball was discovered missing from my home shortly after one of his visits and I was certain Fred took it. He denied the theft, but

Life Between Innings

not too convincingly, and I never let him back into our house after that. I had learned a very valuable lesson; do not trust thieves, regardless of who they are. Fortunately, Fred moved to the East Coast after the eighth grade, which was probably the best for all of us.

In late November of 1959, I caught Ray and Fred whispering about something while out in the schoolyard. All they would tell me was that they had a secret that they couldn't tell me. However, at some point later that day they met me to say that they had decided to tell me their secret. It seemed that over the previous weekend they had somehow discovered the Boys' Club of St. Louis, located on South 11th Street, about a 20-minute walk from our homes. They confessed that they had decided not to tell me about their discovery because there was to be tryouts for the Boys' Club Junior Varsity Basketball Team that next week. Their fear was that if I tried out it was almost a certainty that I would get one of the roster spots and this could cost them a spot that they desired. They also told me that it was a supposed fact that the coach of the team had once pitched for the St. Louis Cardinals and had played on some high-level basketball teams; his name was Ken Wild. As it turned out, their fears where unfounded and we all three made the team. Actually, Ray, who became our starting center, had to do some creative work, with the help of his grandparents, to adjust his birth date on his birth certificate, as Ray would have just otherwise missed the age cut-off. Although not polished by any stretch of the imagination, Ray improved over the season and became a pretty good player. I was the starting "off guard" with the responsibility of being a scorer. Fred was usually one of the first players off the bench at the forward spot and did a fairly good job.

Much like making the Salem All-Star Baseball Team was the thrill of making my first organized basketball team. I

The Teenage Years 1959-1965

was, again, ecstatic! The Boys' Club was a first-class operation in a low-income area of south St. Louis giving kids such as myself an opportunity to grow up around men of good reputations and moral standards. The Club provided our own private locker room where we dressed and where we stored our fully equipped basketball uniforms with our own number and *St. Louis Boys' Club* scripted across the front of the jersey. Here we would also meet with the coach for pre-game and half time talks about strategy. It was here that I would learn to hear my name loudly called out for my many failures, such as not scrambling for a loose ball, for not following my shot for a rebound or for not taking the ball hard to the basket. The Club also had a beautiful gym; in fact it was the most beautiful gym I had ever played in. It was even better than the hallowed floor of the Salem High Tigers that I, on one Sunday in my distant past, had been allowed to practice on. We also had our own specific practice times, just like the Senior Varsity players did. We were big stuff.

Also on our team was a very small and slightly built left-hander, Danny Dixon. Danny played the point (guard) for us and one of our favorite plays was for Danny to break for our end of the court at just about the time Ray would rebound a missed shot. It was a timing play that, surprisingly, worked very often, getting Danny a lot of easy lay-ups.

Danny was involved in one of those, "you-had-to-be-there-to-appreciate-it-stories," while our team was playing in the Boys' Club Regional Tourney in Springfield, Missouri. This was truly big time for all of us, as Coach Wild had arranged to give each of us daily meal money. None of us was worldly wise, to say the least, but Danny certainly was not. At our first meal at a neighborhood restaurant we all mostly ordered the standard fare of hamburgers and French fries. For whatever reason, Danny wanted something different, but became

Life Between Innings

frustrated in his attempts to convey to the waitress what he wanted. So finally, feeling a little embarrassed by his failure to make an order, he finally said rather matter of factly, *I'll just have a baloney sandwich.* I am not sure who laughed the hardest, but it wasn't Danny. I tried to maintain my composure, I really did, as I really felt for Danny. The waitress, having much more class than any of us, tried hard not to further embarrass him and very simply stated, *I'm sorry, but we don't have baloney sandwiches here.* Danny never did understand why we were all losing it. It was not until years later that I realized that Danny had probably not eaten in too many restaurants, and when he had, his mom had probably ordered for him. I think he settled for a grilled cheese.

I also became involved in the Club's House Leagues as well. Our House League was made up of uniformed teams put together by the staff from the Club's membership; the more knowledgeable players were named as captain or coach. Thus, I was named captain and acting coach of my first team, kind of rag-tag group, but we made it to the championship game. We had a tall, lanky player, whose last name sounded like Shagnasty, so Shagnasty he was to most of us. Several of the local bullies put out the word that if Shagnasty played in the championship game they were going to beat him up. I took the issue to Mr. Charlie Nash, the Assistant Director at the Club and Assistant Junior Varsity Basketball Coach. He assured us that nothing would happen to Shagnasty. It took some convincing to get him to the game, but he came, and we won the championship. Shagnasty was never beaten up and I was proud of his courage in playing because he truly was fearful for his health.

For the next six years of my life, the Boys' Club would become my home. Almost all spare moments I had were spent here. The routine was pretty simple: go to school, go home

The Teenage Years 1959-1965

and do my homework, head out to the Boys' Club until they shut the doors at 8:30 PM. While I primarily spent my time that first winter practicing or playing basketball at the Club, there were many other activities to do. I became rather proficient at playing billiards (pool) and ping-pong, with either hand, and became the *Regional Boys' Club of America Chinese Checker Champ* in 1962, beating a young man from Paducah, Kentucky, in the finals. The Club also conducted an annual Christmas Party with dancing girls (and I mean girls) from a local tap dancing school. We would sing Christmas Carols, many of the religious variety, and chow down on cookies and soft drinks. At the end, we would normally be introduced to a surprise guest such as the great Stan Musial of the St. Louis Cardinals or Larry Wilson of the St. Louis Football Cardinals. The Club sports followed the season and with in-house (intra-mural) football, baseball and basketball leagues to play in, as well as the various Varsity Teams, we were kept wonderfully busy.

My basketball coach that first year of 1959-60 and forward was Mr. Ken Wild. The rumors circulating about him were fairly accurate in that he had been an up-and-coming right-handed pitcher with some talent for a St. Louis Cardinal minor league team until hurting his arm. He was also a scout for the San Francisco Giants professional baseball team. Additionally, he had played basketball with Collegiate All-American and Pro-Basketball Hall of Famer Ed McCauley on the St. Louis University Billiken Basketball Team in the mid '40s. As I grew to know Ken Wild, he became the greatest influence on my life, outside of Christ, that I would ever know. He truly became the one and only personal "Hero" that I would know. Even today his influence still follows me in the way that I approach so many things in life. In fact, even now in my 60s, I still catch myself wondering at times, *Is this the way that Mr. Wild would have wanted it done?*

Life Between Innings

Many years later, in fact I was well into my 40s at the time, I saw an article in the *Post-Dispatch* about the Boys' Club of St. Louis. The author had been careful to praise Mr. Wild, as well as the current director, Mr. Charlie Nash, Mr. Wild's assistant for many years. It stirred such emotion within me, calling-up such vivid memories of how these two men had helped to mold and shape me, that I just had to write a letter to the Editor. In the letter I mentioned that at the Club there were plenty of boys like me, boys that grew up without fathers and maybe did not have as much of the material blessings that others might have had. But, I noted, that we were probably more blessed than the richest of kids who had fathers in that we had Mr. Wild as our role model. I saw him a few days after the letter was published at a special Sunday afternoon, Senior Varsity Club game. As he was walking across the basketball court he spotted me up in the stands and called out, *Hey, there is the letter writer,* and he gave me an almost shy-like, blushing smile. A few days later I received a letter from him thanking me for the thoughts expressed in my letter and letting me know how much it meant to him. That Sunday was the last time I saw him before he passed on and I was glad that I had been able to let him know how much he meant to me personally. I have never met anyone like him ever; even in death, I still feel his care and compassion reaching out to me. Ken Wild remains my one and only true hero in life.

On June 16, 1961, I became a grade school graduate from Fremont Elementary. It was a proud moment indeed. This also proved to be a most momentous occasion as our class held its graduation party on the historical Admiral, a large, multi-deck excursion boat that floated the Mississippi River. One of the parents drove Ray Huskey, Fred McGill and me to the boat moored along the banks of where the Gateway Arch was to be built. In those days we did not date at the grade school level,

The Teenage Years 1959-1965

as some do today; we just met up at places and hoped that the girls would be there. At the time, I did not dance, nor drink, nor smoke, or run with girls who did, as the saying goes, but most of my school friends did, at least when the occasion was presented to them.

My exposure to girls was also very limited, although not for a lack of interest. I had this keen interest in girls and sex since the first grade. But, here I was in the eighth grade and still, other than Anna Lee McCarter in the fifth grade and that very short stint with Sharon Eudy in the sixth grade, I had never really had a girlfriend where the feelings were mutual. I did have an eye on Sharon Sommers in the seventh and eighth grade, a beautiful blonde with obvious assets, but I think we only talked once or twice. I had heard through the grade school grapevine that she thought I was cute, so that kind of frightened, yet intrigued me. I would go out of my way to pass her home on the way to the Boys' Club, praying for some random meeting, but it never occurred.

However, here I was on the Admiral when I was approached by Mary Lou Smith, a small dark-headed classmate with a somewhat suspect reputation, even for the eighth grade, who it was rumored had some interest in me. She very boldly agreed, or should I say, solicited, a graduation kiss from me. With as much courage as I could muster, yet somewhat impressed that I was not really nervous or apprehensive, I wrapped my coat around her shoulders as we stood atop the Admiral, and gave, and received, my first real kiss.

Mary Lou went off to McKinley High School while I went off to O'Fallon Tech. You don't forget that first kiss, so I accidentally, on purpose, ran into her as she walked to school during my junior year. I was now driving to school on occasion so it was easy to divert from my normal route to see who I "might" run into. I offered her a ride in my stunning red and white (it

Life Between Innings

was really mom's) Chevrolet Super Sport Impala. I noticed easily that she had developed even more over the past three years into a very attractive young woman and she seemed genuinely excited to see me. However, she was equally and obviously concerned that her boyfriend would see her in my car, an experience she obviously did not want to occur. Although I looked for her several more times, I never saw her again; but the impression she left was lasting!

During the spring of 1961, just before our grade school graduation, the school organized a field trip to O'Fallon Technical High School in mid-city near the famous Italian "Hill" district. I was blown away at the opportunity to get a high school education as well as learn a trade in a number of fields. So, instead of following my sister to McKinley High School, where she had graduated two years hence, I opted to attend O'Fallon. They offered training as electricians, machinists, aircraft mechanics and auto mechanics, plus the field of photography, business, cosmetology, printing and more. The machinist field seemed to be a "manly" occupation with a good future so I decided to go that route.

O'Fallon Tech was the largest high school by population in the state of Missouri and had a freshman class of over 700 students. The population was divided about 70% white and 30% black and, if nothing else, gave me a most valuable education in race relations that I would have not otherwise had. About my only exposure to people of other races and cultures was when we played baseball or basketball against a black team. The backdrop to all of this is that Blacks were just starting to follow the lead of Dr. Martin Luther King, Jr. and his non-violent Civil Rights protest methods for which the '60s became famous. St. Louis and East St. Louis (located in Illinois on the east side of the Mississippi River) were central to this whole protest movement and stories of marches, sit-ins, protests, blockades and such were regular features on the evening news. The papers and the newscasts where peppered with stories daily featuring Blacks in a not-so-favorable light, but the issue was becoming more clear; they were not going to stop their protests and marches until some progress was made in the area of equality across all aspects of life.

At the time I can't say I was truly impressed with their issues nor was I unimpressed. More than anything, I think I was just a little scared, but mainly ambivalent to it all. At school, I had made friends with a number of Blacks and played basketball almost daily with them during our lunch hour and found them to be, for the most part, just like any other kid my age. In truth, I could not really understand why there was so much hatred toward them, they seemed fine to me, but if anything I guess I was just passive about the whole issue. In retrospect, I realize that my attitude was actually part of the problem.

I carried this "passive" feeling toward Blacks and their issues until sometime into my late 20s or early 30s when I began to develop a better appreciation for their plight and their fight for equality. I certainly did not hate them nor did I go out of my way to avoid them. They were just people and their issues, while I was becoming more and more sympathetic, did not seem to affect me personally. But, because I was accepting, if nothing else, I was kind of allowed into their groups as a non-threat.

In all truth, my high school years were fairly uneventful and not too memorable, although I had wonderful experiences and great friends, both at school and especially within the church youth group. My Christian faith continued to grow as well and I began to take on leadership roles within the youth group. It was, however, a historic time and the idyllic America that we had grown up in was changing and life as we had known it

Life Between Innings

was now becoming uneasy. While Blacks and Whites where trying to learn how to deal with each other across America, the Cuban Missile Crisis of 1962 broke out. At the time I was working through the second semester of my freshman year. The school administration kept us appraised as to the latest news reports as we sat in our seats and tried to study. On the day when the crisis came to a head, even the skies were as dark and ominous as I can ever remember them being, even though it was mid-morning. The fact that we were on the brink of a nuclear war made all of our nerves stand on end. Studying was pretty impossible. Then, sometime before noon a voice broke out over the PA saying that Russian President Khrushchev had ordered his fleet to return to Russia at practically the last possible moment and war was averted. It was to be President Kennedy's finest hour in his short-lived term in office.

On November 22, 1963, early in my junior year in high school, another historic moment occurred when President Kennedy was shot and killed while riding in an open car in downtown Dallas, Texas. I was sitting in my New Math class (This was actually the title of the class and I never figured out the purpose for this type of math, but I passed. We would actually add numbers like 2 and 3 and get 6. I just never got it.) when the first rumors began to pop up that the President had been shot. About half way through the class one of the administrators announced on the PA that in fact the President had been shot and was in serious condition in a local Dallas, Texas, hospital. At the close of that hour, the entire student body was ushered into the gymnasium where we were kept apprised of the situation. Finally, word came that the President had died and that each of us should promptly return to our homes. The student body was in shock. The full reality of what had occurred would not set in until later that evening when we were able to view the assassination as it was replayed over and over on television.

The events of that week, including the funeral of the President and the murder of Lee Harvey Oswald, the chief suspect in the Kennedy assassination, are indelibly imprinted on my mind as if they occurred only yesterday. The news of Oswald's murder came on Sunday morning while we were attending church at Carsonville Full Gospel Tabernacle. Just prior to Leland Mooney, my uncle and our Pastor, starting his message, he stopped to announce to us that Jack Ruby had just shot Oswald as police were leading Oswald to a more secure jail. We would find later that these assassinations would only serve as the beginning of more violence poured out across our nation over the '60s. It was a time of "free love," but there was hate everywhere.

While basketball occupied much of my time from seventh grade through the twelfth grade, baseball was still the game. Oddly, I was probably a better basketball player than a baseball player but I still loved baseball with great passion.

In the spring of 1960, the end of my seventh grade year, I met a neighbor boy named Larry, who lived just a few doors up from us on Arsenal Street. Larry would become one of my best friends, even though it was only for a short time. Larry's dad just happened to coach the Stag Athletic Club (or Stag AC) baseball team and I received an invitation to try-out. At this point, I still was not much of a hitter, although my fielding had improved. Yet again, somehow, I made the team. I think coaches from back to my years in Salem saw my intense love and desire to play the game and consequently overlooked some of my flaws that they would have otherwise disqualified me.

The Stag team was not very good as we neither had pitching nor consistent hitting. But, this was an organization that

Life Between Innings

knew how to treat its players. At the end of the season, the Club gave us a banquet, trophies and beautiful green jackets with Stag AC scripted across the back. Since I did not have a dad, mom was invited to come to the Stag Club for the event. For all I know, she was probably the only woman there, but she handled it well and was proud for me. Because of her work, she rarely ever saw me play, be it in Salem or St. Louis, but it was neat having her share in this with me. This was my first such awards event and as you might guess, I was truly impressed. The food and the trappings were great; it was major league.

As I have said over and over to my own children and to those that I have coached, it was through sports that I learned how to use a knife and a fork and how to be comfortable sitting and talking with the rich, the important and the educated. This banquet was the beginning of that education. While this was an important part of my "education," I remain to this day just as comfortable spending time with the poor, the uneducated, the no-bodies, and not be phony.

That was the only year that I played for Stag, as this was the same year that I discovered the Boys' Club. Just as in basketball, the Boys' Club had a Varsity Baseball Team, as well as the intramural baseball House Leagues, and I was fortunate to play on these as well.

During May of my sophomore year came that moment of which all boys dream and that was getting my driver's license. I had actually numbered my calendar back some 100 days and carefully marked off each one as the days slowly slipped past. Finally, on May 2, 1963, my 16th birthday, I rode the bus to the license bureau at Hampton Avenue, just south of Chippewa Street, and passed my written test with a score of 92. A couple weeks later my brother-in-law, Gary Hedrick, allowed me to take the test in his car, a car that was without exaggeration, twice the size of Mom's Pinto, which I had driven frequently

The Teenage Years 1959-1965

with and without my permit. I didn't do too well, although I didn't kill anyone, so I passed with a score of 72. Being able to drive suddenly opened up a whole new world, a world that included girls. In fact, at age 16, most of the things I did seemed to involve girls in one way or the other. A level of my shyness with women was starting to dissipate. Only my issues with acne slowed me down, somewhat, and that was probably good.

So it was at this time I started involving myself in things other than just sports. The Boys' Club and my church activities still kept me busy but I was ready to branch out. I joined the school Pep Club for the sole purpose of meeting girls. I later joined the Citizenship Club, also for the sole purpose of meeting girls. My grades got me into the Honorama Society but there were no meetings to attend and no girls to meet. I was selected by the school administration to serve on the Student Council, which was pretty great, as we got out of class to do our business and some of the prettier, if not smarter, girls were also members. As might be somewhat evident, my participation pretty much revolved around the fact that girls might be involved; but, even though I was breaking through my period of shyness, I never dated a girl from my high school.

I was also developing a more adventurous and daring spirit, at least compared to what I had heretofore demonstrated. I had overhead a couple of the guys talking about how they had gotten in to see an adult film at one of the downtown theaters. Having never seen one, I figured it was time for me to do some investigating of my own. As usual, when I decided to do something that I shouldn't, I went alone. Following basketball practice one evening, I hurried off to the World Theater in downtown St. Louis to catch Jayne Mansfield in *Promises, Promises*. There was only one nude scene in the movie but I was impressed enough to stay for the second showing to

Life Between Innings

watch that scene again. By today's standards this scene and movie would barely get an "R" rating, but at the time it was considered risqué and was certainly an "eye-opener" for me.

Having succeeded at my first great adventure I decided to go on another. This time it was to see if I could get into the Grand Burlesque Theater, likewise downtown near where the current Busch Stadium sets. With my baby face and all, I brazenly walked up to the ticket window and surprisingly was given a ticket without question. My knees were knocking like crazy as I walked in and found a seat about half way back and to the side. The comedians were funny and the women were beautiful. Oddly though, as I sat there half enthralled with the success of my plan and half under conviction for even being there, I began to feel sorry for the women who were performing. Talk about a bag of mixed emotions. I think I even offered a prayer for them at some point. About halfway through the show my religious guilt began to take over and I decided to leave. Several days later some guy at the Boys' Club came up to me and said that he had seen me buying a ticket at the Burlesque Theater as he and his mom drove by. I argued hard that the person he saw wasn't me. I don't know if he bought it or not but I decided that the risk of going far outweighed the reward and I decided not to go back.

During my high school years I remained involved in the Boys' Club playing basketball and baseball and eventually coming on staff as Mr. Wild's Junior Staff Assistant, working at the front desk, greeting visitors, answering the phones and maintaining the initial membership applications. Mr. Wild was very kind to share with me the many compliments he received regarding the courtesy and attention that I had given to visitors and callers.

While the job was better than selling newspapers on the corner of Arsenal and Lemp, my love was still to play the

The Teenage Years 1959-1965

games. I continued to make the varsity basketball teams each year up through my sophomore season. My freshman House League Basketball Team became one of my all time favorite teams, as we were not, as they would say, on paper good enough to win it all. We had a couple of good players but the top team had more good players, including Ken Lehrmann, who was probably the best in the league; he was really smooth and he could really shoot. As player-coach I devised my first real defensive scheme where I and another good defensive player played ball-denial, man-to-man on their two best players, Bill "Lefty" Johnson and Lehrmann (I had Lehrmann). Our other three players set up in a triangle zone under the basket. Many teams now use this defense but when I came up with it, I did not know of anyone else using it. To my great delight, the defense worked very well. We kept their two best shooters well in check and really frustrated them while our zone gave us an opportunity to rebound even though we were not as physical or as tall.

As we were entering the last quarter of the game it had been nip and tuck from the beginning with a number of lead changes. I was beginning to feel it and sense that our opponents were losing some of their confidence, plus, since we were the underdogs, the crowd was clearly on our side. As the fourth quarter continued my teammates kept giving me the ball. Our opponents kept yelling to each other, *Deny Mooney the ball.* The more they tried, the harder my teammates worked to get it to me. Finally, we had reached a point where the clock became our ally and our opponent's enemy. It soon became apparent to them that they were going to have to foul in hopes of our missing the free throws so that they might regain possession. During that critical part of the game the ball seemed to always be in my hands and they had no choice but to foul me. And, I couldn't miss from the free throw line, hitting 8 in

Life Between Innings

a row to clinch the championship while the fans were going wild. What a great feeling; what a great rush! It was one of those natural highs that stays with you a few days and your feet seem to rarely hit the ground. I finished the game with 21 points, 9 of those points coming from 11 free throws. The individual trophy we received for winning the championship may be the smallest that I have ever received, but it remains one of the more meaningful ones that I ever earned.

I never played basketball at the high school level, I just continued playing for the Club. I had to use public transportation to get to and from school and as much as I loved the game, there was no way I wanted to be standing on street corners waiting for a bus at all hours of the night. Since our games would have been all over the city and the county and without a parent that could pick me up following games, it was just too much. In retrospect, I should have transferred from O'Fallon Technical High School to Cleveland High School in south city following my freshman year, which was only a few blocks from our new home at 3105-A Osage Street. There I could have played and realized a life-long dream of playing for my school. After three years on Arsenal Street, Mom sold the four-family flat and bought the two-family flat on Osage located in a nice residential area on the city's south side. It was a tremendous location with the Marquette Park swimming pool located just across the street along with a number of baseball diamonds. By the time we moved here, Bonnie, at age 19, had married Gary Hedrick and it was just Mom and me, except for my cousin Evelyn (Sullivan), who had moved from rural Missouri to live with us following her graduation to live in St. Louis to look for better job prospects.

Evelyn became like a sister to me and I never felt like her living with us was an intrusion. However, Evelyn was an accident waiting to happen and happen it usually did. She is one of the few people I have ever known that was just as adept at falling up the stairs as she was in falling down the stairs, a true talent indeed. Evelyn's most endearing adventure started one morning as she was running late for work, not necessarily an uncommon happenstance. She did not have a car so it was important for her to dress on time and then walk the two blocks to where the #77 Carondelet bus would stop. "Sensing" that she was very late, I offered to drive her to the bus stop, which she readily accepted. Upon arriving at the corner of Minnesota and Meramec Streets, where she normally caught the bus, we saw it departing. We were now in chase mode and finally caught up with the bus at California and Osage. I strategically pulled in front of the bus so that Evelyn could get out and the bus could not get away. She hastily jumped out of the car and attempted to climb the steps into the bus, only to fall up the steps, scattering herself and her belongings all over the bus floor. In tears and in embarrassment, she gathered up her stuff and ran just as quickly down the steps of the bus and back to the car, throwing herself inside. Her tear-stained and anguished face glared at me and with trembling lips said, *I've torn my nylons, take me home.* After she composed herself, changed her panty hose (which I know all about as mom was not shy about asking me to go into the store and pick up nylons and sanitary pads for her) and found that I was agreeable to driving her downtown to the Mart Building where she worked, we laughed. We laughed some more. I am still laughing!

I made the Boys' Club Varsity Baseball Team in the spring of 1961, my eighth grade year and played with the Club for the next three years. In 1961, Mr. Wild was now our baseball coach as well as our basketball coach and he ran our practices much like he had learned during his professional career. He taught us how to take infield and batting practice at the same time without risk of injury, which kept everyone on their toes

Life Between Innings

and made practice fun. I used this technique later on in life as I coached other teams, both youth and adult. It pains me to watch coaches try and practice with young kids when they, the coaches, do not possess practice skills sufficient enough to keep all the kids actively involved throughout practice. Their failure to do so usually means that the kids will lose interest very quickly, unfortunately never returning to the sport in any meaningful way. Our daughter, Whitney, fell victim to this in softball. I coached her for many years in basketball and soccer but needed some time away each year to catch up on other things. The result was that her coaching experience in softball was very poor and she never developed an appreciation for the game until her junior and senior years in high school.

Just as with the Stag Club, our Boys' Club teams were not very good. Again pitching was not a strong suit for us. However, I began to blossom as a hitter. As a left-handed hitter, I learned to open up my stance a little, giving me a better look at the ball, especially from left-handed pitching. For some reason, I hit left-handers pretty well. In one memorable game, in fact one of the few games out of the thousands that I would play where a member of my family attended, that being my brother-in-law Gary, quite a baseball player in his own right, I had an awesome night. The first time up I crushed a tremendous drive to right field. The right field wall was made of brick and was about three stories high. The ball easily cleared that wall and was still climbing when last seen. I have no idea how far it went, but it was a monster. The next time up, I hit another one, not quite the monster shot as the previous one, but it easily cleared the right center field screen. It was at this point that I really had Coach Wild's attention.

Generally, I played shortstop and some second base. I was not blessed with speed; however I was blessed with a keen instinctive sense of knowing from the pitch location which

The Teenage Years 1959-1965

way the ball was going if it was to be hit. This helped me get a jump on balls that I otherwise would not have gotten.

As the years went on, Coach Wild, who was also an ad hoc scout for the San Francisco Giants, told me that if I continued to progress each year as I had these past few years, he would sign me to a contract upon graduation from high school. As he stated, *If you can continue to hit, they will always find a place in the field to play you.* This was the highest compliment that I had ever received in regard to my baseball ability. Due to a number of factors, including, but not limited to, my involvement in youth church activities and leadership and a weakening throwing arm, I did not continue the growth that I needed to move on to the next level. But it was a nice dream, a dream that no one else had ever allowed me to dream, except for Mr. Wild.

For many of the same reasons that I did not play high school basketball, I did not play high school baseball until my senior year. Finally, I decided to try out and had a tremendously successful audition. Coach Droste, who doubled as my Chemistry teacher, positioned me at third base where my weakened arm could still be effective with the much shorter throws to first base. He would hit line shots at me time and time again trying to break me, but rarely could he do it. I even surprised myself, as fielding, as you know by now, was never my strong suit.

I made the team and this time Mr. Droste pulled me aside to verify what I had suspected to be true. He stated that he rarely ever allowed a player to make the team their senior year if they had failed to participate in the years previously. But, he went on to say that he saw a passion and love for the game in me that not many kids possess and he wanted to give me the opportunity. So, once again, I was blessed beyond deserving, which was already becoming a theme for my life.

Playing for the O'Fallon Technical High School *Hornets* became a thrill in more than one way. It was the first

Life Between Innings

successful baseball team I had ever played on as this team won the *St. Louis Public High League Championship* and played well in districts. It was also the first team that I had played on that had any pitching. Several of our players received minor league contracts, including George McDonald, our key starting right-hander, and Tom Cooksey, our best outfielder. None ever reached the big leagues but we had plenty of talent, offensively and defensively.

While I did not date any girls from my own high school, although not from a lack of interest, I did date several girls from other high schools. One was Ronnie (Rhonda) Finch from Ritenour High School, a dark haired beauty, and one of the most beautiful ladies I would ever date. I met her during my senior summer before heading off to college, a neighbor of my cousins, Dennis and Darlene Mooney. Ronnie was Catholic and loved to dance so they were not terribly supportive of me dating her, but how could I resist? Our first date was a double with my friend Ray Huskey and a neighbor friend of Ronnie's named Linda, who ironically had just started attending our church at Carsonville. We decided to go to Fairmount Park near Collinsville, Illinois, a horseracing venue. Ronnie's parents thought this was quite funny that an aspiring minister would take their daughter to the racetrack. However, none of us had ever been to Fairmount in our lives and we were obviously too young to bet on the horses, but we had a ball. Oddly, I never returned to Fairmount again until the night our daughter, Whitney, was born 20 years later.

I had also competed for the attention of another beautiful girl, Connie Cossey, who started attending our church when I was 15. Connie was beautiful in all aspects. She had a great personality, beautiful smile, and beautiful face, loved the Lord, and was slimly built, except that she was, dare I say it, wondrously endowed; and amazingly so! It may have been a church crowd

The Teenage Years 1959-1965

I hung out with but even they would stammer and stare when she was in the vicinity. Connie attended Central High School back in the city so it was an easy drop to take her home after church on Sunday nights once I obtained my driver's license. One of my more memorable dates with her was a double date with my cousin Carol White and her boyfriend Ed Treat who later married. This was the Thanksgiving weekend just following the assassination of President Kennedy. Our parents gave us their approval for a day trip to Salem, Missouri, for the annual Revival Tabernacle Thanksgiving Day services. Since we had never been romantically linked to this point I was very pleasantly surprised when she leaned over and kissed me several times on the trip back. The Bing Crosby Christmas classic, *Do You Hear What I Hear?* had just been released and over the years became a holiday standard. Whenever I hear that song, I can't help but think of her and what turned out to be a really great weekend.

Later that year Connie accompanied me to the Boys' Club Staff Christmas Party at LaRusso's Restaurant on Watson Road. She was absolutely stunning, especially so as she wore the Christmas corsage that I had given her. I was obviously the envy of all present, both boys and men alike. The next morning she gave me the ultimate compliment by wearing the corsage to church, validating our date the evening before among those with whom we attended church.

Unfortunately, Connie and I did not date long. It was not her fault as she was still willing to go out, but I think I felt a little intimidated by her, as she was truly *Big League Stuff.* As a kid who hadn't dated much to that point, and didn't truly know how the game was to be played, I finally decided to back off. It's one of those things that when you get older you realize how stupid and naive you were, letting your lack of self-confidence and dating experience deprive yourself of a potentially

Life Between Innings

great high school relationship. But such is life; we live and learn and then we get old!

While I continued to date a number of young ladies that I would meet at various functions, the most special of them all was a blonde young lady, Sandra (Sandy) Cloud, who started attending our church the summer of 1963. Sandy was a pretty girl with an attractive figure. Yet, she had so much more than just a pretty face and nice figure. She had a tremendous sense of humor and remains to this day one of the most genuine, naturally funny women that I have ever known; she just had a joyful, fun-filled personality that endeared her to her friends and to me. I really loved being with her as she always made me feel very special. And, she was a tomboy who could play softball better than most boys. For some reason, tomboys seemed to catch my attention more quickly than other girls (women), a trend that has extended through most of my life, even before and after meeting Sandy. In fact, in Tina, I married one. Without any reservations, therefore, I give my full endorsement to the dating of *tomboys* as they have proven to be the best companions and women to date and to marry.

Sandy proved to be a great friend and still is, even after all these years. We dated continuously throughout my junior and senior years (her freshman and sophomore years). The two years that we dated are loaded with the best memories of my high school years. Because I was a "trustworthy" lad, her dad, Verdell, allowed me to date Sandy, even though she was only a freshman. Because of that trust, I determined never to let him down; I always got her home on time and in the same condition that she was in when I had picked her up. Verdell and I are still friends to this day.

Sandy and I shared many, many great times and memories, one of which was being selected King and Queen of our Youth Valentine Banquet at church in 1964. We attended a number of Youth for Christ activities together, including other dress-up banquets and general things like going to the movies or just taking a Sunday ride. And, most importantly, she was my high school graduation date. While I made it perfectly clear to her during our dating days that we were never "going steady," she was, in fact, my main girl. Somewhere in the beginning of my dating years I had realized that it was a big mistake to be "committed" to one girl during high school. As much as I enjoyed and cared for her, I have never regretted taking that stance. I was fortunate enough to meet a number of young ladies in a number of different places during my high school and early college years that I would not have been able to meet if I had "gone steady," consequently missing the opportunity to meet some really neat ladies along the way. However, I respected Sandy then as being someone very special and I respect her even more today; we still keep in touch from time to time.

Despite my love, dare I say passion, for the games of baseball and basketball; I also had begun to develop a more personal walk with Christ during my high school years. While we lived in south city and eventually in deep south city, we traveled for 45 minutes to an hour each Sunday, sunshine or rain, to the county to attend my Uncle Leland Mooney's church, Carsonville Full Gospel Tabernacle. It was here that I had been baptized, fully immersed, at about age 14, and would learn to grow in God's grace throughout my high school years. It was not uncommon to make the trip twice on Sunday from our home in the city; however, most of the time I just stayed with my cousin Dennis during the afternoon who lived near the church in Berkeley, and then later in Bridgeton. Most Sunday afternoons were spent playing ball with him or some of the other guys from the church or just hanging out with the kids from our church Youth Group.

Life Between Innings

Our Youth Group was a collection of very special kids. The core group included Dennis and Darlene Mooney (my cousins), Sandy and Judy Cloud, Sharon and Brenda Eddington, Judy Moore, Bob Belyew (who married my cousin Darlene), Dick Wilkerson and Susie and Debbie Wilhelm. This was the Sunday crowd; others joined us from time to time but it was these young people that became family, as we became like brothers and sisters, except without the fighting. Only Darlene and Bobby and Sandy and I dated to any degree from within the group. This group was pretty talented with musicians and singers. One of the highlight memories in being with them was the Sunday afternoon that we gathered at the Trio Restaurant, one of our frequent hangouts near the church by St. Louis Lambert International Airport, and jointly wrote a Christmas play that we were allowed to put on before the church congregation that holiday season. That was a blast and our presentation was a success.

Once I started driving, I was able to attend the Tuesday night youth group meetings regularly. Consequently, I was able to enjoy the friendship and fellowship of this closely-knit group even more so over the last few years of my high school experience. It is neat to know that almost everyone in our closely-knit inner circle of friends is still involved in the Lord's work today. I was elected the Youth Leader, a position that I held for about 2 years until I left for Bible College. It was this responsibility that actually began to eat into my baseball and basketball playing time. However, God has been very gracious in that while I gave up the dream of playing professionally, a dream that most probably would not have materialized anyway, He has allowed me to remain in various areas of sports throughout my entire life. While at the time it seemed to be a big sacrifice, in the light of eternity, it was truly no sacrifice at all.

The Teenage Years 1959-1965

Oddly, going to church did have one negative effect on me, as I became, as mom put it, *"her juvenile delinquent son."* Within about two weeks of obtaining my drivers' license, in fact I still had the pink paper saying that I had passed all my tests but did not yet have the official license in hand, I received a ticket for running a church stop sign while driving home from church. Several weeks later I received another ticket coming home from church for not coming to a complete stop at the stop sign on a very dark side street with no traffic anywhere in sight. Within a month or so of that occasion, and still prior to my 17th birthday, I was coming home from Youth Group, still on a spiritual high from the service, when I was pulled over for doing 40 in a 30. This prompted an invitation from the Juvenile Courts of St. Louis for mom and me to attend a meeting with a judge in his private chambers to discuss my newly established driving record. As mom generally was in these circumstances, she found some humor in the fact that her juvenile delinquent son was being reprimanded indirectly for attending church. On the lighter side, I was again blessed beyond deserving, as mom did not restrict me in any way. I never received another ticket until 1979, some 16-years later during my "angry years."

Some of the greatest times that our group enjoyed came at our church camp that was held in Mountain View, Missouri, every July. Now by today's standards, this wasn't much of a camp. On the other hand, I would challenge any teen that has ever gone to camp to have enjoyed a better, more fun-filled, more spiritually up-lifting week, than we did each year at our camp. No matter the summer obligations, this was something that just could not be missed. We were housed in fairly nice little cabins, joined together to make a dorm. Our showers were across the camp in an outbuilding with cold running water.

Life Between Innings

For entertainment, there was an open field where we played softball with bases made of rags or sticks or rocks or whatever we could find. It was on this rocky, so-called softball field, that during my sophomore year I developed a mad crush on a left-handed pitching and slugging red-head, Ruth Ann Hoover. She was by far the best of the girl players and exceeded the talents but of just a few of the guys; but her real talent was in her looks as she was gentle on the eyes. We actually stayed in touch for a couple years and had a date or two. However, Ruth Ann lived in Bourbon, Missouri, about 70 miles from St. Louis, which was just a tad bit far to begin a dating relationship.

On the campground we also had volleyball net. Actually, the games were quite competitive, and since they were co-ed, it was much more fun than just mere competition. I don't know of a place or a game in which we laughed and laughed and laughed as we did playing this game. We would play for hours until required to come in for supper or head back to the tabernacle for worship. And that was it, at least for entertainment. Well, that is unless you want to call being on the dishwashing crew entertainment. And yet it was entertainment. Sometimes it was hard to get on a crew because that was where the fun truly began; it was also the place where many new and lasting friendships were made. No one left dry and, again, all left laughing. And, to the credit of our adult supervision, they let it happen. I think they knew that it was here, performing this chore that true relationships were being born.

On the spiritual side, we would meet for devotions in the morning in the old outdoor tabernacle with the sawdust floors and the old weathered benches with splinters. We did a lot of repenting kneeling in that sawdust and God honored those repentant prayers time and again. It was neat seeing young people minister to young people and to see those young people begin a new life in Christ. It was rare, very rare, that an

The Teenage Years 1959-1965

unsaved young person could come and stay the week and not leave a born-again-child-of-God. The power of the Holy Spirit swept that place day after day and night after night and year after year. It was such a glorious time that I lay in bed these many years later and still vividly recall how God met me there summer after summer.

Unfortunately, it was here that I experienced the pain of well meaning people, such as my Grandma Anderson, putting their personal spiritual convictions on others, convictions that often could not be backed up by Holy Scripture, convictions that were burdensome and legalistic and simply stumbling blocks in our walk with the Lord. Despite all the good that occurred here, the legalistic bent of just a few of our leaders put some of our young people, including me, under condemnation instead of godly conviction, and that was and is wrong. I know I was pressured and misguided into making a vow that was not of my own personal conviction but that of two strong, well-respected, adult leaders. During one of the services, after an emotional presentation, Mrs. Priest, one of the key leaders, led us to pray to God and make a vow to Him that we would no longer attend movies. This husband-and-wife team preached hard that going to the movies was a sin, an abomination in the sight of God, and that for us to attend was a sin in His sight. Being young and sensitive in heart to what God might want or expect from His children, I am sure that many, like myself, followed her in making that prayer. I have struggled with the issue of that particular vow since; it created an unnecessary spiritual struggle for me in my youth and early adult years that at times was personally painful and so unnecessary. I am comfortable with the fact that as spiritual leaders, in areas of conviction and liberality, we are best served to allow the Holy Spirit to do His work in the lives of those that we minister to rather than to try to usurp that role from Him. Amen!!

Life Between Innings

During my Junior and Senior years I discovered a grand and special new world of gospel music, especially southern gospel quartet music. The Lester Family of St. Louis was a gospel singing family that traveled all over the U.S.A. presenting the gospel musically. They had a nice sound, but more importantly, they hosted a monthly "Gospel Singin" at the old Kingsland Theater on Gravois Avenue in south St. Louis. One hot Saturday evening, after everyone else had cancelled out on mom, she convinced me to go with her to one of these singins. When we arrived, the concert had already started and the theater, lower area and balcony, was packed. There was not an air conditioner in sight, except the cardboard kind that you hold in your hand and wave back and forth, yet from the moment we entered, you could feel the electricity in the air. I do not remember all the groups that were there that night but I do seem to remember that my favorite group that evening was the *Blue Ridge Quartet*. Not only was the quartet style music to my immediate liking but the whole entertainment package itself, with the humor and banter that each group brought to the stage, was unique and enjoyable to a young Christian.

After my initial evening at the Kingsland, I was hooked, and mom did not have to beg me to go from there on out. One of my favorite groups was the *Oak Ridge Boys Quartet*, who later became even more famous as the *Oak Ridge Boys*. I think it was during the summer of 1964 that Smitty Gattlin, their lead singer, resigned. Mom and I got in on a little bit of history one night that summer when the *Oaks* introduced their new lead singer, Duane Allen, who had left his previous group upon being drafted into the military. However, Mr. Allen flunked his physical and the *Oaks* picked him up to replace Gattlin. The rest, as they say, is history.

I continued to follow and enjoy the great gospel groups. My favorites were most everyone's favorites: *The Stamps* with

The Teenage Years 1959-1965

JD Sumner, *The Speers Family, The Weatherford Quartet, Jake Hess and the Imperials, The Happy Goodman Family* and the *Blackwood Brothers.* I was so thankful when Bill Gaither started his Reunion Tours during the '90s featuring many of these great Christian artists. Tina and Whitney, my beautiful wife and daughter, give me a lot of grief (good-naturedly) over my obsession in watching the Gaither program each time I stumble across it; but the music represents great memories and a great time of spiritual renewal for me.

In September of 1964 my senior year began. I was, by this time, doing very well in school. In fact, I think to this point I had been knocking down A's and B's for three years with perhaps two exceptions, that being Biology and Chemistry; I hated both of those classes. But because I was a good student I began to get some of the benefits that go with that accomplishment. One of the "bennies" was being excused from class to make keys in the school office. It just so happened that the Cardinals were in the World Series for the first time since 1946, so I was able to watch most of the games while I worked. However, I finally decided that it was time to skip a day or two so that I could more fully devote myself to watching the games as this was the culmination of many years of frustration in following those Birds. Now, at my school, students skipped school all the time and it was no big deal; well, at least the administration did not call your home unless you were gone for an extended period of time. However, in my case, since I so faithfully attended school, my machinist instructor, Mr. Ledesma, became concerned for my health after just two days of absence so he called mom to inquire. Mom was very understanding and simply told me that all I would have had to do was ask and she would have excused me as she understood my "need" to see the games.

In 1965, my senior year in high school was coming to a conclusion and I was faced with new decisions. First, I had found

Life Between Innings

that I did not like being a machinist, and even after 4 years of extensive training, I wasn't really very good. My grades in the class may not have indicated that, as I was averaging about a B+, but the fact was that I was not a good machinist and really did not desire to become a better one. In retrospect, I find it interesting that no one ever took the time to pull me aside and advise me that maybe I should consider another field of study, except a music teacher with whom I had very little, if any, relationship. One day during my sophomore year she pulled me aside and questioned whether it may be in my best interest to transfer to the Business Department. To this day I do not know what she based her observation on but it was obviously, so obviously, correct. Her comment was so random, plus none of my true advisors had ever questioned or challenged me to consider anything else, so I disregarded her suggestion and continued my training as a machinist.

The lack of skill and aptitude for becoming a machinist became even more evident to me, and finally a number of others outside of the school. During the last semester of my senior year, the school sent me out on a machinist apprentice job at a small shop located just off Manchester Road in Rock Hill, a small St. Louis suburb. I was kindly let go after about two weeks. I was then sent out on another job to a place called Merit Company at 205 East Davis, a much bigger shop just off South Broadway in the Lemay area of south city. There I worked as a screw machine operator; the absolute dirtiest job I have ever had or most likely will ever have. I did not iron my shirts before going off to work, as within minutes of toiling at one of the machines, I would literally be covered with oil from head to toe and all the wrinkles would be gone. My performance here was a little better, but this was obviously not a good career choice for me. The old heads working there strongly encouraged me to get out and do something else with

The Teenage Years 1959-1965

my life as this was not a job I would want to be working 20 years hence. I agreed.

It was also at this time that mom had gotten a call from Mr. Ken Wild at the Boys' Club of St. Louis asking that she attend with me the annual awards presentation being held at the Club. I had recently left my job there as Mr. Wild's Junior Staff Assistant to try my hand as a machinist and to play baseball for the school. So, I could think of no reason he would want mom or me to attend. I also knew that none of my teams had won anything that year. Mom and I arrived and took our seats up in the bleachers of the gymnasium and patiently waited as trophy after trophy was handed out. There seemed to be more awards than normal so the night seemed to be going long; it also was apparent that there were no trophies or awards for me. Finally, the ceremony was over and Mr. Wild came to the microphone and announced that there was one last award to be presented; that it was a new award being presented to the boy that truly exemplified the *Spirit of what the Boys' Club stands for.* The award was to be presented to a boy that was involved deeply in the Club, to a boy that was involved in his school and whose grades were well above standard, to a boy who had been a good citizen in the community and lastly to a boy that was deeply involved in his church. He went on further to state that three members of the Club had been nominated for this award and their resumes had been sent to the headquarters of the Boys' Clubs of America in New York for the final selection. And then he announced, *The winner of the first annual Boy of the Year Award for 1965 is Leo Mooney.* WOW! So unexpected. So really neat. So speechless. It is quite an honor and thrill for me to go back to the Club and see my name engraved on the plaque that still hangs prominently on the wall as the first winner of the award.

Shortly after that Mr. Wild approached me with an offer of a full 4-year scholarship, on behalf of the Boys' Club of

Life Between Innings

St. Louis, to attend Southern Illinois University at Edwardsville (SIU-E). All I had to do was agree to work part time at the Club while attending school and upon graduation agree to give back my services to the Club, services for which I would be paid, for three years. I had been making plans to attend Southeast Missouri State (SEMO) in Cape Girardeau, Missouri, to study for a coaching career, and in fact had already been accepted, and had my room assignment in hand. I was also being heavily persuaded by my Uncle Leland Mooney and Verdell Cloud, Sandy's dad, a minister in his own right, to attend International Bible College (IBC) in San Antonio, Texas, as they were confident that God was calling me into the ministry.

In the absence of a father, I did not receive much good or unbiased counseling regarding this important decision. To follow my dream, I felt that I needed to go to SEMO. We were not rich by any stretch, in fact we were poor, so SIU-E would have been a good and prudent choice. And, most likely, at SIU-E I could have pursued my dream of coaching there as well as I could have at SEMO. However, of all the choices I had, because of the strong influence of Pastor Mooney and Rev. Cloud, I made the choice to attend IBC. Spiritual things aside, I listened to the wrong voices and I made a wrong decision. Yet, out of that decision has come many untold blessings, a fulfillment of Romans 8:28-30 which states, *28And we know that in all things God works for the good of those who love him, who have been called according to his purpose. 29 For those God foreknew he also predestined to be conformed to the likeness of his Son, that he might be the firstborn among many brothers. 30And those he predestined, he also called; those he called, he also justified; those he justified, he also glorified.*

In God's sovereignty, yes, the decision to go to IBC was the right decision, but in human terms, in terms of what I wanted to do with my life and what would have been beneficial

The Teenage Years 1959-1965

(success and money), going to IBC was the wrong choice. And, as I realized a few years later, I certainly did not have a pastoral or ministerial call on my life, regardless of what others may have thought. It was with great relief that this burden would be finally lifted off my shoulders some nine years later and I was able to go on with my life. However, for years, I would, in the honest recesses of my heart, resent the fact that I "wasted" my opportunity to do what I really wanted to do and probably would have been "really" good at doing, if people, good people, with good intent, had not put their "feelings" or their "impressions" of a God call on me. Now, some 45 years later, I truly see God's handprint all over that decision. In the light of eternity, it will prove to have been a great decision. Although I realize and accept that, I still must admit at times, my mind does wonder what it might have been like had I followed my dreams.

The 3rd Inning

THE BIBLE COLLEGE
YEARS 1965-1968

In 1965 Lyndon Baines Johnson was serving his first full term as the President of the United States. After succeeding President Kennedy upon his death in 1963, President Johnson had been elected in his own right in 1964. During this term, President Johnson involved the United States even more deeply in the Viet Nam War and America was seriously divided on the issue. At the same time, he was introducing his "Great Society" plan, an attempt to address many of the concerns that developed out of the Civil Rights demonstrations, but also a way to ensure that no American would go to bed hungry. His plan was marked by a huge tax increase and ultimately, his plan failed miserably. In 1968, President Johnson surprised the nation when he announced that he would not run for a second term saying, "If nominated, I will not accept, and if elected I will not serve." This set the stage for the political comeback of Richard Nixon as he barely defeated the popular Democratic candidate, Hubert H. Humphrey. Unfortunately, the violence that would come to mark the '60's continued. In 1968, the Rev. Martin Luther King, the leader of the NAACP (The National Association for the Advancement of Colored People), and the most visible leader of the Civil Rights Movement, was gunned down on a hotel balcony in Memphis, Tennessee. During the presidential primary campaign that same year, Democratic hopeful, Robert Kennedy, the brother of President John Kennedy, was gunned down

Life Between Innings

in a Los Angeles, California, hotel just after scoring his greatest primary victory. In baseball, the hated Yankees were starting to flounder. Likewise, in 1965 and 1966, the Cardinals returned to their losing ways finishing in seventh and sixth place respectively. However, they rebounded again in 1967, led by League MVP Orlando Cepeda, and earned another trip to the World Series. In a great seven game series, the Cardinals bested the Boston Red Sox with Bob Gibson winning three of the four games. In 1968, the Cardinals returned to the World Series only to blow a 3-1 series lead to the Detroit Tigers and their left-handed ace, Mickey Lolich, who won three of the four games. In 1967 the first Super Bowl was played pitting the Green Bay Packers against the Kansas City Chiefs; the Packers prevailed 35-10.

It was August of 1965, a Thursday, and my cousin Dennis (Mooney) and I had his car packed and ready to leave for San Antonio, Texas, and our new life as Bible College students. Dennis had an old Buick that was grayish looking at its best and to which we affectionately dubbed the "Tank." The car ran fairly well and it had a radio, so what else could two future "Reverends" want. Our trip was uneventful, but was as exciting as all heck, as we were 18 and we were out on our own. The fact that we were living off our parents' money and credit cards was beside the point; that's college life.

The car was not air-conditioned so we enjoyed the August heat as we journeyed through Joplin, Missouri, turned left at Big Cabin, Oklahoma, traveled on through Sherman, Texas, till we reached Dallas and found a fairly nice hotel on the interstate just across from Southern Methodist University. We did not realize it at the time but the contrast between the school across the street and the one that we were attempting to reach was so great that to try to attempt to compare them would not have done justice to either school. As we awoke the following Friday morning we made our beds, just so that the maids would understand that not all teenagers were slobs. The fact

90

that the maids would have to remake the beds anyway, plus would have no way of knowing that teenagers slept here, completely slipped by our thinking.

After a little breakfast, we were off to complete the remaining 300 of the 910 miles we needed to travel to reach San Antonio. Sometime toward 2:00 PM we entered the city and left the city, entered the city and left the city, entered the city and left the city, and so on for several miles. The city, as we found later, was oddly drawn so that the interstate kept coming into and out of the city limits. Upon reaching the Interstate 410 Loop we became enthralled with our new city with its distinctive Hispanic flair. It was easy to close my eyes for just a moment and envision cowboys from the old west riding by. We had learned on this trip that I was the better navigator so at this point Dennis was driving and I was providing directions, per our map, through the city to our new home on Hallelujah Hill, a name affectionately given to the IBC Campus as it sits overlooking the city.

Finally, the last of the 910 miles was upon us and we were approaching the school. The street we were driving on suddenly dead-ended and there, right in front of us, barely seen through a large growth of weeds and behind a small rock retainer wall, was a sign that read *International Bible College*. In smaller letters in script under the school name we could barely make out the words *Impossibilities Become Challenges* and the school's address, *2369 Benrus Boulevard*. To say my heart sank would be an understatement. I am not sure what I had expected, but I certainly hadn't expected what I was seeing and what I was about to see. We made a short left onto Benrus Boulevard and then a quick right onto the graveled, rut filled drive leading onto the school property. If my heart could have sunk any lower, it would have been in my shoes. I simply wanted to cry but couldn't. We passed the library that looked like an old Army outbuilding (because it

Life Between Innings

was), a dorm (this was the men's dorm and would be my home for the following year) that looked like an old Army barracks (because it was), a row of trailers (for the married students) and then a small, oddly shaped, two-story wood framed building with a sign saying, *Office.* Around the corner from the office was another dorm (the girl's dorm) sheltered by a number of large trees, which was just a tad bit better looking than the one we had just passed. Lastly, across from the office we observed a three-story stucco, pinkish looking building (housed several of the staff and served as our dining hall). And, did I mention the weeds? And the dust? And the lack of pavement? And a gymnasium?

Dennis and I did not talk. We just got out and went into the office to introduce ourselves. A couple of women behind the desk greeted us with big Texas-looking smiles and a hearty welcome. After a little chitchat, we were led back to the first dorm that we had passed and into our first floor, small, non-air-conditioned, non-carpeted, pretty drab looking, room; and that is being kind. It was obviously occupied already by another student, although he was not present. Dennis and I had planned to room together but we had not anticipated having another "roomy;" we were told that they were anticipating their largest freshman class in the school's history so we were being "bunched up" a little. As I have stated several times, my family did not come from money, but if we did it was from coin, not paper, so we were not used to living the high life by any stretch, but the conditions of this place were by far the worst that ever I could have imagined; ever. Even the campgrounds and dorms at Mountain View where we had spent a week each summer for camp were a prize compared to this. At that precise moment I wondered how in the world I could have ever given up my dream of coaching and attending Southeast Missouri State University for this. I was in mental anguish!

The Bible College Years 1965-1968

Despite what we were seeing, sensing and feeling, I do not recall Dennis or me making any verbal complaints about this place or our decision to come here until sometime weeks later after we had became acclimated and were sharing, with some levity, our first impression of IBC.

Later, on that first day, a slender, dark complexioned Hispanic young man with Elvis Presley looking black, slicked up hair, came into the room and introduced himself as our roommate. His name was Charles Lashua, an adopted son of a missionary family working in Mexico out of Brownsville, Texas. Charlie would become one of my better friends during our years at IBC. It did not take long to find out that Charlie liked to play basketball, so before the day was out the three of us were on the court, a large concrete slab out in the great outdoors. The court had goals at both ends, but with no nets, something that I would have to remedy immediately; it also doubled as a volleyball court. Dennis and Charlie did not possess my basketball skill so, as we often did, we played me against the two of them. The outcome was hardly ever in doubt but it was fun to beat up on somebody once in awhile and they tried hard.

The following Saturday may have been one of the longer days of my life, as we did not have much to do nor the means to do it with, and the place had not gotten any more attractive overnight. By Sunday, more and more of the students were starting to come in and we had our first visit to the home church of the college, Revival Tabernacle. Rev. John Bell, the brother-in-law to IBC President, Rev. David Coote, pastored the church. David was the son of a missionary to Japan, Rev. Leonard Coote, the founder of IBC colleges, first in Japan and then here in San Antonio. It became evident from the moment that we walked into the church by the banners posted over the podium that this was a church that supported foreign missions. The banner hanging on that particular Sunday read, *The Next Town Crusades.* My favorite banner, later hung for one of the annual mission conferences, read *Go or Send a Substitute,* a theme that later in life became very important to me personally. The light was gradually starting to come on that IBC was more than a school that was training pastors, evangelists, children's workers and Sunday School teachers; they were also training missionaries. Now, at this time, I was not necessarily opposed to being a Pastor, nor was I opposed to supporting missionaries, but to be trained to be one, well, I hardly think not!

On Monday following our arrival we began the day, as we would each day for the next three years, by heading off to chapel. We were then introduced to our new classes, almost all of which were Bible studies, and told what books we would need. However, in many cases, the Bible was the textbook and other books were only source material to help enlighten or validate what we studied.

As the weeks went on, the effect of the initial horror that occurred when we first drove on campus began to diminish and a new life began to break forth that was actually enjoyable, if not exciting. In the classroom, the Bible was coming alive in ways I had never thought it would or could. Many of our studies were outstanding, but none like the *Life of Christ* course taught by President Coote. I seriously doubt that there is a man alive that could have made the scriptures of Matthew, Mark, Luke and John more alive, more real, almost like you were actually there, like you were in the crowd with the disciples and were actually seeing Christ perform His miracles, than Brother Coote could. He easily could have been a great actor with his gifts; I would leave his classes daily so inspired, so challenged, so in awe of our God.

Over the three years my studies went very well, maintaining an A+ average. I found right away that retention of all

94

The Bible College Years 1965-1968

this Biblical knowledge was difficult for me. This was probably a direct result of finding that I did my best work when up against a deadline. Consequently, I was cramming for most of my exams. While I never learned to quote scripture like many of those I studied with, I did learn methods on how to find the answers if given time to do the research. This worked for me then and now.

One of the major contributions to our Biblical education came from the daily chapel services. It was here that select students with preaching skills were allowed to share from time to time. It was also here that various missions clubs and organizations would put on occasional skits highlighting their areas of interest around the world. Since I had absolutely no intentions of being a foreign missionary, I founded the *Missions to North America Club*, with the permission of President Coote, and was actually surprised at the number of students (cowards like me) that joined. In fact, we eventually became one of the larger prayer groups on campus, if not the largest. Later, in my second year, I began to repent of forming such a club as my heart was growing more and more tender toward the world of foreign missions and the call of the *Great Commission* (Matthew 28:19-20). However, as an official mission club, we took our regular turn along with the other missions clubs at hosting a chapel service.

The chapel, not surprisingly, became a source of continual spiritual uplift. It was not uncommon for students to minister to each other right along with the staff. These daily services were marked with students standing in awe of Almighty God with arms raised high in praise and worship as we sang songs and choruses of the heart. And, about once or twice a year, a confessional service would break out with students confessing some of their latest sins or seeking forgiveness from a roommate that they may have offended. I was becoming a little

Life Between Innings

more aware of the "worldly life" so I was not shocked necessarily at some of the revealed sins, but I did find it interesting that so much was going on around me that I knew little about.

In retrospect I now realize that it was in these chapel services that God began to teach me a lot about living the Christian life while facing the struggles and weaknesses that we Christians confront daily, but hate to admit. I certainly did not realize it at the time but I had become a very self-righteous, narrow-minded person over the span of my Christian life. I began to learn slowly, but at least I began to learn, that sin in the life of a Christian did not necessarily make that person a hypocrite, as Christians are commonly accused of being. But as Christ said, He had come to heal the sick, not the well (Matthew 9:12-14). Translated, that simply meant to me that the church was a place for sinners, that the church was full of sinners and was a place where sinners could be ministered to and find forgiveness and peace. My favorite bumper sticker probably says it best, *Christians Are Not Perfect, Only Forgiven.*

Not all that happened in chapel was good and spiritually pure. One of the shameful rites of fall and our return to school was the assessment of the new overly spiritual, overly zealous students that had arrived on campus. They were easy to spot, as they would usually be overly demonstrative in their worship, often accompanied by outburst of prophecy that just smelled of "fleshly exhortation." This was horribly wrong for us to do, but we were rarely wrong in guessing, with some accuracy, how long one of these students would last before bailing out, often in the middle of the night, leaving for destinations unknown. We would have better spent our time in praying for these souls or at least attempting to draw along side of them in an attempt to help them through some of the inevitable trials and tribulations of being a student at IBC and a Christian. We regretfully failed them.

The list of guest speakers at chapel that came year after year, including a great number of missionaries, could have made a *Who's Who* listing. While IBC was on humble turf, I found that its mission was highly thought of worldwide in our non-denominational circles. It was here, during my sophomore year, that I first heard and met John Hagee. After hearing him speak at chapel, Dennis and I, with permission from President Coote, started attending his new church. At the time, the church had just opened its new building on Nacodocus Road that would seat about 300. It was not long until the church was packed out. After graduation, Pastor Hagee and the Trinity Assembly Church moved on to another newly built church that seated 600. Just as in the first instance, the first Sunday that the church opened the congregation overflowed and they had to immediately move to two services. Within the year, that service was likewise packed. Pastor Hagee went on to write a number of books, develop an international TV and crusade ministry and, by God's grace, build the Cornerstone Church and TV ministry widely broadcast on cable (Trinity Broadcasting Network as well as others). His messages were dynamic and he became one of the greatest pulpit speakers I have ever heard.

It also became very evident that our class, the *Trumpeters*, comparatively speaking, was highly intelligent and talented, and we soon began a rather spirited competition in all areas of college life with another talented class just ahead of us named the *Swordsmen*. Even now, some 40 years later, these two classes have probably produced collectively the finest group of pastors, teachers, singers, musicians and missionaries that the school has ever turned out. The current President of IBC (IBC closed its doors in the fall of 2010 due to a lack of students and funding) is David Cook who was a member of the Trumpeter class. The fact that David was almost expelled his

Life Between Innings

sophomore year from the school for assisting in the sabotage of a Swordsman class project, makes the story even better.

As part of preparation for ministry, the school arranged *Home Missions Assignments* for students where we would travel in teams to churches all over San Antonio or all points east, west, south and north of the city. We would travel to such places as Corpus Christi, Kerrville, Austin, Laredo, as well as to some of the local military bases, especially Fort Sam Houston. These assignments were on a voluntary basis but were a great opportunity to occasionally speak or sing or just tag along for prayer support; there were also a lot of girls on these assignments. The churches welcomed us with open arms and gave us a lot of liberty to minister. Also, the congregational members would generally bring a large dinner for us to enjoy following the AM services on Sunday. We ate well. During the afternoon, while we waited for the evening services, we could catch up on some of our studies, prepare for our ministry that evening or just hang out and get to know many of our classmates better. Home Missions assignments provided great memories that I still cherish. The Community Church at Kerrville, the home of Mooney Aircraft (no relations), was clearly my favorite mission assignment and for which I volunteered often.

An opportunity for those who had stayed in town was to preach, speak or witness on the street corners of downtown San Antonio. We would board the old battered school bus at the campus and take the 20-minute ride to the heart of the downtown area of the city. Along the way, the bus became a place of song, worship and prayer as we prepared for the spiritual battle ahead of us. We usually had a fairly large group and we would divide the group up so that we would never have any of the girls out alone on a street corner. We would take turns speaking, usually giving our messages in five minutes

The Bible College Years 1965-1968

or less, as our "congregation" represented a moving target. The best goal was to present the gospel message with clarity and with an invitation to accept Christ during the length of one red light. Don't say it is impossible. Mostly we ministered to servicemen from the nearby military bases that had earned a weekend pass and had headed to the *River Walk* area of downtown and its nightclubs and outdoor restaurants. It was not uncommon for one or two of those we met to accompany the team back to Revival Tabernacle for the evening service where we had more time to explain God's great plan of salvation.

It was also during these times that Charlie Lashua and I hooked up with a rather short, robust young man with red hair named Richard Wilson, who somehow had earned the nickname of "Mother Goose," to form a trio. Now Richard was a different sort of guy that didn't necessarily fit in with the "cool crowd," but I enjoyed Richard and sharing time with him. For whatever reason I had the knack of hooking up with the "cool" crowd, yet I could also connect with the "not so cool" crowd. In Richard's case, once I was able to get through the superficial stuff, in other words the defensive barriers that he had placed in his life to protect himself, I found him to be engaging, intelligent, talented and fun. Charlie had by far the best voice of us three and he sang bass, or at least sang in the lower keys. Richard sang tenor and had a very good voice. That left me to sing the lead part and we actually sounded pretty good.

At one point we had considered doing a daily 15-minute radio broadcast spotlighting our music. There was also a dynamic group that had been formed primarily from the Trumpeters and Swordsmen classes called the Waymark Quartet that had traveled extensively for the school during the 1966 summer break. It was our plan to use them as well as a number of other talented musicians on the campus. Feeling confident of his approval, especially since we had a

Life Between Innings

potential sponsor waiting in the wings, we decided to discuss this opportunity with President Coote. We were never really sure of his reasoning but he discouraged us from doing it and the project died a quick death.

However disappointed we were, it did not deter us from taking on many home mission assignments and from traveling into Mexico a couple times to minister with Charlie's adoptive mom and dad. Charlie spoke Spanish fluently, but of course Richard, a product of the state of Indiana, and I could not. So, while we would sing in English, the Mexicans poured over us like we were "somebodies." The defining moment for me was the day we were invited into a very small, one room hut of a house with a very cleanly swept dirt floor. The Mexican family that was hosting us that afternoon gave us each a warm Coca-Cola to drink. They obviously did not have enough for every-one but they gave us the soda and then sat there and smiled at us as we drank it. It was humbling to know that these people were so excited to have us in their home, sharing their best with us. Then, WOW!! Sitting there in this hut it suddenly hit me that, in comparison, IBC looked beautiful.

I had also decided to try out for the IBC choir during the beginning of my freshman year. One incentive was that a lot of beautiful co-eds were also trying out. I made the choir and we had an eventful year as we jointly made an album with the Waymark Quartet. The IBC choir, directed by Brother Daniel Quizzenberry, was featured on one side and the Waymark Quartet was featured on the other. It is still one of my trea-sured vinyls. The choir often sang at Revival Temple, espe-cially at the annual mid-year and year-ending conferences.

In March of my freshman year, we also took a tour to Dallas, Texas, and ministered over the weekend to a church pastored by Brother Charles Dufee, an I.B.C. alumni. It was also a momentous weekend in that an upstart Texas Western

Miners basketball team from El Paso, Texas, with an all-black starting line-up clashed with the all-white basketball royalty, Kentucky Wildcats, for the 1966 NCAA Tournament title. The Miners were coached by Don Haskins, a white man. No NCAA basketball team had ever reached the finals playing an all-black starting line-up. Kentucky was known as a racist school and some wondered if Kentucky would even play the game. Adoff Ruff, the Kentucky coach, after much consternation and considerable pressure from folks on both sides of the issue, decided to play the game. The game was being held in College Park, Maryland. The *Baltimore Sun* ran the following observation regarding the Miners: *They can do everything with the basketball but autograph it. The running, gunning Texas quintet can do more things with a basketball than a monkey on a 50-foot jungle wire.* Actually the author's assessment, which was racially biased in and of itself, was also flawed in that the Miners played a very deliberate, very effective passing game and were distinguished by their voracious defense and a lot of poise. All those traits were evident in the Miners' great victory, 72-65, as they held Kentucky to 27 of 70 field goal attempts while they hit on 22 of 49. However, the flustered Wildcats committed 23 fouls to Texas Western's 12 and that became the final difference in the game. This game made a significant impact on the NCAA and Kentucky basketball as blacks gradually become more and more a significant part of the fabric of the game and Kentucky, not too long afterward, began to actually recruit a few blacks.

While IBC did not a have a gymnasium, there was a lot of basketball played after classes and on the weekends on our outdoor, open-air "arena." It soon became obvious that first fall that there was actually some talent here and I began to get anxious for the season to start. IBC at the time was not affiliated with any league and they played an independent schedule that included other small schools and industry teams. We

Life Between Innings

rented out a beautiful facility for our games at Woodlawn Park, located just around the corner from Revival Tabernacle. Jack Gunn, a former student, was the coach, but we did not hold practices in the traditional sense as most of the players had jobs from which to work around. However, the talent soon began to mesh and our first season was upon us.

In the backcourt we had a very talented point guard, Daylon Stoldorf, who was about 5'7, quick off the dribble with either hand and who possessed a nice jump shot. Daylon had that "Ed Kookie Burnes'" look, from the old *77 Sunset Strip* detective television series. Daylon's long, carefully contoured hair was never out of place, never ever. If we told him that his hair was the least bit disheveled, he would immediately head for the nearest mirror. At 5'9", and still at my high school playing weight of 129 pounds, was me at the off guard position. I could shoot the ball a little but I was not the ball-handler that Daylon was. However, I could pass the ball very well and was always one of the team leaders in assists. I was honored to be elected captain of the team both of my first two seasons *(1965-66 and 1966-67)* and co-captain my final season *(1967-68)*. At forward we had good height and size with two of my best friends, Richard "Shade Tree" Riles at 6'2" and John Elmore at 6'3". Richard earned the nickname of Shade Tree as he would commonly stand at the corner of our outdoor court just under the shade provided by one of the big trees and shoot his jumper from that area. Richard worked hard in games but rarely moved from that spot during practice or pick-up games. At center was David Yeager, a tall, lanky guy with the biggest ears you'll ever find on anyone, standing all of 6'6" or better; he could jump out of the building and was a great rebounder. Over the years, even after college, David and I remained good friends. David, one of the Swordsmen, was the most gentle of people you would ever meet, truly a godly man, full of joy

The Bible College Years 1965-1968

and life. David and his college sweetheart, my classmate, Karen McSorley, married right after David graduated, moving to Mexico and immediately began to work as missionaries. A few short years after I had visited with him and Karen in their home in the early '70s, David was tragically killed in a fall from atop an old building in Oklahoma that he and a team were tearing down. Dave had wanted to take the lumber from the building back to Mexico to help construct a church.

Our bench was not that strong but we had guys that liked to play like my roomies, Dennis and Charlie, Ted Ketterling, a tall man at about 6'3" who actually developed into a pretty nice player, David Sellers, also about 6'3 or so and a terrific player and person, Harry Croft, and Ray Reavis, who later married my high school sweetheart, Sandy. We finished the season at 17-9 and it was one of the better seasons in school history. The fact is, we had a few guys who could have played at a higher level had they desired to pass on ministerial training at IBC.

When the 1966-67 season rolled around a 6'1", sharp shooting redhead from California, Tom Pendergrass, enrolled at IBC. Tom had been the object of a number of college recruiters as he was the real deal in every department. Tom transformed our team in a number of ways, as he suddenly became the focal point. Tom could play either of the guard positions or as a small forward; consequently, his playing time came out of mine and a few other previous year's starters. We certainly could not complain as Tom obviously was our best player, a great teammate, a very gracious person and usually led us in scoring. The team continued to be successful but it seemed our chemistry was not the same as it had been in the 65-66 season. However, to blame Tom would have been unfair as he was as humble as he was good. It was during this season, however, that I had my top game at IBC pouring in 21 points while gaining a victory over one of our top industrial team

Life Between Innings

competitors, scoring mostly from the free throw line, much as I had done in the old Boys' Club House League championship game back in 1962. I cut out the newspaper box score clipping from the next morning's *San Antonio Light* and have kept it among my memorabilia all these years.

Our winning ways continued into our third and my final season as most of our key players were back. However, David Yaeger was selected as captain, and while I was but a little disappointed, the team did honor me by selecting me as co-captain. However, just as in the second season, newer and better players were coming in and I also lost my starting position. I still got ample playing time but I missed being one of the key clogs. But, being able to play the great game was still a thrill. On game day, starting or not, I would still feel that tingle of excitement that begins to build as you sit in class nervously waiting for the day to end so as to get to the important things of life, like basketball. At age 60 and still coaching, I would still get those same sensations that run down through the arms and into the legs on game day. I think I would realize that I had finally died if that "game day condition" ever ceased.

Christmas, our first year away, came upon us much more quickly than I would have imagined. Dennis and I had become acclimated to IBC much sooner than I would have dreamed and now it was simply home. In fact, it was not with much sadness to have the holidays end and find that it was time to return to school. However, while home, I made the most of it. I had wanted to reconnect with Ronnie during those two weeks at home but once back in town it seemed that most of the days were occupied with either the holidays themselves or attending parties with the old gang from the church youth group. And, of course, Sandy was still there and it was great to be able to spend time with her. While neither of us had ever used the "Love" word, I truly did have a passion for her beyond just

The Bible College Years 1965-1968

a boyfriend, girlfriend thing. However, I was determined not to get hooked into a long distance relationship since she was still just a junior in high school and I was a college freshman.

It was good to get back to IBC. I loved my mom; she truly was the best a kid could have ever hoped for, as she trusted me beyond what most parents do their kids. I was given a tremendous amount of liberty about where I was going, what time I should be in and with whom I would be spending time. I had most always been careful not to abuse that liberty or take it for granted. Even at IBC I did not stray far from the rather strict rules that were in place. But, IBC was home and there was a certain freedom that I had as a young adult, even here, that I was enjoying very much as I began to expand my wings.

Getting back to classes also meant getting back to work. I had obtained a bus-driving job in the fall with the local school district so I needed to get back and return to work. Previous to this I had worked for just a few weeks as a stocker at the local Piggly Wiggly supermarket chain. I found quickly that this was a job not to my liking. I primarily stocked shelves, which meant that I never knew exactly when I was allowed to go home. That uncertainty drove me crazy, plus the supervisor and I didn't seem to mesh. He was one of those kind of bosses that would like to get in your face a little, which I was actually used to from my baseball and basketball coaches. Mr. Wild and Mr. Nash from the Boys' Club had not been shy about getting in my face and I respected those two men greatly. However, this seemed different. I think the final straw that ended my grocery career was when he said, *You know, Mooney, you need to lighten up a little; you take things too seriously.* This was a rather odd comment I thought as most of my friends and family found me to be very laid back, hardly ever serious, rather sarcastic in a humorous, not hurtful, way, and if not the life of the party, certainly I contributed to it. But whatever

Life Between Innings

it was, since I didn't have to work for him (I had a small but adequate Social Security check coming in every month as a result of my dad being a deceased veteran), I didn't, and I quit. Thus, the start of my bus driving career, which was actually pretty exciting for me and the students, as we would rock and roll down the highway as I learned how to double-clutch the big "Yellow."

Soon after arriving back from that first Christmas vacation, rumors began to surface that a young lady on campus, Shirley Redman, was planning on asking me to the Sadie Hawkins Valentine's Day school party. Prentice Woods, an upper class student at IBC and a good friend from one of the St. Louis area churches, had dated her for a while and still had a large crush on her. That, and because of impressions, rightly or wrongly, I had made about her from afar, gave me the impetus to avoid her with all abandon until after the Sadie Hawkins event. With the help of Charlie and Richard, I was able to pull it off. But, just as a safeguard against some unforeseen accident occurring where she would be able to find me, we decided to put together a musical skit for the party so that I could use this as an excuse as to why I could not go with her should an excuse become necessary. It worked. I was able to avoid her long enough that finally I received word that she had invited someone else. However, Charlie, Goose and I proceeded with our plans and received permission to bring our musical act to the party and perform. Prior to the party we had set down over a couple days and had written some original songs put to the tune of several pop hits of the time. We were a surprise hit. And, just as the evening ended, I ran unavoidably face to face with this stunning-looking blonde coming down the stairs of the Admin Hall (where the party had been held) dressed in a beautiful black dress . . . it was Shirley. We casually greeted each other and I quickly moved on.

The Bible College Years 1965-1968

Several weeks passed and the end of the 1965-66 basketball season was coming upon us. One of our final games was to be played in Houston, Texas, against Gulf Coast Bible College. Our cheerleaders, who were some of the more attractive ladies enrolled at IBC, were allowed to accompany us on this trip. Shirley was one of those cheerleaders. As we were boarding the bus for our return back to San Antonio, it became pretty evident that everyone was taking this opportunity to couple off. At IBC, there was no such thing as "coupling off" legally, as students were not allowed to date until their second year, and even then, with one of the staff serving as a chaperone. Even with this rather large restriction, the number of IBC couples that married over each summer was amazing. Thus, IBC had earned the mantle of International Bridal College.

Being one of the last to board, the only available seat that I could find was next to Shirley. Since our brief face-to-face confrontation at the Sadie Hawkins party, I had reevaluated my thinking somewhat and was not as opposed to getting acquainted with her as I had been originally. For the next two to three hours we rode together through the moonlit evening getting acquainted and talking like two old friends. I found her to be very interesting and charming and not at all like I had been impressioned to think. For the remainder of the school year, we continued to look for each other at various school functions or after class and began to build a relationship.

As my freshman year ended and it was time to head back to St. Louis for the summer, Shirley and I had become an item. We both were anxious to be away from IBC and its restrictive dating rules for a time; however, the summer job that I obtained happened to be as a camp counselor in Pevely, Missouri, for the *Teamsters Union, Local 688, Summer Kids Camp*. While this job took me away for most of the summer and interfered with my summer dating plans, I had the time of

Life Between Innings

my life. My new counselor friends quickly nicknamed me the *Deacon*. Even though I had this religious bent and was preparing for the ministry, they openly included me into their fellowship *as a religious guy that didn't seem like most religious guys.* I took that as a compliment. About the only time I was not included was on those occasions when I would be asked to baby-sit the camp during one of those evenings when the counselors would take up residence elsewhere in one of the vacant cabins and indulge in a few activities that a minister-in-training should not.

I had a great time at the camp as I had the joy of teaching beginners, usually the eight to ten year olds, how to swim, an event that most parents should have wanted to experience personally with their kids, but for a variety of reasons had not. Just getting the heads of some of these children under water was the mark of a successful day, and then to see them actually swim by the end of the two weeks was really enjoyable. I took great pride in showing the parents what their kid had been able to accomplish. We also did a lot of hiking, some archery and directed a number of skits. I also got a crack at playing golf on the Teamster's beautifully sculptured course with a group of the counselors including Sue Boyer, a particularly attractive blonde . . . did I say particularly attractive . . . and this made for some great laughs and memories.

Soon, the summer had ended and it was time to return to IBC. Shirley and I had gotten a few dates in just prior to leaving so all was not lost. However, my biggest failure and regret was not getting to Sandy to tell her about my dating Shirley. I always felt bad that she got the news about Shirley and me through the grapevine; she had not deserved that. While Shirley and I had not specifically said to each other that we were "going steady," it was clearly understood by us both that we were not dating anyone else.

The Bible College Years 1965-1968

Back at IBC, Dennis and I moved into the new boys dorm that had arrived over the summer. Yes, I said, "arrived," not "built." And when I say new, I mean that it was new to the college as they had obtained two used wooden military dorms from nearby Lackland Air Force Base and had them picked up and delivered to IBC just prior to our leaving the school for summer break. When we arrived back, there was still much construction to be done to get the buildings adjoined and back into livable shape. However, we were moved in and they were much better than the old dorm that had become home the previous year. In fact, the outside of the dorms were deceiving in that the rooms, halls and visiting areas were quite nice. These dorms had hardwood floors, much larger showers and pretty much doubled the occupancy space. Consequently, Dennis and I had our own room, which, frankly, we fixed up quite nicely. From time to time, the Dean of Men would conduct room inspections and Dennis and I were often selected as having the cleanest and neatest room. That kind of news about two guys spreads fast on a small campus and we were chided by both genders of the student body, but always in good fun. Unfortunately, the parking lot and roads into and out of the new dorm area had not yet been constructed so the least amount of rain created some rather muddy, tracking conditions.

Shirley was in tight with the Girls Dean, Meta Miess, so we were given permission to meet off campus from time to time to "talk." However, since we still could not publicly date, we did arrange for one chaperoned date with Bernice Freeborn (probably in her mid 70s at this time), the mother of our class sponsor and one of the newest professors at the college, Rev. Andrew Freeborn. Several of the nationally popular gospel quartets were in concert at one of the local schools so we met up with Sister Freeborn, went out for a nice dinner and on to

Life Between Innings

the concert. It was a terrific evening. However, Sister Freeborn continually apologized throughout the evening that she was there crashing our party; she felt that the dating rules were just a little too restrictive. The fact was, she was not crashing the party as she was so delightful and enjoyed the evening as if it was her own date.

Early in the fall of 1966, I was still driving the school bus but had discovered that there were several Boys' Clubs in San Antonio. I contacted the main office and found that there was an opening for an Athletic Director at Boys' Club #4 located in one of the toughest, more dangerous parts of town in what was called the Zarsamora District. This district held one of the largest Spanish-speaking populations of the entire city. I made an appointment to meet with the director of the Club and drove out to where the Club was located. Dennis, had been very kind in allowing me to drive his car while he hitched rides to his work much closer to the college.

A very short Hispanic man, who just may be the roundest individual that I have ever met, greeted me at the door of the Club. He was introduced as Bola, which the kids at the Club later told me was translated, "Round Man" or "Ball." He and I clicked in short order and he offered me the job, starting immediately. The Club was small with a half-size gymnasium with a tile floor, an office area and a large activities room with a television, pool table, ping pong table and few other tables used for reading or doing a craft. It was on that very television, on April 4, 1968, that I heard the news bulletin saying that the Rev. Martin Luther King had just been assassinated in Memphis, Tennessee. Beyond the outside entry door was a large field, perfect for our softball, soccer and football programs. The only problem, unfortunately, was that there were only about 30 active boys in the club ranging from age 8-18. This was hardly the mixture of ages to put together leagues and teams.

The Bible College Years 1965-1968

With basketball being the easiest game to play with less people, I put together two leagues with boys 8-12 and another for boys ages 13-15. I was initially able to form 3 teams in each division with 3 players each. But, the word spread quickly that a Gringo had been hired to direct the athletic programs and before I could begin play we had enough boys for several more teams with 4 players on a team. I could never have envisioned the success that this program would have. Boys seemed to come from everywhere as we took regular t-shirts and painted them as individual team shirts, which each player wore with pride, kept scores and stats, offered trophies for the winners and played each game with a fully qualified official; me. I was told that none of the previous Athletic Directors had ever put together organized programs such as I was attempting and the boys loved it. We shortened the season and began a new winter league right after the holidays so that we could get more teams in and, of course, more boys.

Immediately following basketball season we moved into soccer and then softball. I knew absolutely nothing about soccer, but the kids did, so I pretty much let them play and blew my whistle if the rough stuff broke out. For softball, I selected a varsity team and we traveled to some of the other Clubs for games. Bola would load up the boys in the back of the Club's pickup truck and away we would go. Today, this would be a lawsuit waiting to happen. I would ride with Bola upfront and I could see that he took some joy in seeing his Club coming alive. When I came back after the summer break between my sophomore and junior year, I put a touch football program into place. By now the Club was gaining quite a reputation and parents and friends were starting to come and watch the boys play their games. I carefully kept stats for each sport and the players eyed the posted charts daily. These became fodder for some mild, good-humored trash talk. Not being able to speak

Life Between Innings

Spanish I could not understand all their chatter, but I could tell by their faces when the sarcasm and talk was getting a little mean-spirited and we would try to hold that in check. You could see the boys begin to take pride in their accomplishments and the community was obviously behind us.

During the 67-68 season, my last one at the Club, I picked a Junior Varsity basketball team from our *House Leagues* and took them to Houston, Texas, for the Boys' Club Regional Tournament, something that they had not experienced before. The boys had to stay in some cramped quarters on the floors of the Houston Club, but they did not complain. And, just as I had when I traveled with the Boys' Club of St. Louis to Springfield, Missouri, some years back in my youth, I provided the boys with meal money, truly a first for these young men. We did not receive a very good seed in the tournament so we lost our first game pretty handily. However, in our second game we played our opponent very tough and narrowly lost out in the end. The boys were emotionally down as we left the court. However, I was so proud of them that day for the fight they carried into those waning minutes. Seeing that, they rebounded fairly quickly and the good-natured, spirited conversation picked up as we journeyed back to San Antonio.

As we were practicing softball in the spring of the 1968 season, I discovered that my personal glove was missing. I posted a notice on the Club bulletin board announcing that all Club athletic programs would be cancelled until my glove was returned. Bola supported me and understood the important lesson that I was trying to teach. At first, I met with some gentle resistance from the boys as they stated that this was being unfair. Finally, late on the second day following my posting of the bulletin, several of the boys came to me to inquire that, if the glove should be returned, would there be any questions and would the softball season and other activities resume.

I responded that there would be no questions asked and as soon as the glove was squarely in my hands, I would pull the bulletin and all activities would resume. Within the hour the glove was back in my hands and all was well with our world. Activities were resumed and I never asked who had the glove or how they happened to get it back, and I was never told.

I truly marveled then, even as I do now, how God kept his hand on me while working in this violent area. No doubt the boys took care of me, much more in fact than just the glove incident. During my two years at the Club nothing was ever stolen from me, other than the glove, I was never confronted in any threatening way, my car was never tampered with and I was given respect by each of the boys, young and old alike. Even at my age of 60, my experience with these boys and the community of the Boys' Club of San Antonio #4, still live on in my memory bank as perhaps one of, if not the most, rewarding experience in my life. I had modeled all that I had done by that which Mr. Wild and Mr. Nash had taught me while playing and working at the Boys' Club of St. Louis. As I walked away, tearfully, in May of 1968, I knew that Mr. Wild would have been proud, and that made me proud.

In 1994, while on a trip back to Texas, I drove by the spot where the old Club used to stand. It is now gone and only a memory remains. Yet, it was easy, for just a short moment, to close my eyes and see Bola sitting in the doorway as he did every day, ready to give me his normal greeting. I missed the old place and the boys; I tear up just thinking of it.

In the fall leading up to Thanksgiving of 1966, there was a sudden rash of engagements announced at IBC. I had never really given much thought to marriage. It donned on me that perhaps I should be giving it some consideration since so many of the other students, my friends, were moving in that direction. It is almost embarrassing to admit that I probably would

Life Between Innings

not have given it much consideration if so many others had not been making their announcements. I was generally not one prone to peer pressure. Gosh, I had faced it almost from the moment I started the seventh grade at Fremont Elementary and had with some ease and grace, resisted most of the temptations that they offered. However, I did begin to think about the idea more and more and to consider that this really was something I could do. Shirley was working at one of the local malls and it was not uncustomary for the guys to pick their girlfriends up after work to escort them back to the campus. Early in November of '66, I decided that the timing was perfect so I arranged to pick Shirley up at her work. Driving back I stopped along Hillcrest Road, a side road located on a hillside that overlooked a portion of the city. We had stopped a few times here in the past "just to talk." As we talked on this particular evening, I popped the question of marriage; she accepted immediately.

We kept our engagement quiet, except for just a few friends, for a few days. However, it did not take long for the news to make the grapevine and the secret was out. However, as we moved toward the Christmas holiday I began to have second thoughts and began to look for a way out. After several weeks of indifference by me, it became obvious to us both that something was amiss. And then, almost in a flash, just prior to our departure back to St. Louis for the Christmas and New Year holidays, the doubts seemed to be lifted. Consequently, it was agreed, since we would be driving straight through to St. Louis, that Shirley could ride with Dennis and me. We had barely entered Oklahoma when a sudden snowstorm hit, blocking the highways and making driving impossible. Shirley had a grandmother that lived in Skiatook, Oklahoma, just outside of Tulsa, so we decided to try to make it there, stay over night, and leave the next morning. By morning the snow had ceased

The Bible College Years 1965-1968

falling, although there were six or seven inches of it lying on the ground, and the roads around Skiatook did not seem overly bad. Our guess was that the major roads like Interstate 44, and especially the toll roads that we would be traveling, would be getting priority attention, so it was good to start out for home.

Our judgment was greatly flawed and the interstates were so bad we could hardly make 25 miles per hour. The driving was tedious and problems began to develop with the car, including problems with the heater. After another night's stay in Rolla, Missouri, and some adjustments with the car, we were able to be back on our way and successfully navigate our way home. Our 18-hour, straight through trip, ended up taking about 64 hours instead. This trip and two others from San Antonio to St. Louis while in college took similar turns with bad weather and car troubles. The effect of those trips was such that only in recent years have I been willing to even consider such lengthy car trips.

Following the holidays, Shirley and I set an August 11 date for our wedding. It was also decided that she would return to St. Louis at the end of the first semester and begin to work, save and plan toward our wedding. Consequently, from late January '67 through early May we did not see each other, although we maintained contact by mail and weekly phone calls. At first, the days seemed to drag by but the busyness of work at the Boys' Club and studies at school, plus a great class trip to the HEB Camp near Kerrville, hurried the days on by. Also, Dennis and I had made friends with Sharon Steadman, whose family lived on a ranch several hours away and not far from President Johnson's ranch, and we were invited frequently to spend time with her and her family riding horses and playing moonlight tag in our vehicles. Moonlight tag was not as dangerous as it might sound as the mesquite tree-covered plains were very clearly lit by the huge Southwest Texas moon.

Life Between Innings

However, I do wonder sometimes whether Shirley and I would have ever gotten married had we actually spent more time together. After finally meeting in March of our freshmen year, we spent the remainder of the semester (less than three months) getting to know each other. We then spent the summer apart as I was working at the Teamster's Camp. That fall we came back to IBC for another 4 months, the last 6 weeks of which we were engaged but already experiencing some doubts. Lastly, we were apart again for four more months in the spring of my sophomore year when she went back home to save money and start planning for the wedding. The truth is we really did not know each other that well. I take full responsibility for going forward with the wedding, but it would have been good had someone, someone who loved us and cared for us, to have put us through the grill a little before we made that "fatal" step down the aisle. However, such a "grilling" never occurred.

My sophomore year finally concluded and Dennis and I packed the car and headed for St. Louis. For once we had an uneventful trip traveling home, only to find that Mom's car was in the shop and I had no way to get over to East St. Louis, Illinois, where Shirley lived. The day after arriving, my brother-in-law, Gary, loaned me his car and we finally had our long awaited reunion.

From the beginning things did not seem right. We still enjoyed each other's company but there just wasn't that passion, that spark that two people should have for each other just prior to entering the greatest commitment that two people can make with each other. It was not until a few years later that we admitted to each other that we both would have liked to have delayed our marriage plans that summer of 1967, at least for a little while, if not canceled all together. The immediate question that most would ask would be, *Well, idiots, why*

The Bible College Years 1965-1968

did you not postpone things if you had doubts? I cannot speak for Shirley but I think I was a little intimidated by the fact that Shirley's dad was the Rev. Henry Redman, a great pastor and missionary known world wide. Plus, so much information had already gone out about the pending wedding. I did not want to embarrass her or the family and never really gave much thought that canceling was an option, in fact, a very good option. And, having doubts was supposed to be normal, right? So, we did the immature thing and continued to venture on despite the fact that we did not have, nor were ever offered, any pre-marriage counseling, which would have undoubtedly been most valuable to us.

One evening, around 8:30 PM, just a couple weeks prior to our wedding, I was attending a youth group meeting at Carsonville Full Gospel when I was summoned to the phone. Answering the phone I was surprised to hear the voice of Pastor Redman. He told me that there was an emergency and that he needed me to come to their residence immediately. I, of course agreed to do so and sped off down I-70 toward their home. Their home was actually the church parsonage that sat above and behind Full Gospel Tabernacle at 25th and State Streets in East St. Louis. Upon arrival, Shirley met me at the door with her hair all askew, as she had just finished washing it, and was obviously surprised to see me. I quickly explained that her father had called me at church and asked that I come quickly as there had been an emergency. Pastor Redman was summoned and he promptly sat us down and handed us an article from a newspaper published in Greenup, Illinois. I tried to read the words but the words were not sinking in. Finally, like a ton of bricks, it hit us both at about the same time that the article was detailing the drowning death of Velma Grissom near Pensacola Beach, Florida. Velma was the youngest sister of the three Grissom sisters that were attending IBC and who

Life Between Innings

were all to have been bridesmaids in our wedding. The sisters formed a singing trio and were out on the road for the summer touring on behalf of IBC and had stopped for just a few hours in their travels to enjoy the beautiful white beaches. Unfortunately, Velma had gotten caught in a strong undertow from which she could not recover.

President Coote came to Greenup to officiate the funeral and did a magnificent job. Not until my own mother's death and funeral would I again be in a funeral that impacted me so. Velma was such a beautiful young lady, with long blonde hair and an engaging smile and laugh, herself just engaged to Danny McMasters, a young man and future minister that she had met at IBC. Rev. Coote emphasized throughout his message that God is sovereign and does not make mistakes, that our trust in Him should not waver as the events that led to Velma's death were not a surprise to our awesome God. While the situation was obviously heartbreaking, the fact that Velma was a solid Christian who died serving her Lord helped to alleviate a lot of the pain that would have otherwise been there.

Shortly after Velma's funeral, Shirley asked one of her long time friends, Faith Tenlaudo, to take Velma's spot in our wedding and she graciously consented. Finally our wedding day, August 11, 1967 arrived. We were met at Full Gospel Tabernacle by a packed house for the 6:00 PM, Friday evening wedding. Pastor Redman did the honors of both giving his daughter away and officiating the service. Things went off without a hitch. Our reception was held at the nearby VFW Hall and again the place was packed.

Some weeks before, I had secretly booked the Collinsville, Illinois, Howard Johnson's for our Honeymoon Night. Certainly the booking does not seem too impressive here in 2011 but at the time it was nice, plus we had very limited funds. Mr. Wild had given me a summer job working at the Boys' Club of

The Bible College Years 1965-1968

St. Louis and Shirley had been working for Famous-Barr, neither of which paid great money, let alone provided much to put aside as extra for a wedding and for a honeymoon. I had not registered at many motels in my life, and never with a woman, so I was a little nervous as I signed us in. More importantly, we were both virgins, so we had an interesting evening ahead that called for some nervousness.

The next morning was Saturday and we headed to the Lake of the Ozarks for a couple days of honeymooning. As we traveled down Interstate 44 toward the Lake, things just seemed so very odd. Shirley was not feeling too well and I do not remember either of us talking a whole lot, although I am sure we talked some. I do vividly remember, however, thinking to myself that this had not been such a great idea. I even more vividly remember thinking *how long life suddenly now seemed as it stretched out in front of me.* These were not the thoughts that a newly married young man should have been having within just hours of his own wedding and wedding night. I felt bad for Shirley and I felt bad for me. I kind of suspected that she might have been having some of the same thoughts as I was, although I never asked.

Our honeymoon was not too eventful. With very little money we could only stay two nights, again at a Howard Johnson's, and we could not afford to partake in many of the Lake activities. Shirley was still not feeling too well so basically we just hung out, ate a few meals, drove around to do a little sightseeing and found a church for us to attend on Sunday. One thing that we did splurge for was a helicopter ride, which gave us a great view of the Lake.

Finally, it was Monday morning and time to return to St. Louis. It was actually a relief to be heading back as we really did not know what to do with each other in those moments and hours of inactivity. This time we decided to go back on

Life Between Innings

Interstate 70 just to experience some different scenery. It was during this trip that my new (new to me as it was my first car) 1964 Blue Ford Fairlane began to experience some difficulties that unfortunately turned out to be the transmission. This was the last thing we needed, as it would potentially put us in a financial bind on day four of our marriage. I can't remember exactly how we got it fixed; probably Pastor Redman paid for most of it, as he was very good about doing things like that for us throughout those early years of our marriage.

Upon returning to East St. Louis, we met at the Redmans home, my mom included, and opened our wedding gifts. We had gotten quite a bit; it didn't hurt being married to the daughter of a very popular pastor of a nice size church, missionary friend to many and a long-time voice on KSTL - 690, a Christian radio station.

Within scant days we were packed up and heading back to IBC for my final year. We had been notified that our application for on-campus housing had been approved and that we were to receive one of the new (to IBC) house trailers that President Coote had purchased over the summer to help accommodate all the newly married couples returning to the college. Upon arriving in San Antonio and on the campus, we found that our trailer had not yet been moved and was still located quite a distance from the campus just off the I-410 loop in far west San Antonio. This was not particularly good news as Shirley would not be able to start work until we were able to get on campus where she could get a ride to one of the malls; I needed the car to get to my job at the Boys' Club. To compound the bad news, Hurricane Beulah, one of the most destructive hurricanes in U.S. history, was bearing down on Corpus Christi and slamming against Padre Island, some 150 miles to the southwest of us. Because of a crack in the coil the car would die when it became wet, leaving us stranded wherever we were until it could dry out. Sometimes, the drying-out process could take a hour or two. Needless to say, with a hurricane bearing down on us, we were stranded several times. The good news was, however, that we had gotten one of the nicer trailers and President Coote worked hard to get us back on campus within the month. For this we praised God.

When I had started at IBC, it was a three-year college with graduates receiving a Ministerial Diploma upon successful completion of all the requirements. But, the school had decided, sometime after my freshman year, to begin a four-year undergraduate degree program for those who wanted to continue. However, even before returning, I had pretty much decided that I wanted to get my Bachelor's degree from an accredited and better-known college. I had already begun to investigate the possibility of transferring my credits to Central Bible College (CBC) in Springfield, Missouri, the college of choice of the Assemblies of God. The denomination was likewise headquartered in Springfield.

I had grown to like the Assemblies of God much better than I did the Full Gospel non-denominational circles that my family had been associated with for most of my life. While the Assemblies were still Pentecostal, they were not quite as demonstrative in their worship and did not, as a general rule, "enjoy" the frequent interruption of "prophecies" popping up from all over the congregation during their services, a practice that was customary in many Full Gospel services. Although I refuse, even to this day, to deny that there is a place for tongues and prophecy in the church, despite my very strong reformed Presbyterian bent, I had become increasingly uncomfortable with those outburst in our worship services as they tended to drive the unsaved and unlearned away and created a lot of confusion for those that were visiting. I just could not see then, or now, that this was a good thing, or that in the context that these gifts were most often used, even biblical.

Life Between Innings

As my junior year at IBC continued, I received word from CBC that I had been accepted and that many of my credits would transfer, so all seemed well with my plans of becoming an Assembly of God pastor at some point in the foreseeable future.

In the fall of 1967, Shirley surprised me with the announcement that she had been to the doctor and, despite our best efforts, she was pregnant. That was not news that I wanted to hear, as a family was not something that I wanted this soon into our marriage. Within weeks of the announcement Shirley began to show signs that the pregnancy was not going well. Sometime before Thanksgiving, the doctor informed us that the baby had miscarried. The doctor tried to comfort us by saying that this was nature's way of correcting a problem. While I had not initially been too excited about the prospects of being a parent at this time, the miscarriage was still tough, especially on Shirley, physically and psychologically.

My final year was fairly uneventful except for one tragic event, the death of my brother's very good friend, and a friend of the entire family, Bill Boatman. Bill had surprised me by attending our wedding just a few months previously, but evidently he had succumbed to a disease that he had contacted while serving in the military in Panama, some years prior. Financially, we had no business attempting or even thinking about going back home for the funeral, but we (I) decided to go. We never made the funeral, although we attempted the trip, as our car continued to give us trouble, trouble that was very costly to repair. This very immature decision on my part put us in a bit of financial straits from which it took considerable time to recover.

I did have a rather odd event happen to me in one of the chapel services toward the end of the school year and just prior to graduation. We were having one of those services

The Bible College Years 1965-1968

where the Holy Spirit was moving across the room and a lot of students were really being refreshed, worshipping and praising our Lord while praying and ministering to one another. To be honest, I was kind of enjoying the service, but mostly from the role of a spectator. For some reason, during the course of it all, I had moved myself from my assigned seat to a place upon the platform. At some point, Rev. Bill (Wilford) Hammon, our professor of Old Testament studies, came over and placed his hand on my head and began to prophecy, but not in a loud voice, as he would occasionally do. I do not remember all that he said but it was something along the lines of, *Your life and ministry will go through some hard and difficult times and will take you in a direction of which you have not expected. But, do not be discouraged as God will see you through those times and in your later days give you a ministry and work that will be fruitful.* And then it was over.

I was then, even as now, one that had a problem with these personal prophecies that get offered up around Pentecostal circles. When I say that I have seen more of these personal prophecies not come true than have come true, I would really be largely understating the fact. However, our class advisor, Rev. Andrew Freeborn, had encouraged us many times that when we receive such "truths," and our hearts do not feel a witness to it, just put this "truth" on our spiritual shelf and look back at it occasionally to see if God has given any revelation on it since it was first received. If He has, reflect on it. If He has not, don't worry about it. I decided to apply that principle to this word that Rev. Hammon had given me because I did not have a clue as to what he was talking about. Whether Rev. Hammon truly had a "word from God for me" or not, I do not know. I can say, in retrospect, the words he gave me that morning in chapel have seemed to be fulfilled in large part as my ministry did take me down a path that was unexpected; in

Life Between Innings

fact, I got out of the pastoral ministry, and about as far away from it as I could. With my later divorce from Shirley, my life also suffered some difficulties I had not expected, especially with my two older children. But, here in the later years of my life, it does seem that God has given (did give) me a ministry that I did not expect, but one that He is has certainly blessed as the Director of World Missions at the Twin Oaks Presbyterian Church (PCA). I will be interested to see how the story completely plays out as my "later" years continue.

May 1968 was upon us, as was my graduation from IBC. The three years that I had spent there had truly flown by. The memories of that first day had long since dissipated and I had developed a fondness for the place. Spiritually, I had grown a lot, although I still had much to learn and still had some very narrow minded views of people who fail, especially Christians, who need or needed a second, or heaven-forbid, a third chance. I was not much into the "second chance business" at this time of my life. But, I had developed a new found love for world missions over the past three years. At this point, I had truly become convinced that world missions was and is truly the heartbeat of our God; I am even more convinced of that fact today. So, I was glad for what I had learned, but I was anxious to get off to a "real" Bible College and begin my studies at CBC.

Just prior to graduation, Pastor Hagee invited us to attend Trinity Church's annual graduation dinner for high school and college graduates. This was such a nice event and one that we appreciated. The thing that I was going to miss the most upon graduation was Trinity Church and this church body, the great times of worshipping here and listening to the Word of God proclaimed as only Pastor John could. Trinity Church was a church on the move and I would not personally experience anything like it again until 1991 when I was blessed to find

The Bible College Years 1965-1968

Twin Oaks Church starting up in my own backyard, and that was another lifetime away. But, in between, I never lacked for a good church with good, solid, Biblical preaching. I will always thank God for this great blessing.

May 24, 1968, the Friday night of graduation finally came, and I donned my cap and gown and headed to Revival Temple were the ceremony was to be held. While I certainly had not been the valedictorian of the class, I had finished with a very good overall grade point average of better than 97 (Equivalent to being an A+ student or something like 4.85 on a scale of 5). I was pleased to see that I had been able to maintain my grades from my freshman year without much fluctuation. One of the highlights of the graduation ceremony was that my father-in-law, Rev. Henry Redman, was the graduation speaker. As usual, he had plenty of great stories mixed with a lot of humor and an inspiring message for the graduates that was right on point. Finally, the time came when President David Coote called my name, shook my hand and conferred on me my *Ministerial Diploma*. Immediately, I swung my tassel from the left side of my cap to the right, hugged a number of great and endearing friends, jumped into our loaded car, waved good-bye and soon was headed out I-410 and back to St. Louis to work the summer prior to moving on to Springfield. But, as President Coote would often say, *Our destiny swings on small hinges,* and in our case, he was right on as our plans were not God's plans and our plans were about to change.

Since we were to be home only for the summer prior to heading off to CBC in August, our plans were to live with Shirley's parents in East St. Louis. We had barely moved in and settled when news of the shooting death of Robert Kennedy, brother of John Kennedy, our President who had previously been assassinated; the nation was shocked. Robert Kennedy had been a late entry into the Democratic Presidential Primaries

125

Life Between Innings

but he had just won a major victory in California when killed. A young man named Sirhan Sirhan had gunned him down during the celebration party at a Los Angeles hotel; he was wrestled to the floor and arrested immediately. The violence and bloodshed of the 60s seemed as if it would never end.

However, we were about to face another tragedy of our own as Shirley, again, became pregnant. This was a stunning blow to us, just as in the first instance, as we were taking great precautions to prevent such a thing. Obviously, we did not have any insurance as we both were unemployed. And, this was a blow to our plans to attend CBC in the fall, as any money that we could raise would not be going to my college fund but to medical bills. Since I had been looking for a short-term job, and not too successfully at this point, it became necessary for us to reevaluate our plans. Before the evaluation process had gotten too far Shirley began to show signs that this pregnancy, like the first, may be in trouble. And, within just a few short weeks of our discovery of her pregnancy, Shirley again miscarried.

Evidently this pregnancy had been of a little longer length than the first and her miscarriage required her to be admitted to the hospital. These hospital bills were larger than what a simple birth and delivery would have cost so it became apparent that I needed to get a long-term job and give up the idea of going to CBC until the spring semester of 1969, at the earliest. Our plans had now become uncertain, in fact, just about everything about our plans at this point were uncertain. Because I still wanted to go to CBC, but was not sure if or when I would be able to make the move, I held off calling CBC because I was not sure what to tell them.

As a result of Shirley's short hospitalization stay we received word on two fronts, one that we ignored and one that would dramatically affect us in regard to these miscarriages that Shirley was having. We had been married right at a year at this point and she had been on birth control for the entire period, yet she had already become pregnant twice and had miscarried twice.

The first notice involved Shirley and came from her attending physician's assessment of her. For some reason the doctor never talked with me but he did pull Henry (Pastor Redman) aside to tell him that Shirley probably needed to see a psychologist, as he was certain that she was fighting some issues. Henry never explained to me if the doctor's diagnosis was based on issues that may have developed due to the two rapid fire miscarriages or if he was talking about other physiological issues; but regardless, we all laughed it off, literally, and ignored his diagnosis. Understand that in 1968, Pentecostals did not go to see psychologists. It was the general thinking by Fundamentalists that to open one's mind and thoughts to a liberal thinking doctor was an open invitation for Satan and Satanic thoughts to enter the mind. It was reasoned that psychologists did not base their thoughts or counsel on biblical principles but on their own human reasoning, putting Christians in a very vulnerable spot and open to satanic attack. Consequently, seeing a psychologist was not a viable option or even a consideration.

But secondly, as Shirley continued to see her doctor and to be evaluated, the reason for her pregnancies and her miscarriages was discovered. It was found that she was ovulating twice a month, instead of the normal once, so that the birth control pills were not able to prevent a pregnancy, but certainly would create a problem with having a healthy pregnancy. With proper medication and doctor's care, this problem was resolved and was one that we did not face again.

We were now getting into late July and I set out looking for a job with renewed intensity. Based on a tip I had received from an acquaintance at church, I stopped in at Cardinal Snacks, Inc.

Life Between Innings

on Manchester Road in Rock Hill, Missouri. Cardinal Snacks was a division of Kitty Clover of Kansas City, Missouri. I filled out an application and within a few days received a call asking me to come back in for an interview. I met with Mr. Charlie Nachbar who explained that they were looking for several new route delivery/salesmen as a couple of their routes had grown and needed to be divided. He explained that my salary would be a small base fee, but that most of my salary would come from a percentage of products sold. Charlie and I hit it off and he hired me, asking that I start the following Monday.

Since I was the first of the new hires, I was given the best route resulting from the splits. The guy that had driven the full route previously had decided that he preferred the half of the split that was mostly local city driving. The city portion had less driving and as any salesman knows, you do not make sales while you're driving, only when you are delivering, so this looked to be a wise decision on his part. This was a tremendous break, however, for me as my route, while it involved more miles than most of the drivers had, was out in the growing, rapidly expanding St. Charles, Missouri, area and the upscale area of Chesterfield, a west county community of St. Louis. New supermarkets were being built all over this area, plus it was an area of considerable discretionary income that could be spent on items like snacks.

It was truly a case of God blessing me beyond what I deserved as I was consistently in the top three of products sold from the very beginning. I think the former driver of the area was a little jealous, although never resentful, as his city sales never really seemed to grow much after the split. However, week after week, God blessed my efforts. As I would be bringing products into the store and stocking the shelves assigned to Kitty Clover, I would find myself on my knees a lot trying to reach the lower shelves. I decided that this was a good position to be in to pray, so I did, asking God that he would bless the products and those that purchased them. I do not know if the people who purchased them were blessed, although we had a very good product line, but I know I was as my check continued to grow beyond what Mr. Nachbar or I had projected. While I was not real good at drumming up new business, Mr. Nachbar seemed pleased with the efforts.

The new job also helped to get us back on our feet financially much quicker than we had anticipated. I am not sure what happened to Shirley's medical bills as they never reached my home. Again, I think Pastor Redman must have had something to do with paying them or making them go away, as it was typical of him to do something like this, and then never make a big splash about it. However, it soon became evident that while we could not yet afford to head off to CBC, we could now afford our own apartment and move out from the in-laws. They had been very gracious in allowing us to live there for a little over two months but I was anxious, as was Shirley, to get our own place. Over the year that we had been married, and its somewhat inauspicious start, we were starting to grow and become much more comfortable in our new life together.

Again God showed himself so gracious. We had found a brand new apartment just off 39th Street in Rosemount, Illinois, only about a six or seven minute drive from the church. We signed a six-month lease and prepared to move in with what little we had. But, as moving day approached, word had gone throughout the church of our need of furniture, at no doing of our own, that by the time we had settled in we had all the bedroom, living room and dining room furniture needed to furnish our apartment very nicely. And, to top it off and show God's hand in it all, the pieces all matched or complemented each other. What a blessing!

Life Between Innings

It was now clear to me that we were not going to make it to CBC until at least the following fall semester, a full year from when we had expected to arrive. As a consequence, I was asked to take the leadership of the youth group at Full Gospel Tabernacle. While the Carsonville Full Gospel youth group had been a nice sized group of about 20 or so, the East St. Louis Full Gospel youth group was much larger and much more active. I would guess that we had perhaps 75, maybe even 100 or so, very church-active young people and I became attached to these young people very quickly. It was like pastoring my own church, but in a much, much smaller way. We had our Sunday evening youth service at 6:00 PM, just prior to the regular evening worship service at 7:30 PM. It was my custom to go home after the AM services on Sunday, and our usual dinner out with the Redmans, and take a nap, awakening in time to listen to two very inspiring services on the radio, *Harvest Time*, sponsored by the United Pentecostal Church, a very, very, very conservative denomination, and my favorite, *Revival Time*, sponsored by the Assemblies of God, featuring their radio voice, Rev. C.M. Ward. These broadcasts, coupled with my own preparation, gave me a tremendous spiritual boost as the time of the youth service would approach. Again God was kind in that I doubt that I had any great words to share on each of those Sunday evenings, but it was not uncommon for our services to be going so well it would be hard, in fact, at times impossible, to break off so that we could get upstairs for the regular evening service. This was a special time for me and the growth of our youth, both in numbers and spiritually.

Now that I was actively working in ministry, Pastor Redman approached me about the possibility of being ordained; the time seemed to be appropriate. So, we set about arranging the date and decided on September 25, 1968. About midway though the service Pastor Redman called Shirley and me to

The Bible College Years 1965-1968

the platform where we were met by the Elders of the church. We were given a charge to be faithful in our preaching of the Word and in the examples of our lives. Then, as in the example of Barnabas and Saul (Acts 13:2-3), the Elders set us apart for the work of the ministry by the laying on of their hands. Following the service I was given my certificate of ordination from the Independent Assemblies of God International (IAGI) signed by Henry Redman, John Schrieber (Clerk of the Board of Elders) and Rev. A. Rasmussen, the Secretary of the IAGI.

By early fall we had gotten into a routine of work and church and both seemed to be blessed. We were in need of new car so we began to shop around and decided to purchase a brand new 1969, bright red, Datsun Station Wagon. Our very good friends, Ed and Barb Givens, Ed being the Assistant Pastor at the church, had just purchased his second Datsun and had enjoyed really good luck with them. With my long drive to work and the good gas mileage that the Datsun offered, this seemed to be a good buy. Our payments were not outlandish and we reasoned that even if and when we landed in Springfield, Missouri, at CBC, we would still need a good reliable car.

The ink was barely dry on the loan papers for the car when I received a nice letter from Uncle Sam and the Selective Service asking that I come by their office for a physical. It seemed to them that since I had not returned to CBC as planned that past August, and since I had not sought reinstatement for enrollment at CBC for the spring of 1969, that I probably had decided not to return to my religious training. Therefore, they had changed my 4-F designation, a designation given seminary and religious students draft exemption status, to 1-A, meaning that I was now a priority for induction into the military. It was my own fault that this happened but there had been so much uncertainty in our lives due to health, medical bills and

Life Between Innings

raising and saving money, that I had just not gotten around to getting re-accepted at CBC.

Sometime just prior to Thanksgiving, I journeyed over to the Mart Building in St. Louis and received my induction physical. I passed with flying colors and was told that I could probably expect an induction notice within a month or so because the Viet Nam War was still in full bloom and I had a low draft lottery number, something like 76. At this particular time in our nation every draft eligible young man's birth date was annually dropped into a random lottery drawing to establish a priority system for induction. With my birth date having been selected in the upper one-fifth of the lottery, it was pretty certain I was going and was going very soon.

At this time my registration was in the state of Missouri since I had not changed my home of record to Illinois with the government. And, in the state of Missouri, a good majority of their inductees where being assigned to the Marines, as they were having trouble getting their monthly quotas filled. I looked into the mirror and was convinced that what I saw was not Marine material, so I decided that it might be in my best interest to see what the Army and the Air Force had to offer to someone who enlisted versus being inducted.

Following work one evening I stopped off in Brentwood, Missouri, to talk to the Army and Air Force recruiters. They both had me scheduled for some aptitude testing within a very short time and both gave me some pretty good offers. The Army, for a seven-year commitment, offered me the best deal. I would go to basic training and then be assigned to attend classes up East, much like a college student, and study television production. After three years of accredited studies, I would be assigned military duty in the field of television production somewhere in the world for the final four years of my commitment.

The Bible College Years 1965-1968

The Air Force offer was not quite as good but they were willing to place me into electronic technician work that would potentially offer quite a few job opportunities after I completed my four-year tour of duty. After some quick deductions and assessment of the opportunities, because I knew my time was running short, I decided on the Air Force because it had a much shorter commitment. I notified the Air Force recruiter of my decision and he began to search for a slot for me to be inducted. A slot was found and I was to be inducted into the Air Force sometime in the mid to latter part of March 1969. Just as I was convinced that all was OK, I received a notice from the Selective Service saying that I should report for induction into military service, the branch of service unknown, on March 5. I took the letter the next day to my recruiter who was not the bearer of good news. He stated that since the Selective Service date was earlier than the Air Force induction date, I was stuck with the Selective Service date unless he could find a spot in Missouri that would open up unexpectedly for me to take prior to the March 5 date. If that would happen, I could still go Air Force.

The next couple weeks leading up to and past Christmas were tough. I knew that I was going into the military but at this point I did not know if I would wake up on March 5 in the Marines, Army or Air Force. Certainly this was a matter of prayer but I was not sure which way God was going to take me. Finally, the call that I had been hoping and praying for came; my recruiter had secured a spot for me on March 4, one day prior to my induction into the Army or Marines. It seems that someone in out-state Missouri, near Cape Girardeau, had to be slotted to a later date for personal reasons and I was awarded his spot. Praise God!

Once my Air Force commitment had been confirmed, it was time to tie up loose ends at home. One of the glaring problems

Life Between Innings

was what to do with the new car that we had just purchased. Even if I was stationed stateside after basic training, I did not think it would be possible to make the payments on an airmen's salary. Substantial salary increases for military personnel had just been approved by President Nixon, but it would be a while before I began to earn any real money. Again, my father-in-law stepped in to save us by agreeing to purchase the car from us to use in doing his various church related duties. It was greatly appreciated, in fact it was humbling; I always felt bad, really bad, when I would see this man, who could barely squeeze into the front seat of the vehicle, plus had long ago earned the right to drive a bigger, more luxurious car, start out on his hospital runs or other church business in that compact car. Long after I had served my tour of duty in the Air Force, Pastor Redman was still driving that car. He said he fell in love with it the more he drove it because he could go just about anywhere and park it without any problem.

The youth group at church gave me a tremendous send-off with a party and gifts. It was tough to leave them as I had become quite attached to this group in the short time I had been given the privilege to minister among them. Also, I needed to give notice to Mr. Nachbar at Cardinal. This was tough as he and the other men had been genuinely kind to me over the past six months. On my final day of work, Mr. Nachbar and the other drivers held a party for me and also gave me a couple of gifts. Mr. Nachbar commented that a number of people had left the company over the years but this was the first party he could remember that a party had been given to anyone as they left. He made a number of very kind remarks, which I appreciated so much. It gave testimony to me that a Christian in the work place can leave a mark if he is willing to walk the fine line of being a Christian while not alienating the workers with a self-righteous attitude. I thanked God for helping me do this as it came time to leave. God had shown once again that He was committed to blessing me, even though I was so undeserving.

The 4ᵗʰ Inning
THE MILITARY YEARS
(1969-1973)

As the year of 1969 began, Richard M. Nixon was inaugurated, having been elected President of the United States in November of the previous year. In 1972 he would be reelected by a landslide for a second term. However, due to a political scandal called "Watergate," much of his time was taken with fighting a potential impeachment from office. From 1969 and on into 1973, the Viet Nam War continued to rage, further dividing the U.S.A. War protests were becoming much more vocal and much more violent. On the positive side, in July of 1969, U.S. Astronaut Neil Armstrong became the first person to set foot on the Moon, a very important accomplishment as the U.S.A. had finally overcome the Russians in space exploration. In January of 1969, Cardinal great Stan Musial was elected into the Baseball Hall of Fame and the "Miracle Mets" stunned the baseball world by getting into the World Series that October with a record just better than .500. The nation was further stunned when they proceeded to knock off the highly favored Baltimore Orioles in four straight games after losing the first. The Cardinals reverted back to their disappointing ways of the 50s, losing more than winning. In 1973, the Supreme Court handed down its decision known as Roe vs. Wade, legalizing abortion by overturning all state prohibitions prohibiting them.

It was a chilly, rainy morning on March 4, 1969, when Shirley drove me to the Mart Building in downtown St. Louis, Missouri,

Life Between Innings

for my induction into the U.S. Air Force. Our marriage, after a somewhat inauspicious start, had begun to improve and we knew that separation while I was in basic training would be tough, even if it were only for a couple months. Upon arrival at the induction center, we kissed each other a teary goodbye and I quickly exited the car, a "saying goodbye technique" I had learned from my father-in-law when Helen, my mother-in-law, would drop him off at the airport as he departed for one of his frequent, sometimes long and dangerous missions trips.

As I entered the building I was greeted by a number of other recruits milling around waiting for our appointed time to start the induction process. It looked like there were easily 100 or more men to be processed. We were about to receive our first lesson in regard to the military way of doing things; simply, it was "hurry up and wait." Finally, we were ushered into a much larger room. All the men going into the Air Force were instructed to go to one side of the room while those going into the Army or Marines were told to go to a different corner. At that point, all those that had not been designated a branch of military service by the Selective Service were told to get in line and count off. About two-thirds of that group was told to go stand with the Marines and the rest with the Army guys. It was at that exact point that I realized I had made the right choice by going Air Force; there were no questions about it. One look again in the mirror convinced me that I was not one of those "few good men" that the Marines were looking for.

Once it was clear who was going where we were directed to come to attention and receive instructions regarding a physical that we were to take. Everyone was told to drop their clothes, except for their skivvies, and then come back to attention. This was ugly; this was not a pretty scene in any shape, way or form. It was going to take more than just a few days to get these bodies in fighting shape. The physical was almost

The Military Years (1969-1973)

identical to the one given us at this same location the previous year upon receiving our induction notices. We heard all the standard lines again, like the one you always hear during the rectal exam, *Bend over, spread your cheeks (butt that is) and say,* "Ah!" It was always good for a few laughs. However, contrary to my first physical, this doctor became a little more than just concerned as he determined that I was marginally flat-footed.

I was shuffled off to another doctor for a second opinion and I spent what time I was allotted with him to argue that I was an athlete and that there was no way that I could be flat-footed. I tried hard to scrunch up my insteps as best I could as I paraded around for his observation. I had heard that being flat-footed was a sure fire way of being disqualified from military service and at this point in time after quitting my job, saying all my goodbyes and having mentally come to grips with the fact that I was going into the military during wartime, I wanted no part of that diagnosis. Finally, after much conversation and a pregnant pause, he said that he thought I would be all right and sent me on to the next station.

After that scare I was sent to various paper pushers and began to sign document after document. This process continued until the afternoon when I was summoned to another room where the final paper check on all personnel were being conducted. This was the final step in the process just prior to our induction ceremony. I was told that during the final check it had been discovered that for some reason the doctor who had given me my original physical in the fall of 1968 had failed to note that I was colorblind. I was not aware of the fact either as I couldn't recall ever being administered a color blindness test. While I was assured that being colorblind would not disqualify me from military service, it would however mean that I would have to make a career field change from Electronic Technician Specialist. I was given a booklet that detailed the available career choices that were open at that time from which I could choose a new career field. I was further told that I had only about five minutes to make a decision, as my group was moving on to the induction ceremony.

With the clock running I didn't have time to get too frustrated as I hurriedly looked through the booklet. Nothing stood out at first blush as the material I was given to read seemed only a blur. I did see one choice, *Communication Specialist,* that sounded somewhat important and significant, and it certainly sounded better than *Military Cook* or *Military Security,* so I selected it. I had no clue what a *Communication Specialist* did, what kind of training they would go through or where they trained. I was able to ascertain that training was only for 12 weeks, which actually was disappointing in that I reasonably deducted that whatever it was I was about to learn probably did not translate into a good civilian job somewhere down the road. Obtaining a viable skill had been one of my primary goals coming into the military, although I would have selected the Air Force over the Marines, and probably the Army as well, regardless of the career path I might have been placed in. However, beyond the limited training, all I knew was that I was about to become one, a *Communication Specialist,* that is. I wasn't even in the military yet and I was already on a bumpy journey. Fortunately, the bumpy road ended for me personally after the sudden career switch.

The hour was starting to get late when we were ushered into another room and told to get in several lines and come to attention. With that, an officer stood before us and instructed us to raise our right hands. With our right hands raised, we all stood facing the U.S. flag and we repeated the oath that was being recited. The Officer smiled and welcomed us jointly into the United States Air Force. After so many unexpected obstacles I was finally in; I was finally an Airman preparing to serve in the greatest Air Force in the world.

The Military Years (1969-1973)

We were again dismissed to another room and the waiting process started all over again. 4:00 PM came and went and most of those working at the center were headed home. Around 5:00 PM, with darkness now starting to replace the small amount of daylight that had been filtering through the window, we were summoned to pick up our little duffle bags and head to a bus that was waiting for us at the curb. Out of all the inductees of the day, we Air Force guys were the last to finally depart for whereabouts unknown. As I approached the bus I heard one of the non-commissioned officers call out, *Who is Mooney?* My first reaction was, *What now?* I identified myself and he walked over to me, handed me a large packet, and stated that since I was the oldest man in the group (at 21 years and 10 months) I was to carry this packet to our destination and give it to the person that would meet us. I was relieved to find that this was all that he wanted.

We boarded the bus and headed to the *St. Louis Lambert International Airport* where we boarded a Trans World Airlines (TWA) Series 707 airliner, destination San Antonio, Texas. I had assumed that this was where I would be going for basic training but no one had to this point made it official. This was my first airplane flight, except for the helicopter ride that Shirley and I had taken on our honeymoon. I thought to myself how cool and how fitting that on my first day in the Air Force I would also take my first flight. Somehow, I was able to get a window seat and I sat captivated looking out the window at the many lights that blinked off and on in the distant darkness below.

Our flight into San Antonio lasted a little over two hours. Upon landing we were greeted by several military types, I handed over the package, and we were hustled onto another waiting bus. As the bus turned from the airport onto the I-410 Loop that circles the city, it seemed so odd, even a little surreal,

141

Life Between Innings

as it all looked so familiar. Plus, this was not where I was supposed to be on March 4, 1969. I was supposed to have been in Springfield, Missouri, working on my final few credits and a Bachelor's degree, preparing for the ministry. Yet, here I was, a little over ten months removed from my IBC graduation here in San Antonio heading into training on a whole new career path. Again, President Coote's words rang clearly in my head, *Your destiny swings on small hinges.*

By the time the bus swung into Lackland Air Force Base, which literally is within eyesight of IBC, it was nearing 11:00 PM and I was hungry. However, I would have willingly given up a meal to find a bed and get some sleep, as I had not slept all that well the night before and this had turned into a rather long day. It was to get longer. As luck would have it, the bus pulled up in front of one of the all-night Mess Halls located on the base and we all filed out for supper. I must say the food was surprisingly good and we had all that we wanted. Finally, we were loaded back on the bus again and this time the bus headed to one of the nearby Student Squadrons, stopping directly in front of one of the barracks, my new home for the next seven weeks or more. Inside, recruits from other parts of the U.S. joined us and we were instructed to go stand at the foot of one of the beds. Inside was a typical military dorm with about 20 double-decker beds. As we stood at attention we were introduced to a Staff Sergeant who was about 30 years old and not very tall. He introduced himself as our NCOIC (Non-Commissioned Officer In Charge) and began to tell us, or should I say, yell at us something about his not being there to be our Mommy. He went on further to say that every "swinging dick" in the room would learn to hate his guts before we got out of Lackland, but he was determined to make soldiers out of us whether we liked it or not. It was at this point that I determined he must be some kind of prophet because I was already learning to hate his guts.

142

The Military Years (1969-1973)

At about 12:30 AM we were finally allowed to go to bed with a reminder that we would be up promptly at 5:00 AM to start our day. 5:00 AM came way too soon and with much commotion as our NCOIC awoke us and had us come to attention at the foot of our beds. We were instructed to make our beds and then we were each given a brand new razor, blade included. Believe it or not I continued to use that razor until the summer of 2004 (35 years) when I accidentally left it at a vacation home that we had rented on Sanibel Island, Florida. Once everyone had their new razors we were instructed to go shave, whether we thought we needed it or not, get dressed and be out front of the barracks in three minutes. I had never used a blade before, having opted for an electric razor in my mid-teens. With the clock running I spread on the shaving lotion and began the process of shaving. Within seconds momentary panic set in as I knew that something was wrong as I was not getting anywhere. Out of the corner of my eye I noticed another Airman having the same problem but he had just discovered that there was a paper protective shield covering the blade. After removing the shield, things were bloody, but they went much more smoothly.

I don't know if we actually made time or not but in short order we were all shaved and dressed and were standing at attention in front of the barracks enjoying, well, not enjoying, a nice little rain shower. I noticed quickly that it was cool in San Antonio at this time of the morning and we did not have coats. I also noticed that a number of guys were sporting fresh bloodstains on their necks that were much greater than mine from our initial military shave. I took some solace in their pain. I think the NCOIC kind of enjoyed seeing that as well as he made mention, with a noticeable smirk on his face, of all these rookies assigned to him who were just learning to shave.

Life Between Innings

Fortunately for us, our barracks was located right across the street from the Mess Hall. We marched over to the Mess Hall for one of the finest breakfast meals that a man could hope for. We were told to eat all we wanted, just don't take any food out of the Mess Hall. Oddly enough, I reported to Lackland AFB at my married weight of 153. After eating three square meals a day for seven weeks with all the seconds and all the dessert that I wanted, somehow I graduated from basic at my high school weight of 129.

Following breakfast we met outside the Mess Hall, as we would do following all meals, except for those on the weekend, and marched back to the barracks. We were again ordered to go inside and stand at the foot of our bunks and await further instruction. Once inside, we promptly started a class on *Bed Making 101*, which was really an adventure in humiliation for some of the guys. The sheets and coverings had to fit tight enough so that if you dropped a quarter in the middle of the bed, the quarter would bounce. The higher the quarter bounced, the better your bed was made. With the upbringing that I had and Mom's insistence that our beds be made daily, plus with Dennis and I wanting our room at IBC to be considered one of the neatest each month, this was not a problem for me. At some point our NCOIC conducted several up close and personal conversations with a few guys about their lack of comprehension regarding this basic skill. Most of the guys understood this part of the "military game" but a couple had a hard time handling it. Finally one of the guys felt it necessary to stand up for his rights so he began to shout back at the NCOIC. He was ushered out of our presence and we never saw him again. It was right there that I decided that my best strategy was to take a low-profile position and try hard not to let the NCOIC learn my name. It was a strategy that proved to work well for me.

The Military Years (1969-1973)

Following our bed making class we came to attention outside of our barracks again and proceeded to march to the base barbershop. The rain had stopped as we stepped sprightly along the road to the count of, one, *two, three, hut, one, two, three, hut, one, two* . . . and on and on. From time to time I could hear a passerby say something derogatory or sarcastic about the *Rainbows*, which obviously was us. I later found out that one of the rites endured by new recruits was to be called *Rainbows* as they marched, adorned in their multi-colored civilian clothing, on their first full day in the military. As we stood in line for our hairstyling appointment, you could see that some were taking it better than others. Of course I had worn long hair even before Beatlemania so this was not something I was necessarily looking forward to, yet I kind of found it exciting. When it came my turn, the barber slowly trimmed up the sides and for a moment I thought maybe he was going to leave me a little hair on top. That thought had scarcely graced my mind when he suddenly made three or four fast cuts down the middle and promptly dismissed me. So much for getting a break. We were later posed the question, *When does an Airman need a haircut?* The answer was that an Airman should never "need" a haircut; it should be cut before the "need" arises.

Following our trip to the barber, we again came to attention and proceeded to march several blocks to the base clothier. As we would pass through the various stations those in charge of handing out our new military clothes would take a guess at our size and that was what we got. We were provided everything a man would need from socks, underwear, fatigues, khakis, dress uniforms, hats, coats, plus a coat that was made of wool and was so heavy that the only possible need for it would be if assigned somewhere in Alaska or Siberia. If the garments were too big, you were lucky. If the garments were too small, you were not so lucky. We were instructed to try

Life Between Innings

each item on but even if it did not fit, it took an act of Congress to get the item exchanged. This was all part of the games that we were subjected to in order to find out how we would react. A day or two later we found that certain times had been set up where we could exchange any non-fitting item with no hassle if we wanted to. I was one of the fortunate ones in that all my clothes were guessed properly and I did not have to exchange any items. We were finally beginning to look like military men even if we did not know how to act like one.

Upon receiving our clothing we again marched back to the barracks where we were instructed to carefully go through each item and remove every manufacturer's inspection sticker or tag in the garment, except the manufactures tag. It was unbelievable the amount of these stickers and tags that we found. When we finished, the NCOIC selected the pile of clothing of one of the Airmen and began to look for and find numerous tags and stickers that had been overlooked the first time through. I am sure that with his experience he knew where a lot of these stickers and tags were located that were not necessarily visible at first blush. After going through our items a second time we were instructed to go through them again a third time. It was amazing how many stickers and tags we found even on our third time through. After completing this exercise, we were shown how to properly hang and fold our clothes. Finally, after all this was concluded, the NCOIC told us that most likely within the next few days or week, our barracks would be inspected by his superior, a Captain, and that it would be in our best interests, and in the best interest of the squadron, if the Captain did not find clothing hung improperly or find any stickers or tags in our uniforms and clothing. The inspection did occur a few weeks later just as we were warned; unfortunately, the Captain found much more than just stickers and tags.

The Military Years (1969-1973)

Now that we were all styled in identical military uniforms and our heads were cleanly sheared, our class distinctions of being rich and poor were somewhat eliminated. I actually enjoyed this as it really did put the squad on more equal footing. We only had a couple of Hispanics and Blacks assigned to our squad and the group for the most part seemed to mesh together pretty well. However, there was one class distinction that color, hair and clothing could not cure. Two young men, good old white boys from Alabama, were assigned to the squadron and, bless their hearts, they just may have been about as intelligent as a bag of rocks. If nothing else, they were the two most naive guys I have ever met. Now, I am sure they are not representative of all the good men from Alabama, but these two made quite a duo. No one, including our NCOIC, could figure how in the world they were able to get into the military period, let alone the Air Force. I do not remember them being with us long. If they were, they were not in my squad for which I am humbly thankful and appreciative.

My first Sunday at Lackland I searched out the Protestant Chapel. There I saw a few of the guys that I had gotten to know so I sat with them. The service had barely started when I felt tears slowly, gently, trickling down my cheeks. I know that part of the emotion that I was feeling was simply missing Full Gospel Tabernacle, a church that I had grown to love in a very short period of time. I missed the worship and I missed hearing Pastor Redman preach. However, when the worship leader began to lead us in the first verse of *All Hail the Power of Jesus Name*, the trickle became a stream. The song had inspired me so many times as I listened to it lead into and out of the *Revival Time* radio broadcast each Sunday prior to heading out to our youth services. Here I was worshipping with those "cold, non-spirit-filled and ritualistic" Presbyterians, Methodists, Baptists and Episcopalians, yet God was blessing me and stirring my

Life Between Innings

heart. God wasted no time as he began schooling me that first Sunday worshipping in a military chapel that His Kingdom stretched far beyond my little Pentecostal world. It was a lesson I badly needed to learn.

About two weeks into basic training one of the guys decided to take an ice cream bar from the Mess Hall and finish it outside before our NCOIC came around. This was not too uncommon, although we had been instructed not to do so. However, on occasion someone, usually the smokers who wanted to get an extra puff or two in, would hurriedly eat their meal and then take an ice cream bar or cupcake with them to eat outside while they smoked. In each instance, the offender had been successful in finishing off the item in time. On this particular day the NCOIC appeared almost out of nowhere and the guy with the ice cream hastily shoved it into his coat pocket to avoid detection with thoughts of removing it as soon as the NCOIC's attention was not directed at us. We moved into formation and marched the short trip back to the barracks. While standing at attention we were instructed to go inside the barracks and change into our shorts and workout gear, hang up the uniforms that we had been wearing and report back in formation in three minutes. At this point we were getting used to these three-minute drills without too much of a problem.

When all were back and accounted for we marched out to the tarmac and proceeded to do our normal drills. After what seemed a little longer than normal, we marched back to the barracks and were dismissed but told to meet up with the NCOIC in the barracks in about ten minutes. This was not unusual at this time of the day as he normally would come in and give us any further orders or instruction for the evening, such as guard duty assignments, if there were any. However, on this particular day it was obvious as he entered the room that he was not happy. Well, let's be a little more accurate and

The Military Years (1969-1973)

say he was furious as he came storming through the doors. He wasn't yelling like he normally would; it was kind of a softer, yet more volatile anger than normal that made us really sit up and listen. He began to tell us that while we were on drills our barracks had been inspected and we had failed. He further went on to say that it was not only stickers and tags that were found, but his boss, his superior, had dipped his hand into the pocket of someone's coat and had pulled it out covered with a sticky, white, yet chocolaty substance. He wondered aloud if anyone just might know anything about such a thing that would have caused this. With great apprehension on his face, speaking with a voice excruciating with pained fear, the offending Airmen raised his hand and proceeded to explain the error of his ways. From that point he was forever branded as the *Ice Cream Man*. The *Ice Cream Man* and the NCOIC went back to his office to privately finish their up-close and personal conversation; from the sounds emanating from behind those closed doors, it did not sound pretty. The *Ice Cream Man* stayed with us for a few more days but eventually he was gone and we did not hear from him again. It was rumored that he had been sent back to start basic training all over again with a new unit. If that was all that he faced, he was lucky.

The ice cream incident was big, but it was only a visible sign or symptom of our squadron's overall inability to get the little details done correctly. Shortly after the incident the NCOIC told us that the Squadron Commander was seriously thinking about extending our training a week or two because we were just not getting it. Toward the end of the third week we were all summoned to the barracks where the NCOIC told us that it had been decided to fire the four squad leaders and put four new ones in place in a final attempt to turn our squadron around. He pulled the duty sheet roster out and began to review it to see who in our squadron had received the least amount of "gigs" up to this point. I was one of several who was low so by turn he called us individually into his office for an interview. I am not sure he and I had ever spoken a full sentence to each other at this point because of my low-profile strategy and ability to play the game. To date, I had not had any problem adapting to military life.

He began the interview asking me a series of non-related questions. Finally, he decided to cut right to the chase. *Mooney, do you think you can lead a squad and help us get out of this mess?* Without hesitation I responded with a firm, *Yes Sir!* He turned toward me and looked squarely at my innocent, baby face, his eyes kind of laughing while sporting a little chuckle and said, *You do?* I again responded with as much confidence as I could muster, *Yes Sir!* This time he did laugh and said, *Well, OK, you got the job.* I was dismissed and a few minutes later he came back out to where the squad was waiting and announced the names of all the new squad leaders. I knew I had blown my cover but it was time for action if I wanted to get out of basic and on to my tech school training assignment on time.

As squad leader, I was moved from my bed and locker near the rear of the room to the front. One of the guys was still having trouble making his bed so I took care of that while in exchange he polished my boots from time to time. I liked the arrangement. Other guys could not iron if their lives depended on it, so I would help them out as needed. When it came time for our first weekend pass and the wearing of the required tie, I conducted a tie tying class for a number of the fellows. Although I looked like a high schooler at best, the guys learned that I was willing to take care of them if they worked with me; with that, our problems began to diminish rather quickly. We did have one guy whose sloppiness was annoying and finally I reported him to the NCOIC. Shortly thereafter he was removed from our barracks. I do not know if my report did him in or if

The Military Years (1969-1973)

it was just the straw that broke his back; however he was gone and I sure did not miss him.

The routine of an Air Force Base sat in quickly. Unlike what Army and Marine personnel are subjected to, our days were fairly mild. From midweek of our first week we were normally in class for half a day in the morning learning about all the various facets of military life from saluting to claiming our many benefits. The rest of the day we spent on the tarmac learning how to march, doing calisthenics or heading off for some other function like getting more shots. However, practicing our marching drills were a must as we were not very good. Unfortunately, our last test before getting orders to Tech School was to perform and be scored in front of the Base Commander and this was truly our squadron's bug-a-boo. For some reason this was a skill that our squadron just could not seem to master no matter how hard we worked. We certainly did not have any rhythm, probably due in large part to our extreme "whiteness."

As we moved into our final weeks we were assigned KP (Kitchen Police: translated washing dishes and cleaning the Mess kitchen) duty twice. I was surprised that it was not more often but nevertheless that was all we were given. I discovered upon arrival for my first KP duty that the job hardly anyone wanted was the job I found to be the easiest. I would suppose the reason most tried to avoid it was that it looked pretty messy, and consequently not too desirable. The job was to take the trays as they came down the line, remove the dishes and scrape the remains into a rubber funnel. This allowed the food to drop below into several garbage pails. Someone else removed the pails so that was no problem. While utensils were furnished for doing the job, I just scraped the plates with my hand, which actually was quite fun. This made the job appear even more disgusting, so the job was mine. The

Life Between Innings

greatest benefit was that it fit my low profile strategy as I was never subjected to up-close and personal conversations from those in charge about a dish not being clean or dry or properly put away. What a great life!

We were also ordered to appear at the Base Obstacle Course during the fifth week of basic training. We all had to successfully complete it or we had to do it over. However, our squad found it to be fun and challenging so we volunteered to do it again. By this time, our problem children had been pretty much weeded out and our NCOIC was turning out to be a pretty nice guy. Although it was not easy to get it scheduled, he worked it out where we were able to go a second time. The best part was crawling through the minefield with all the explosions going off all around and live ammunition being fired overhead. The only way you could get hurt was to stand up or veer off course. Should that happen, the control tower would have shut things down immediately.

Our last challenge was to appear at the Rifle Range to be tested on firing the M-16, the rifle of choice by those serving in Viet Nam. I had not fired a rifle since I was about eight or nine years old and that was my BB gun. I remember shooting a sparrow with it. After finding my prey and looking at its lifeless body lying on the ground before me, I never shot at a bird or animal again; ever. After receiving our instructions on how to safely handle and fire the weapon we were led out to the actual firing range. We were each placed in position in front of a target, I don't know, maybe 75 yards out. If we were successful in scoring 57 of the allotted 60 shots, we were to be awarded a military ribbon for marksmanship that could be worn on our dress uniform, and occasionally, on our khakis. After I had fired off a couple shots I realized that I was shooting at the target of the guy next to me. When the scores were totaled it was found that I had scored 54 out of 60. However,

The Military Years (1969-1973)

my partner had scored 62 shots out of his 60 that were allotted. He got a ribbon and I did not although I figured that if truth were known, I probably had scored at least 57 on the two targets combined. This was the first and last time that I fired a rifle the entire four years and five months that I served in Uncle Sam's Air Force.

Early on at Lackland, in fact I believe it was immediately following that first chapel service, a newly converted young Christian man, Bob Wilson, from Wisconsin, introduced himself to me. Bob and I became fast friends and spent most of our off time together. As basic training was drawing to a close, we were given a one-day pass to go into San Antonio if we liked. My cousin Dennis had returned to IBC for his fourth year to earn his Bachelor's degree. Consequently, I called Dennis and he graciously loaned me his car to use on Sunday. Bob was more than willing to go with me to Trinity Assembly that Sunday to hear Pastor Hagee preach. All I can remember about the service was that it was just great to once again be in such a place of worship and praise and to hear Pastor Hagee preach God's Word. Afterward, I became tour guide as I chauffeured Bob to my favorite restaurant and other haunts that I had frequented while a student at IBC. Bob and I remained in contact for a few years following our time in basic but, unfortunately, we eventually lost touch with each other.

At long last the final day of basic training was upon us. It was a bright, hot, muggy day in April with the humidity hovering around 70 or 80 percent. We had one final test that we had to do before getting our orders for Tech School and that was to participate in the parade of squadrons that would march before the reviewing stand and the Base Commander. There were approximately 12 or so squadrons participating and as we marched past the reviewing stand a panel of officers would score us. Our final score was not very high but we

Life Between Innings

had performed well enough to illicit a few compliments from our Squadron Commander. I think the fact that none of our guys passed out in the humidity and heat must have given us some extra credit as a few guys were dropping in the squadrons surrounding us.

Final test concluded, it was time to march back to the barracks where we would receive what we all had been working toward, our first set of orders directing us to our technical schools. I still did not know where Communication Specialists were trained, although I had heard of a couple options, so I was getting very excited as we were called to attention to receive orders. When our name was called out, we were to drop out of formation and report to the Squadron Commander, give salute, obtain orders and be dismissed. Finally my name was called and I went forward. Upon receiving orders I quickly hustled to the side and began to read it. Not being familiar, at this point, on how orders are laid out, it took a moment or two for me to decipher that I was being assigned to the 3752 Student Squadron at Sheppard Air Force Base, an Air Training Command (ATC) base, located in Wichita Falls, Texas. Once training started, and the orders did not have a firm starting date for training to begin, the training would last for 12 weeks. From what I could find out, the reputation of the base and city was not all that good, but as I was learning, it would not take me long to adjust to any of the assignments I was given, and this would be no exception.

On April 15, 1969, the day following graduation, I boarded a Greyhound bus and headed to Wichita Falls. It was also on this date I received my first promotion from Airman Basic (Pay Grade E-1) to Airman (Pay Grade E-2) and was able to sew on my first stripe. The bus ride took several hours, as Wichita Falls is located near the Texas and Oklahoma border and the Red River. Upon arrival, I reported in at the Base Office and

The Military Years (1969-1973)

was immediately told to report to my new squadron. There, I was given a room and barracks assignment. I met my two roommates, both being black Airmen, one whose name was Roy Rogers. I only spent a few days in the barracks before moving into town so I rarely saw either of my two roommates. One Saturday evening I came in to go to bed and found that one of the guys was sitting staring off into a purplish light listening intently to some type of Oriental stringed music, getting high. I slipped into bed and drifted off to sleep thinking how this scene looked so reminiscent of that which I had seen in a number of movies, but never thought I would experience.

Before I left Lackland, I had contacted Shirley regarding the assignment and she began to make preparations to meet me. We had purchased an old white Plymouth, probably a 1962 or 1963, with the real long sloping back window, just prior to my induction. With the help of her Dad, she promptly arrived within the week after my arrival. While waiting for my class start date, I had been assigned KP duty, working an 8-hour day shift. Her first night there, I eagerly met her at the motel where we were to stay until we were able to find an apartment. That first night, because I did not trust the wake up service, she agreed to stay up so that she could awaken me in time to get back to base.

After finishing my shift of KP duty that morning, I was off for a few days so we immediately started looking for a place to live. On that first day we struck gold as we found a second floor, furnished, one-room flat with a kitchen on the main road running through Wichita Falls, not far from the base. About half a block away was a nice park where we could walk and talk after finishing up at school each day. It was also convenient to all the places we needed to go. For us, it was perfect. The living quarters had a couch and chair and a couple tables with the kitchen nook off to the side. When bedtime came, we

155

would move the furniture as necessary, go to the closet, and then pull the bed down and out into the room. In the morning, the bed was made and then was returned upright into the closet. Pretty cool!

We could not afford much in the way of entertainment. We did have a small black and white TV and a Monopoly Board to keep us busy in our spare time. We played a lot of Monopoly over the three-plus months that we were there. Since I rarely lost, we rarely played the game after leaving Wichita Falls.

We did find a pretty nice Assembly of God church to attend. While they did not go overboard to make us feel at home, we did not go out of our way to get too acquainted, knowing that we would be gone in just a few short weeks. However, we were spiritually fed there and did not lack for the hearing of God's Word.

One of the highlights for us while here was a visit in July from mom and the Sullivan family (Uncle Floyd, Aunt Enzie and Cousin Evelyn). They had been on a vacation out west and decided to detour our way on their way back to St. Louis. One of the nights that they were there was the day that Neil Armstrong, an American Astronaut, landed and walked on the moon, a first for any human being.

Upon arrival at Sheppard AFB, I had developed a clicking sound in my neck so I was instructed to go by the hospital each morning for treatments. This process lasted about six weeks and then the doctor released me. However, I had never been instructed to do anything else during the mornings after that so I would show up at my squadron around 11:00 AM, fall into formation and march the half-mile or so to the building where our Communication classes were held. Class ran from Noon until 4:00 PM wherein we would fall back into formation, march back to the squadron and be dismissed. Other than my studies in the evening, that was my schedule.

The Military Years (1969-1973)

I also learned quickly what a *Communication Specialist* was. Our primary skill was typing, a skill which fortunately I had developed fairly well at IBC. In order to pass, an Airman had to be able to type 40 words a minute with minimal errors. Again, not a problem for me. The job of a *Communication Specialist* was to work in a telecom (Communication) center typing messages and sending and receiving messages that would go throughout the world regarding military issues and personnel. The Communication Center was the hub of any base and while we were sworn not to reveal to anyone the things we would learn in the process of doing our jobs, it was neat having the inside "know" on so many issues.

Several weeks into training a couple of us were directed to an interview room regarding a possible assignment in the White House, or better yet, traveling with the President of these United States of America wherever he was to go. The first order of business was to make application for a Top Secret – Crypto security clearance followed by the interview session. Here I was faced with a mountain of paper to be filled out citing friends and relatives, places of work, etc. that could be checked to verify my security liability. I was told that this security background check could take awhile, in fact a month or more at a minimum. I was pretty excited about the possibility of this assignment and I knew that any background search on me would not be troublesome. However, the interviewer, upon finding that I was married, held out little hope for me as he implied that they preferred unmarried guys. The basic reason given was that the cost of living was so great in Washington, D.C. that it was tough, if not impossible, for a low-ranking Airman like me to make it financially. I guess I understood, but man did I covet that job. When the assignments came down following graduation I found that indeed I had not been accepted.

Life Between Innings

While living in Wichita Falls, the weather was setting new records. At one point, the temperature reached 100 degrees or more for over thirty straight days, that in and of itself was a record. We had also endured some tremendous storms that passed that way, as Wichita Falls lies right in the middle of what is known as Tornado Alley, a path that cuts through Texas, Oklahoma and parts of Kansas and Missouri. On one of those extremely hot Saturdays, Shirley and I decided to drive up to a beautiful park and lake situated near Stillwater, Oklahoma, maybe an hour's drive from home. We had a great day basking in the sun and sand and swimming in the beautiful, cool lake. Unfortunately, I had enjoyed it a little too much and came back with a painful sunburn.

Now we had been warned numerous times in our various meetings that we could be disciplined for getting severe sunburn because we were *damaging military property*. So, I applied whatever known cure I could find that night and throughout the next day to my skin but I was still in a lot of pain by the time I reported to the squadron to march to class on that following Monday. Marching was still not one of my best military skills. In fact, it was not uncommon for Airman White, our Squad Leader, to turn and bark out at me while we marched to or from class, *Hey Mooney, you're bouncing up and down like a rubber ball.* I can only guess that my marginally flat feet would not allow me the "heel to toe rhythm" necessary to march and not bounce. Fortunately, Airman White had little authority to do anything about it so I escaped any repercussions. However, I had no choice but to go on, no matter how much the pain or how much the stiffness set in or how much the sweat on my back would pull my rough uniform shirt to the burn. Toward the end of the week I had made it through, but it was close.

At the end of each week we were tested over the material that we had covered. My first grade was a disappointing 85 or

The Military Years (1969-1973)

86; most of the guys it seemed scored in the mid to upper 90s. I decided to hit the books a little harder and thereafter consistently scored in the upper 90s, including a few aces, the rest of the way. Upon graduation day, the instructor had additional certificates to hand out to all that had graduated with honors. I had been keeping score and I knew that despite that low score the first week, I had gradually overcome and was due for an honors' certificate. When the instructor got to my name he commented in kind of a surprised tone, *Mooney, you made Honor Graduate?* I just smiled and took my certificate knowing that he has misjudged me based on that first test, plus, with my low-profile strategy still much in play, he truly was surprised. That made receiving the award even that much greater.

As my final week was coming to an end I had an occasion to meet up with one of the NCOICs assigned to our squadron. As we talked it became evident that somehow I had slipped through the cracks as I was to have had daily duties assigned to me on the AM prior to class. Consequently, I was assigned to dust and straighten up the squadron recreation room the following day and that was it; that was the only daily assignment that they were ever able to assign to me. Again, what a great life!

The weeks at Wichita Falls had flown by. Shirley and I had really enjoyed our time here, contrary to what we had been told to expect, perhaps due in great part to my less-than-pressure-filled schedule. On an Airman's pay we obviously did not have much income, but we ate fairly well, had minimal expenses and had really enjoyed our first military experience together. It was July 22, 1969, and I found myself again in formation on the base tarmac, following graduation, outside our Tech School building awaiting orders. This time I was even more clueless than I was the first time about where we, or I, may be going. Finally, the moment of truth came and I found that I was being

Life Between Innings

assigned to the 6948th *Security Squadron (Mobile)* at *Goodfellow Air Force Base* in San Angelo, Texas. Goodfellow AFB was part of the *United States Air Force Security Service (USAFSS)* and the assignment was to a Mobile Unit. Mobile Units are trained and prepared to activate on a moment's notice for Temporary Duty Assignments (TDY) worldwide and could involve a single Airman or the whole unit. I was told to report on or about August 8, 1969.

In the Air Force you are given four weeks of vacation a year, in advance. Consequently, I could report to Goodfellow right away or anytime within the next four weeks. Shirley and I decided to leave directly from Wichita Falls for San Angelo, located in southwest Texas about 100 miles due west of Abilene and 200 miles to the northwest of Wichita Falls. We would take whatever vacation time we needed to look for a new place to live and then I would report. So, sometime around the third week of July, we packed up what little belongings we had and set sail for our next assignment. Again the report was that Goodfellow was not that great of an assignment, although for families, San Angelo was not too bad. As it was, San Angelo and Goodfellow turned out to be the best stateside assignment I would have.

On the first day, as was our luck in Wichita Falls, we found a nice first-floor, three-room, furnished flat right on the outskirts of the midtown area, not too far from the base. We were allowed to move in right away; however, we decided to do some major cleaning, especially on the kitchen, before we moved in. Consequently, we spent the entire first night, including the early morning hours of the next day, cleaning and scrubbing and waxing the floors. Finally, it was ready and we quickly made ourselves at home.

Since we had gotten settled so quickly, I decided to go ahead and report to work so that we could save our vacation

The Military Years (1969-1973)

time. Upon reporting I found that my security clearance had not yet come through and, in fact, could possibly take some time since it was for the Top Secret – Crypto level. Therefore, in the interim I was assigned to work as a clerk at the Base Housing Department. Again, I had a really tough job (well, not really) playing hotel clerk to all kinds of military types coming into Goodfellow for training or meetings. I worked five days a week, usually including the weekends, on an eight-hour PM shift. I worked for two civilians who couldn't have treated me nicer. I almost regretted when after six or seven weeks passed by, my security clearance came in. I did find out later that many of the people I had listed on my background check sheet were in fact contacted and interviewed.

At last, as the middle of September rolled around, I was able to finally meet and work with the men and women in our squadron. It soon became apparent that as a mobile unit, we really did not do much except wait around for an emergency to erupt somewhere in the world that would require the deployment of the full squadron or an individual Airman. However, since I was a neophyte in this field, I was loaned out to work, slash train, in the base communication center for a time. At Goodfellow, I found that in the Base Communication Center the day shift was for working, the PM shift was for reading and the Midnight or Owl shift was for sleeping, undetected of course. I am not sure how much I learned at the base communication center, although the exposure to live operations was good for me. But, after about two weeks, I was sent back to our squad to continue training.

Our squad met daily in an old brown military trailer that sat out in the compound along with our mobile equipment, including a mobile communication center. If or when the call came, this equipment would be loaded on our various tractor-trailer diesel trucks or on large military air transports and

Life Between Innings

shipped wherever needed around the world. The schedule ran something like, report at 6:00 AM, head over to the Mess Hall for breakfast around 7:00 AM before the crowd got there, come back to the trailer around 8:00 AM for training, and then on occasion head back to the Mess Hall around 11:00 AM for lunch before being dismissed around noon. During our training time we read a lot, but not always the prescribed manuals that we had been instructed to read. We also told lots of stories (I mainly listened as I had no military stories to tell), played cards and played a football game that we had invented played with paper clips and small wads of paper. On occasion, we would be told by our NCOIC to do some training in the mobile communication center, but that did not happen on any regular basis. I know this all sounds rather sloppy, especially during war time (technically, Viet Nam War was never a declared war), but except for us seven new guys, this was an experienced lot.

Many of the guys had already served in Viet Nam and most had lost a friend or two along the way. One or two had actually killed some Viet Cong while patrolling the compounds around their particular communication center. I did not detect in the voices of those that had killed a Cong any sense of pride in their accomplishment; mostly there seemed to be regret that it had to happen. Most of the guys who had been in that situation talked very little about it; it was like it was a closed door that they rarely wanted to open.

I found it odd, if not interesting, that some of the guys hated Viet Nam passionately while others were trying hard to obtain another assignment to go back. For those that wanted to go back, the reasons varied from the excitement of being in war, the bigger pay check, the booze, the plethora of available women and cheap sex. From the stories that were told, it was amazing the amount and types of sexual experiences

The Military Years (1969-1973)

that could be obtained for a chocolate bar, some nylons, a little money or even a Christmas tree. Some just frankly wanted to get away from their wives and families.

The Christmas tree story was sad, if not sordid. One of the young men, in fact an airman from Kansas City, Missouri, told the story of how he had left for Viet Nam just after getting married. He really missed his wife and had remained faithful to her for a number of months despite the harassment he had received from his peers. His wife, knowing that they would not be together on their first Christmas, sent him a small Christmas tree as a reminder of her love and thoughts during the holiday season. But finally, in a very weak moment, he agreed to give one of the house ladies the Christmas tree for her sexual favors. I think he regretted telling us the story as the guys brought the incident up a little too often. It was easy to see that he was uncomfortable with the teasing and harassment that was being meted out to him and it was obvious that his actions had affected him more than what he tried to let on.

Although we had a highly trained group ready for some action, the calls rarely came for any of the Airman to report somewhere, and never was the full squadron ordered to move. It seemed that the most popular spot to send the few guys who received a TDY assignment was to a base at Shemya, Alaska, located on an extremely cold peninsula along the coastline that is actually just a few miles from the coast of Russia. This lack of activity was making a lot of the guys antsy as most wanted to work and not just sit around.

Since we were a mobile unit, it was also necessary that we become proficient in driving the big diesel tractor-trailer trucks. For most guys, learning how to back one up was the real trick. Fortunately for me I picked it up quickly, most likely because of the bus driving skills I had learned while attending IBC and the truck driving experience I had gained working for

Life Between Innings

Cardinal Chips. Certainly, I could now double clutch the old rigs, thanks to my previous experience of driving "Big Yellow."

For us, finding a local church was a top priority. We set out immediately to look for a church and found that there were two fairly good-sized Assembly of God churches in town, Evangel and First Assembly. We visited them both and decided that we liked the worship much better at Evangel, located on Campus Boulevard, and the ministry of Reverend and Mrs. Mack. The Macks were a great couple in their mid 30's and were a delight to work and fellowship with. Airman Richard Leake, a good friend who was likewise a Communication Specialist at the base, and his wife, had already decided on First Assembly, but neither of us wanted to change our decision, so we stayed with our respective churches. Despite that, we quickly became right at home at Evangel and made some wonderful, caring friends. Contrary to our experience in Wichita Falls, we had no idea how long we would be in San Angelo so we were quick to make friends and get involved. In fact, I became the Sunday School superintendent for a short time during the latter part of our stay; it was a great experience for me.

On October 1, 1969, just two months after arriving at Goodfellow AFB, I received my second military promotion, this time to Airman First Class (Pay Grade E-3). Consequently, I was able to sew on my second stripe. Promotions were obviously exciting times. It was neat to gather up all my uniforms and take them to the local seamstress to have the old stripes removed and the new ones placed in their stead.

Soon after arriving in San Angelo I had noticed an ad in the local newspaper seeking referees for the Pop Warner football league. The pay was something like $15 a game so I figured what the heck, I may not know a whole lot about the rules of football but I probably know more than the kids. Plus, $15 for an hour of work didn't seem all that bad. Since I had ample time on my hands, usually being relieved of duty on the base shortly after lunch, I applied and was readily accepted. There were no tests or physicals to take so the process was easy. I was normally assigned to watch the line play, as that was an easier assignment for an inexperienced official. It was an easy few bucks that it didn't hurt to have on my military salary. Although the Pop Warner league was not associated with Goodfellow AFB, it was here that I became aware that the military base had a basketball league each fall and winter and they were always looking for officials. It also hit me that sports officiating just might be a way to make a few bucks the year round while doing something I really enjoyed.

Consequently, I dropped by the air base athletic office one day and struck up a conversation with one of the Air Force guys who actually had an assignment at Goodfellow to assist in running the athletic program. How neat a job is that? I discussed with him that I did not have any experience as an official but that I had played basketball all my life, had some small college experience and had worked as the athletic director for the San Antonio Boys' Club, which included a lot of basketball officiating. He was very interested in me and decided to put me right to work. He also recommended that I contact the local area *Southwest Basketball Officials Association (SBOA)* to see about additional work if I wanted it. Plus, the SBOA could help me get the rules and mechanics training that I would need if I wanted to get serious about officiating. He gave me the number of the guy to contact and I made an appointment to meet him right away.

Like the base, the SBOA was always on the lookout for fresh blood to be recruited into their program. I attended their classes and began to find out how much I did not know about officiating, especially the mechanics of officiating. However, I passed the prerequisite *Texas State High School Basketball*

Life Between Innings

Officiating Test and they likewise were ready to put me to work. At this time, officials assigned one of the regular junior high or high school games, were paid about $30 per game, plus travel. Should we get assigned a really big game, we also got a portion of the gate receipts. As a rookie I knew that I would not get many of those games, if any. If you were the driver to a game away from San Angelo, you were paid a nice fee per mile. Driving of course was easy money that could add up quickly so the privilege of first refusal went to the senior man. As a rookie, I didn't expect to get many of those opportunities either; however, I was surprised at the generosity of a number of the old timers that would allow me to drive so that I could pick up the extra cash. The wage for a military game was a little less but still in the $20 range.

The SBOA met weekly to discuss situations that had occurred at various games. It was here that we also picked up our schedule for the following week. I obviously was assigned on a regular basis with one of the more experienced guys. We would discuss all that we anticipated would or could happen as we drove to the game, met again at halftime to discuss the game and receive some constructive criticism, and then do it all over again on the way home. It was great; I enjoyed every moment of the whole process. Apparently word was getting back to the head of the Association and the guy that made out the schedule that this "Mooney Kid" knew his stuff and was progressing very well. I did not know it at the time but the school officials also sent in evaluations on all the officials and evidently many of them liked my work. I had already begun to develop a style of hustling to get in position to make my calls, and making them decisively and fairly. Coaches found it harder to complain about calls or effort if I was doing this, plus these attributes are important in keeping a game under control.

The Military Years (1969-1973)

I had not been working too long when I received my first break. The two local high schools in the city were meeting in their annual league game and they were major rivals. Fortunately for me, I was not scheduled to work a game on this particular night. A couple hours before game time, one of the officials scheduled to work the game had an emergency and the Association was scrambling to find an experienced official to take it. Finding none available, the brother of the famous professional wrestler, Cowboy Bob Ellis, mentioned that he had worked with me before and that I had handled myself very well. It was not an ideal situation to put a rookie into but Mr. Ellis was very experienced and well respected by the athletic departments of both schools so it was decided that with him there, we probably should be able to handle the intensity that surely would be present both on the floor and in the stands.

Prior to the game Mr. Ellis took me to both of the coaches and introduced me. You could see that both coaches were a little leery but they had other things more important than me to worry about. Finally, tip-off came and went and sure enough we were involved in an emotional, highly charged, nip-and-tuck battle. For the most part, however, things went well throughout the first quarter. As we moved into the early moments of the second quarter, things were starting to get a little physical and Mr. Ellis and I both were taking pains to keep things under control. One of the players made a drive for the basket and was getting fouled with his opponent's lower body and I whistled a foul. The coach jumped up and began to protest the call and asked me for an explanation. Not liking my answer to his protest, which I had politely given him, he threw his towel to the floor and stomped back to the bench. Without hesitation I hit him with a technical foul; all he could do was just stand there and glare back at me.

Life Between Innings

The remainder of the half was uneventful as the players saw that we were not going to tolerate any funny busy. As our halftime break was nearing the end, the coach on whom I had called the technical stuck his head in the door and asked if he could ask me a question. I gave him permission. With that, he politely asked, *Why did you hit me with a technical since I did not curse you?* I explained, *I was OK with your outburst, as I understand that this is an emotional game; however, once you threw the towel it was apparent that you were trying to show me up and in a game like this I could not allow that to happen.* Again, very politely, he said, *Thank you, I was just wondering.*

The game continued without incident and remained an exciting, well-played game; it was fun being in such a great atmosphere. Following the game, both coaches approached Mr. Ellis and me to shake our hands and to thank us for doing such a good job. After they left, Mr. Ellis gave me the ultimate compliment, *Mooney, I would be glad to recommend you for any game; it was a real pleasure working with you. You handled yourself well.* From that point forward my reputation began to climb as a good, fair, proficient and hard-working official. Of course, at the air base it was a little bit different in that I knew and worked with many of the players. When players would see me around at various functions, especially after I had refereed one of their military league games, they couldn't help but take a good-natured jab at me, and that was fine; it was all part of the game. It was also not unusual to be out shopping and have someone approach me and tell me they had seen me officiating their kid's game someplace in the area. The people were always polite and positive in their remarks, which I really enjoyed.

One of the neat things I was assigned to do was officiate a number of girls' games. Girls' basketball was big in Texas at this time but long before it became the popular game it now

The Military Years (1969-1973)

is across the USA. In addition, the girls' game was played a little different from today where girls and boys play by the same rules. At that time each team would have six players on the court, three on the offensive end and three on the defensive end. Neither was allowed to go past the midcourt stripe or it was a violation and loss of ball. My reputation for working girls' games was even better than for working boys' games and I would have a coach or two around the area who would specifically ask for me. I think what they liked was that the typical official would not call the girls' game as close as they would the boys' games. I did not believe in differentiating and called both games the same way. As a coach myself later in years, I would likewise become agitated at officials that tried to pull that stuff; I wanted my games called the same way that I had seen them call the boys' games.

Needless to say, I was starting to make a decent amount of extra cash. In fact, at this point, with my extra work, Shirley and I were living much higher on the hog, so to speak, than the average Airman and his family. Not to brag, but we were eating steak and roast while many of our friends were eating potpies as their regular staple. With the additional cash it was also possible to move and live in a better apartment than the flat that we were living in. The walls at our flat were pretty thin and it was not too hard to hear the conversations coming through our walls from other flats. Before we moved from the flat, my sister, Bonnie, and her husband, Gary, came through on vacation and got to experience with us some of the sounds and joys of living there.

By January or February of 1970, we began to look for a better, perhaps quieter, more private apartment than the flat we were living in near mid-town. We were thrilled when we came across the Magdalen Apartments, a brand new apartment complex across town from the base, but very affordable. It was a second-story apartment located at 2818 North Magdalen Street. It was furnished fairly well and had a kitchen that Shirley just loved. It was also a nice place to begin to raise our new baby that was on the way.

Not all of my basketball officiating experiences turned out to be as rewarding as the junior and senior high school games and the military games I was doing. Even though I was working games both in the community and West Texas area, plus on the base, I still had a few nights available that I could work. I am not sure how it began but somewhere around the turn of the year I agreed to work some church and industrial league games. Hardly ever would I come away from these games having had a good experience. With no authority to back me up, like the school system or the military, these games often got out of control. On one particular night I had made a call that resulted in a rather large player fouling out of the game. After the game I was walking toward the door when this mammoth of a guy, in a fit of anger, picked up a basketball and fired it at me from behind, just missing my head. The ball ricocheted off the wall with a terrific thud, scaring the bah-gee-bees out of me. Several of his players restrained him for which I was thankful. I vowed never to work church or industrial leagues again and I didn't; there just wasn't enough money in it for the abuse that officials were subjected to. I figured it was their loss.

However, with the success that I had with basketball, I decided to try my hand at baseball and softball. As an umpire, I was required to join the local baseball umpiring association and the *Amateur Softball Association (ASA)*. I was getting in kind of late for high school baseball as in Texas they start very early in the spring, often before basketball is completed. Even with the late start, I worked over 100 baseball and softball games that season. By now, I was making almost equal in pay as an official, if not more, than I was with my military salary.

The Military Years (1969-1973)

On Friday, July 25, 1970, Shirley was now several days overdue and the doctor told her that there was no use waiting any longer. As he put it, *Come back on Monday and we will have us a baby.* It was kind of fun having the weekend off knowing that Monday we were going to have the baby. It gave us time to get things set up and ready to go so when Monday arrived, we were ready. On Sunday morning we went to church as usual and then decided to go to the drive-in theatre that evening to enjoy one last evening without crying in the background. We saw what was considered to be a rather risqué movie at the time, *Lolita*. The movie was not very interesting, but we did have a pleasant evening out.

On Monday, July 28, we arrived early at the hospital and Shirley was induced to begin labor. The doctor projected that the baby would probably arrive around noon. However, we waited and waited and waited and nothing seemed to be happening. Shirley was quite miserable, as would be expected, and she was as anxious as anyone to get this over with. Now the AM had moved toward late afternoon and I was getting nervous as I had a game I was supposed to work at 5:00 PM. From what we had been told, there was no reason to expect that this was to be a problem, as the baby would be born around noon. With this schedule, I could be there for the "blessed event" and still have a lot of time to welcome visitors from the church, make sure Shirley and the baby were both comfortable, make my game and then get back to the hospital in short order.

I soon learned that with baby birthing, things do not always go as planned. So, I waited and waited, finally checking back in with the nurses at about 4:30 PM. I was assured that all was well but that the birth was not imminent. I hurried off to do my game and then rushed right back, getting back to the hospital around 6:15 PM. I was shocked to see friends from church there laughing and smiling and congratulating me on the birth of my new girl. Evidently, just as I was pulling away from the hospital, the course of events began to pick up very rapidly and Dionne Reshea was born somewhere around 5:15 PM. Unbelievable!

Shirley and baby Dionne had come though the ordeal very well. I would now be a bachelor for two days and then my life would change forever. On Wednesday, I picked up the girls and brought them home. I would be the primary caregiver for a few days until Shirley's Mom, Helen, was able to fly in. She was a lifesaver, staying for about two weeks to help us get acclimated. Unfortunately, Dionne developed a very good case of colic that would hang on for about nine months. Over the next few months, we took many car rides trying to get her little stomach to settle down. We also slept in a variety of positions because whenever and wherever Dionne decided to go to sleep, whoever was holding her or walking her at that precise moment, that is also where they would sleep. We did find a nice red wind-up swing that would swing back and forth for up to 10 minutes at a time. Dionne lived and slept in that swing a lot of days and night. Perhaps it was child abuse, sobeit if it was, but if that was where she went to sleep, that was the place she was going to stay.

One of the fatherly tasks that I became rather good at was changing diapers. However, Dionne gave me an initiation that I would never forget. On the day that we brought her home it became obvious moments after we arrived that it was time for a diaper change. I got all the necessary equipment ready to go, took off the old stinky one, cleaned her up pretty well and prepared to put on a fresh one. Just as I was finishing the task it became clear, very clear in fact, that I was going to have to repeat the chore as she had made "new provisions" for me. For several minutes I performed another thorough cleaning job. Just as I was about to fold up the diaper and pin

The Military Years (1969-1973)

it, more disgusting pooh-pooh came rushing out. I honestly do not know how many attempts I made to get her clean and changed but it was more than just a few. Evidently she had developed a very nice case of diarrhea for ole dad to attend to and attend to I did for quite some time. Finally, after a number of attempted changes, her little system settled down and I was able to take a momentary break.

Toward the end of summer I was assigned to my first and only TDY assignment. I had found out earlier that men whose wives were pregnant were rarely sent on TDY unless it was an emergency or a short exercise. Security Command was to be part of a two-week maneuver that the Military was conducting near Goldsboro, South Carolina. Since the baby was now born, the military decided to send me out on the exercise. I was actually looking forward to the assignment as I had not really done much of anything for the 10 months or so that I had been at Goodfellow, except train. Finally the day came to depart so we loaded up our mobile equipment and headed for Dyess AFB in Abilene, Texas. We hung around the flight terminal at the base most of the day and were finally summoned aboard a big C-137. It was like a house. The front of the aircraft opened up into a ramp and several vehicles, including our mobile communication center, were driven on board and strapped into place. We were told to sit wherever we could find a place, as there were no seats. I found a little window and sit viewing the scenes down below. Our flight seemed much shorter than I expected and it was still daylight when we landed at the airbase in Goldsboro. We unloaded and were assigned some very comfortable pre-fab huts out in an open field, which served as our temporary quarters. Over the course of the next two weeks, military games were played out; however, our little communication center had very little business and I ended up working about two nights for a total of about

Life Between Innings

4 hours out of the 10 days we were there. Finally the games were concluded and we boarded a C-47, another large military cargo plane, somewhat similar to the C-137 that we had flown up in, and we were whisked away and headed back to Abilene and then home.

During my time at Goodfellow, seven different airmen of my rank (E-3) were assigned to our squadron. Supposedly, we trained together, but obviously not much training occurred. As September of 1970 came around, one by one, those in our little group began to get reassignment orders. None of the assignments had been great with the majority going into Thailand, a neighbor of Viet Nam. Finally, we were down to my good Christian friend, Airman Leake, his best friend and me. Several days passed and finally both Airman Leake and his buddy, Airman Arthur Nunn, received their assignments to Ankara, Turkey. The only good thing about this assignment was that they would be able to take their wives. So far, they were the only ones of the group to get such an assignment.

The days passed and then a week or two and still no assignment came down for me. I could only picture what dreadful place they must be sending me, perhaps to the jungles of Viet Nam, because it sure was taking a long time to put it all together. Finally, one early September morning I was sitting in the training trailer when the call came down for me to report to the office for orders. I was nervous, yet excited as I fumbled through them to see where I was going. As I read it, I could not believe it; the U.S. Air Force was sending me to the 6931st *Security Group*, like Goodfellow, a part of the USAF Security Service, located at Iraklion Air Station, Crete, Greece, an island sitting squarely in the middle of the Mediterranean Sea between North Africa and the mainland of Greece. I was in delightful disbelief. Not only was I being sent to an island, but I was also being sent to one of the most beautiful places

The Military Years (1969-1973)

in the world where the water is so unbelievably blue and clear and laps up on sandy or pebbled white beaches beneath huge rocky clefts. The Cretan culture was very much a mixture of the present and that of Bible days. The history of the island was fascinating with so many historical spots to visit. This was going to be neat; no, it was going to be fascinating!

I was truly embarrassed to go back to the trailer and tell the guys where I was going. Most of them where going to the armpits of the world, yet God had graciously blessed me again beyond deserving. A war was being waged in a far away country where many of our men were being sent, including some of the guys sitting in that trailer with me. Yet, for some unknown reason, God was sending me to Greece. Embarrassed; yes! But, *Praise God and Hallelujah,* for God's wonderful blessing. And, while I was thankful, I also knew that I could and would soon get over the embarrassment. Yes, it was a great life!

We had loved San Angelo. God had been good to us here and we had made a lot of good friends. The last weekend before our early October 1970, departure, the church gave us a wonderful party, a sit-down dinner in a banquet room of a nice restaurant downtown. We did not deserve such a send off, but we accepted it as humbly as we could. In our short time of ministering and worshiping and growing in God with the folks from Evangel, we had made some tremendous friends and we had been very blessed. Yes, I must say it again; it truly was a great life.

Shirley and I decided that we would drive back to St. Louis and take a couple weeks of vacation. Then, I would leave her and Dionne there with her parents and I would travel on to Crete and begin the search for new living quarters. So far, God had blessed us on each move and we had been able to find a nice place to live immediately upon arrival. The two weeks passed quickly and I packed up to leave St. Louis. It was never

Life Between Innings

easy to leave home but this time it was even more difficult. As the time approached for my departure, I became keenly aware that it might be awhile before I could save enough money to fly Shirley and Dionne over the Atlantic and into the Mediterranean to join me.

The day finally arrived and it was time to leave St. Louis, say the many obligatory goodbyes and kiss Shirley and Dionne goodbye as well, and then head out for the next great adventure. I left St. Louis on October 14, 1970 on a flight into New York where my late flight out became even later as the flight mechanics had to make some "adjustments" on our aircraft. Around midnight we were finally airborne enroute to Frankfurt, Germany, where I would transfer to another flight that would take me into Athens, Greece. At Athens, I would need to take a cab from the Athena International Airport over to the Olympic Airline Terminal for the last leg of my flight into Iraklion, Crete. About all I can remember about the flights was that cumulatively it was long, but I did eat very well. I also watched two pretty good movies while crossing the Atlantic entitled, *To Sir With Love,* starring Sydney Pointier and *They Call Me Mr. Tibbs,* likewise staring Mr. Pointier.

The trip was uneventful once we were out of New York. My only scare was in the cab driving over to the Olympic Airline Terminal from the Athena International Airport, about a 15-minute trip. It was late in the evening, probably about 11:00 PM, it was dark and we were pretty much alone on the road. Suddenly, my cabby came to an abrupt halt at a red light and promptly turned off his motor. I figured this was it, he was going to turn around and assault and rob this "rich" American right on the spot. Seconds later, the light turned green, he started the motor and off we went. We repeated this little ritual several times but finally made it to the airport. I learned

176

later that Greek cabbies believe that this procedure saves gas and gas is expensive, so the logic goes.

It was now very late, probably somewhere around 1:00 AM on October 16, when our prop driven Olympic airliner landed at the international airport of Iraklion, Crete, Greece. As I shuffled through the small terminal I anxiously looked for someone who might be there to pick me up. I was told that every incoming airman is assigned a sponsor who meets you at the airport and helps you to become more quickly acclimated to the base. My sponsor and I had communicated about my arrival before leaving the States but I heard no one calling my name or lifting a sign indicating that they were looking for some guy named *Mooney*. Suddenly a guy, obviously an American, but in civilian clothes, politely and quietly asked if I might be Norman Mooney. I responded that I was he, and with that he introduced himself as my sponsor and a guy that I would be working with at the military base Communication Center. Our first joint project however was to find my luggage. After several exasperating minutes, we were informed that my luggage had missed a transfer somewhere during the flight and they would begin an immediate search for it. My sponsor reassured me that this was not uncommon and that I probably could expect my bags to arrive in about three or four days.

We proceeded to his car and began the 12-13 mile trip to the base. Almost immediately he began to explain why he had not held up a sign indicating who he was or why he had not called out my name in search of me. It seems that the word *Mooney, or moonie,* in Greek is translated to mean *vagina*, or more literally it means *pussy*. He recommended that for my health and welfare, it might be best to pronounce my name Moonae (moo nay) while living in Greece. I was more than willing to do that

Life Between Innings

but it still played into some interesting situations for me over the next 18 months.

It was pitch black outside as we left the airport and drove out to Iraklion Air Station, the U.S. Air Force Security Forces air base that would become home for the next 18 months and 10 days. Consequently, I was unable to see the breathtakingly gorgeous view that we were passing as we drove. In fact, once I got settled in, I would drive this road almost daily and it was awesome, a view you never tired of seeing. The road was winding and narrow and ran along the edge of the steep cliffs that plunged straight down to the Mediterranean Sea below. I later learned that driving to the base was not too scary as you hugged the hillside going that direction. However, driving back toward the airport and into town, you drove right next to the drop off and most of the places did not have guardrails to protect you. Every trip was an adventure as it was not uncommon for the big buses, the main transport for many Cretans into town and then back to their rural homes and farms, to take more than their share of these winding narrow roads. I was surprised however at how few accidents actually occurred on this strip of highway, although there were a few. Fortunately, what few accidents did occur did not involve anyone who I was familiar with.

At the base, I was checked into guest housing. I was to report to my new squadron later that day at a time of my own choosing. I was still technically on vacation until I decided to report. Of course I awoke very late in the AM the morning of my arrival as I was suffering jet lag and had not slept much on the way over. Crete is 7 time zones ahead of St. Louis so noon in Crete was 5:00 AM back home. I dressed in the only outfit I had, my travel blue military dress uniform, and ventured out the door. I was blinded immediately by the brilliance of the sun flashing off of the deep blue color of the Mediterranean

Sea that was staring me right in the face. Our base, which I could not tell the night before, was right on the beach. WOW!! Some distance off shore, but very much in sight, lay Dia Island, affectionately called Dragon Island, as it clearly resembled such a seafaring behemoth. After catching my breath and taking a small "walk-about," I thought I would check in at the squadron to see what I should do about housing, food and my luggage and to get acquainted with the CO (*Commissioned Officer*) and my new NCOIC (*Non-Commissioned Officer In Charge*).

I was assigned a room with a roommate. However, we did not work in the same facility nor did he work the same hours that I did, so I saw very little of him. He was single and spent most of his off time at the Airmen's Club, which basically served as a nightclub for non-commissioned officers like me. The roomie, like me, was an E-3, but his drinking and gambling were taking their toll. Unfortunately for him, the month lasted longer than his money and it was not long before he was asking me for a "loan." I had no relationship with this guy, and really didn't want one, so I politely, but firmly pointed out that I had only been there a few weeks and I had already saved some money, sent some money home to my wife and had some money in my pocket, money that I was not going to share with him. After that encounter it was even more rare that I saw him.

I had arrived in Iraklion just a little over a month prior to Thanksgiving. My sponsor turned out to be a pretty great guy who had already been on the air base, affectionately called *Little America* by the residents, for about four years and was trying to get extended another three. At that time, the military was just starting to allow career military people to do such things in an attempt to save dollars. Once an airman reached E-5 status (Staff Sergeant), the military was responsible for shipping the airman's entire household goods and a car, if you needed it shipped. Obviously, that could create quite a bill for Uncle Sam so he was looking for ways to cut back. They very graciously invited me to their family Thanksgiving Day dinner. While it was not like being with my family back home, where the holidays around my mom's home were a haven for great food and laughs, it still was nice. Without family, holidays on the base could be very lonely. In fact, a lot of the single guys would prefer to work the holidays than to have them off as it made the day easier on their emotions.

After a day of getting settled, I had reported for duty and was escorted into the secured communication compound by my NCOIC. Once inside, I was introduced to C-Group, the collection of men and women I would be working with in the communication center. The communication center had two basic rooms. One was manned by hundreds of personnel whose job it was to monitor the airwaves around the Middle East and electronically capture any conversations, especially those that were encoded, for review by experts in dissecting messages that might give them insights into enemy activities. The smaller room, although really not small, was where I was to work. It was here that we sent and received messages of all types, from unclassified personnel information to highly classified Top Secret Crypto messages, which we would then pass on to the appropriate officials at the base or to other stations worldwide as routed. We would also type up the many messages leaving our station for worldwide destinations and transmit them via our telegraphic equipment. The folks in the large adjoining room kept us busy much of the time typing 5-digit coded messages that had been retrieved from the airwaves across the Middle East and the countries surrounding the Mediterranean Sea. These had to be redrafted and reformatted and then sent on to Washington, D.C. for breakdown and further review.

The Military Years (1969-1973)

I actually learned to love the hustle and bustle of the communication center, as we were truly the "heartbeat" of the base and in the know of much that was ongoing around the base, both militarily and personal. But, even when we knew really neat stuff, translated "the dirt," on various base personnel, because of our security clearances we could never discuss any of it once we left the secured compound. During my 18 months at Iraklion, I was twice honored as the *Communicator of the Quarter* for my error free and proficient work. I worked with some really good Communicators, like my good friend Fred (Larry), so I truly felt honored to receive those awards.

Staff Sergeant "Moe" Modzelewski was the NCO that I reported to daily. He was a laid back guy with a good sense of humor who was great to work for. As long as we got the job done, he was not too particular with all the military protocol. Also on crew were Larry, Tom, another Tom and a young lady named Sue, whose husband was a Security Officer. His claim to fame was pulling a Barney Fife and shooting himself in the foot demonstrating his quick draw to one of his fellow security officers a few months after my arrival. Thereafter, he was only allowed to carry one bullet, which was a little embarrassing for him. Later, I would actually car pool with him and his wife as they had a home back in the city of Iraklion near me.

On my first night working with the crew, I was taken around and introduced to everyone, but of course I could not remember all their names immediately. Tom and Moe consistently called Larry by the name of Fred, because they thought he resembled Freddy Farkle of *Rowan and Martin's Laugh-In Show*. I wasn't in on the joke when I arrived and was not aware that Fred was really Larry. For practically the entire 18 months that we served together I called Larry by the name of Fred. Only in the latter days of our assignment did I find out that Fred was Larry. Now Fred (Larry) had been my best friend on base the entire time on Crete as we played basketball, racquetball and softball together. However, he said he never thought anything about me calling him Fred, he just figured that I was carrying on the joke started by Tom and Moe. I was a little embarrassed.

About seven months into my tour of duty, one of the Toms was reassigned to South Korea where his wife resided. As a result, a good old boy from Georgia was assigned to take his spot. He was really a nice kid but not too far removed from the two boys from Alabama that I had met in basic training.

Shortly after my arrival at the base I was notified that I would be promoted to Sergeant (Pay Grade E-4) on January 1, 1971. This would mean a major jump in pay and the resumption of that happy ritual of taking off the old stripes and having the 3 new ones sewn on each of my uniforms. The pay increase was almost double my current military salary, thanks to President Richard Nixon's magic pen that had initiated a significant pay raise for all military personnel about the time I had enlisted.

Also, since I had been officially notified of my upcoming promotion, I was scheduled right away to take the test for my next promotion to Staff Sergeant. It was at this time that the military had just begun to enact new promotional criteria that the "old heads" simply hated and complained vigorously about. For years promotions had been based primarily on evaluations given by an airman's supervising NCOIC. While personal evaluations were still a part of the new procedure, the military was also administering weighted tests covering the large spectrum of military life, policy and activities. The results of these tests, more than the evaluations, weighed heavily on who was to receive future promotions and who would not.

Knowing how much the "old heads" hated this process and their lack of preparation for taking the tests, I decided to do something novel and actually study for it, something most of them refused to do. On my first attempt I knew that I did not do well but I immediately left the test area and went back to the barracks and wrote down every question I could remember from the test. Subsequently, when I was scheduled to take the test again six months later, I used my notes from the previous test to help me study for this one. This paid off with great dividends.

Almost immediately I began to referee basketball games on the base to help raise the finances needed to get Shirley and Dionne to Crete. Even with my upcoming promotion to Sergeant on January 1, 1971, the airfares of family and the shipping of any household items were our responsibility, not the military's, so every penny counted. However, God truly blessed us and things began to fall together rather quickly. Other than airfare and shipping, the first major obstacle was hurtled when one of the guys on base was notified that he and his family were to be transferred out just before Christmas. Consequently, I was able to take over his first floor, four-room flat right on the bus line in the near part of town in an area called Five Corners (A popular restaurant area where 3 streets intersected). It was perfect.

Shirley and Dionne arrived in mid December of 1970, just in time to enjoy our first Christmas together on the island of Crete. We quickly settled into life on the island. That life consisted of most of the same things that we would normally be doing back in the States. However, they arrived during the brief rainy and cold season that probably seemed more unpleasant than it really was. It was so good to see them; Dionne had grown in the short two months apart and she would immediately become the focal point of all our neighbors and friends with her flowing strawberry-blonde hair. Our house was not quite ready so it was necessary to spend the

Life Between Innings

first three days in the Xenia Hotel, a nice hotel by Cretan standards, in downtown Iraklion across from Eleftherias Square. Here in the square was a nice park where fathers loved to walk on Sundays to show off their families. Even though the place was nice, it was tough for Shirley to take care of a small baby in a hotel room while I was trying to get some sleep. In the communication center, we worked a typical rotating shift of seven day shifts followed by seven evening-shifts and then six midnight-shifts. Fortunately, we were able to move into our home rather quickly and so the inconvenience was minimal.

As I stated, the house was perfect. The floors had a Greeky pattern embedded into the ceramic tile. There were two nice size bedrooms, a living room and a kitchen. To get to the restroom you had to walk through a glassed in patio where the washer sat, but it also doubled as a nice study area. The bathtub was one of those small ones with a seat that you sat in to bathe; Dionne loved the tub as she grew and began to walk and become a real toddler. Also, we had a small yard with grass and a high stone fence all around with an orange tree, a lemon tree and the overhang of a pomegranate tree. The yard also served as the place to hang the clothes out for drying. Yards were scarce in Iraklion so we were rather fortunate. When it was time to cut the grass, I would get down on my hands and knees and take out a pair of clippers to do the job, which still only took about a half an hour or so to do.

Cretan homes as a rule do not have any kind of heating system and certainly no air conditioning systems as the temperature rarely dips below 40 or gets above 88 degrees. January and February are called the rainy season, when it does get a little chilly, maybe in the low 40s, but most of the year the weather was pretty nice. We were the envy of our neighboring Greeks, however, as we were the proud owners of a kerosene kettle heater that took the chill out of the air, especially important

The Military Years (1969-1973)

to us with a new baby. The fall weather, September until well into December, was absolutely gorgeous with clear blue skies being the rule. During the summer we would occasionally get some hot winds coming in from North Africa, which carried a lot of sand. When this happened, it was very difficult to keep it from coming into the house, as it would find ways to come under the doors or around the windows. The water pressure was not great and it was not unusual to have to save the bath water to use to flush the toilets, if necessary, but that is making it sound worse than it really was. It was just a way of life that we got used to. The toughest part, actually, was having the electricity go off and on at frequent and unexpected times. Certainly, the alarm clock had to be a wind up because you never knew when the electricity was going off or for how long.

Another problem with the electricity being out any lengthy period was the loss of foodstuff in the refrigerator, plus the use of the electric range. Now the Greeks rarely cooked at home anyway so this was not a problem for the rank and file Iraklionian. Generally their hot meal came on Sunday after a Saturday visit to the market for meat. The ladies would place the meat in their baking pan, along with their vegetables and whatever other items they may have, and then take it to the local bakery Sunday morning or afternoon to be cooked.

One of the great benefits we enjoyed, that we certainly could not have enjoyed back home, was having a maid come in once a week to clean the house and do the washing and ironing. In fact, the military encouraged airmen to do this when possible as it provided jobs for the locals. Our maid was the absolute very best. She worked for 30 drachmas a day, which was equivalent to $10.00. It was hard to believe but with that salary, she actually was better paid than her husband who drove a taxi.

We were also able to secure a Greek babysitter for Dionne. She was a very attractive young lady from a well-to-do family

Life Between Innings

who spoke English fluently. She was great with Dionne and loved to sit and chat with us about her plans to study and eventually marry. She was from a very traditional Greek family in which marriages are often arranged. However, she was fairly confident that "Daddy" would do right by her and not make her marry a man that she found undesirable.

Iraklion was a safe town. While the Greek guys did not mind stopping to stare at the American women, especially the blondes, it was safe to walk the streets at night. In the whole time we were there, no one reported any incident that we knew of regarding our women being harassed.

It took awhile to get used to the Greek life style and their way of doing things. For the most part Greeks were never in a hurry, that is, unless they were driving a car. In their cars they had only one speed and that was "fast." But in all other things, the pace was slow, very slow. For instance, I was able to purchase a little green Fiat while I was there. It was nice when it was running but I used to joke that I needed a second job just to keep it running. When I would have to take it in for one of its frequent breakdowns, I soon learned that there was no need to ask when it would be ready because whatever I would be told was meaningless. Whereas you take a car into the garage in the U.S. today, you expect that it better be ready tomorrow. In Crete, you're lucky, really lucky, if you get it back the next week. Often, they would have my car for at least two weeks if it were a day.

It was drilled into our heads by the military to drive defensively in Crete for a number of reasons. Number one, should you be sent to jail, know that their jails are not like the "nice" ones we have here in the U.S. Once in jail, you better have a loving family willing to take care of you because the "state" only did the bare necessities to keep you alive; it was the family's obligation to take care of an inmate's need. Also know

The Military Years (1969-1973)

that it may take a while to get you out. And, heaven forbid, if there was any hint of drugs in your car or on your person; if and when you were released, you could pretty well be assured you were being released to go stateside; but of course in that case, that was good. Should you hit a farm animal on the highway the common advice was *drive like hell and get out of there.* If it was confirmed that you were the driver of the vehicle that killed the animal, not only did you have to pay for the animal but also for several generations of animals that this particular one may have produced. Another oddity, at least for us, was that it was unusual to have a police car follow and pull you over. You were ticketed by photo taken by an officer standing on the corner with a camera who would shoot your license plate number. Then, in a few days, you open your mail and find a ticket that you had no idea was coming. Another major problem for drivers was the number of motorcycles, motorized three-wheelers (affectionately called "Manole Carts," which I will explain later), bicycles and large buses that you encounter while dealing with very narrow streets and roads. Defensively was the only way to drive.

As I had found out in Athens, many Greeks stopped at red lights and turned their motors off. Even though this was their practice, the moment, and I mean the very moment, that the light appeared, yes, I said "appeared," to be turning green, the horns were blaring for those in front to get going. After awhile I just became numb to it because it made no difference how fast of a get-away was made, you still were going to get a horn.

The Greek business world was also different. I don't like to barter over things but a lot of the Americans did and the Greeks loved it. Also, much like in Mexico or South America, the Greeks open their stores about 9:00 AM and close at 1:00 PM for a siesta. They would reopen around 4:00 PM and stay open, depending on the store, until sometime between 7:00 PM

Life Between Innings

and 9:00 PM. If I was going out to dinner, I never needed to worry about reservations as we Americans would eat around 6:00 PM or so. However the Greeks would start straggling in about the time we would be leaving, but generally around 8:00 PM. And, if you drove back by that restaurant later on that evening, it was not uncommon to find those that came in while we were leaving were still there eating and partying well past midnight. Partying was another thing that was different in that it was very common, in fact it was the rule, to see the guys dancing with each other and having a ball while the women would sit at their tables and talk. It was also hard to get used to seeing guys walking down the street holding hands, as well as the women, and yet this did not mean they were gay. Of course, it also did not mean that they weren't.

Going to market was fun. This was a great place to learn and practice your Greek language skills while getting a great cross-cultural experience. Most of our grocery shopping was done at the Base PX but you could get some great vegetables, fruit and meat buys at the market. We never bought the fish, lamb, pork or beef that hung open on hooks in the marketplace, as the flies and bugs made that idea unappetizing. But, right in the middle of the market area was a little store that carried frozen rib eyes, which were unbelievable, and the best, leanest hamburger meat you will ever find. In fact, it was so lean it was necessary to add grease to it when frying so that the meat would not burn. They also had just about any other type of meat you might want, all of which was shipped in from Austria. The meat was reasonably priced; consequently, we never lacked for good, quality meat. So, just like in the states, we ate well, in fact, we ate very well.

One of the highlights for me would be to go downtown and sit at one of the many local outdoor eateries and have a Nescafe or Greek coffee with a pastry. Nescafe was the closest thing to

The Military Years (1969-1973)

American coffee you could find. I loved their pastries. In fact, I craved their pastries. Also, on every corner was what we called "Manole Shops." It seemed every man in Iraklion was named Manole, including my landlord, so the handle was coined "Manole Shops" and "Manole Carts" for the many corner stores and three wheeled gas-powered carts you would see. Literally attached to, hanging on or located inside one of these little Manole Shops you could find almost anything. They were our equivalent to 7-Eleven Stores back in the States, except about 20 times smaller in size. My favorite purchase at these stands was an ice cream cone similar to what we call a *Nutty Buddy Bar*. The only difference was that these were made with goat's milk, and I loved them. Also, although the base had a theatre that ran fairly new releases, it was fun to go downtown and catch a movie. Usually they were in English with subtitles for the Greeks. Watching a movie at the local theater, or just going downtown period, really helped to accentuate the experience of a different culture, and I tried to make the most of it.

However, one funny incident occurred when I decided to venture over to the side of Iraklion that I rarely went to take in a matinee at one of the larger movie houses. Upon entering the large auditorium, I chose my seat about halfway back from the screen and settled in. After my eyes became better focused in the dark I noticed that for this matinee I was only one of about three people in the entire theater. Just as the movie was about to start, a young gentleman, probably in his late teens or early twenties, came in. To my utter astonishment and/or amazement, with all the seats available, he decided to sit right next to me. His butt had barely hit his seat when in a flash, I jumped up and literally hurtled myself back over the seat in which I was sitting, and with great haste, ran back down the aisle to the nearest exit, quickly finding myself back on the bright sunlit streets. I never visited that theater again.

Life Between Innings

Saving money was always an important issue for us, as we knew our time on Crete would be short and the time for purchasing tickets for my girls' return to the states would be upon us quickly. As my first basketball season was coming to an end, I found a new place of employment working in the Communication Center compound in the Snack Shop making sandwiches and selling soft drinks and candy. I must say we put together what may have been the greatest roast beef sandwich you would ever want to taste plus an egg salad sandwich to die for. I did not like egg salad before I got there and I have eaten very few since leaving; however, that was one grand sandwich, if I do say so myself.

So, with working rotating shifts in the communication center, rotating shifts in the Snack Shop and working a full schedule of basketball games during the season, my time was stretched pretty thin. But even with that, I took on the duties of writing a sports column for the base newspaper featuring the various sports activities ongoing on the base. After a few months, Shirley put the clamps on the sports reporting activities, effectively ending my budding career as a Sports' Columnist.

In March of 1971, as the basketball season wound down, I received some very nice recognition and a special invitation from the Air Force. Because of my good work and reputation as an official back in San Angelo, coupled with the good work I had done at the Air Base in Crete, I was invited to go to Athens and help referee the *Air Force Regional Basketball Championships*. This was a great honor, which I had to refuse, as Uncle Sam agreed to pay for everything, including game fees and room and board, but they would not pay my airfare. While the cost was not prohibitive, in fact, I would have probably broke even at worst based on my game fees, Shirley wasn't too receptive to the idea of my being in Athens for a week or more without

The Military Years (1969-1973)

her, so I decided to stay home and continue working at the Snack Bar.

However, in the meantime, I was asked to referee several games of the annual airbase basketball tourney. As a result, I became embroiled in a potential international scandal, for real. The local Greek team, with players primarily from the Iraklion area, was invited to participate. This team included one of the star players from the Greek national team, plus his brother. Assigned to work the game with me was a Captain, with whom I had worked games previously and we meshed pretty well. The Greeks normally got a kick out of seeing me referee because it appeared to them that the local airmen, many who knew me personally, were unabashedly unkind with their comments. Remember what my last name means in Greek and you can easily understand that often one of my calls might be accompanied by fans from the stand yelling out, *Hey Mooney, that call stinks.* Oblivious to my "fan friends," the Greek's understanding of these catcalls, of course, interpreting my name in their own language heard, *Hey Pussy, that call stinks.* The Greeks loved it.

But on this particular night, the Greeks did not love me. About midway through the first half the American Team and the Greek Team were locked in a close battle. I was the "out" official (the official away from the basket on this particular play) when the brother of the Greek national team player drove the paint (the painted area under and out from the basket which makes up the free throw lane) and committed what I clearly saw and believed to be a charging foul. I made the call and turned to the scorer's table to relay the foul information. As I turned back around, the player was in my face and "accidentally" bumped me. Whether accidental or not, that is an action that I would not tolerate from any player and I immediately hit him with a technical foul. I did not see it, but

Life Between Innings

evidently, the Greek national player "flipped me five." This is similar to giving someone the finger in the USA only with a much more significant meaning. In fact we were told that the Greeks consider "flipping five" as one of the most offensive things you can do to another human being, and in this case it was observed by my partner, the Captain. With that, he immediately called another technical foul on him and ejected him from the game. The Greeks, and especially the Greek coach, went ballistic. After much shouting and stomping and carrying on, the coach of the Greek team motioned for his players to follow him and leave the court. I went to the coach, who spoke very good English, and strongly, but tactfully, urged him not to do this and to please bring his players back on the court. He refused. The Greek players gathered up their stuff, headed for the bus, and promptly left the base.

The next morning the Captain and I were summoned to the Base Commanders Office to give him a full and complete accounting of what had happened. The Iraklion newspaper that morning had run a large headline stating, *Greek Team Kicked Off Air Base*. Actually, the Commander was very understanding but he did want a complete written report from both of us as the local officials from the city were already calling for the Captain to be transferred immediately. For some reason, probably because I had very little military rank, they did not request my ouster. We gave our full reports and received assurances from the Commander that this should be the end of it. Unfortunately, it wasn't. Evidently the controversy did not settle down and the demand to have the Captain removed from the island of Crete intensified. Finally, after a few short weeks, the Captain was notified that he was being transferred. This was truly unfortunate and unfair. For me, I continued to live in the city and at peace with all my neighbors and was never restricted in any way regarding my movements around the city or the island.

The Military Years (1969-1973)

Spiritually, life on the island had its ups and downs. On the upside was the opportunity to worship and fellowship at the Base Chapel. For us Pentecostals, this was truly a time of stretching and growing as we worked with many folks from a variety of mainline denominations. This was an entirely new experience for me. As a young man growing up I had been peppered with the ideology that Methodists, Lutherans, Presbyterians, Church of Christ and some Baptists were at best involved in "dead and lifeless" religion. What I found was a group of people from all these denominations that truly loved the Lord, had enjoyed a valid new birth experience and were passionately in love with our Lord and Savior, Jesus Christ. The word "shocked" would probably not be too strong of a word to express my surprise at this discovery.

Our Chaplain was a Methodist minister who did an excellent job in the pulpit and bringing us together as a congregation. Through some of my close, personal, Pentecostal friends, namely Carl and Bonnie (Assembly of God) and Bill and Alma (Church of God), he became aware that I was an ordained minister. He was very supportive and gave me opportunities to speak in the evening chapel services from time to time. I can only remember one evening message that I preached which I had entitled, *God Never Promised Us a Rose Garden.* Of course the evening services were not attended to the degree that the Sunday morning services were, but it was still a great opportunity given to me and those that attended seem to respond very well.

My Chapel ministry highlight occurred when our Chaplain asked if I would be willing to preach and plan one of the upcoming Sunday morning services, as it was necessary that he be off the island and away at a conference. I could tell he was nervous about entrusting me with this responsibility with so many potential feet to step on but I guess he did not have a

Life Between Innings

lot of options available to him. Part of his fear, I am sure, was the fact that the service was broadcast over *Armed Forces Radio* in that area of Crete and it was important that I be sensitive to hearers of the message beyond the immediate congregation. As the designated Sunday approached I prepared and practiced like never before. I might add that I prayed a little bit more than normal, as well. As it turned out, the Chaplain was unable to attend the conference as planned but he allowed me take the service anyway. Without a doubt, God truly blessed me that day, as it may have been one of the better efforts from the pulpit that I would ever give. And, it did not create any international incidents, for which I was thankful.

Another great source of spiritual encouragement came in the form of great teaching and preaching via cassette tape. Full Gospel Tabernacle sent tapes occasionally featuring the Full Gospel Tabernacle Choir and ministry of Pastor Redman. These services were always exciting to receive and hear. However, the *Assembly of God* radio ministry, *Revivaltime*, sent out, free of charge, copies of their weekly radio services featuring the ministry of Dr. C.M. Ward, including inspiring music by the *Revivaltime Choir,* to military personnel around the globe. There were two half-hour services on each tape and Shirley and I would hang on each word and each note when a new tape arrived. It was like manna from heaven to hear such inspiring messages and songs. I can still clearly hear Reverend Ward's booming voice giving the benediction to each service from Zechariah 4:6 as he would emphatically declare, . . . *for we confess that it is not by might nor by power, but by my Spirit saith the Lord* . . . This verse has become a source of strength and part of my prayers in my life-long struggle to learn that in <u>all</u> things the battle belongs to the Lord, not me.

Despite the encouragement we received from worshipping on base and from the cassette ministry, there were also

The Military Years (1969-1973)

lengthy dry spiritual times, especially during the last half of our stay on Crete. Shirley and I were starting to experience some marital issues, although not evident to the naked eye, and probably not too evident even to ourselves. I think I recognized them perhaps for the first time during a visit to Crete by my mother in June of 1971. It seemed that Shirley and I were constantly on edge with each other during her entire visit, something that did not escape mom's attention.

It was during this "dry" time, however, that God gave me a verse of Scripture that has become my life's verse. After several months of praying and seeking God, only to sense that my prayers were going no higher than the ceiling, I came across Proverbs 3:5-6. Here I read from the *Amplified Old Testament: Lean on, trust and be confident in the Lord with all your heart and mind, and do not rely on your own insight or understanding. In all your ways know, recognize and acknowledge Him, and He will direct and make straight and plain your paths.* The entire chapter offers keen insights into successful Christian living, but the phrase, *. . . Acknowledge Him, and He will direct and make straight and plain your path . . .* hit a cord with me that even during my darkest hours, even during those times when I could not feel God near me or in me, I knew that if I would simply acknowledge Him, He would make my paths plain and make them straight. What a tremendous promise. And, those have not just been mere words to me; they have in fact been fulfilled time and time again as God has made my paths straight and plain, even during times of complete ignorance as to what direction He would want me to go. For this His promise, I am most thankful.

Shirley and I had taken the opportunity to see many of the sites found in and around Iraklion during our first few months on the island, but had not had the opportunity to see much of the island itself during the first half of our assignment. As a consequence, we were excitedly awaiting the visit of my mom

Life Between Innings

as we planned to tour the island and then take a few days to visit the mainland, first in Athens and then on inland to old Corinth. Old Corinth is where the Apostle Paul had worked as a tentmaker while preaching and planting a church among the Corinthian saints.

It was exciting to see mom at the airport. She loved to travel and she too was excited about coming to visit with us. The day after her arrival we began our vacation by taking her on the beautiful mountainous drive along the shoreline on our way to the Air Base to show her "Little America." We then drove back into the city of Iraklion, showing her the big ships tied up in the harbor, the hustle and bustle of downtown, the shops, the theatres, the restaurants and the open-air markets. It was also a joy to share with her my favorite pastime of exploring the numerous sidewalk cafes with their unbelievable pastries while enjoying a cup of Nescafe or Greek Coffee. Greek Coffee is served in the tiniest of cups and is very rich and thick and served with a large glass of water. Oh, my mouth is watering!!

The city is typical by European standards in that the streets are very narrow and the buildings located right at the street's edge. Most of the streets are kept very clean as the merchants and homeowners take great pains to wash down and sweep the roadway in front of their businesses and homes. Iraklion (spelled "Heraklion" in Greek) is a medieval town, founded in 824 A.D, and is the largest city on the Cretan Island. In fact, it is the fifth largest city in Greece after Athens, Thessaloniki, Piraeus and Patras with a population of about 100,000 during the time of my stay, or about 1/5 of the total population of the island. This city had been the main seat of the famous Minoan Civilization (2600-1100 B.C.) and it is here that the incredibly intricate palaces of Knossos (about 3 miles outside of Iraklion) and Phaistos (about 40 miles outside of Iraklion) had been excavated. Knossos was the most prominent city of Minoan

Crete and was the capital of the legendary and mighty monarch, Minos. The palace had its own version of indoor plumbing that I found simply fascinating. One of the more interesting items found among the ruins here was the *Throne of Minos*, the oldest throne in Europe. One of my treasured photos is of Dionne setting on this throne.

Iraklion's Venetian Harbor serves as the hub for export shipping of the island's rich products of raisins, grapes and olive oil. While driving through the countryside, one will see the rolling hills covered with grapes lying on cloth sheets as they dry and become raisins. Mom found this quite interesting and confessed, to her embarrassment, that she did not know that this was how raisins came to be. And, as one might imagine, inexpensive, but delicious wines can be and are easily purchased throughout the island. Many Greek's daily sustenance is nothing more than bottled wine and bread. With the abundance of olive trees scattered across the island, olives and olive oil, the staple of any Greek salad, were easily and cheaply obtained.

The Island of Crete is approximately 175 miles long and 40 miles wide at its narrowest point. Iraklion, and most of the major cities, are located on the north coast facing Greece. The southern coast is steep and harborless and affords little communication with Africa. A high mountain range runs east to west (the length of the island), covering most of the 175 miles. The range is divided into three quite distinct groups of mountains. To the west are the Lefka Ori (White) Mountains with an altitude of 2452 m. In the center is the massive Idi Mountains with an altitude of 2456 m. I could see these snow capped mountains from my home in Iraklion on any clear day of the year and they were simply magnificent! To the east are the mountains of Kiki with an altitude of 2148 m.

Life Between Innings

We visited most of the major cities of Crete. On the first day we headed east along the northern coastline to visit Neopolis and the quaint town of St. (Ag.) Niklolaos, and then turned south to Ierapetra, located on the southern coast. On the way back we visited the Plateau of Lassithi, near St. (Ag.) Georgios, with its 6000 windmills. Wow! What an impressive site as you first come up over the outer ridge of the plateau, and suddenly, laid out in great splendor below, is the *Valley of the Windmills,* as it is so appropriately called. All along our trail that day we observed numerous active excavation sites (digs), as many old ruins were being unearthed. After a while, they became so commonplace we would just casually mention as we passed, *… it looks like they are <u>building</u> some new ruins over there.*

The following day we headed west from Iraklion, along the northern coastal highway to Rethymnon and Chania, where we stayed all night at the Hotel Canea before heading back. Souda Bay is located at Chania and is the island's best-protected bay. It is a refuge for merchant and warships when a storm occurs and is the base for the Greek Royal Navy. The U.S. Navy had a base located there as well and used the bay to dock their big ships during their many patrols in the Mediterranean Sea. The great comedian, Bob Hope, and his caravan, visited the Navy troops at Souda Bay during my stay at the Iraklion Air Station but regrettably we were not able to drive up to Chania to see the show.

On the way back from Chania to Iraklion, Shirley and I had a nice little fight in front of mom. This was rather embarrassing for me *(although a similar incident some six years later would have an even greater impact on me and our little family)* and elicited some interesting observations on which mom commented some time later when Shirley was not in our presence. Obviously I am not a psychologist, although I like to play the part of one every once in a while, but it was apparent, at least to me, that

The Military Years (1969-1973)

Shirley was often jealous of the attention that I would give mom, and even of our family in general, to the point of acting out that jealousy at some awkward moments. I was never a "Momma's Boy," so even to this day I do not understand her reactions, but nevertheless, there was an undeniable problem there that the family was aware of but did not discuss with me until months after we were divorced in 1978. Mom, being very astute and very observant, was careful to keep her distance so as not to create problems for me. Unfortunately, while we still had a great trip, this incident left a distinct mark on me as we had always been careful not to display our dirty laundry, and I mean never, in front of anyone, especially family. This cloud hung over our heads the remainder of mom's visit.

As the first phase of our trip was coming to an end, we became very conscious of the fact that we had visited many remarkable sights and had enjoyed some of the most beautiful scenery that one could enjoy. On one hand, Iraklion was somewhat a modern European city. Yet, just a mere few miles outside the city, it was like entering a time machine and going back several centuries. I can close my eyes and still see visions of a Greek wife walking on the road behind her husband who always led the way. Often he would lead the way while riding on a mule or ox while she walked along behind him. I can still vividly see in my mind's eye an old woman that I had observed out in the field thrashing the grain. She was "riding" in an old rocking chair with no wheels being pulled by an ox that was going around and around in a circle, pulling her over the stalks of grain until all the grain had been extracted. It must have worked but it sure looked strange to this city boy from St. Louis.

It was not uncommon during our travels to stop on the highway and let the shepherds drive their sheep across the road or at least separate them long enough for us to get by.

Life Between Innings

We also noted that every few miles, it seemed, we would see a small, usually white, church or religious memorial built along side the road where a passersby could stop and offer a prayer, or perhaps leave an offering. The rolling hills were filled with grape vines and raisins drying in the sun along with a plentiful amount of olive groves. The scenery was very much like what I envisioned the Holy Lands to look like and I never tired of taking it all in.

And, of course, everywhere we went we ate some of the best Greek foods you could ever hope to find. Not speaking Greek, we were often ushered into the kitchen of the restaurant where the food was being prepared and we then would be able to point out the various dishes that we would like to have served. I could hardly ever pass up a typical Greek salad of cucumbers, tomatoes, big hunks of feta cheese, all smothered in olive oil, accompanied by my favorite meal of mousika, a dish made of egg plant and cheese over a hearty, tasty layer of ground beef laid over a tasty, flaky layer of crust. A fabulous Greek pastry, which more often than not was a piece of Baklava, a flaky crust smothered in rich syrup and chopped nuts, followed this great meal. Life does not get much better than this!

About the fifth day following mom's arrival we boarded the Olympic Airline turbo prop for our hour-long flight to Athens. What a treat was awaiting us! After checking in at our hotel we arranged to take a tour of Athens. Representatives of ABC Tours met us at the hotel and our first stop was the famous Parthenon on the site of the equally historic Acropolis that majestically overlooks the city. The Parthenon is an awesome structure, and especially so when viewed at night when it is illuminated in spectacular fashion. The Parthenon and the Acropolis are typical of many ancient sites that we visited where silence is almost demanded as you walk about in total awe and amazement, only imagining what might have been happening on or around these very stones so many years before.

From there the tour guide took us over to a small hill, just a few paces west of the site of the Acropolis where we had been. This little hill, maybe more like a knoll than a true hill, was not impressive by any stretch of the imagination. After some searching, we found a small marker that revealed that we were standing on *Mars Hill*, the spot where the Apostle Paul had stood in the meeting of the Areopagus and preached to the men of Athens (Acts 17:15-34). He noted in his sermon that as he walked around, and looked carefully at their objects of worship, he had found an altar with the inscription, *To An Unknown God*. The Athenians had constructed this altar because they were superstitious and did not want to offend any god, especially one that they might have overlooked. Paul very astutely took that bit of knowledge to go on and explain to them the miraculous work of the God of Holy Scripture who had recently sent His Son, Jesus, who had come from glory, died and was buried and then raised to life as the perfect sacrifice for their sins. Most rejected Paul's message; however, a few were interested and intrigued enough to ask Paul to come back and talk with them some more about this God, this Jesus, that he served.

The next morning we again boarded our ABC Tour Bus and headed out of Athens toward the Isthmus of Corinth. The 50-mile drive to Corinth was a trip back in time, much like our trips out of Iraklion just a few days earlier. Athens, the modern city, was barely absent from the rearview mirror, when our surroundings changed dramatically. Once again our view was filled with small, simple rock and mud homes, olive trees, rolling hills, farms and farmers out in the field, oxen and sheep, small white churches and religious boxes scattered along the road.

Life Between Innings

As we pulled into the ancient city of Corinth I was struck by its size, or lack of. It was much smaller than I had anticipated but the awe that I felt, as the ruins of this once great city came into view, was indescribable. Both economically and strategically, the Isthmus of Corinth, as this narrow stretch of land was called, had played a very important role in the history of Greece as well as the history of the Christian Church. The isthmus was about four miles wide and separated the Saronic Gulf in the east from the Gulf of Corinth to the west. Peoples, armies and valuable commodities had crossed this narrow piece of land in a variety of ways over the years making Corinth a very strategic, rich and influential city. In 1893 a Greek firm completed what is now called the Corinth Canal connecting the two seas and greatly enhancing the ability to move commodities quickly and safely.

The ancient city of Corinth was mainly a city of Roman times, first founded by Julius Caesar. It once was renowned for its beautiful buildings, large temples, public offices, trading establishments and industry. It was also known for its illustrious prostitutes that were highly admired for their beauty, culture and wit. I thought this to be somewhat interesting in that I had never considered one of the attributes of a "successful" prostitute as being her "wit." It was here that the Apostle Paul stayed for a period of about 18 months. The Bible says (Acts 18:1-18) that, *Every Sabbath he reasoned in the synagogue, trying to persuade Jews and Greeks.* While most of the Corinthian Jews rejected Paul's message, the Bible says that many of the Gentiles living here believed and were baptized. While staying here, Paul supported himself working as a tentmaker, refusing to take any money for his ministry among them. As we viewed the ruins of the old marketplace where Paul very likely had labored, I paused to visualize him working on a tent in one of the small shops. It was pretty cool.

The Military Years (1969-1973)

Here we also viewed the ruins of the Temple of Apollo. Apollo was the divinity worshipped most devoutly by the ancient Corinthians; the temple was built in the sixth century B.C. Originally the temple had some 42 columns; however, only seven of the columns still remain. In my Bible is a picture of this exact site. There was so much to be seen here in Corinth. Now, among all the excavated ruins lies only a very small village. Tour buses wait for no one so it was time to move on; but without a doubt, visiting Corinth was the highlight of this trip for me.

From Corinth, we began to head back in the direction of Athens stopping along the way to visit the Lion Gate in Mycene, the famous open-air theatre of Epidaurus located in the city of that same name, and the acropolis of Nauplion. The theatre at Epidaurus had been so intricately designed that one could speak in a low tone standing on the floor of the theatre and be heard very clearly on the top row, and do so without a microphone. I know this to be true because we tried it. Amazing! At Nauplion we stopped at the Xenia Hotel, setting just beneath the acropolis, for a great Greek dinner that had been especially made for us.

At the close of the day we all marveled at what we had just seen. Truly this trip was an experience of a lifetime as we had the opportunity to trace the steps of Paul while visiting some of the most historic grounds and sites in all of history.

Our last day in Athens was upon us and it too would prove just as exhilarating as the previous two. At approximately 8:00 AM the ABC Tour Bus picked us up at our hotel and shuttled us off for a very short trip over to Piraeus and its world famous seaport. There we met representatives of Dolfin Cruises and boarded the M/V Delfini, a small tour boat, for our visit to the first of three islands on our agenda.

We sailed for approximately an hour and a half across the clear, blue, sparkling waters of the Aegean Sea and into the

Life Between Innings

Aghia Marina located on the shore of Aegina Island. Here we disembarked for a brief walk around the city and viewed the famous temple of Aphaea. Around 11:30 AM we reboarded our boat and set sail for the Island of Poros, a short trip of about a half hour. Here we had a really good lunch laid out for us at the first class Xenia Hotel (I was beginning to think that all hotels in Greece were an Xenia Hotel.). From Poros we headed to our last stop at the island of Hydra. Again the trip lasted about a half hour. At Hydra, we disembarked again and were given plenty of time to shop and walk about this really beautiful city embedded into the hillside. Finally, at approximately 4:00 PM we boarded the boat for our three-hour ride back to the port at Piraeus. The scenery that we enjoyed that day was nothing short of spectacular. My eyes could barely take it all in as the beauty of these islands, sitting up in such rugged form amidst the gleam of these breathtaking waters, was something I knew that I would never forget.

After arriving back at our hotel in Athens we dressed for our final excursion into the city and one last special meal at one of the local restaurants we had been encouraged to visit by friends back at the Air Base. We set outdoors that night in an open-air restaurant and simply basked in the atmosphere of this glorious city. What a way to end one of the most memorable weeks of my entire life.

The next morning we hailed a taxi and headed to the Olympic Airport where we boarded our plane back to Iraklion. Mom stayed on for a few more days and we used those days to finish up purchasing and packing (for shipping) the fabulous authentic pottery, the flokotti rugs and pictures that had been purchased on our travels. We were amazed in the end that very little of the pottery was damaged in shipping. And then, it was time for her to leave us. Except for the unfortunate marital spat that Shirley and I had as we were heading back to Iraklion from

The Military Years (1969-1973)

Chania, the trip could not have been more enjoyable. We put mom on the plane and we went back to our normal lives, which all in all, was still part of an exciting adventure, an adventure that had a few more great moments in store.

The summer of 1971 passed on into fall and fall into winter. I remained spiritually dry, but our time spent with friends from the base and the chapel was still exciting. Bonnie and Carl, our black friends who had taken care of Dionne while we were visiting Athens with mom, became even dearer friends. I regret that somehow we lost track of these dear people after a couple of years. During the summer I had decided to take some time off from officiating and played fast pitch softball on the Operations team. Our team was not very good; however, my friend Fred (Larry) was an athlete and sports fan much like me and he likewise played on the team. Fred and I also played a lot of racket ball that summer and all the way up till I finally left the island in April of 1972. We often would get off the Owl shift and head over to the Rec Center and play a few games before heading off to home or the barracks, exhausted and ready for a full day of sleep.

For Shirley and me, life was still fairly hectic, but a nice hectic. Our time was fairly planned out. In fact, even watching TV was a planned activity in that we only had the one *Armed Forces Network* channel, so you selected the few shows that were of some interests to watch, and planned accordingly. The few sporting events that were carried were rarely live so generally the outcome was known long before we got a chance to see it, like the *World Series* or the *Super Bowl*. The new hit television series that they were carrying that year were *All In the Family* and the *Flip Wilson Show*. Flip's line, "... *the Devil made me do it*," became a popular catch phrase that was tossed out frequently when someone did something out of character. *Laugh-in* and *Perry Mason* reruns were also a hit.

Life Between Innings

In early December of the year we received exciting news on two fronts. One was that I had finally passed my color vision tests and had been accepted for Air Traffic Control training school. It was stated that I would be assigned to a class starting in May of 1972, most likely in Biloxi, Mississippi at Kessler AFB. At first my application for training had been in jeopardy because I could not read many of the numbers on the multi-colored dot vision charts. Finally, they agreed to let me test by use of a "color wheel," and from that I could easily distinguish my colors. I also had to agree to extend my military service for 11 additional months for the training, which I was glad to do, as Shirley and I both were enjoying military life and were exploring the opportunity of perhaps making it a career. At the time, the re-up bonus for an Air Traffic Controller was at the top of the Variable Re-enlistment Bonus (VRB-10) scale; the rather large size of this bonus was becoming a strong enticement for us to consider staying in.

The second bit of news was that Shirley was pregnant and that the baby would be due on or about July 22, which was perfect timing as we would be back in the states. Since it would be necessary to divest ourselves of our furniture and car before leaving Crete, we decided that it would be best for Shirley and Dionne to head back to the States sometime after Christmas and live with her parents while I worked to save some money for our next move in April and the birth of our new baby. Consequently, sometime in mid-February or early March, we found a buyer for our stuff, a new airman coming in much like I had over a year earlier. With the sale finalized, I accompanied the girls back to Athens where they boarded a big red and white TWA 747 and headed back to the good ole US of A. I must admit, however, that our parting was not necessarily sweet sorrow. It is hard to explain in that at times while on Crete we seemed to grow more closely together and at other times

The Military Years (1969-1973)

there seemed to be a large gulf between us. Any tears that I shed that day, and I'm not sure there were any, would have been at losing Dionne for a couple months. Inwardly, although I was incapable of allowing myself to think it, I was glad to see Shirley leave. In fact, I was already looking forward to a couple months of being on my own and not burdened with "working" on the relationship. That was sad to have to admit to myself.

Back at the Air Base, I moved into the barracks again, but this time I was fortunate in that I did not have a roommate. Frankly, I enjoyed the peace and quite. It also allowed me time to further explore the city and island and the freedom to enjoy the foreign experience. My favorite thing to do in her absence should not be a surprise as I would, as often as I could, head into town and catch a movie at one of the downtown theatres, followed by a casual evening setting in the open-air cafes while enjoying those great pastries and a cup of Nescafe.

One more piece of good news came to me around April 1. It seemed that my study for the promotional military testing had paid off as notification came that I was to be promoted to E-5, Staff Sergeant (4-stripes). Because I had so little service time, I was told that I would most likely be one of the last to sew on my new stripes during that promotional period. It was surmised that I would sew them on in October or November, but regardless, what a blessing. The old-timers called men like me "Fast Burners," as the normal airman did not receive such a promotion until he or she had served six to seven years. Here I was, right at three years in the service, and receiving arguably the most important promotion for an airman to receive because of all the significant additional benefits and pay. To say that I was elated would be an understatement. It also meant that if I did decide to stay in the military, my re-enlistment bonus would be even higher because my VRB would be multiplied against a higher salary.

Life Between Innings

One of my final highlights on Crete was a trip that I took early that April to the island's southern shore, sometimes called the Libyan coast. My goal was to find the village port of Kali Limenes, better known in Scripture as *The Fair Havens*, population 48, near the ancient town of Lassaia. It was one of those typically beautiful days on the island when the weather was neither too hot nor rainy and the skies were a brilliant blue. At this time I still had possession of my little Fiat, so I bravely engaged it, bravely because it was never known if or when it might break down, and headed out across the mountains to this small port mentioned in the Book of Acts 27:7-13. It was here that the Apostle Paul, a prisoner on his way to Rome to report to Caesar, was forced to anchor for several days due to a storm. He admonished the centurion and the owner of the boat not to leave this port but instead to winter here or face much pain and damage, not only of the lading and the ship, but also to the lives of all those on the ship. Paul's advice was not heeded and we know that his prophecy came graphically true.

Upon arriving at Kali Limenes, I found a small sign pointing to the sandy, isolated beach area, hidden from view by tall pussy willows, identifying this as the place that I sought. I parked my Fiat off to the side of the narrow road, picked up my Bible and began to walk slowly out to the beach. It was so quite and isolated that it was almost eerie. Opening my Bible, I slowly read the pertinent passage from Acts regarding Paul's warning. It was one of those moments where I experienced some chill-bumps as again my mind, just as it did in Old Corinth, raced with visions of Paul walking this same beach discussing the weather with all those involved. It was definitely a "Kodak Moment."

Back toward Iraklion, just a few kilometers from Kali Limenes, is the town of Gorty's, an important ancient city,

The Military Years (1969-1973)

that Paul later returned to following his release from Rome, bringing the message of Christ with him. In fact, Gorty's was the first town on Crete to become Christian. It was here that Paul ordained Saint Titus to the ministry and Titus became the first Christian Bishop of Crete. The small church that Titus pastored here had been somewhat restored; it obviously held great interest for me. However, the interesting thing about all the historical religious sites on Crete, and throughout Greece for that matter, is how little the established national religious denomination, the *Greek Orthodox Catholic Church,* works to make these Christian sites known. In most cases, such as with my trip to Kali Limenes and Gorty's, it was necessary to know what I was looking for as there are few, if any markers, to identify these historical Christian places.

The last week of April was quickly approaching and my days on Crete were passing much too soon. I hated to see the day of departure approach as I had loved it here and the experiences that God had allowed me to enjoy. Also, the time away from Shirley had been good for me, as I felt somewhat renewed.

I had also taken this little respite to experiment with a mustache, which I wore home. The mustache was not received with much enthusiasm by Shirley, or anyone else for that matter, except Dionne; I think she was mildly amused. With orders in hand to report to Kessler AFB on or about May 16, 1972, for Air Traffic Controller training, I bid everyone good-bye and boarded the Olympic Airliner for Athens and then a TWA 707 back to the USA. Upon arrival at Lambert Airport in St. Louis, the family and a number of other relatives and friends met me. It was time to begin the next chapter in my military life and I was anxious to get it started.

With the baby due in July, Shirley was obviously showing pretty well by the time I returned home. My two weeks of

Life Between Innings

leave were packed with visits with family and church folks, plus looking for a new car. I finally settled on a 1967 white Pontiac that seemed to simply float down the highway, especially after driving the little green Fiat for over a year. Except for one incident, "Old Whitey" was an excellent purchase and served us well for the next 6 years.

I was eager to leave St. Louis and living with the in-laws to get back to our military life routine. Henry and Helen were actually pretty great in-laws but one can only live under someone else's roof for just so long and two weeks was plenty for me. I was to report to the 3398th *Student Squadron* at Kessler AFB sometime before May 16, 1972, so I wanted to get there and try to find us an apartment before training started. I arrived late in the afternoon on a Friday, checked into temporary quarters at the base and prepared for a weekend of looking for a decent place to live for the next six months.

As had been our fortune to date, I found an excellent place right away only a few miles from the base. Our new address was 119 McDonnell Avenue, Apartment 12. It was a fairly new, first floor, furnished apartment with a very nice pool right outside my front door. The property had been kept very clean by whomever was managing the place and the neighborhood around us was likewise neat and safe. In walking distance were a number of shops and restaurants that we would come to know and frequent, especially the family style restaurant just around the corner that featured strawberry pie. And, it was less than a block from the Gulf of Mexico. The only problem was that swimming in the ocean in and around Biloxi, Mississippi was still forbidden due to contamination caused by Hurricane Camille back in 1969 that had cut a path through parts of Mississippi, Louisiana and Virginia.

At the time of our arrival in Biloxi the town served basically as a stop off place between New Orleans, Louisiana, and

The Military Years (1969-1973)

Pensacola, Florida. There were a few noted nightclubs and eateries along the costal main thoroughfare, but Biloxi at this time was not the mega gambling center it is today with the various casinos. The beaches were really nice and sandy with plenty of palm trees to give it a distinctive flair.

Since I had been able to find a place to live much sooner than expected, I was able to contact Shirley and make arrangements for her and Dionne to join me immediately, which they did within the week. As usual, our first order of business was to check out the local Assembly of God churches. The first church that we visited was the Northside Assembly of God on LeMoyne Boulevard, which we liked very much, so we stayed. It was a fairly large church near the heart of the city with a good pulpit ministry and worship. However, much like the situation in Wichita Falls, Texas, we knew that we would only be there a short time so we did not try to get involved in the church nor did we socialize too much with the people.

Finally, in mid-May, my six-month training began. Right away it was easy to discern that this course was going to be much tougher than the one I had completed at Sheppard AFB to become a Communication Center Specialist. We were in class for four hours in the morning, which often included a lab made up much like a Radar Control Facility (called a RAPCON). At noon, I would then head home for lunch and several hours of homework. Dionne and I quickly got into a great afternoon routine whereby she would take her nap and I would study. My studies normally ended about the time she was awakening and we would immediately head to the pool for a couple hours of swimming, basically until suppertime. Dionne would not be two until July 28; however, she developed a great fondness for the water. So we strapped her into her life jacket and off she would go, jumping into the pool without any help from dad. With her golden hair and flashing smile, she quickly became

Life Between Innings

the darling of the complex. Residents were always stopping by to watch her swim and dive and talk. These were some of the best times I ever had with Dionne and we became quite good buddies.

Unfortunately, about our second week in Biloxi, the timing chain went out on the Pontiac. The price of the timing chain was something like $20 but the total cost of repair was over $300. The idiots that had designed this car made it where it was necessary to dismantle the front end of the car to get at the chain, thus the cost. We just did not have the money for such an expense as I was not able to work games as I had been able at other stops. Here in Tech School, I did not have the time for that luxury. We did not want to ask the in-laws to help us, although we were confident that they would have helped had we asked, so we just parked the car. For the next six weeks I was able to hitch a ride with one of the other students who lived nearby and we walked to one of the near-by stores to do our grocery shopping. After a couple weeks, we got used to not having the car and really did not miss it all that much, except on Sunday, which we needed so as to be able to attend church. But, with Shirley having a due date less than a month away, we knew that we needed to get the car back soon. Finally, we were able to save up the necessary funds for the repair and we were back in business.

Early in our stay Shirley became concerned that Dionne's left foot was turning inward so we had her examined by one of the base doctors. After a good examination he decided to put Dionne in a special foot brace that she would wear at night that would force the in-turning foot back outward. Basically, the apparatus was a piece of metal about 18 inches long with a shoe attached to each end. It was so funny watching Dionne try to sleep in this contraption, especially when she tried to turn over. She obviously balked at wearing it at first. As she

The Military Years (1969-1973)

got used to it, if we tried to put her to sleep without it, she would make sure that we did in fact put her into it before falling asleep. Several months later when the doctor felt that the brace had done its job, we had the reverse problem of convincing her that she no longer needed to wear it. She would lie there in her bed begging us to come and put her brace on. Finally, after a few nights, she thankfully got over it.

Our time at Biloxi was flying passed due to a number of reasons. One, we were enjoying our routine here and secondly my class studies were moving at a rapid pace. Also, we were anticipating the birth of our next child, so times were good. As her date to deliver approached, her stomach got bigger and bigger, and yes, bigger. When asked what we hoped to have, a boy or a girl, we would just usually comment that, *"… we don't really care if it is a boy or girl but we are afraid it might be a horse."* Later, we would find that this statement was not too far from the truth.

Finally, on the morning of July 22, the labor pains intensified, her water broke and we were grabbing our emergency bag and heading to the base hospital. Contrary to the long induced labor that Shirley had with Dionne, this delivery seemed to be moving much quicker. By early afternoon we were moving toward having a baby. The final act of delivery became a double miracle of sorts, but with a serious twist, as a problem began to develop just as the baby began to move down the birth canal. As the doctor described it, the baby was coming breech, which obviously was not good, but then at the very last moment the baby did a complete reversal, a flip-flop if you would, and came out headfirst. While this may have saved the baby's life, it really messed up Shirley's insides. After further examination, the doctor advised us that it would be his recommendation that she have her tubes tied while in the hospital as she was at risk of serious, future health problems if she

Life Between Innings

was to become pregnant again. After this experience, we both readily accepted the doctor's recommendation.

On the positive side, we were rewarded with an 8 pound, 11 ounce boy that we named Marcus Vaughn. Marc, contrary to Dionne's first 9 months, was a great baby that began to sleep through the night quickly and did not have the serious colic issues of his sister. Dionne readily accepted her "not so little" brother and became his caretaker immediately. Marc also proved to be the better buy in that Dionne's hospital bill was $25 while Marc's was $12 and some change. Love those military hospitals.

Within a couple days, both Shirley's mom (Helen) and my mom (Janie) made their way into Biloxi to help us through the first couple of weeks. First Helen flew in as she had done in San Angelo when Dionne was born and was a tremendous blessing. After she left, my mom came in to take up where Helen had left off, and she was equally a blessing. Before the time my mom left, Shirley was feeling good enough to drive with mom and me down Interstate 10 to New Orleans for a day. New Orleans was interesting to mom, as she had spent some time with my dad here during his military service. For me, it was just one of those exotic cities that I had heard about all my life and its allure (as bad as that might be) was exciting to me. We had a great day of walking, shopping, sightseeing and eating and came back home exhausted. After both of our mothers had come and gone, we were very thankful for the help that they had given us as I still had class and daily home-work to do. But, finally we were back to our normal routine, only with one more mouth to feed

You might say our stay in Biloxi was uneventful, except for the birth of Marc. However, God gave us one more really nice blessing in that I received my promotion to E-5, Staff Sergeant, on October 1, 1972. What this meant was that as an E-5, not

The Military Years (1969-1973)

only would I receive a very substantial pay raise, but the military would come to our apartment and pack all our stuff in a big United Van Line truck and ship it to our next assignment. Almost simultaneously I received orders for my first assignment as an Air Traffic Controller at Laredo AFB, Texas, an Air Training Command (ATC) base. While we had hoped to get an assignment in Arizona or Florida, or an overseas assignment to someplace like Taiwan, we were not totally unhappy about this move, as it would be close to San Antonio and an area very familiar to us. Those "nay sayers" familiar with Laredo tried to discourage us as they painted the city as a pretty pathetic place to live and work. Most controllers do not like working ATC bases and having to put up with all the rookie flyers. But, we had been given the same discouraging words with regard to Wichita Falls and San Angelo, our previous Texas assignments, but in each case we had really enjoyed our stay. We had no reason to believe that this assignment would be any different, and we were not disappointed.

Finally, November came and time for our graduation ceremony. I did not achieve Honor Graduate as I had at Sheppard AFB, scoring in the high 80s instead. However, I did achieve the class high score on the *Federal Aviation Association (FAA) Exam*, which was quite an achievement. I must say I was pretty proud as the test was tough and we had some pretty sharp guys in the class. All of us had to pass this test before we could move on to our new assignments, and not all the men passed it that first time.

The second week of November came, as did the United Van Line truck to pack up and pick up our stuff. This was very cool as they pretty much did it all. And, following the custom that we were becoming quite familiar with, we packed our few remaining things into the trunk of "Big Whitey," strapped the two children into the back seat, said our goodbyes to our

Life Between Innings

friends at the apartment complex, said our prayers asking for safety on this trip and headed West on Interstate 10 out of Biloxi toward New Orleans, Houston, San Antonio and ultimately Laredo. It was for us, in many ways, like heading back home, and we were pretty happy.

We were told to report sometime on or around November 15, 1972. The military gave us three days of travel time plus whatever time we might want to take from our Leave Bank. We decided that there was no real need to take an extended leave at this point so we drove straight through to Laredo. The drive was pleasant as the kids were in good behavior. And again, upon arrival, God blessed us beyond deserving in that we were able to find an acceptable place to live our first day out. It was a nicely furnished, 2 bed-room house trailer that had been maintained very well, located in the outskirts of the city in a better than average (as trailer parks go) trailer park. It was not a place that we would want to stay during our whole assignment, but for the present it wasn't half bad. I even had a Rural Route and Box Number for a mailing address; this is the only such time in this city boy's life that this has ever occurred. We settled in very quickly and I reported to duty with the *2107th Communication Squadron*, part of the 38th *Flying Training Wing* of the *Air Training Command (ATC)*, located just off the base flight line.

At this time President Nixon was beginning to bring the Viet Nam War, at least as far as to the USA's involvement, to a close. Conversely, the need for Air Traffic Controllers in the military was lessening in the short few months since I had left Iraklion. And, ultimately, the Variable Re-Enlistment Bonus (VRB) for Air Traffic Controllers had been reduced to half of what it was when I had agreed to be retrained. Consequently, reenlistment did not look as good to me at this time as it did back in March or April.

The Military Years (1969-1973)

To get the Air Traffic Control training I had agreed to extend my service time an additional 11 months, which gave me an expected discharge date of February 3, 1974, or just a little over 14 months from this point in time. With such a short amount of service time left without a commitment to reenlist, my Superiors decided to place me in the Control Tower in lieu of the RAPCON *(the radar controllers)* where most new guys were placed. This was fine with me, as I preferred tower work anyway to being cooped up inside a small-darkened room out in the middle of the airfield watching small blips on a screen.

As a new Controller, there were a lot of regulations and procedures I needed to learn that were pertinent to the Laredo Air Force Base, the surrounding area and to tower work in general. While in Tech School at Kessler AFB we had not been exposed to tower operations in any great detail as most of our emphasis had been on radar work. However, I seemed to catch on quickly and necessary items in my Consolidated Training Records were consistently checked off. What helped was that I was assigned with some pretty experienced guys, several that had served at the Saigon Air Port in Viet Nam at the time that it was the busiest airport in the world, surpassing even Chicago's own O'Hare International. Now that is busy!

I discovered one of the nice perks of being an Air Traffic Controller very early in the game. While officers and airmen rarely associate outside of the work area, the officers did treat us much more respectfully than they normally treated other non-commissioned officers. I suppose with us having some degree of control over their lives and their safety, it was in their best interest to be more civil to us. Also, because of the importance of being sharp and alert at all times, most of our shifts were four hours or six, but rarely, very rarely, much more than that. In fact, it was not uncommon to even work a two-hour shift and go home. Not a bad life!

217

Life Between Innings

Laredo Air Force Base airfield was somewhat unique in that we had three parallel runways running east and west and two others that crossed these at an angle running northeast and southwest. Fortunately, we rarely used the diagonal runways. Here at Laredo the pilots were being trained to fly T-36 and T-37 jet aircraft. The T-36's were a good training model for the beginners. Once they mastered the T-36, they were able to move on to the sleeker, faster, T-37's. As part of their training they would run missions all over the Southwest and then come back to Laredo and run touch-and-go's. Consequently, it was not uncommon for us to have aircraft landing on all three parallel runways at the same time. We had to be very careful to clearly state to the pilots, who were for the most part trainees, what runway that they were cleared to land on, be it Runway 35 Center, 35 Left or 35 Right. That distinction was obviously very important.

To complicate things even more was that to our south, only two to three miles away, was the Mexico border. The airspace over Mexico was "Restricted Air Space" and the pilots were required to avoid this area unless they had received prior approval. This meant that those running touch-and-go's on the inside runway had to make some sharp turns to avoid getting flagged. Another complication was that the Laredo International Municipal Airport set off to our northwest about five miles away which had a steady flow of commercial and private aircraft taking off and landing. Add all of these restrictions with the afternoon rain clouds that came rolling in regularly and it could get interesting as the pilots had to avoid these while trying to stay "inbounds."

For the most part, my color blindness had little affect on my ability to control air traffic. I really have more of a color deficiency than color blindness in that I can easily identify colors that are separated out, like those of a normal signal light

The Military Years (1969-1973)

at an intersection. Where I had a problem was pulling certain colors out of other colors such as a silver plane coming out of a white cloud. At times it was necessary to tell an aircraft that we had him in sight and then give him further landing instructions. Most of the controllers could look out across the horizon and spot the plane easily. For me, it would usually take a little longer. To be honest, in those circumstances, I usually spotted him about the time he was close enough in for me to see the lights on his wings or landing gear.

It was not uncommon while all this was going on for us to be playing a game of Hearts or Spades while drinking our coffee. I know it sounds risky at best, if not just plain careless and lacking in responsibility, but things were very much under control. In fact, to the old experienced guys, this was a piece of cake compared to what they had seen and done in Viet Nam.

In the 9 ½ months that I actually performed the job of an Air Traffic Controller, I was fortunate to have made only one major error. We had the morning shift, which started on this day at 6:00 AM. On this particular day it was rainy and the field was socked in with fog. Our weather monitor listed the visibility at zero, and it was accurate, as I could not see the end of the runway at either end. As was the custom, Ground Service, the men down on the tarmac driving around in their little trucks, called to say that the barrier was up on such and such end of the center runway. This being a training base, a very strong net would be raised at the departure end of the runway just in case one of the jets flamed out on takeoff or the brakes failed on landing and was simply unable to stop. The message from Ground Service was garbled so three times I tried to get him to clarify on which end the barrier was in the up position. Ground Service never responded and I failed to seek confirmation prior to opening the airfield. Sometime later that morning when the fog began to clear, one of the

Life Between Innings

instructors decided to take a short run to get a bird's-eye view of the weather situation before letting his students take off. As he was cleared and readied for takeoff, he called back to say that the barrier was up on the end of the runway that he was taking off from. While, obviously, he was in no danger of hitting it, anyone who might have attempted a landing coming in from that direction, could have gotten their landing gear tangled in the netting and would most likely have crashed. Rarely does anyone landing touch down that close to the end of the runway, but conceivably it could have happened. An *Incident Report* was filed by the pilot resulting in my crew chief, Staff Sergeant (SSGT) Davey Deaton, getting a good "ass-chewing," which quite frankly was mine to receive. However, Davey endured the pain in my stead and was very kind in his discussion with me later about my error.

Davey was a real interesting guy. He was generally crew chief on my shift. He was one of the guys assigned to our squadron who had served in Saigon. He was a very slender man, standing a little over six feet tall. When he was working, he would stand in the tower and point in the direction of any aircraft that he was talking to. This was a trick he had learned during those busy days in Nam, which helped him to mentally maintain location for all those he was responsible. Away from work, his life was a mess. Loving the Mexican nightlife in Nuevo Laredo, the sister city to Laredo, Texas, just across the international bridge and the Rio Grande River, he had fallen in love with Rose, a prostitute, and had married her. Rose kept pretty good tabs on Davey so his partying became a little bit restricted except for the rock concerts that he and his fellow rockers traveled great distances to attend. He carefully greased down his hair while at work so that it would "appear" to meet military regulation. As much as he could, he avoided anyone in authority so as to bring as little attention to himself

The Military Years (1969-1973)

as possible. During his off time, however, the grease came out and he had a fairly representative rock hairdo. Despite his attempts to conceal the unlawful length of his hair, Davey was one of those types who seemed to always gain the spotlight, no matter how hard he tried not to; consequently, his hair was a constant issue.

Now this was good for me as my hair was rather long by military standards also, but since I rarely ran afoul of my superiors, I was never questioned about it or given any directives to have it cut. While I did not really get a directive, I did get a very strong suggestion once from my NCOIC, Master Sergeant (MSGT) Roy McEntyre, a man I really enjoyed working for, just before I was to be discharged from service. On that day we were finishing up our shift about noon when he asked if I would like to go play a round of golf on the base course as soon as we got off. I suggested that this was a great idea and that I would meet him there. At that, MSGT McEntyre smiled and made his own suggestion, which I heeded, *I tell you what, Mooney, why don't we first meet over at the barber shop and both of us get a hair cut and then go on over to the course.* I quickly responded to his suggestion stating, *Sir, that is a great idea; I will first meet you there!* He smiled again knowing that his objective had been accomplished!

Finding a church at each of our different assignments was one of the things we looked forward to with some anticipation. Church life was such an important function of who we were as a family and investigating new ministries and places to worship was actually fun. And, it was always more fun in places like Laredo, much as it was in San Angelo, as we knew that we would be here for some time. Knowing this, we were willing to try and make a lot more friends than at the shorter assignments, plus our chances of getting more involved in the church was enhanced. In Laredo, our options were somewhat

Life Between Innings

limited as there was only one English-speaking Assembly of God church of any size and one Spanish- speaking Assembly of God church. Since we did not speak Spanish, the choice was pretty much made up for us.

In this case our one option was not a bad option as we began to feel at home with the saints of the First Assembly of God church immediately. I think the Pastor, Reverend Sword, and isn't that a great name for a gospel minister (*The word "Sword" is often used as a synonym for "Bible".*), took a liking to us almost immediately, if for no other reason than we were faithful tithe payers. Once we decided that his would be our church, I dropped in a rather sizable tithe check into the offering because the amount had been accumulating since our departure from Biloxi.

There were several military families that attended plus a good number of locals. It was probably the smallest of all the churches we had attended since joining the Air Force but it did not lack for friendliness. Pastor Sword and I became pretty good friends in short order. He and his wife had been in the pastorate for about 40 years and retirement was obviously not too far in the distant future. He had a good grasp of the Word and preached some really good sermons. One that I will never forget was a sermon he preached on a Sunday night entitled *Snares and Traps*, using Joshua 23:13 as his text which read, *Know for a certainty that the Lord your God will no more drive out any of these nations from before you; but they shall be <u>snares and traps</u> unto you, and scourges in your sides, and thorns in your eyes, until ye perish from off this good land which the Lord your God hath given you. (KJ)*

After a couple months of worshiping at First Assembly, the primary worship leader at the church was transferred out of Laredo. Pastor Sword asked if I would be willing to lead the worship, which I was more than glad to do. As youth leader

The Military Years (1969-1973)

in the church and at IBC, I had led the worship services many times and felt very comfortable doing so. My style was a little different from the previous leader in that I normally mixed in a number of contemporary courses along with the traditional hymns. I also liked to have the congregation stand near the close of the worship service so that they could more easily raise their hands in an act of worship. The services did seem to have a more marked spiritual emphasis leading up to the message and Pastor Sword encouraged me strongly in continuing with this style. He said he found it much easier to preach following a good worship service.

Thanksgiving 1972 came quickly after our arrival in Laredo. We had not had time to really make any friends, since we had only been there a couple weeks, so our little family of four celebrated the holiday by ourselves in our trailer home. It wasn't quite as sad as it might sound; we actually had a great meal and some time to kind of slow down. We had been going nonstop since leaving Biloxi and this relaxing holiday came at just the right time.

I was fortunate that our arrival in Laredo coincided with the start of the high school and military basketball season. The latest promotion to Staff Sergeant had helped with the finances but still officiating was good easy money, plus it helped me stay in shape. I sought out the key men that ran the Laredo area basketball association and was put to work immediately doing high school and junior high games all over the area. I was also in quite demand on the base, so I was back doing something I loved to do. I was surprised, a little, how much I had missed working sports activities over the summer when I was unable to work due to tech school.

My reputation grew here as a good, hard-working young official, much like it did in San Angelo. Also, as in San Angelo, I found that the coaches liked the way I handled the girls'

Life Between Innings

game. For some reason, this close to the U.S. and Mexican border, there was not quite as much girls' basketball as there was in the San Angelo area but I enjoyed the games that I was able to get.

As basketball ended we immediately moved right into softball and volleyball. I had not worked volleyball games up to this point but it may have been the easiest money that I have ever made. Counting to 15 was the toughest part of the job and the scoreboard usually took care of that for me. However, just being back around the game of softball and baseball was fun, especially after missing all of the 1972 season. Again, there was not quite as much local area softball going on in this part of the country but I was able to consistently work the base games.

Shortly before Christmas of 1972 we relocated to an apartment complex at 605 Bustamante Street (Apartment #101). It was a very clean two-bedroom, first floor apartment with a washer and dryer in the apartment, which was nice to have with two growing kids. The location was also great in that it was about a mile from the base, which made it convenient for me to get to work and for Shirley to get on base to do the grocery shopping or drop the kids off at the day care. The base was located toward the northeastern edge of town and this was one of the newer apartments in this fast growing area of the city. In retrospect, I am amazed at how timely God provided really nice places for us to live the entire time that we were in the military. He was faithful to do so as we came to each new assignment. I firmly believe it to have been more than just luck or happenstance.

Along with a rare ground cover of snow that we received in March, 1973, came the announcement that Congress had decided to close the Laredo Air Force Base by year's end, and even sooner if possible, and move the training wing elsewhere.

The Military Years (1969-1973)

A number of bases were selected for closure because Viet Nam continued to wind down. With that, I was asked again about my desire to re-enlist. I really had mixed feelings as I was enjoying military life. If I had been an officer, there is little doubt that I would have stayed in, but then that was something that was not going to happen. My major bone of contention was twofold; they could not assure me that they would assign me to any of my choice locations and the VRB for Controllers had dropped off to a point that it was now negligible and not worth consideration.

Knowing that Arizona was my number one stateside choice, the Air Force finally came across with an assignment to, are you ready for this, Gila Bend, Arizona. Gila Bend is located about 70 miles south of Phoenix right smack in the middle of the desert. If you look on the weather map, about once or twice a week, it is listed as the place with the highest temperature of the day. At the time I am writing this, the expected high is 116 degrees. Gila Bend was not really a military base as much as it was just a military outpost, of sorts. At the time, the base had a one-lane bowling alley; for a theatre, it had a sheet, posing as a screen, hanging on the wall of the joint Officer's/Airmen's Club. There were approximately one hundred military personnel assigned there plus a few hundred local Indians that lived in the area. Now, I love the desert, but with a family, this would be just a little too much. I declined their kind offer. I also declined their offer to reenlist. They very kindly gave me a discharge date of September 21, 1973, which was about five months earlier than my actual discharge date.

Shirley and I decided it would be best to send her home early, as had been our practice, so that we might be able to save a few extra dollars to ease our re-entry into civilian life. So, around the 1st of July, we once again packed all our belongings into "Old Whitey," except for the few things that I could

Life Between Innings

use in the dorm, and headed back to St. Louis. We had seriously given thought to settling in Dallas or Fort Worth, but being near family won out. After getting the family settled in at my mom's home on Osage Street in St. Louis, I boarded a military hop at Scott AFB in Belleville, Illinois, and flew back to Kelly AFB in San Antonio. There I met up with the Trailways Bus and returned to Laredo for the last two and half months of military life.

Upon my return, one of the ladies at the church loaned me her little Volkswagen bug to drive. This enabled me to stay involved in the church for the last couple months and have the freedom to move about. Of course, just as it was on the Island of Crete, one of my favorite pastimes was to go downtown Laredo to taste some of the authentic fare. The Mexican food served in the local downtown restaurants was nothing like the Tex-Mex restaurants that we were used to back in the Mid-West. The food was for the most part a little bit more bland, yet it had a unique flavor that I loved. Having my choice, however, I would have preferred to be back on the quaint little streets of Iraklion eating Greek desserts.

As much as I enjoyed going into Laredo's downtown area, I was not real keen in crossing over the border to shop or eat in Nuevo Laredo. For whatever reason, I just never felt comfortable. In fact, Shirley and I rarely ventured across the international bridge to do much shopping. Shirley enjoyed the bartering but I did not, plus that side of the border just seemed evil. I did not feel the heavy spiritual oppression as badly in Nuevo Laredo as I had crossing over from Brownsville, Texas, into Matamoros, Mexico, as I had several times while taking short missions trips as a student at IBC. So, we had made enough trips to gain the experience, but otherwise I felt no great need to make the short trip across the Rio Grande River and the international bridge to visit after Shirley had left.

The Military Years (1969-1973)

My basketball buddy from IBC, David Yaeger, was serving on the mission field at Zapata, Texas, less than 100 miles away, right on the Mexican border with his Father-in-law, Reverend Jerry McSorley. Jerry was a successful, life-long missionary to Mexico who was committed to the call. David had married my classmate, the very beautiful and blonde, Karen McSorley, and had moved to the mission field right after his graduation in 1967. David was every bit of 6'6" or more and Karen was hardly 5'2", if that. Despite their great differences in height, they made a very handsome couple; two of the neatest people I will ever know. On one of my last weekends prior to my discharge, they invited me down to their home to visit with them in the local church at Zapata where they worshipped. It was such a great weekend. Little did I know, or could have known, that this would be the last time that I would see David. Sometime around 1977, David was on the top of the roof of an old building in Oklahoma, helping to tear it down so as to retrieve the lumber to take back to Mexico for use in building a new church. David fell through the roof and was killed. I can only guess that God needed a really great guy, a great husband and a dad, to work in His heavenly home. On this side of heaven, although I am convinced that there are no mistakes in Christ, it just didn't make sense.

Things at the base were closing down quickly and friends were either being discharged early, like me, or being reassigned. I was able to get a room with no roommate in one of the barracks, which was nice, and went about winding down my career. There were still softball games being played so I stayed busy working them. Our tower operations slowed down dramatically to where our once "busy" schedules became very ho-hum. If not working a game or working in the tower, I usually spent the time on the golf course. I never played so much golf in all my life. I soon came to the realization, however, that

Life Between Innings

golf, no matter how much I played, was a game that I was only going to get so good at, and I might as well accept it as fact. Actually, this realization, allowed me to enjoy the game of golf without the frustration that I would have otherwise had, being as competitive as I am. While my buddies were swearing and throwing clubs, I was usually laughing at them or myself. What else could I do?

Finally, there just was not enough air traffic to keep very many guys on shifts, so I was temporarily assigned to work the switchboard at the base telephone office for my final two weeks. It was an old-fashioned type switchboard with cords and plugs. I got to wear the headset and the little microphone like you see in old pictures or movies. I would answer incoming calls from off the base saying, *Laredo Air Force Base; may I help you?* Or, if it were a call from inside the base to another location on the base, I would say, *Number please,* and patch them in. It was actually kind of fun. I felt like I was working at *Petticoat Junction* (Old TV Series).

Finally, September 21, my day of departure arrived. All in all, I had served 4 years, 6 months and 18 days, getting out 4 months and 12 days early. Man, the time had flown. I had joined the Air Force at age 21, and now here I was at 26, starting a new life all over again. We had figured that during our time in the service, including the move to basic training and then my final move back home, that we had made at least 11 specific moves during those 52 months, or an average of about one move every 5 months. Yet, it was a great life. And God had blessed us in many ways with great assignments, great people for which to work, good jobs and sufficient finances, great experiences and some travel, good churches, a good chapel and the friendship of many people. I really hated to see it end.

I could not help but wonder where in the world the time had gone. March 4, 1969, the date of my induction, seemed like

The Military Years (1969-1973)

only yesterday, yet here it was, time to move on and see what the next chapter in my life had in store. I figured that this would be, however, a tough chapter to follow.

Shortly after 10:00 AM on September 21, 1973, I was given my Honorable Discharge. All the goodbyes had already been offered so I made my way to the Laredo bus station and my ride back to the San Antonio International Airport for my flight back home. I was glad for the 150-mile bus ride back to San Antonio as it allowed me some time to soak in what I had experienced over these past four-plus years and contemplate the future. On the bus the familiar scenes of Laredo, then the Texas plains and finally San Antonio itself, helped to accentuate those memories as we moved slowly down the highway. I had really loved this experience and would miss it, but, it was time to move on; there were new experiences waiting, some of which I never, ever would have anticipated happening in my lifetime.

The 5ᵗʰ Inning
THE LIBERATING YEARS (1973-1977)

On October 15, 1973, Republican Vice-President Spiro Agnew resigned as the result of income tax evasion committed back in 1967 while serving as Governor of the state of Maryland. Gerald Ford, the highly respected Republican Senator from Michigan, was promptly appointed as the new Vice-President. On August 8, 1974, Republican President Richard M. Nixon resigned from office as the result of his involvement in the cover-up in the infamous Watergate Scandal of 1972. Vice-President Gerald Ford was sworn in as the new President of the United States. A few days after taking office, President Ford issued a pardon to former President Nixon for any wrongdoings he committed while in office for "the betterment of the nation and to put this dark period behind us." In 1974 Hank Aaron of the Atlanta Braves broke Babe Ruth's career home record when he hit number 715. In 1975, Bill Gates founded Microsoft launching the personal computer and electronic age. On April 30 of that same year, Communist forces captured the Saigon presidential palace in Viet Nam ending the war that had never officially been declared. It was a sad day, regardless of the position that any individual had taken regarding the war/conflict. In January of 1977, a peanut farmer and former Governor from Georgia, Democrat Jimmy Carter, was sworn in as the President of the United States, having defeated Gerald Ford the previous November. It was also in this year that pop legend Elvis Presley died unexpectedly at

Life Between Innings

his beloved Graceland Mansion in Memphis, Tennessee. Following the successes of the '60s, the St. Louis Cardinals returned to their mediocre play of the '50s during the entire 1970's era. Cardinal great and future Hall of Famer, Bob Gibson, pitched his final game on September 1, 1975.

For the past four and one-half years, at each stop we made, God had shown Himself faithful to provide a comfortable place to live and the additional work that we needed to help make ends meet. I was confident that God would do the same for us in this situation, but I was also keenly aware that this transition back into civilian life would be different. In reality, from San Angelo until our departure from Laredo, we really never had the pressure of finding work, as my primary job was always there waiting for me, as was the supplemental work of officiating sports. All of the other moves had an element of excitement that was much different than this move home, and a certain amount of dread and anxiety began to set in.

After reuniting with my family and marveling over how much the kids had grown in those two-plus months that we had been apart, especially the barrel-chested, very blonde, Marcus, I immediately began to look for work. This time we were living with my mother in south St. Louis on Osage Street. Mom was very gracious during this entire time and made it very easy for us as a family, not always an easy feat when there is a wife, a mother in-law and two children sharing space in a small two-bedroom, upstairs, city flat. But, somehow it worked.

My first goal was to get registered at the Unemployment Office so that I could draw unemployment while looking for work. To my dismay I found that since I had cashed in 28 days of military leave that I had saved, I could not draw any unemployment for at least four weeks. Four weeks of military pay in my pocket was nice to have but it seemed wrong that I was being penalized for being thrifty.

Looking for work can be one of the more humbling experiences in life. It is very similar to that humbling feeling that we guys have experienced when we finally get enough nerve to ask a special lady for a date or dance, only to be rejected. Unfortunately, in job hunting, the pain goes on and on as the rejection continues over and over and over again, usually on a daily basis. However, lest we starve, we are compelled to continue to ask. Oh, the humanity!

By law, and due to my previous good work record, I knew I had a job waiting for me at Cardinal Chip Company, if I wanted. My former boss, Mr. Charlie Nachbar, had strongly emphasized to me just prior to leaving for the Air Force, that they would really like to have me back after my service time expired. While I had made good money, I really could not envision doing that type of work for the rest of my life.

I was fortunate, and again it was a God-thing, as *United Parcel Service (UPS)* gave me a call about two weeks into my job search to come in and take a physical. Here in early November of 1973, they were doing their annual hiring of new package delivery drivers as they geared up for the holidays. The pay of $6.67 an hour, plus union benefits secured by Local 688 of the Teamsters Union, was a welcomed sight. I passed the physical and was immediately ushered back to personnel and was hired. Their promise to me was that out of the pool of drivers that they hire for the holidays they usually select a certain few that perform well to become permanent employees. This was very promising in that UPS was certainly a solid company, one that I could possibly move up in over time. I was thankful for the opportunity and very glad to put the job-hunting behind me, at least temporarily.

Life Between Innings

My supervisor, Mr. Mike Lady, went with me my first day out. Mike was a real pleasant guy and it seemed that he would be easy to work for. I was assigned an industrial route along Washington Avenue in downtown St. Louis. The first day, I was given 35 stops to make that we accomplished in a timely fashion. We took a nice leisurely lunch and then began our pick-ups that started promptly at 2:30 PM. The next day, I found that we had been given about 45 stops plus our pick-ups. However, we still had time for a nice lunch before having to begin our pick-ups. On the third day, I was given about 55 stops. Around 11:00 A.M. that morning, Mr. Lady asked me to drive him back to the Jefferson Street office. Here he excused himself saying that he was needed elsewhere, plus he felt confident that I could handle the rest of the route very well, which I did. On the fourth day I was given 65 stops and had to bust my butt to get them completed. In fact, to do so, meant that I missed lunch, which I was not too thrilled about, in order to finish in time to begin my pick-ups as required. On the fifth day, I was given 70 stops. I was not able to complete all these stops prior to the start of making my pick-ups, so I brought a few packages back to the station with me. I quickly found that this is a practice that is not condoned by the management of UPS.

Over the next few weeks I found that when I made all of my stops as required, nothing was said. However, I could expect to have more stops added the next day. If I failed to get my stops completed before time to start my pick-ups and needed to ask for help, Mr. Lady would let me know that my efforts were not acceptable. This seesaw battle continued to the point that I began to really hate the job. To compound things, the officials responsible for the *Veiled Prophet Ball,* an exquisite affair for the debutantes of St. Louis' high society, used the services of UPS during these already busy weeks leading up to Christmas to send out those personal and prized invitations to their big

The Liberating Years (1973-1977)

gala. This meant adding several extra hours to the end of our already long day. I rarely slept well and dreaded each new day. Friday and Saturday nights were the best time of the week for sleep, but Sunday afternoon and into the evening I could feel the tension build as I anticipated going back to work that Monday. It did not matter to me that the "old heads" (the union guys) kept saying that it would get better after my six months probation had expired; I simply had learned to hate this job.

During my job-hunting weeks prior to obtaining the UPS position I had left an employment application with Union Electric Company (UE), the major electrical utility in the St. Louis area. Midway through December came a call from the UE Personnel Office asking if I was still interested in employment with them. I wasn't too interested in the starting pay, as it was $4.17 an hour, well over a two dollar an hour decrease from what I was making at UPS. However, my mother was insistent that UE would probably offer me a tremendous opportunity for the long haul. Hating the job as I did at UPS, I reluctantly, but without much regret, said, *Yes, I am interested.* The lady from personnel ended the phone call by simply saying that they would call me when something came open.

I continued to work for UPS until the conclusion of Christmas week. Since I had been hired to work through Christmas and no one from UPS had given me any indication that they wanted me to stay on, I simply did not report for work that last week of December. By this time I was feeling much better about my decision to work for UE, even though I had no real assurance as to if or when I might start. On Tuesday of the last week of the year, I received a call from Mr. Lady asking why I had not reported to work the previous day and ask me to come by his office on Wednesday. On Wednesday I did as he had requested and went to visit him. After some light pleasantries he asked why I had not reported and I told him that when I was hired I

Life Between Innings

was told that I would work through Christmas and that if they liked my work they might offer to keep me on full time. I went on to explain that as of the Friday following Christmas, no one had offered me a job so I believed the job to have concluded. At this point he went on to say that he and the UPS management had been very pleased with my performance and that they had wanted me to stay on. He further stated that since no one had told me the job was over I should have understood that I was still working until receiving such a message.

After Mr. Lady finished his complimentary summary of my performance and offering me a full-time job, he asked if I was interested in staying on; my reply was fairly simple and to the point, *No.*

Since I was again unemployed, although somewhat promised a job, it appeared that I was free to accept an opportunity offered by the church (Full Gospel Tabernacle) to go to the Central American country of Nicaragua to help put on a roof on an orphanage. A year earlier, on December 23, 1972, Nicaragua had suffered a devastating earthquake and they were still trying to recover from its horrible destruction. Somewhere during that first week in January of 1974, while preparations were being made to go, the call came from UE checking again of my interest in employment. I told them that of course I was interested, but asked if it would be possible for me to participate in the Nicaraguan mission before I began work. After seeking some assurances from the UE personnel employee that I would not be dropped from consideration if I went, my brother-in-law, Don Redman, and I flew to Miami and met up with a wonderful Pastor from Atlanta, Rev. Marty Tharp, who was leading our three-man team. Marty not only pastored his church, but he and his wife and daughter formed a singing group that was in much demand and they traveled extensively in their huge bus. Even today, after 50-years of

The Liberating Years (1973-1977)

ministry, he is going strong traveling nationally and internationally working with churches and youth in the spread of the gospel in both word and deed.

After staying overnight in Miami, we left the next morning for the capital city of Managua. While I had seen a few military clad personnel at the airport in Athens, Greece, during my time of military service, I was really taken aback by the number of military personnel in full gear at the Managua airport. It was, to say the least, a little intimidating and I was not too unhappy to find our driver and host ready to whisk us away. Driving through the city on our way out to his village, some 50-60 miles from the city, I was amazed at the level of destruction that was all around us. One of the most amazing scenes was to see buildings several stories high crumpled in a stack piled up like pancakes standing perhaps no higher than what would have been a one- or two-story home or office. You could look at this pile of rubble and actually see the stories of these buildings clearly defined; obviously, no one could have survived had they been inside at the time of the earthquake. We were told that at final count some 6000 people from among 400,000 residents had been killed in this earthquake. Looking it over from our brief vantage point, that total did not seem the least bit exaggerated.

At the little village where the orphanage was being built we found our lodging. Actually our cabins were rather nice, although certainly roughly built by any standards. It did not take long for us to fall in love with the children that were already being housed in crowded conditions in a single building where they waited for teams like ours to come and finish putting on the roof of both orphanage buildings. Daily, for one full week, we climbed atop the newly constructed buildings and hammered in the new tile for the roof. Don and I were not exactly what you would call experts at this new trade.

Life Between Innings

I have often wondered how many repairs had to be made after we left and the first rains came, revealing our inadequacy as roofers. Although we had worked hard, when our week was up there was still work to be done on both buildings before the children could move in.

As we prepared to leave the orphanage and begin our return to the States, the children, with the help of the cooks, had made for us a special cake to show their appreciation for our labors. The finished product did look delicious and we were anxious to share in this delicacy with the children. As I received my huge piece I very quickly noticed that it was full of fleas, baked nevertheless, but they were still fleas. However, Don and I never flinched; we ate our piece with a smile and a big thank you but politely refused the offer of seconds, as we "wanted" the children to have more. There was no way that we were going to hurt the feelings of these children who had so lovingly made this special treat for us. And, I guess in reality, the fleas probably added some protein to the mix and were cooked well, so we were safe!

I did have some conflicting feelings as we departed. As I looked over the beautiful plateau surrounded by mountains, I briefly considered accepting the invitation of the American who was building and operating the orphanage to return and be on their staff. However, the timing for such a move was not right so I only briefly considered the offer. We soon returned to the States and it was time to contact UE to see if there still might be a job waiting for me. I was very pleased at the response I received as they indicated that a call might come soon.

In fact the call did come soon and I was told to report to the Employment Office to fill out some papers and receive my assignment. All that I knew was that everybody, except professional folks like lawyers, engineers and such, all started at the

The Liberating Years (1973-1977)

bottom in entry-level jobs, so it could be one of a variety of jobs in a variety of locations. After filling out my paperwork I was given a proper welcome and told to report to Mr. Sanlin on the PM shift working in the Building Services Department, right there in the headquarters' building at the corner of 14th and Gratiot Streets. My official job title: Janitor. My hours of work would be from 3:30 PM until 12:00 midnight, Monday through Friday, and I would be working on the cleaning crew that cleans the offices each evening. I was also told that upon my employment, I was required to join the *International Brotherhood of Electrical Workers (IBEW), Local 1439,* within 30 days.

My first evening of work was memorable, not for the work we did, but for the work we did not do. I was assigned to a scrub crew with two guys that had been on the job for several months; Jim Hip, a white gentleman, and Wardell Jones, a black gentleman, both of whom were about my age. Who could have imagined on this particular night that 15-20 years down the road I would be in a position to represent both men before the company on behalf of the Union in an attempt to either save their jobs or help them to avoid serious discipline due to work place issues; such are the ironies of life.

We were assigned to strip, mop and wax the floor of a small office and I was told by my partners that it was a job that we had to make last the entire night. Our first chore was to move the small amount of furniture out into the hall, which took only a few minutes. We then did a quick dust mopping of the floor, again a chore that only took a few minutes. We then spread the stripper on the floor, need I say again, a chore that took only minutes, and then we began the waiting process necessary for the stripper to do its thing. I immediately began to fear for my job as we sat and read the newspaper or listened to the radio for long, long periods of time. The more I fidgeted, the more relaxed Hip and Jones seemed to be.

Life Between Innings

It must be remembered that I was only a few months removed from military life and only weeks removed from my hectic pace with UPS. Could this job be for real?

Well, it was for real. Several hours into the shift we removed the stripper from the floor, mopped up any residue that we may have left behind, and then went back to our reading and listening to the radio. It was on this night that I first heard of radio station KSLQ, a fairly new station evidently in the St. Louis market, which featured current rock artists. Throughout the night during various record breaks, the DJ offered his latest "Q-tip" for his listeners. But the thing I will remember most from that night was hearing for the first time Elton John singing his smash hit, *Benny and the Jets*. By the time my first night had ended, I already knew the words to *Benny and the Jets,* as it must have played at least once an hour every hour of the evening. However, no complaints here, I love the song!

As we approached our last two hours of "work," we decided it was time to put a coat of fresh new wax on the floor, which we did with precision. With the wax now dry and the approaching "free time" coming upon us, we put the furniture back in place and waited for Mr. Sanlin to come by and give us his approval. "Free time" was the last half hour of the shift when Mr. Sanlin wanted all work to have been completed. The half-hour margin gave him the security he needed that all work would be finished and no overtime work would have to been done. All he asked was that we come back to our "gathering room" and play cards, read or just hang out, which was easy work for the pay we received.

Mr. Sanlin, a black gentleman who had started out on these same scrub and cleaning crews and had later become the supervisor of same, was cool. All Mr. Sanlin wanted was for the work to be done and for his workers to stay out of trouble or at least out of sight. When he approached our work area, he always let us know of his soon arrival with the jingling of his keys. How cool was that? And, as apprehensive as I might have been, the floor of our assigned office shone with such a gleam as to make one blink from the glare; and, we had not gotten fired. The first night had been a success.

For the next seven months this would be my workplace. The job assignments would differ from night to night but mainly our jobs consisted of stripping, mopping, waxing or cleaning the various offices by dusting and emptying waste-baskets. You knew you had arrived when you were given a regular assignment to clean a block of offices on a given floor as your only job assignment. After about two months I was given one of these plush assignments, which was pretty neat as one of the offices had a TV where I could hang out when my duties were complete. The secret was not to tell anyone of the "perks" you received in your area and you never had to worry about someone messing it up for you.

It was while working here that I came to know a number of men, and a few women, that I would be working with and around for my entire Union Electric (UE) career. One of these guys was Paul Helfrich. I am not sure why we clicked, as we really did not talk much or spend any time with each other, but we became very good friends down the road when I eventually transferred to the Labadie Power Plant.

Another gentleman that proved to be a good friend over the years and also provided a couple of my most memorable stories while working as a Janitor was Don Travis. Donnie was a short black man with a good size Afro, young and mod and aggressive and one who had this air of confidence about him. After a few nights with Hip and Jones, Mr. Sanlin assigned me to work with Don cleaning, mopping and buffing a room used by the Company as an outreach to area youth in one of their many social programs. The room had a combination radio and

Life Between Innings

record player, so we were set for the night as we began our assignment. Just prior to starting our work, Mr. Sanlin had given us the usual instruction to work carefully and safe.

At times Don could get a little out of control, not seriously mind you, but in those days he was kind of a free spirit and a lot of small, but odd, things seemed to happen to him. On this particular night Don wanted to run the buffer, which can be fun to operate but you have to know how to handle it or it will get away from you real fast. What happened next is one of those stories that is funnier if you are there than when it is told, but nevertheless, we were well into our evening with the radio blaring, Don singing along and rather nonchalantly running the big buffer. Suddenly, without warning, the buffer grabbed the cord of the radio – record player and slung it high into the air. For a very brief moment it was like the record player was suspended in air and then with a sudden jerk it was thrust to the ground, much in the same fashion as one might imagine a football player spiking the ball after scoring a touchdown. Pieces were dancing all over the floor and then back up into the air to slowly cascade back to earth a second or third time before coming to rest. I remember seeing little springs literally bouncing up and down on the floor in some weird kind of exotic dance. The buffer and the music stopped simultaneously; so did Don. The look on his face was priceless as he first was in shock, then appropriate fear, and then finally contemplation as he immediately began to think of how he was going to explain this to Mr. Sanlin. Talking nervously, yet with some element of collected thought, he begin to verbally form the story he was going to tell. After a brief moment of reflection, he picked up the phone and called Mr. Sanlin. His phone conversation went something like this, *Mr. Sanlin, I do not want you to be alarmed; everything is OK and I am safe. I need to tell you that the buffer somehow became entangled in the cord of a*

The Liberating Years (1973-1977)

record player and it smashed into pieces on the floor. However, I had my safety-toed shoes on and I am not injured; everything is OK. With that he hung up the phone and I went into hysterical laughter. First, what a great crash scene. Secondly, what an unbelievable, B.S. story. And thirdly, Mr. Sanlin bought it. We cleaned up the mess and nothing was ever said; Mr. Sanlin covered for us. What a guy, what a boss.

On another occasion we were equally as fortunate, but almost not. We had been assigned to do a strip job on a small office so we gathered all our tools and equipment and reported to the site. We quickly moved into the routine of moving the furniture, dust mopping the floor and pouring the stripping product on the floor. We then moved to the adjoining room, rolled some industrial white cotton gloves into a couple of balls and began to shoot baskets (into a wastebasket) from across the room. First he would shoot at my basket on my side of the room and then I would return my shots to his basket on his side of the room. We were fully engaged in this activity when our game was suddenly interrupted by the voice of the Superintendent over the entire department speaking directly to me saying; *I think you missed your shot.* This particular room had at least three doors and Donnie just happened to be screened from view (he was actually hiding behind it at this point) by the door my visitor had just darkened. I clumsily said something to the affect that, "*Yes, I need to work on my shot.*" As quickly as he had appeared, he disappeared, leaving us to think that this had not been a big deal. However, in mere seconds he appeared at one of the other doors and immediately began to question me about what I was doing and why I was not working? I quickly replied that, *Sir, I just poured the stripper on the floor and there is nothing I can do until the stripper has done its work.* Then, he was gone. Later Mr. Sanlin told us that the Superintendent had come directly to his office after our little

243

Life Between Innings

encounter to verify my story (It should have been our story but Don left me hanging high and dry as he continued to hide behind the door.). Had it not been a fact that we really could not do anything while the stripper was on the floor, I imagine my career at UE would have been short-lived. As it turned out, Mr. Sanlin saved me this time.

Working those late shifts in Building Maintenance provided a real study in human nature. For some, this was a job of a lifetime and was all that they wanted until they reached that glorious day of retirement. For others, like me, this was the starting point. It was the first step in taking me, or any of the employees, in a variety of directions as Union Electric offered a wide range of job opportunities in a wide range of fields. And, the way to get to one of those desired fields was through the system-wide bidding procedure. Each day all the starting level jobs throughout the UE system were posted in various places around our work areas listing the job, the associated union, the starting pay and the qualifications of the job. Even starting positions in "Company Level" jobs were posted for those who wanted to climb the levels of management in lieu of working the various bargaining unit (regular union work forces) jobs. I did not know a whole lot about the company but it had been made pretty clear that the best money, and the quickest path to it, was made in the power plants.

Those words rang rather positively in my head so I began signing every bid sheet that was posted that listed a job in the power plants. It was not long, probably sometime in May, that I received a bid as a Laborer at the Venice Power Plant in Venice, Illinois, at the foot of the McKinley Bridge crossing over the Mississippi River. The Venice Power Plant at one time was called the *Mammoth of the River,* as it was the workhorse of the UE system. Now, it was a coal-fired plant that was in much decline and was being used basically as a back-up plant. But,

The Liberating Years (1973-1977)

nevertheless, I was making my first move and I was anxious to get there as soon as I could because my union and plant seniority would not start until my first day at the plant. In determining seniority, every day can be critical as it is used for determining bids on jobs, vacation selection, forced overtime and many other considerations. The Building Services department continued to hold onto me saying that they needed to hire a replacement before I could be released. They were not in any hurry so it was August before they finally let me go. By that time, some guys hired off the street after I had accepted my bid, were already in place at Venice and building seniority.

Shortly after my employment with UE began, Shirley and I found a nice duplex at 1-B Cameron Drive on the outskirts of Belleville, Illinois, to rent. Our stay with mom had extended a little longer than we would have hoped, but she was very gracious to us and our stay had been a pleasant one. Our new place was furnished, which was what we needed, as we had gotten rid of all our furniture upon my entry into the military five years earlier. We also liked the location, as it was only a few miles from our church, Full Gospel Tabernacle, which was now meeting in Fairview Heights, Illinois, in their new building. It was also close to Shirley's mom and dad and our relationship with them was very good. And, now that I was at Venice, the prospects for a significant promotion and pay raise were much more attainable and the future began to again look bright.

When I was finally released from my job as Janitor and the Building Services department, I immediately reported to Venice and my new Laborer supervisor, Mr. Gildersleeve. Power Plant workers were represented by the *International Union of Operating Engineers (IUOE), Local 148,* and were arguably the strongest union on the UE property. IBEW 1439 was likewise a strong union, primarily because they represented the

245

Life Between Innings

all-important line crews as well as the Janitors and a number of outside crews. But the Linemen walked to a different drummer and it appeared at times could write their own ticket, as they could find work easily, should a strike occur, while most other workers were stuck walking the picket line and lining up for unemployment. But, the IUOE wielded the larger power as they controlled the very reason the company existed, the production of electrical power.

Mr. Gildersleeve was a slender white man who had spent his life around power plants and was now nearing retirement. He was not a complex man, he just wanted everyone to do the work that they were assigned and then get lost. This sounded like a man I could work for! Getting lost in the Venice Power Plant was a walk in the dark, literally, as there were tunnels and caverns and rooms all over and under this 10-12-story mega-complex. And, now that Venice was winding down as a key player in power production, there just weren't many people around to watch what you were doing. In the summer you could go up on the roof and look out over the entire Metro St. Louis region and watch all the Mississippi River activity. It was not uncommon for some of the guys on weekends to head to the roof and work on their tans. There was a lot of our work that had to be done on the roof so to be up on the roof was not considered being out of our work area by supervision, so there was a lot of time spent on the roof during the summer months. Now in the winter, the roof was not a great place to work as the winds would swirl around and make it seem like it was 20 degrees colder than it was.

On my initial day at Venice, following some brief introductions to the other Laborers on the crew, I was assigned with another new guy named Perry Dones, an educated, intelligent black guy, big into tennis and going to college at one of the local schools. Mr. Gildersleeve asked us to pick up a shovel and a pick and follow him around to the side of the complex to the Mill House door. I gathered up the shovel and Perry picked up the pick and away we went. Once at the door Mr. Gildersleeve explained that during a recent storm the heavy rain had washed a good amount of coal in front of the mill house door and he wanted us to shovel it up and move it away. There was a lot of coal in that area as it was not uncommon for coal to spill off of the overhead conveyors that was bringing coal from the coal pile, some 75-100 yards away, and into the building to the silos that fed the boilers that heated the water into steam that ran the turbines that created the electricity.

I started shoveling while Perry and Mr. Gildersleeve observed. The coal had mixed with the rain and at times was somewhat hard to shovel. So, Mr. Gildersleeve instructed Perry to take the pick and break it up to make it easier for me to shovel. Perry looked at the pick and then looked at Mr. Gildersleeve and with the straightest face possible said, *How do you use one of these?* While I could hardly hold my laughter at such an inane question, Mr. Gildersleeve, without even a blink, took the pick from Perry's hand, lifted it high over his head and rammed it into the coal, breaking the coal apart easily. He did it one more time and again without even a hint of, *You stupid SOB,* handed the pick back to Perry and said, *That is all there is to it,* and walked off around the corner not to be seen again until noon. Although Perry and I worked together for years, in fact for 28 years, I never asked him if he was serious with his question or not; I can't believe I never asked!

Such were my early days at Venice. We did all kinds of odd jobs from dusting railings inside the plant (A coal-fired power plant is always filled with dust and at first blush you wonder, *Why even bother?* But the fact is that accumulating coal dust can be very explosive, plus it is just hazardous to breathe, so you eliminate as much of it as you can; which is not much.),

Life Between Innings

cleaning up coal spills inside and outside the plant, sweeping various areas of the plant, picking up trash and replacing rail ties on the various tracks used by trains bringing coal into the plant and moving it from the coal dump pit out to the pile where it was stored. Working the rails was a great summer job, as we would work in teams using a variety of tools that we had stored in our little pushcart that ran on the rails. This cart was very heavy and when it would derail, it took a large bulldozer to come and help lift it back on the track. After derailing it twice in just a few days, Mr. Gildersleeve decided that he might better use my talents elsewhere.

Because of so much down time the guys had a lot of time to spend perfecting the art of "water throwing." Because a power plant uses grates for walkways and flooring so that heat, steam and dust will not be trapped in any particular area, you can look down through the grates at men working (or standing around) who may be three, four or more stories below. Most power plants are 15 or more stories high. Once you get used to walking on grates and realizing that you're just as safe as if you were walking on a regular tiled floor, it is actually pretty neat.

There were many techniques to throwing water, depending on what you wanted to do and for what purpose you wanted to hit someone with it: fun, revenge, bored, etc. Throwers would use styrofoam cups, coffee cans, 5-gallon oil cans and even the infamous 55 gallon drums to dump water on their unsuspecting targets. Depending on where this evil deed was to occur and the height from which it might fall, the chances of picking up considerable coal dust along the way could be from negligible to significant. For the thrower, he usually took this all into consideration. To say that it was not uncommon for someone to spend more time plotting out and executing their water throwing plan than actually doing work would not

The Liberating Years (1973-1977)

be an untruth. While management certainly did not condone our activities, they really didn't attempt to stop the practice as most of the supervisors had come up through the ranks and had been throwers themselves through the years.

The stories are unending, they are even classic, with regards to successful shots that were taken. One of the great stories was about a young employee named Ed Wingron who had taken a shot with a small cup at one of the senior guys, Joe Robinson. It was OK to do this, you just can't get caught, nor can you brag about it as there are no secrets in a power house; Ed failed to keep the secret, being young and brash and wanting his success known. Ed was working on the turbine deck a few days following sweeping the floor with a push broom. Joe had strategically plotted that when Ed reached a section of the floor away from any power sources, he would get his revenge. Joe found a nice hiding spot several stories up, filled a 55 gallon drum to the top and somehow maneuvered it into position. At the precise moment Joe tilted the drum and a torrent of water came crashing down on Ed, hitting him with such force that it broke his broom and tossed him to the ground. Success!! This was a story of which legends are born.

One that I personally saw of equal magnitude occurred late on a PM shift on my second tour of Venice. To this day I do not know who threw it but, again, it involved a 55-gallon drum of water. Rarely did you try to hit the "good" supervisors or foremen, but for some reason someone made an exception. Old Jack Campbell, perhaps the best supervisor on the floor, was making his regular walk up and down the Boiler Operations aisle. This aisle is where the control boards of all eight units are lined up side by side down the full length of the boiler room. I was working on Unit 6 when Jack came by. Suddenly, and without any warning, 55-gallons of water came cascading down from above. Now, this wasn't just a hit and it was

Life Between Innings

over; the water just kept coming and coming. Poor Jack was knocked over onto the operator's desk. I could see that he was trying hard to get up but the water just kept forcing his face back down on the desk. It was hilarious!! As I write this I can hardly keep my fingers on the keyboard as I laugh and snort. Jack was drenched. Once he was able to recover, Jack stood up, composed himself and we never heard a word about it.

Old John McConnell had been an operator at Venice probably since the time before God formed the Mississippi River. John had perfected his art over the years. His favorite tactic was to get a small cup of water, put a firecracker under it tied to a string. He would light the string and the string would burn up to the fuse and then the firecracker would go off, toppling the cup and spilling the water on the target below. Now John had obviously had way too much free time on his hands over the years as he had been able to determine how long it would take certain lengths of string to burn before it would reach the fuse of the firecracker. John had one-minute strings, he had two-minute strings, he had five-minute strings. Because of the different times of the strings, John could set his trap, then go off to the lunch room or be down a unit or two talking with some guys, and wait rather inauspiciously for his trap to go off. Because a firecracker was involved, no matter how much John would cry his innocence, we knew it was him, even though the circumstances would seem impossible. I made it my job to get John on his last day of work before he retired. He walked around all day looking up, hiding underneath the small canopies that shielded the operator's boards, darting from one to the other, trying to escape me and others. I would imagine his neck still hurts from looking up all day. There were several near misses but he basically left unscathed; he was a Pro.

My favorite episode occurred one Day Shift while working on units #7 & #8 of the Boiler Floor. Over off the Boiler Floor

The Liberating Years (1973-1977)

at Venice was an area called the Heater Bay. Back in between units #4 and #5 an open-air restroom had been constructed surrounded by a wall, but it had no roof. At the time it was constructed only men were working in the power plants so complete privacy was not an issue. Also, a roof was not desirable, as it would hold in the heat creating some unsanitary situations in what was probably the hottest part of the plant. Spotting a fellow worker sitting on the "throne" with his pants down around his legs I took the opportunity to quickly find a quart-sized can, filled it with water and got into position. From my vantage point I had a perfect shot, was well hidden and had an easy get away path marked out. I unloaded my can of water and watched as it fell in a nice full wave and hit the target below. After seeing the shot hit my target I booked and never did confess my success to anyone. However, as he told the story to the guys on shift, he remarked at how well he had been targeted, his pants and shorts being fully soaked and covered with wet coal dust. His only complaint was that the toilet paper had also been soaked, which created a bit of a dilemma.

The stories of water throwing are legendary and endless. Even after transferring to Rush Island some time later this art form followed. At Rush Island we really did work but from receiving our work assignment in the morning till clocking out that evening, each man was on alert looking for shadows and moving creatures above; if you didn't, you paid the price. Over the years I had became rather proficient at my craft. But, being secretive as I am by nature, I was often suspected of committing a crime by my water soaked comrades; however, I was rarely convicted.

There are many, many more stories to tell. However, my last story did not involve me but I saw it; it was classic. I was at the Rush Island Plant walking along mill row with my good

Life Between Innings

friend, Craig Phillips. All I saw was Craig's hard hat flying through the air with a large red object bouncing up and down on the walkway in front of us. It was obvious this object had hit Craig solidly on the head. Craig immediately began to cry out, *My God, someone has hit me in the head with a brick; they are trying to kill me!* Actually, what happened was that someone had targeted Craig with a red water balloon thinking it would be funny to hit him with it, the balloon would break and he would summarily become soaked. However, the balloon failed to burst and it did look, momentarily, like a brick bouncing along ahead of us. Once it was determined that Craig had not been "bricked," we had a new classic story to add to our collection. I admit it, I laughed! This practice ended once I got to Labadie. By this time management had taken a much stricter position on such tomfoolery and at least one aspect of the enjoyment of going to work was taken away.

Sometime in late August 1974, our former pastor from Laredo, Rev. Sword, called to tell me that he had resigned his pastorate at the church and wanted to know if I had any interest in applying for the position. We had loved our time in Laredo and at the church and I was immediately intrigued, to say the least. I huddled with Pastor Redman to see what he thought and he concurred that it might be a good move, certainly a good opportunity to see what God might have in store for us in pastoral ministry. He also offered to provide support from Full Gospel for an unspecified length of time, as it was not likely that the church could fully support us initially. There was also the issue of my ordination being with the Independent Assemblies of God and I was not sure if the Assembly of God organization would allow me to accept the pastorate of one of its pulpits. A few calls were made by those on the other end and the extension of a call was made to us to come.

The Liberating Years (1973-1977)

Having just arrived at the Venice power plant some six weeks earlier, I hated to meet with Mr. Ernie Kohlenberger, the Superintendent of Operations, and tell him I was resigning to take a pastorate in Laredo. However, that meeting went well and sometime in mid September we packed up Old Whitey, our smooth riding white Pontiac, hitched a U-Hall on the back, and headed back to Texas. It was almost a year to the day that I had boarded the Greyhound Bus in Laredo to begin my journey home after being discharged from the Air Force. Life does take some strange twists and turns and there were more strange ones to come.

Upon arrival we were greeted by several women of the church who helped us get settled into the parsonage, a very nice, two bedroom trailer home that sat on the church property. The church property consisted of the church with an attached educational wing and the trailer home. The church itself was a cozy little building with a slight Spanish flair and a sanctuary that would probably hold 150 people comfortably. The church had both an organ and a piano and had several musicians who had been faithful during the time that Pastor Sword had been in leadership. When I was last there, I had actually led the worship, but I was hopeful that I could find someone to take that responsibility so that I could concentrate on teaching and preaching.

Dionne and Marc, now ages four and two respectively, seemed to be doing very well and had taken the move in stride. Shirley seemed to be comfortable with her new prospective role; I was somewhat apprehensive, due more to what our financial situation would look like than what my ministry outcome would be. I think that I felt that with God's blessing, we could actually make this work. Of course the immediate problem was to begin to re-establish the congregation. The numbers had fallen off significantly since I had left due to the

Life Between Innings

base closure. Consequently, what had been a nice sized congregation a little over a year ago now stood at about 35 or so.

I found that I enjoyed preaching in our youth services back home and God had been very gracious to bless those efforts. However, sermon preparation had always been a struggle for me when preaching to adult congregations, and fortunately or unfortunately, I had not done much of it. Shirley, in one of her more honest moments with me regarding my potential ministry, had pointed out that part of the problem was that I did not pray enough to ever be an effective minister. She pointed out that her father was a man given to much prayer and that her previous ministerial boyfriends (two of them, I think) of the past had likewise been men whose lives were marked by prayer. While those statements hurt my "spiritual feelings," the truth was that she was right. And, as I began preparation for my first sermon at First Assembly of God in Laredo, I keenly recognized that this was an effort that I could not do alone; I definitely needed the power of the Holy Spirit to enlighten me and to put words and thoughts into my heart and mouth.

I decided to do what I do best and that was to basically take a book of the Bible and begin to work systematically through it verse by verse. For my first book I chose I Corinthians, as it is basically the Apostle Paul's exaltations on *How to do Church; 101.* For our first Sunday morning service we had about 30 or so in attendance. I had enough of the appropriate assistance in place with music and worship that I was able to concentrate on the message and it seemed to go well and seemed to be accepted by the congregation. The Sunday evening service was pretty much of the same, but again a good service with the same usual suspects in attendance.

One of the first things I decided to do was post a financial report each week of our congregational giving and expenses. After paying expenses, there was no money left over for salary but the support that Full Gospel was sending was sufficient to meet our needs since we did not have to pay rent or utilities. However, I felt it was important that the congregation know the financial status of the church so that they could more properly and specifically pray about the matter and hopefully be moved to pay their tithes consistently.

Within days after our arrival a representative of the local presbytery of the Assembly of God called and asked if I would be willing to preach at the quarterly Fellowship Meeting in a nearby town; this meeting was scheduled about two weeks hence on a Friday night. He was hoping that I could come so that I could become acquainted with the other regional pastors and evangelists of the Assemblies of God. I readily accepted the opportunity. I had also been approached by the *Ministerial Alliance of Laredo* to join with them in a weekly fellowship, which I again agreed to do. It seemed good that I was getting plugged in so quickly with the various other ministries of the city and the region.

About the third week that we were in town I received a call from the local Spanish Assembly of God pastor. He told me that he had been approached by a couple from outside his church asking if he would marry them. He wondered if I would be willing to meet with them and perhaps fulfill their requests. I responded that I would be happy to discuss this with them if he wanted to give them my number. Shortly I received a call from the prospective groom and I told him that if they would allow me to counsel with them a day or two prior to the marriage, I would be willing to perform the ceremony. To this they agreed, so we set a date to meet and to discuss the wedding and participate in my counseling session.

I have to admit that I was very pleased and impressed at how well the counseling had gone and how well they both seemed to receive it. They were a handsome couple to say the

Life Between Innings

least and obviously had a little money on which to start their new lives together. Neither confessed to being a Christian, in fact I strongly suspect that they were Roman Catholic in background. This being my first wedding I probably did not ask all the right questions but again I suspected that this wedding was obviously a decision made quickly and time was of the essence.

The couple had a beautiful wedding and a wonderful reception. They treated Shirley and me with great honor and we felt blessed to have been part of their special day. I was not the least bit nervous and I never let on to them that this was my first wedding. They followed my every lead and the ceremony as a whole went as perfectly as one could hope. Unfortunately, our situation would change quickly in Laredo and we never had the opportunity to follow up with them.

The night of the Fellowship Meeting came so we journeyed over to the nearby city that was about an hour away. I had chosen to speak on *God's Peculiar People*, from I Peter 2:9. The message went well and those in attendance and the other pastors from the presbytery wonderfully received us. More and more it seemed as if we were off to a good start.

Another thing I felt strongly about was that we needed to begin to develop a World Missions ministry sooner rather than later. From my time at IBC, then at Trinity under Pastor Hagee and then most certainly in working with my father-in-law, Henry Redman, a great missionary statesman and pastor, I knew that missions speaks to the very heart of God and I wanted that working in our church immediately. It seemed key to me that any church that expected to grow and to do effective ministry, had to have a vibrant, active World Missions Ministry. As I was considering this, Rev. McSorley, the father of my former classmate at IBC, Karen McSorley (now Yaeger), gave me a call, having heard that I was ministering in the area. The McSorleys were doing some effective missions work in Northern Mexico working out of the border city of Zapata, Texas, about an hour or so drive from Laredo. On what was probably our fourth Sunday evening service since arriving, I asked Rev. McSorley to preach. I immediately signed him on as our first missionary.

Somewhere along about the 5th week of my pastorate I began to sense in my own spirit that, while things were going well, very well in fact, this was just not what I was suppose to be doing. I would go back to my study at the church, and for the first time perhaps in my whole life, began to have some very honest conversations with myself about my call and about my gifts and desire to be a pastor. To be a pastor is a very special call and not all men are gifted to be one. I could readily tell within my spirit that I was not enjoying most of the aspects of pastoring from making visitation calls to homes and hospitals to welcoming people into my home at all hours of the night, usually to hear about their problems, problems which, for the most part, seemed rather petty. As noted earlier, sermon preparation was not a joy, but a real struggle. I did not like being available to anyone and everyone 24 hours a day, seven days a week. And, it seemed to me that a lot of the spiritual types that I had to deal with were simply kooks, and my patience level with them was not good. All these attributes combined together do not make a good recipe for pastoral service.

So it went. I kept tossing this thing back and forth in my mind, and the more I thought about it the more it was becoming increasingly clear that my call was a "man" call and not a "godly," personal call. In my mind I finally articulated what I had felt from the beginning of this whole adventure and that was that my Pastor, Rev. Leland Mooney, and Rev. Verdell Cloud (a close friend), were speaking out of their own heart, not mine, when they strongly urged and counseled me to go

Life Between Innings

to IBC and prepare for the ministry. And, after all these years, I was still trying to live up to a calling that I did not have. Finally, for the first time ever, I was starting to come to grips with the fact that I had simply missed the mark with the decision to come here and the decision to seek pastoral ministry period. I recognized that both Pastor Mooney and Pastor Cloud were very well-intentioned and had most likely focused on my love for the Lord and strong Christian faith as evidence of a call, but the fact was that I did not sense a call, had truly never sensed a call, and in fact, did not have a call, and I knew it. But, regardless of how I got here, the decisions, all of the decisions, in the end were of my own making and there was no one to blame but myself. And, consequently, I was the only one who could make the decision to right the wrong that I had been perpetuating since 1965.

After wrestling with this issue the whole week I told Shirley that I was going to ask the congregation, on this our sixth week, to give me a vote of confidence. I knew that my coming to the church had not been at their specific request but at the invitation of the Assembly of God presbytery. My hope was that they would waffle with their approval or that at the very least the vote would not be overwhelming. Both of those scenarios would give me the impetus that I needed to resign. That Sunday I preached my sermon and God seemed to bless the effort again. However, as the service was coming to a close I announced to the congregation that we were going to be voting on my status and I explained the rationale for it. As the votes were tallied, I could not help but be amused, as the vote was unanimous that we stay. That was clearly not what I had been hoping for.

While on a personal level the vote was a great compliment, on another level I still knew that it did not make it right for me to stay, nor did it confirm that I had a call from God to preach

The Liberating Years (1973-1977)

and to pastor. Some might disagree. For a few brief moments I did wrestle with several questions, but the important question was this: could it be possible that all these people from the congregation and all those who had encouraged me in this endeavor from high school to the present, could they all be right about this and I be wrong? I finally concluded that none of them could know my heart and that it was God, and God alone, that I needed to deal with about this issue. Now in my early 60s and having gained some valuable experiences along the way, I am a strong proponent of good counseling and mentorship, something that I never received during my formative years of pastoral training. I simply find that to be abhorrent and a real issue that needs to be addressed by those working in non-denominational circles; this lack of accountability and oversight is simply unacceptable, if not a violation of biblical principle on its face. Just as in other major life decisions that I had made to date, like marriage, no one had really ever sat me down, except in passing, and talked to me heart to heart; no one had ever asked me the tough questions, no one ever pursued these important issues with me or said, *Let's talk about whether you should go to IBC or whether you should pursue your dream of coaching,* no one. The counsel that I did receive was more of a strong suggestion, and never was a dialogue to seek out what was in my heart. In fact, I do not recall anyone ever asking if I felt that I had a call from God to preach or whether I didn't, and now here I was again facing a dilemma where good men wanted one thing and my heart was telling me to do something else.

Finally, about Tuesday of the week following the vote, I decided that I needed to resign and I needed to get out of the ministry. Upon making that decision it was like a tremendous load had been lifted off my shoulders. I truly cannot describe the relief that I felt. It had been a long, long time since I had felt

Life Between Innings

so at peace with myself and with a decision that I was making. I sat down with Shirley and told her my heart. She was very supportive of what I was going to do and we began to make preparation to pack again and head back home. For ten years I had struggled with this question, and finally it was resolved. I could not have been more relieved; I could not have been any happier!!

I contacted Pastor Redman and explained to him the situation and he too was very understanding and supportive. In fact, I think he confirmed with me that my decision was right and strongly believed that my gifts were much better suited in the area of "helps" or "administration" in the church and not in the pulpit. I then drafted a letter to the chairman of the presbytery and explained to him that I felt compelled to return to St. Louis and to leave the church in Laredo and hoped that my decision did not in any way bring embarrassment on the church or the Assemblies of God.

On what would be our seventh and final Sunday, I preached perhaps my best sermon to date and then asked the congregation to be seated just before closing the service in prayer. I explained to them my appreciation for their overwhelming vote of confidence the previous week but that I was resigning, effective immediately. I explained that my actions were not due to any fault of theirs, but just a genuine sense that God had not called me here as their pastor or to continue the work. I could see from the facial expressions of a few that they were disappointed. On the faces of others I could see a slight sense of confusion and wondering what was "really" going on. After some tearful goodbyes, we loaded up Old Whitey and the U-Haul and the following Tuesday we headed back up I-35 North, leaving my 7-week pastorate and call to pastoral ministry in the rearview mirror.

I must say that the ride back home was a joyous one for me. It was as if the monkey that had been on my back for "oh

The Liberating Years (1973-1977)

so many years" was finally lifted and I was now totally free. I had no idea what the church or family back home would think. Would they think that we came and failed, and that is why we returned? What would they really think? I finally concluded that it really did not matter. I had finally made a decision that was right in my own heart and it felt really, really good! I was finally at peace!

While my spiritual burden had been lifted, there was a queasiness that was gradually starting to build in the pit of my stomach as we reached Joplin near the Oklahoma and Missouri border. I truly hated the prospect of starting to job hunt all over again. I hoped that Union Electric might hire me back but I figured that was a long shot, but decided it was a shot that I needed to take before I started looking elsewhere.

Once home, the Redmans welcomed us back into their home until I could find work. The church folk were exceptional and welcomed us back warmly and without questioning. I am not sure what they had been told before we got back but they sure treated us well and loved on us in a big way.

Ed Givens, the Assistant Pastor at Full Gospel Tabernacle, and his wife Barbara, were close friends to Shirley and me. I soon confessed to Ed how my heart had been freed from the decisions regarding ministry and the spiritual battle that I had encountered while in Laredo. I told him that I had no desire to ever seek pulpit ministry again. He was a wonderful guy to have come alongside me as he was very mature in the faith and sensed strongly that the decision that I had made was right. Like Pastor Redman, he believed that while pastoral ministry may not be my gift, certainly there were many other things in the church where my talents and gifts could be effectively used. It was about this time that he began to look for someone to help teach an adult Sunday School class and wondered if I would be willing to help co-teach it with Roy Higgerson, an

Life Between Innings

Elder and the worship leader in the church. It seemed like a good fit and would not be a burdensome chore for me, as we would have a specific subject every other week to teach.

But, first of all, my primary consideration was finding a new job and a new place to live, and do so in short order. Before heading off to the Union Electric's employment office, I offered up a brief prayer, swallowed my pride and went in. I was sent in to see Mr. Joe Nesselhoff, the man who had hired me in January of this same year. Now, here I was standing in front of him asking him to hire me again some 10 months later. I do not know if it was an act or not, although it sure did not feel like an act, but Mr. Nesselhoff was not glad to see me. Whereas he had been very gracious to me when he first hired me and whereas we hit it off pretty well the first time after we discovered that we both had been Communication Specialists in the Air Force, that same warmth was missing this time.

As we talked Mr. Nesselhoff let me know that it was not the Company's policy to hire people back that had previously quit. In fact, to the best of his recollection, only one other person in the history of the Company had ever been hired back after quitting. At one point he said, *I don't know why I am even talking to you about this!* But, for whatever reason he continued to talk. We reviewed my previous work record at UE at both the headquarters building and at Venice and found that in my short stay I had built a pretty good work record. However, at some point in the conversation he asked me about something I did at the power plant and my mind just went blank; I could not think of the name of the power plant, I simply could not think of the word "Venice" no matter how I struggled. My mind was frozen! Finally, in closing the interview he simply said, *If you can remember the name of the plant that you use to work at, call me back and I may give you another chance, but I really do not know why!*

The Liberating Years (1973-1977)

I left the office feeling so stupid. How in the world could I not remember the name of the power plant where I had been working no less than two months ago? Tell me, how can that be? Then suddenly out of the blue it hit me, *Venice, you idiot, it is Venice!!*

With some intrepidation I picked up the phone and called Mr. Nesselhoff at his office to inform him that I had finally gotten my memory back and that the power plant that I had worked at previously was "Venice." I really don't remember getting much of a reaction but he did say that they might call me back. All I could do was hold my breath; it was totally in God's hands if I was to have my job restored. In the meantime, I needed to keep on looking to see if a job might materialize, but nothing did.

However, I did not have to wait long as the call that I had hoped would come finally came sometime around the second week of December. I was told to report back to the Employment Office, only this time I did not have to meet with Mr. Nesselhoff. However, he did get in one last gig at me as the subject of my being hired for the second time came up with the lady that was administering my employment papers. She reminded me that I was only the second person ever rehired after quitting and that Nesselhoff had commented that he did not know why he was doing it this time for me. I didn't know either, except that God must be intervening in some way. Whatever, I knew that I did not deserve it, but I was sure thankful to have it back. The theme of being blessed beyond deserving was becoming fairly prevalent in my life and there were still many more undeserved blessings to come.

In somewhat of an oddity of sorts I was hired to start work that last week of December. UE did not normally like to do this, as they would have to pay me holiday pay three times (Christmas Eve, Christmas Day and New Year's Day), pay for

Life Between Innings

which I would not be doing any work. Another added benefit to my return in December in lieu of January was that when it came time to pick vacation, each time there was an incremental jump from a one-week to two-week benefit, or two-weeks to three-weeks, etc., I got the extra week a year earlier than those who got hired after New Year's. On the negative side, I lost all the seniority I had earned during my previous employment and truly was starting over in every respect. As far as UE was concerned, my previous employment never occurred.

I had hoped they would send me right back to Venice but instead it was back to Building Services and the Janitor position again. This time I was assigned to work in the East Wing of the Headquarters Building working for a Mr. Anderson. Anderson was not as easy to work for as Mr. Sanlin, but once he knew he could trust me, he pretty much left me alone. Consequently, after a few weeks, I rarely saw him except at shift changeover. I also received my own square to clean daily within just a few weeks of being re-employed and I was sitting pretty and on easy street from that point forward waiting for my first opportunity to get back to Venice. In one of the ironies of life, the very offices that I was cleaning would eventually be the very offices I would be using for various meetings with company officials for discussions regarding contract issues, disciplinary matters and even contract negotiations. God does have a sense of humor; just ask Joseph.

With a steady job in place, we once again began to look for a new place to live. In the spring of 1975 we stumbled onto a beautiful duplex near the church at 9633 Ridge Heights Road. The duplex was located right in the middle of a very nice residential area of Fairview Heights, Illinois and provided a really nice place for Dionne and Marc to play and to grow up. It was while living here that Dionne started kindergarten and began riding the school bus. Yes, we were typical parents, standing

The Liberating Years (1973-1977)

at the bus stop crying and waving on that first day as our little one peered out the window at us.

The house on Ridge Heights Road will forever be known to the kids as the "Pink House," as the brick had a kind of a pinkish hue. And, this is probably the one home whose walls hold their most cherished memories as they were growing up with their mom and dad. For the kids, our two years here probably represented the most stability and joy that they would ever enjoy. Unfortunately, it would be short-lived.

While I was enjoying my renewed employment at UE, Pastor Redman had come upon an idea to start a bookstore to be supported by the World Missions Ministry of the church. He also thought it would be a good idea for me to be the manager of the store, an idea that I was not opposed to as it would be work that I would enjoy, on a part time basis, and would be paid for doing it. Our finances were still tight on my Janitor wages so the extra income was greatly appreciated. Since Pastor Redman's missionary organization was the *Christian Missionary Association*, he named the bookstore the *Christian Missionary Bookstore*. I would have a fulltime assistant, named Sherri, who would basically run the day-to-day operations, which would allow me to come and go as necessary, at any time of the day or night, to do the books, order supplies and oversee in general the work of my assistant.

It was at this time that the Charismatic move was coming into full bloom within many of the mainline denominational churches, including a number of Catholic groups, but certainly within the non-denominational churches like ours. It was also the advent of the cassette tape, which helped Christians and non-Christians alike hear the gospel preached by their favorite speakers while in their cars, or as part of their private devotions or in groups with other believers. One of the big sellers in our bookstore was portable cassette players as automobile

Life Between Innings

manufacturers, for the most part, had not yet started installing them at the factory. One of the first things that my assistant and I did was to start and build a large lending library of popular messages by popular Charismatic speakers such as Derek Prince, Bob Mumford, John Hagee, Don Basham, and others. It was also the era of the Jesus People movement, which was kind of the catalyst of the informative bumper sticker, T-shirts with your favorite Christian message, Christian jewelry, new Bible translations and paraphrases, Christian rock, etc. that were not heretofore popular in mainstream Christian circles. Our bookstore was the perfect place to pick up some of these popular items and "trinkets." More importantly, it was a time of refreshing and renewal within the church and our church was growing in numbers and in the Word.

One of the great stories that came out of our church during this period began when a group (maybe ten or so) of Jesus People came on a Sunday morning and marched down the aisle to take a seat in the front row of the sanctuary. They were dressed in their brightly colored, borderline psychedelic, loose-fitting clothes and sandals. They enjoyed the worship and joined right in and obviously loved hearing the Word that was preached by Pastor Redman. However, some of the Elders took offense to the way that these folks came to the Lord's House dressed so "inappropriately." A meeting was called by the Elders and they were rather insistent that Pastor Redman meet with this group and explain to them that they needed to dress more appropriately as they entered the Lord's House, especially on a Sunday morning. They felt it was important that as Christians we should always give God our best, which included wearing our best when we came to worship.

Pastor Redman handled the situation with Solomon-like wisdom, though many of the Elders did not necessarily agree with him. He took the position that if he told them how to

The Liberating Years (1973-1977)

dress in order to worship at Full Gospel, there was a great chance, in fact a very likely chance, that they would leave and not darken the doors of our church again. However, if they were allowed to come dressed as they were, he would have the opportunity to preach to them, something he obviously could not do if we ran them off. And, if he was allowed to preach to them, we should trust the Holy Spirit to do His work in their lives, and if "He" decided that their clothing was inappropriate, "He" could convict them of it. As a result of this wise decision, several of them stayed in the church and grew in spiritual maturity and love for the Kingdom of God. One of the men eventually became a missionary to South America; one of the ladies (Sherri) became my assistant in the Book Store and another became active in our youth ministry. Pretty neat stuff, I would say!!

As I was taking on the new bookstore duties I was also becoming involved again with the youth in a ministry role as the current Youth Pastor had received a call to pastor a church in Edgemont, a small community only minutes away from Fairview Heights and our church. The move seemed to be a good one for him and his wife and they went with the blessing of the church. It was an easy move for me to follow right in behind him as the new Youth Pastor as I had filled this role in a similar fashion before I had left for the military. While the faces in the youth group had changed over the past 6 years, I was well known and respected by many of the parents at Full Gospel and by the kids that had now reached their teen years; so we were accepted back in quickly and it seemed that we hit the ground running without much interference. However, what was different this time was that I did not envision myself as using this role to prepare for my next "big step" in the ministry. In other words, there was no big step to prepare for, ministry wise, as I was no longer pursuing ministry, per se.

Life Between Innings

Having this knowledge was really freeing; this was my niche for this time and God began to bless it immediately.

Because of the fervor for Christ sweeping across our area, I was able to secure some solid ministry, music and musicians for our regular and special youth services. One of our favorite local Christian singing groups, *Harvest*, came by several times. I had also become good friends with Ron Tucker, the Pastor of Youth at New Covenant Church, affectionately called the Sheep Shed, located in Maryland Heights, Missouri, and had him in to speak on several occasions. At the time, New Covenant Church was kind of the central hub of Charismatic teaching, preaching and singing in the Metro St. Louis area and our young people, as well as Pastor Givens and I, frequented their worship services as often as we could. After some division developed within New Covenant, Ron Tucker founded Grace Church, likewise in Maryland Heights, which has carried the Charismatic flag for the area through the years starting with a large congregation and maintaining it even to the present.

Opportunities for ministry continued to fall into my lap. Roy Higgerson, our worship leader, had to be away from time to time during the Sunday night evening services so I was asked to fill in for him. This was not a difficult role for me as I had actually ministered in this role as the Youth Leader at the Carsonville Full Gospel Church, at the Mountain View Youth Camp and in the services at the Laredo Assembly of God Church when Pastor Sword was there.

At about this same time I had accepted Ed Given's invitation to co-teach one of the Adult Sunday School classes. It is so funny how things turn out in life. While seeking to become a pastor, my ministry efforts seemed to be futile and meaningless (except with the youth). Now that I had put that goal behind me, my teaching efforts seemed to be blessed in many ways. I cannot explain it; all I know was that I was enjoying my salvation and my Christian service more than at any time in my life to this point. And, my abilities to teach, by God's grace, improved dramatically and people seemed to be encouraged by it. The two key studies that I recall doing during this time was an exhaustive study of I Peter, still one of my favorite books of the Bible, and a series on *Healing the Broken Hearted* from Isaiah 61: 1-3. These verses hold much truth to those who are hurting (the NIV translation):

(1) *The Spirit of the Sovereign Lord is on me, because the Lord has anointed me to preach good news to the poor. He has sent me to bind up the brokenhearted, to proclaim freedom for the captives and release from darkness for the prisoners,*

(2) *to proclaim the year of the Lord's favor and the day of vengeance of our God, to comfort all who mourn,*

(3) *and provide for those who grieve in Zion — to bestow on them a crown of beauty instead of ashes, the oil of gladness instead of mourning, and a garment of praise instead of a spirit of despair. They will be called oaks of righteousness, a planting of the Lord for the display of his splendor.*

Herein lies another of God's great ironies in life as verse 3 would become the theme verse of Twin Oaks Presbyterian Church, a church that would become a solid foundation for spiritual growth and a safe haven for continued restoration for me especially, but also for my family, many years in the distant future.

However, there was a new struggle developing that I needed to face. It seems that if Satan cannot attack from one side, he will attack from another. Now the struggle was finding the balance that I needed between my two jobs and ministry and with my growing family. I also had decided to start back to school and I was taking two classes a week at Belleville Community College using my GI Bill. If I did not use it, I would eventually lose it and it only seemed prudent not to waste such a great opportunity. Shirley was a great mom and did not complain much at how little time we had for each other. But it did not take long for me to realize that I was out of balance and that something would have to change, and it needed to change sooner than later. How serious this issue would become was much greater than I could have ever anticipated, but should have.

My bid to Venice came sometime in April of 1975 and I was released to return to Venice sometime in May. I was back working in the Laborer group, but it was interesting to see that the turnover in my group had been about 100%, except for a few Old Timers that had no ambition to do anything else with their careers. It was also encouraging to see that the old crew for the most part had already received promotions and were working at various jobs in Operations.

One of the key jobs of a Laborer was to be trained as vacation relief and unexpected fill-in assignments for the guys who worked in Operations. Operations consisted of the Turbine Side, which was much more difficult to learn, and the Boiler Side, which was easier, but dirtier. Each side had various levels of work and the pay was within pennies of each other regardless of what side you were trained. The Laborers were allowed to pick which side they wanted to train based on seniority. Since I had the least seniority of anyone in the group, by default I was assigned to train on the Turbine Side. This would not have been my pick.

My first training was for the position of 2nd Turbine Auxiliary Operator or TAO. Once trained our job was to assist the 1st Turbine Auxiliary Operator, or simply called the First Operator. The First had a pretty difficult job and I was amazed at how well these guys ran their units. The First were working directly for the Turbine Operators who worked on the floor

The Liberating Years (1973-1977)

above ours. As a 2nd, once I learned the perfunctory tasks, the job was not too difficult. Venice used to run around the clock, but not anymore, due in large part to the fact that the new Rush Island Plant had recently come on line and they could produce many more megawatts and do so much cheaper than we could. Venice had six units that would produce about 50 megawatts each and two units that would produce 100 mega-watts each for a total of 500 megawatts for the whole plant if everything was running. One Labadie or Rush Island unit could produce 600 megawatts by itself.

We were also aware that as soon as the new Callaway Nuclear Plant came on line, there may be times that we would be "dead in the water," so to speak, and not have much to do except cleanup chores and making oil changes. However, when the units were up and running OK, my main job was to make hourly checks on the auxiliary equipment and to make sure that all the oil levels were maintained and that the water-cooling apparatus on each piece of equipment was cooling as designed. The work was important but the pace was not as hectic as when the units were coming on or coming down or in an upset (not running smoothly). This equipment was very old, but somehow the guys managed to keep things running. Having heard so many bad things about unions and union guys over the years, I was impressed at how much pride these guys collectively took in doing their work and doing it well.

I had only been at Venice a few weeks when I received my first opportunity for a permanent promotion to the 2nd's job. I had already completed my training in the turbine auxiliary area (the basement of the plant) and had worked a week or two of vacation relief. My promotion was to be effective on the AM Shift of Sunday, July 5th and I was to report at 6:45 AM for work. On Saturday, the 4th of July, Greg Maxwell, one of his girl friends, Shirley and I traveled to Effingham, Illinois, to a nearby lake for some water skiing and bar-b-que. None of us were drinkers but we did stay out a little longer than we probably should have and got a lot more sun than is advisable. The main reason that we stayed on at the lake longer than we had planned was that the radio was reporting that the IBEW 1439 union was planning to strike at midnight over a contract dispute. While I was no longer a member of that union, in sympathy, as good Union Brothers do, we would obviously not cross their picket line. Sure enough, as I was going to bed, it was reported that they had gone on strike and picket lines were being prepared to go up.

We had been advised on Friday before leaving work that if the IBEW went on strike we were to come to the plant gate at our scheduled work time and receive further instructions from our union stewards regarding our "strike" responsibilities. We were of course also instructed not to cross the IBEW picket line that would surely be set up at the gate. So, I got up and headed to work as scheduled, but was certainly not expecting to work, as the IBEW was on strike. I was also not prepared mentally or physically for work, as I was feeling really sick from being overexposed to the sun the day before. Upon reaching the gate I could not believe that there was not a picket line in sight, meaning that I had to go on in to work. I do not think in my 10 years of actual employment with UE that I ever experienced a day on the job where I was as sick as I was on this Sunday; I was throwing up from both ends and could barely navigate, let alone concentrate on my job duties. What a way to start a new job and make an initial impression on my First Operator; what a way to enjoy a new promotion! I will forever be indebted to my First Operator that day as he did his job and mine. After the longest eight-hour shift of my life, we were told that we could leave as the picket line was now in place and that management personnel were prepared to take over for us. Since we were in the building, by contract, they

The Liberating Years (1973-1977)

could have made us stay an extra eight-hour shift. Thankfully, management did not think it wise to do so. What a day!!

Promotions at Venice began to come quickly and often. I had only been in the 2nd Turbine Auxiliary Operator position for about a month when I became aware that a Mill Tender job was opening up on the Boiler Side. What I had also learned confidentially was that one of the guys working as an Assistant Boiler Operator (ABO), one of the major operating positions on the boiler floor might be leaving soon. The ABO position represented a very nice promotion with good pay and I would be in the line for the promotion to that job if I could get the Mill Tender position before the bid for the ABO job was posted. One of the things that I quickly learned was that you do not need to share all the things you know with those you work with if you have designs on making a move. With the Mill Tender job being a very dirty and noisy job, not many guys wanted to take the job unless they thought they could move out of it quickly and up the promotional chain. When I was approached about taking the job, knowing what I knew, and not liking the turbine work, I jumped on the bid.

Within just a few days of taking the Mill Tender job I was again approached by management to see if I was willing to start training for the Assistant Boiler Operator position. They made no promises as to when or if I would be able to utilize the training but certainly it would put me in line for future vacation relief and other temporary assignments that almost certainly would come along. I had barely finished my training when the permanent position as an ABO opened up as I had expected and I obviously pounced on it. Some of the guys on the Turbine Side were not too happy with my quick rise on the Boiler Side, but that was their issue not mine, as they had the same opportunity to take the original Mill Tender job that I did and had passed it up. Praise the Lord that they did!!

Life Between Innings

As they say, *Timing is everything*, and in this case it was certainly true. Prior to Rush Island coming on line and training commencing for work at the new Callaway nuclear plant, it was not uncommon for it to take 10-20 years to get the Assistant Boiler Operator job. Here I had arrived at Venice in April, and now in less than a year I had jumped from Laborer to Assistant Boiler Operator. And, this was the year in which we had an extended cold spell with snow on the ground for over 100 days. Cold weather at a coal fired power plant means overtime and overtime means the opportunity to make some serious cash. God continued to bless us and we were gradually getting our feet on the ground financially.

The 6ᵗʰ Inning

THE SEARCHING YEARS
1978-1982

In 1978 Georgia Democrat, Jimmy Carter, was in the middle of his one-term Presidency, having been elected to office in 1976 following the Watergate Scandal of the Nixon administration. In 1980, the office went back to the Republicans as Ronald Reagan was elected to his first of two full terms. Reagan, at age 69, was the oldest man ever elected to the Presidential Office. In 1980, the world was shocked with the news that John Lennon of the famed Beatles was shot and killed by a "fan" on the steps of his apartment in New York City. The St. Louis Cardinals were awful in 1978 finishing 24 games under .500. They righted the ship somewhat in '79 finishing 3rd at 10 games over .500. However, the big story occurred on September 23, 1979, when Lou Brock, the future Hall of Famer, stole the last of his record 938 bases to become the #1 base-burglar of all-time, plus he joined the 3,000 hit club prior to sliding into retirement. In 1980, the Cardinal fortunes turned for the better when Ken Boyer was fired as manager and Whitney Herzog, affectionately called the "White Rat," replaced him. In 1981, former Cardinals, Bob Gibson and Johnny Mize, were elected to the Hall of Fame; however, the big story was that MLB went on strike. In 1982 the Cardinals traded malcontent Gary Templeton to the Padres for Ozzie Smith and welcomed fan-favorite rookie, Willie McGee, to the team. Later that year the pieces came together and the Cardinals won their division with a 92-70 record, beat Atlanta in

Life Between Innings

3 straight in the National League Championship Series and then beat the American League Champions, the Milwaukee Brewers, in a dramatic 7th game to win the World Series. Yours truly, sitting with lovely wife Tina, was situated in the 4th row of the right-centerfield bleachers as we watched future Hall of Famer, Bruce Sutter, use his famed "split-finger fast ball" to mow down the Brewers in the ninth inning of game seven to secure the World Series title by a score of 6-3. Life was good!!

The late '70s were a time of great change as our society was already in the midst of major sociological changes that had been ushered in by way of the Watergate Scandal, the Jesus (People) Movement, the sexual revolution and the end of the Viet Nam Conflict. In 1978, churches in large part were pushing Jimmy Carter for a second-term as President because of his very public faith in Christ. However, I did not vote for Mr. Carter as it was already fairly evident that Carter was a pretty great guy who would make a pretty lousy president. And, I was right!! So, in 1980 I voted for Ronald Reagan, the last Republican that I would vote for until 2004 when I voted for George W. Bush, Jr., The Bush vote was one that I began to regret within just months of giving it. I had thought Carter was bad but Reagan, in my opinion, was worse. I know that the majority of Americans, especially Christians, have put Reagan on a pedestal, but I count Reagan as the second-worst President to take office in my lifetime, slightly edging out George W. Bush, Jr., as he personally altered the face of Organized Labor, put our nation into unprecedented debt and widened the gap between the middle class and the rich to levels not known since the Industrial Revolution. Reagan became the author of deregulation of the airline industry, utility industry, communication industry, milk and bread industry, etc. under the guise of increasing competition, only to see the competition eat up the little guys with the resultant high prices and decreased

The Searching Years 1978-1982

services that we "enjoy" today. You can say what you want but President Reagan was not a friend of the people, he was a friend of Big Business, and our lives and standard of living have steadily declined ever since.

As the calendar turned to 1978, a number of dramatic changes were also occurring in the Mooney household. The changes actually began in April of 1977 as we had been told by Union Electric Company that the Venice Power Plant manpower was being scaled back dramatically due to the success of the new Rush Island Plant and the soon start-up of the Callaway Nuclear Plant. So I, along with 10 other Venice employees, were shipped off to the new Rush Island Power Plant on the Mississippi River near the twin cities of Festus and Crystal City, Missouri. The Twin Cities were located about 30 miles south of St. Louis off Interstate 55. Even though we were being shipped in as Stationmen (glorified laborers), the *International Union of Operating Engineers (IUOE), Local 148,* our bargaining unit, had negotiated for us to carry a protected rate (*the pay rate of the final classification that we held at Venice*) to Rush Island. This was a great blessing, as my base pay would remain around $18,000 a year in lieu of having to take a drastic pay cut.

The drive from my home in Fairview Heights, Illinois, to Rush Island took about an hour and half one-way. This made for some long days, especially on those few occasions where we were needed to work overtime. I also had the compounding problem of participating in a car pool with a bunch of guys whose work schedules did not always match up with mine. Finally, around August of that summer, Shirley and I found and purchased our first home, a very nice split-foyer located in a small subdivision on the outskirts of Festus at 26 Holly Lane. We negotiated a price of $32,500 for the home which, at the time, was kind of a reach for us. The downside of our

Life Between Innings

purchase was that while the home was beautiful, as it had been built for the contractor working that subdivision, it was located amongst several low-income homes that devalued our property and dampened our enthusiasm about living there. It was not that we were so pompous or uppity, it was simply the clutter that most of our neighbors let build up in their driveways and yards that somewhat affected our pride of ownership. Despite the location, I was excited about the move. Foremost in my mind was that my hour and half drive would immediately be reduced to about 25 minutes one-way with no more car pools.

Another joy for me was that at Rush Island I began to make friends with a number of guys who wanted to form a competitive slow-pitch softball team to play at the Pevely Softball Complex, located between St. Louis and Festus along Interstate 55. It was not long until we had formed the *Rush Island* team and had entered our team in one of the fall leagues. To say we were bad would be an understatement. I had not played competitively in years and could neither hit too well nor field too well, but I at least looked the part. The major components of our team consisted of Bill Dorner, who would become my best friend, at first base; I played second; Craig Phillips, our manager, was at short-stop; Dave Bell was at third; Barry Sizemore was the pitcher and Ken Edmondson was our catcher. The outfield was made up of Tom Kasmarzik, Tom Almany, Randy Hyde and occasionally Tom Kaczeroski, plus a variety of other guys. I am not sure how many games we won that first year, but it was not many.

It was not long after our league started that my competitive juices began to be rejuvenated. One of the things that simply drove me crazy was our pitcher and my good friend, Barry Sizemore, walking so many hitters. For goodness sake, it was slow-pitch; how hard could it be? Finally, I could take it

The Searching Years 1978-1982

no longer and insisted that I be given an opportunity to pitch. Tra-la, I found my niche; for the next 19 years I would pitch and pitch quite well, I might add. I soon found that although it might be slow-pitch, there were things that I could do with the ball that would enhance my ability. I could actually make the ball curve and knuckle, depending on wind conditions and I could vary the height of the arc on the flight of the ball to induce fly balls on weak hitters and lower the arch to induce line drives and ground balls on the power hitters. I was also able to put the ball inside or outside on the corners with consistency and vary the arc to allow the ball to drop at the front of the plate, for ground balls, and behind the plate, for pop-ups. For a good pitcher, it was more than just tossing a slow pitch over the plate, and this became a real challenge for me.

My final pitching characteristic came about after watching a short, squatty, non-athletic looking guy pitching for another team. I had never seen this before but he pitched like a bowler who was delivering the ball off the wrong foot. On a lark I tried it myself a few days later and found that I had much more control and could do some of the things with the ball that I had not been able to do with my conventional delivery. It was also an odd look that most hitters had not seen so that gave me an advantage, even if slight. It was also easier to field my position with this delivery, which at times could be a life-saver with the frequent line shots that hitters liked to take "right up the middle." This new delivery worked well for me and I used it for the last 17 years of my amateur career.

It was while playing ball with these guys that, at age 30, I began to drink for the first time. Shirley too found for the first time a taste for wine, beer and the assorted mixed drinks and admitted a desire to experiment with smoking. Up till then I had tasted beer a couple times and found it rather disgusting. However, one hot day after finishing a game, I took a drink of

Life Between Innings

a teammate's ice-cold Schlitz draft and it went down smooth; very, very smooth. I have no explanation as to why it suddenly tasted so good, but it did. I rarely had more than one beer, at the most two, a pattern that has followed me to this day. To sit around and drink beer, fortunately for me, never became a passion or a habit. From that day forward, however, I began to enjoy a nice cold beer on occasion, especially a Michelob Light or a blue-collar favorite, Pabst Blue Ribbon.

With a shorter drive to work and the opportunity to once again enjoy the great game of base(soft)ball, I was quickly acclimating myself to living in Festus. The downside was that financially this move to Rush Island was not very profitable. Usually a move to a new plant like Rush Island meant the opportunity to work a lot of overtime, which for me was great. At Venice, in just less than a year, I had moved up quickly from Plant Laborer to Turbine Auxiliary Operator to Mill Tender and finally Assistant Boiler Operator (ABO). ABOs made pretty good money at just under $7.00 an hour, plus I was able to get about all the overtime that I wanted. However, Union Electric took note of the errors that it had made in building previous power plants and built Rush Island to be basically overtime free, especially in its early years.

With two growing kids, a new home and tight finances, it was important that I find some additional money quickly. For me, the place to find it was an easy choice and that was to again use my GI Bill and resume my college studies. The GI Bill paid a flat monthly rate for any college course, and fortunately, I could usually pay for the tuition and books with just one monthly check, the rest being mine to spend as I wanted, tax-free. It was a win-win situation for me so I enrolled at Jefferson Junior College in Hillsboro, Missouri, and continued to build onto my transcript that I had started the previous year as a student at Belleville Junior College.

The Searching Years 1978-1982

The biggest adjustment for us was the move away from Full Gospel Tabernacle, our church. As noted previously I was actively working at the church in a variety of capacities such as Youth Pastor, Sunday School Teacher and Deacon, plus I frequently led the worship service when our regular leader was absent. I had also been the Manager of the *Christian Missionary Bookstore*, a job that I could no longer do with our move to Festus. The change really was not that difficult for me but it was a major change and a major issue for Shirley. I would not know just how important this change would be for her until several months down the road.

At first, each Sunday morning we would pack up the kids and head out on the long trek back to Fairview Heights and Full Gospel Church for services. I had resigned most of my obligations at the church by this time as we just lived too far away to truly be involved. We would attend Sunday School and the AM service, eat dinner with the Redmans, hang out at their home throughout the afternoon, attend the evening worship service and then arrive back home, usually about 9:00 or 9:30 that evening. I got real tired of this routine quickly.

After several months of traveling back and forth to Fairview Heights for Sunday services, we decided to shorten the drive and start attending New Covenant Fellowship. This became our place for regular Sunday worship for about a three-month period. They only had one service on Sunday, which was kind of revolutionary for churches with a Pentecostal bent at that time, but it fit our schedule very well in that we could worship and then return home with a Sunday afternoon and evening free. The Redmans were very gracious to us, making us always feel welcome in their home, but I must admit that I did not mind having "in-law free" weekends on a regular basis. Plus, worshiping at the "Sheep Shed" was at times electrifying, as we would stand and worship with uplifted hands sometimes for an hour or so with the power of God very evident in our midst. And the ministry, well, it was some of the best that I have ever sat under. The messages were not filled with just "religious speak," as we often had heard in Pentecostal circles, but contained the scriptural "nuts and bolts" needed for daily Christian living. Truly the gospel came alive in ways I had not noted since my days of sitting under Pastor Hagee's ministry in San Antonio. Pastor Redman was an exceptional speaker in his own right, in fact one of the best, but he had never fully embraced the charismatic move as Shirley and I had, so we were feasting on the Word that we were now receiving. But, it did not take long for me to begin to get antsy, as I missed the close fellowship of a true home church such as we had enjoyed at Full Gospel. We both longed to attend a church wherein we could sink our roots, one located near our home. Like Full Gospel, New Covenant was just too far away to get involved on any kind of regular basis and I knew that.

For me the solution was very easy, but for Shirley it was very hard. Less than a mile from our home was the Second Baptist Church, a nice church with a congregation about the size of Full Gospel, with a ministry that was not great, but certainly one that was acceptable and biblical on the essentials of the Faith. The worship was much more formal than that found at Full Gospel or at New Covenant, but this was not an issue for me. It was, however, an issue with Shirley; in fact, it was a big issue. After attending a couple times I was ready to try it for the long haul. Shirley would have no part of it and insisted that we make the drive back to Fairview Heights for "real church." I just couldn't do it. In retrospect, this clash between us, which was never resolved, was much more serious than even I thought as it kind of signaled the beginning of the downward spiral that our marriage would take.

The Searching Years 1978-1982

It was around this time, late 1977 or early 1978, that Shirley woke in the middle of the night with a frightful dream that plagued her for weeks, perhaps months. She said that in her dream she was literally in a life and death struggle wrestling with Satan who was trying to steal Dionne and Marc out of her arms. She said the battle was intense, but that as she was awakening, she sensed a voice saying to her that Satan was in a battle with us for the lives of our children and that their only hope was for us to faithfully pray for them. I can close my eyes today and still visualize her face, an expression of intense fear and agony. She said that it was the most vivid dream that she had ever had and that she was very frightened for the kids. I tried to comfort her, but I did not put too much stock in the dream; in retrospect, we both should have!!

In the spring of 1978 Disco Fever was in full bloom; it was a contagious fever and we caught it. With the release of the movie, *Saturday Night Fever,* and the accompanying Bee Gees' sound track, the fever intensified. We had heard about a club that was "hot" atop the Marriott Hotel just across Interstate 70 from Lambert International Airport. One Saturday night we made arrangements with a baby sitter and headed out to the club, passing New Covenant Fellowship on our way. I'll never forget the blast of pure excitement and adrenalin that hit me full face as we walked through the door of the club to the rhythmic sounds of the Tramps and their pulsating hit, *Disco Inferno.* The fever grabbed us both as we watched the dancers move about the floor as if possessed by the beat of the music. After getting our drinks and finally finding a table, it was not long until our nerve was such that we too hit the floor. I must say, it was a tremendous high for me, and not so much the alcohol, but the music hit me perfectly and I was hooked. Little did I know that at this precise moment this "fever" would be the tonic, if not the vehicle, that would carry our marriage

Life Between Innings

to its smashing conclusion. I was hooked, but Shirley became really hooked by the whole scene, and our lives quickly, in fact very quickly, began to unravel and go in different directions.

I cannot recall any specific event or occasion in early 1978 that I can point to and say this is the issue where the wall began to form between us, except for our standing issue over where to attend church. The church issue was hanging out there unresolved, I was working as much overtime as I could get for financial reason and was at school during most evenings. We began to frequent the discos a little more and Shirley had hooked up with a couple that was teaching the various disco dance steps. We both were drinking more than we previously had, but not to excess. We really did not argue that much and there were no outward signs, per se, that trouble for us was just over the horizon. But, it was noticeable enough to us both that we decided to seek some counsel from my father-in-law, Pastor Redman. This was kind of hard for me to do but I made the call requesting an appointment for a Sunday afternoon. I explained to him briefly what we wanted to discuss; I think we were both surprised that he put us off as he *had some other important issues to take care of.*

Helen, my mother-in-law, was a little more sensitive to our need and arranged for us to meet with a visiting minister at the church who was renowned for his marital counseling abilities. We were both anxious to meet with him but we both came away chuckling as we were totally astounded at his lack of insight or help. His final words of encouragement, after talking for about an hour or so about really nothing was, *I have met with a number of young couples like you and have found that the best solution is just to go home and make love to each other.* That was it. That was his counsel. As we got back in the car and headed back home we actually laughed out loud together; sex was not a problem for us, in fact we were both rather liberated in that

The Searching Years 1978-1982

area, but getting through this stale period in our relationship, or whatever it was, was no closer to being resolved after his "insightful counseling" than it was before we received it.

As the month of May, 1978 came into focus, softball was starting back up, the spring term at school was ending, finances were still tight, we had not come to an agreement on a home church and our relationship was not improving. I am not sure what brought it on but one evening we did have a rare, but rather intense argument, which resulted in her asking the one question that should not be asked in the heat of any conflict and that is, *Do you still love me?* I also made the fateful mistake in answering that question a little too honestly in that I replied rather emphatically, *I really don't know!* At that point, all hell broke loose!! The immediate suspicion was that I must be involved with another woman, which was totally untrue. I had been true blue, without exception, throughout our marriage, and her unfounded jealousies were something we had to deal with from time to time. Even though our marriage had gotten off to an inauspicious start some 10 years prior, the thought of actually having an affair did not even compute with me. At this stage of my life I would not have even known how or where to start one; I really wouldn't have.

Somehow we managed to coexist over the next few days until that fateful "Mother's Day" a few days later. For Mother's Day we had invited my mom to come down after church so that we could take her to lunch. That spawned an argument in and of itself. By inviting mom to lunch on Mother's Day I had somehow ... *dishonor her, who was my wife and the mother of my children, by showing honor to my mother over her.* Don't ask.

Mom arrived and we headed out Interstate 55 to Ozora, Missouri, to Frieda's, a local family restaurant well known in the area for its outstanding buffet and fried chicken. Upon arriving we found the waiting list way too long and so we

Life Between Innings

decided to travel over to New Bloomsfield, a small town not too far back up the road. After locating a small, but nice restaurant on the main street, we sat down to eat. Just as our meal was served, for absolutely no reason, in fact just totally and completely out of the blue, Shirley blurted out, *Janie, Leo says he does not love us anymore and wants to leave us!* Wow!! Talk about dropping a bomb right in the middle of the salad; I was speechless and totally taken aback at this abrupt, blindsided allegation. Through all our arguments over the past few days, not once had I said I did not love the children or that I was desirous of leaving or planning on leaving. The fact is, I had never even given it a moment of serious consideration, that is, until that very moment!

Obviously, I stumbled through some verbiage about how the allegations were not true. Quickly, in deafening silence, we finished our lunch, paid the bill and took mom back to her car. I don't think mom even said good-bye as she knew this was not a time for pleasantries. Once in the house, hell broke loose like it had never broken loose before. Through the years, our home had seen very little yelling or anger-induced fits of rage. This day was to be the exception. We were both screaming at each other as I was utterly beside myself over the inappropriateness of her comments to my mother. Somewhere in the middle of the screaming, she came at me with arms swinging wildly. I avoided her punches but was able to grab her arms and held them tight as a scramble ensued for several minutes. She went absolutely wild and I had to literally wrestle with her to keep her from inflicting some serious pain on me. I later was accused of hitting her, which was totally untrue; the bruises that she had on her arms and upper body were strictly from the tightness of the grip that I had on her and her arms as she was flailing at me as I was trying to bring her under control. It was a wild scene. Not to make light of the situation

The Searching Years 1978-1982

but it was somewhat reminiscent of one of the fight scenes in the movie *The War of the Roses*.

After things calmed down a bit, for the first time I actually began to consider leaving. The more I thought about it the more the idea had merit. As darkness began to set in and the tension of the day still hanging heavily over our heads, I abruptly decided to leave. It didn't take too long for me to pack up about all that I needed, throw it into the Pinto Station Wagon and leave. I was not sure where I was going but I was going. That first night I found a little motel in Festus on the main drag in town and was actually surprised at how much I enjoyed the peace and quiet that surrounded me that night. I obviously did not have the money to live in motels every night so I began to stake out some of the more secure areas in the local commuter parking lots where I could sleep. Sleep did not always come easy but I got enough to get by. For most of that first week I would awaken in time to find one of the cleaner filling station rest rooms in the area to clean up in and then head out to work. I had too much pride to acknowledge to anyone, especially family, that I was now separated from my wife and living out of my car. And, it was not obvious to any of those that I worked with, as I did not miss work, nor was I tardy, nor was I physically unkempt.

Late in that week Bill Dorner, who I was playing softball with but really did not know all that well, stopped me and said he couldn't help but notice that I had "my stuff" stashed in my car. He went on to say that the signs were very obvious to him as he had recently separated and became divorced from his wife and he too had carried his belongings in the back seat of his car for sometime. He asked me where I was staying and I finally acknowledged that I was living out of my car. He very graciously offered to let me stay a few days in his home. Thankfully, Bill was very insistent and I finally acquiesced. It was nice, so very nice, to be able to take a hot shower and sleep in a nice cozy bed again. Bill was a Godsend for me as I am not sure where I would have eventually gone or what I would have eventually done if it had not been for his friendship.

As the weekend was coming to a conclusion I finally made contact with Shirley and we discussed our situation in some detail. Not much was resolved but we were both civil to each other, which helped. We also decided that regardless of what transpired between us we needed to sell the house and move back into the St. Louis area. It was also decided that I would move back in, which I did. We put the house up for sale and got a buyer much quicker than what we had expected. In fact, after all was said and done we even made a little profit off of the deal.

With the house sold we moved to 5250 Salinas Valley Drive in the Sesson Woods Apartment Complex in South St. Louis Country. For a short period of time we found some peace and tranquility. As August rolled in Shirley became acquainted with several ladies in the area who were "enjoying" their divorces. The timing was not real good as there were still many unresolved issues between us, despite the current "cease fire." With their urging, I was taken aback one evening when Shirley asked me what I thought about her going on a date with some guy that the girls were anxious to "fix" her up with. I suppose the wisdom of my response could be questioned, but I simply replied that if that was something she wanted to do, do it. My rationale was that if that was what was truly in her heart to do, my "yes" or "no" was not going to stop her or change much. She went. While she went out, I had a great evening with the kids, as we took in a *Three Stooges Festival*, with several of the features in 3-D, at the Tivoli Theatre in University City. The kids loved it as I did. Not only did it become one of the more memorable evenings for me and the kids, it was also

The Searching Years 1978-1982

memorable in that this evening marked the beginning of the end for our marriage.

After Shirley's date I figured I really needed to get away. A few days later Shirley and I sat down with Dionne and Marc to tell them I was leaving. The kids were ages eight and six so I am not sure what all they understood but they knew enough to understand that Daddy was leaving and would probably not be living with them for awhile, if ever. The event was very tearful, as you might imagine. The date was September 1, 1978. I left the apartment after our little meeting and headed out to St. Charles, Missouri. My sister, Bonnie, who became my angel of mercy during this very dark hour, had extended an invitation to me to move in with her and her kids in her duplex if I wanted. I wanted!

Bonnie's gracious welcome into her home was very much appreciated. She had recently gone through an emotionally tough divorce as her husband, Gary, the Pastor of Christian Fellowship Center in north St. Louis County (formerly the Carsonville Full Gospel Tabernacle that I grew up in as a teenager), had ran off with one of the deacon's wives. The details of their affair were something right out of a drugstore novel. Bonnie was left to try to raise her two kids, Dewayne and Cassie, on a shoestring as Gary obviously lost his job as Pastor and could not offer much immediate financial support. Bonnie's two bedroom apartment was taken obviously by her and the kids but she made a place for me in the basement. Now this basement was no palace as it was damp and dingy, and did I mention damp? But for the next year this became home, and a very much appreciated home at that. At the time, mom was still single but there was no way that I would have gone to live with her. She would have welcomed me, I am sure, but I would have slept in my car, living on the street, before I would have "bothered" her with my troubled life.

Life Between Innings

Bonnie had just begun dating a guy named Joe (McKee) about the time that I moved in with her. Joe was a job-shopper, an Electrical Engineer that Bonnie had met while working as a secretary for one of the job shops in the area. Joe was contracted at McDonnell-Douglas and was scheduled to be in St. Louis only a short time, a short time that extended out over seven years.

It just so happened that Joe had to be out of town that first weekend, which included Labor Day, so Bonnie and I were stuck trying to entertain each other as best we could. Bonnie and I now joke and laugh about how horrible a day this was, but at the time it was truly the worst day, the longest day, the most miserable day of my entire life. As I later described to Bonnie, I would rather drink cod liver oil straight from the bottle than to experience such a day again. We were both broke, so we could not splurge on any fancy foods, or even get a good drunk going, if we had been so inclined. I think Bonnie did have some chicken pieces that we put out on our pitiful little grill. It was pathetic, an absolutely pathetic day! The hours lingered on much like the hours of the day in the Old Testament story where God held the sun and moon in place, not allowing the sun to go down nor the moon to rise up, so that Joshua would have the light he needed to continue to fight (Joshua 10:13). Being "thankful" on that day simply meant it was time to go to bed. I could hardly wait to fall asleep, awaken and get back to work and into some kind of routine. Finally, the *Holiday from Hell* was over and I was in bed and I did go to sleep. Thank goodness for sleep!!

It was during this time that I found out how to live on basically nothing. All my salary went to buying gasoline for the car, paying the bills for Shirley and keeping me supplied with peanut butter as my main, if not my only, means of sustenance. I was careful not to complain because the stress of not

The Searching Years 1978-1982

living at home was diminishing day by day. Other than missing the kids, I was happy to be away from it all.

Since Shirley needed the Pinto Station Wagon for her needs, I rushed out to find a car ASAP. Not having much money I finally settled on a little brown, kind of purplish, 1974 GMC Gremlin. The Gremlin was perfect for my needs, but as I was soon to find out, it was not perfect for my wallet. I am not sure I had ever heard the words "Freeze Plugs" until I purchased this car but I soon found out that you are not going to drive a vehicle if the freeze plugs are not in place. Three times I had to have the car in the shop to have the freeze plugs worked on. The first time I was able to stretch some dollars and pay for it myself. The second and third time, my precious mother came to the rescue without me asking. It was the only time in my adult life that I ever let her help me financially, but it was sure appreciated and was a grace that was never forgotten.

It was early on a Saturday morning in October that I received a call from Shirley asking that I come and pick up the kids as she was sick and could not properly look after them. I did as was requested and picked up the kids and returned back to St. Charles. Late Sunday, I returned the kids back to the apartment without suspecting that anything was awry. I guess I was surprised, but not overly so, when she revealed that her sickness was only a ruse so that she could spend Saturday night with her date from several weeks back at his apartment. When I asked why she had done such a thing, the only response that I got was that she knew that I would be doing the same thing myself, sooner or later. That revelation closed the book on our marriage and I never ever again considered trying to work it out. Up to that point it still had not sunk in that this whole process was likely to end in divorce; now, it was only how soon!

Life Between Innings

It was amazing what had transpired in such a short time. In less than a year we had gone from what appeared to most outsiders as the perfect couple who attended church with two beautiful kids, a nice car in the driveway of an equally nice home, to a separated couple with alcohol, drug and relationship issues that were not going to be worked out.

About three to four weeks or so following "the revelation," I received a call late in the day at work from my supervisor saying that I was to report to the Guard Shack at the Rush Island Plant entrance. I could not imagine for what reason I was being called there. Upon arrival, I was met by an officer of the law who asked my name. Upon reply, he handed me a summons that stated that I was being sued for divorce. I think that somehow Shirley had convinced her parents that I was involved with another woman and they had given her the money to file. Again, nothing could have been further from the truth. Yet, as I received those papers I can't honestly say that I was disappointed that the process had begun. I was a little embarrassed to be served at my place of employment; I found being served in front of my peers being a little demeaning. Her only response to that question was, *I didn't know where else to have it done.* I guess she forgot I had an address in St. Charles.

I contacted a lawyer and, of course, Shirley was already in contact with hers. My lawyer convinced me of what was in store, what kind of child support I could expect and that I could expect to walk away with all the bills. Consequently, he did not think I had much to lose, since I was going to lose everything anyway, should I want to work jointly with her attorney. I lucked out, to say the least, as I would never recommend that anyone go through a divorce proceedings without an attorney specifically looking after their own needs. Call it being lucky, unlucky or whatever, but when the final divorce draft was written, I had truly lost everything except the clothes on my

The Searching Years 1978-1982

back and my little Gremlin, with the exception of a few key, but important, personal items of which I was able to negotiate.

Since the papers had been filed, I wanted to push the process along as fast as possible. Shirley on the other hand wanted to drag the process out asking for "separate maintenance." Success on her part would mean that I would be required to pay all her bills, child support and rent for an extended, and unspecified, period of time. However, there was no way that I wanted to play that game so I insisted on pushing the process through as I wanted this over by year's end if at all possible. After a number of "bumps" in the road, translated as calls from her and her attorney, a date was set, canceled, set again, canceled, and then finally set for December 28, 1978. I could not think of a better Christmas present, as cruel as that might sound.

As noted, during the process I received many calls from Shirley, and at times her attorney, badgering me over money and kid issues. I was paying all her bills and I was doing as best by the kids as I could, taking them every other weekend, and glad to do so. I had even agreed to her moving to an even better apartment with a higher price tag to help keep the peace. The calls would come at all hours of the night and it was very obvious that prior to many of the calls she had been drinking heavily. Several times the attorney would call me and complain about the "bitch" that wouldn't leave him alone. It was almost funny at times hearing him complain about the frequent late night calls he was getting. I figured that at least he was getting paid to take the calls and I wasn't; better him than me.

Finally, the big day came and I arrived at the St. Louis County courthouse in Clayton to meet with the attorney and Shirley prior to going into court. She had made two major concessions that I was eager to sign off on in exchange for a fairly

Life Between Innings

nice, and not unreasonable, child support obligation and my agreement to allow her to take the children out of state to set up a new residence. Again my wisdom can be challenged here for allowing her to do this, but despite all of our recent issues, she had always been a good mom who took exceptional care of the children. I also did not think it fair that I try to control her life or tell her where she could live and work. In return she had agreed that for the price of one dollar, she would never come after my pension or seek any alimony. Plus, she had also agreed that since I was paying child support, I could take the tax deduction for both of the kids on my annual income tax form. I was very appreciative of the fact that she was willing to move on those two major issues and avoid a contentious fight. Of course I had to agree to be responsible for the $7,000 of debt that we had which was mainly bills associated with the new furniture that we had purchased when we moved into the home in Festus and the remaining amount due on the Pinto. I had no clue how I was going to pay for all this, and live on my own as well, as my income by this time was stretched to the max. But again, I was not going to complain; I was at peace literally and figuratively with my decision.

I am really not sure what occurred on that morning at the courthouse just prior to the time that we were supposed to go before the judge, but something certainly had happened. Following a private meeting between Shirley and the attorney, the attorney came up to me in a huff and stated emphatically, *I quit! I have had all of that bitch that I am going to take! I am sorry to do this to you, but I've had it with her!* I immediately went into "negotiation mode" trying to convince him that quitting now, after putting up with all her late night calls, all of her non-sense, all of her aggravation, meant that she "won" and that he would not get paid a single nickel for all his work and aggrava-

The Searching Years 1978-1982

tion. Finally he settled down, and to my great relief, agreed to go forward. Close call!

If it wasn't so sad it would have been funny when we finally reached the courtroom. The judge put Shirley on the stand first and her attorney began to question her. When she would respond to his questionings, the attorney would say, *Speak up, I can't hear you,* in very terse tones. Finally the judge had his fill of the attorney and told him that he could hear her fine and to move on. Fortunately, he did. My turn went smoothly and the gavel finally dropped; *Divorce granted!!*

As we left the courtroom to go into the hallway to say our goodbyes, her attorney stopped me, stuck out his hand and said, *Young man, I have no idea how much money this divorce has cost you, but it is worth every penny!* With that, he turned and hastily shuffled off on down the hallway and out an exit door, never to be seen again. He was truly a beaten man on this particular day.

Shirley had contacted her brother Don, a successful businessman in Atlanta, who had agreed that she could come there to stay until she could find work and get set up. The next morning, December 29, 1978, Shirley, Dionne and Marc met with me at mom's house for a tearful goodbye. With the Pinto packed to the hilt, I waved as the kids drove away. Life for them would never be as it was. I am sure the kids were hurting much more than I thought or could imagine, but at this point I was helpless to do anything. They were gone, the nightmare was over, at least I thought.

Soon after arriving in Atlanta, Shirley took on a job as a cocktail waitress. After about three months she met a guy at the bar named Dave who worked for United Parcel. Three months after that meeting I received a call that she and Dave had gotten married. I couldn't have been happier . . . for me!

Life Between Innings

Shortly before the divorce I was introduced to Sandra Meador. Sandra, whose nickname was Sam, was a beautiful, full-blooded Indian lady, who had been raised on an Indian reservation in Arizona as a young girl; we hit it off quickly. I am not proud of the fact but we did start seeing each other late in the year prior to the divorce; after the divorce, we were seeing each other regularly. From the first few hours that we were together it just seemed a very comfortable fit for us both. About three months in she broached the idea of moving in together and later marriage. I was not ready for such a commitment and there were just too many pieces that did not fit together for me. First and foremost was the fact that she was not a Christian (not that my life much exemplified Christian principles by this time), although she was very interested in religious things. I later discovered that those interests, however, were headed in the wrong direction as she had strong leanings toward the Mormon faith. The Mormons hold some of the mystical ideas that true-blooded Indians commonly hold to.

Sam was also a heavy marijuana smoker, something acceptable, if not spiritual, on the reservation. This was also a practice conducive to her Mormon leanings, howbeit not the Mormon's doctrine. However, it was no sudden revelation to discover that when she was high, she was absolutely a wonderful woman. When she wasn't high, she had a strong penchant for being, can I say it, a real bitch. The fact that I did not want to get high became a major obstacle in our relationship. I did try a couple times to get high with her but I never succeeded; somehow I just could not get the hang of inhaling properly. Darn the luck!

From the beginning Sam encouraged me to quit college and follow her into the job shop field working as a blueprint draftsman. She had found this work to be lucrative for her and

The Searching Years 1978-1982

her brothers and saw it as a way for us to stay together and for me to upgrade my employment. It was a vocation very similar to what Joe McKee, my future brother-in-law, was doing. I was not so inclined to follow her lead, due in some part to the fact that I still needed the extra money afforded me through the GI Bill. After moving in with Bonnie, I had transferred my credits from Belleville Junior College and Jefferson Junior College and began taking classes at Meramec Junior College located in Kirkwood, Missouri, a suburb in St. Louis County. I was also in the early stages of considering things that I should be doing to get my life back on course and this seemed to be one of the positive things I needed to do.

It was during this time that I had become involved in union leadership at the Rush Island plant, which Sam did not like. Craig Phillips was serving as the Shop Steward for the Stationmen Gang when I first arrived at Rush Island. After a couple months, Craig was trained and temporarily promoted into the Operations Department for vacation relief, so he asked if I would be willing to fill in for him during his absence. I was a little bit leery, as I was still not too sure about unions and what all they allegedly do, but I agreed to help out. During this interim period I found that I actually enjoyed the work and found that the Company was not all that difficult to work with. Not soon thereafter, Craig received a permanent job in Operations so some of the guys asked if I would consider running for the vacated Shop Steward's position. Looking over some of the other candidates and deciding that some of these guys I would not want balancing my checkbook, let alone making decisions that could impact my job or career, I decided to run. I won my first election in a landslide and began working with the new Chief Steward of the Plant, Carmen LaPresta. Carmen was a 100% bona fide union man who could argue anything, and while doing so, leave you believing that he truly

Life Between Innings

believed whatever it was that he was arguing. There were times in meetings I could hardly keep a straight face as his arguments seemed to be really "off the wall." There were other times that I was actually embarrassed at the position that he would take on some issues as they seemed to be so unrealistic and so far-fetched as to be believable, let alone acceptable by management or any other reasonable person. However, I learned a tremendous amount from him. Over the ensuing months and years, Carmen became a very good friend and later proved very influential in getting me involved in Union Business as a career choice.

Sam's saving grace was that she wanted me to gain weight as she felt that I was too skinny; her theory was that real men had a little bit of a tummy. At this time in my life I could actually wear a muscle shirt, the result of a lot of sit-ups, push-ups and a daily running regimen that several of us guys at work had started to do during our lunch-hour. However, it was time to really concentrate on getting my life back in some semblance of order and that was not going to happen with her around.

Sam and I continued to see each other until September of 1979. At one point I finally came to the realization that the reason I had felt so comfortable in this relationship was that it was one in which I was very familiar; duh, it was one like that which I had just come out of. It was hard to do but I finally made my break and just simply quit calling her. The tough part about any break-up, even the ones that you want to make, is those first few days and weeks when the loneliness sets in. Finally one evening, out of the blue, she called me at work to see why I was no longer calling; we agreed to meet together for dinner that weekend. I reluctantly went. About half way through the dinner she acknowledged that she was bored. That was all I needed to hear as I was bored too. I paid the bill,

The Searching Years 1978-1982

took her back to her residence and said good-bye; I didn't even bother to walk her to the door. That was the last I ever saw of her. It was a strange departure to say the least. I didn't dislike her, I just didn't like being around her and her condescending attitude anymore.

Just as my relationship with Sam was coming to an end, I received a tremendous opportunity to improve my financial status and get out from behind the indebtedness that I had incurred from the divorce. Union Electric had a bidding procedure in place that had just been modified by the last union contract that would allow me to bid, by my Local 148 seniority, to any starting job in the line of promotion within the UE system. A bid came available at the Labadie Power Plant in June of 1979 for a Control Attendant Operator (CAO), a job that paid very well, plus had more overtime than I could possibly want. The bid finally came to me, which I readily accepted, but I had to wait for a CAO training class to start before Rush Island would release me. Finally, in mid July I was released to start my 9-weeks of training at Labadie. I was told by a lot of the guys that I had worked with at Rush Island that I would hate Labadie as Labadie was not known to be worker friendly, and neither were the people. As it turned out, I enjoyed the people and the job. Out of all the plants that I worked during my career, Venice, Rush Island and Labadie, Labadie became my favorite place to work.

My move to Labadie coincided with my sister Bonnie's marriage to Joe. Bill Dorner's roommate and friend, Dave Bell, had just gotten remarried so Bill was looking for a new roommate. One year from the September 1st date I had moved in with my sister in St. Charles, I moved in with Bill in his South St. Louis home in Affton at 9603 Dana. This was a major upgrade from the basement home at Bonnie's; it was dry for one thing. Bill had a lot of my characteristics in that he liked the place to look neat. Without it ever being said I kind of took over the chore of keeping the house straight inside and Bill took care of the outside work and yard. Like me, Bill worked rotating shifts, and we now worked in two different power plants, so we did not really see each other all that often except on the softball diamond.

Bill was a rather quite man in social circles, not at all like the demonstrative demeanor that he displayed on the softball diamond. Bill had a few detractors but he quickly became a very good personal friend. Bill was also not one to stick his nose into my personal affairs; however, one day he made a statement that in many ways altered my thinking from that day till now. Whatever the issue was that we were discussing was irrelevant; but, right in the middle of it he simply stated, *Leo, if you think you played no part in this divorce happening to you and that it was all her fault, you will find yourself making the same mistakes again.* While not necessarily profound, it was exactly what I needed to hear because up to that point I had pretty much put the total blame on Shirley.

While living with Bonnie I had developed a practice of driving up to Pierre Marquette State Park over in Illinois, taking the scenic Highway 100, known as the River Road, located past Grafton about 35 miles or so from Alton, Illinois. Being broke it was a good place to spend a relaxing day sitting under a very large oak tree out in front of the lodge. Here I truly began to re-draft my life, making decisions that would impact me until now. This is where I developed the "Game Plan" that I hoped would right my ship. After moving in with Bill, I still continued to drive to this beautiful place to reflect and Bill's words often rang in my ears as I considered the errors that I had made in my life and in my marriage.

After my move from Bonnie's to Bill's, I became keenly aware that my time was once again becoming a premium. I

The Searching Years 1978-1982

think the busyness that my life took on, as I was to working my way out of the mess that I had somehow created for myself, was, however, good for me mentally. The very first night that I went on line (started working in lieu of training) at Labadie, I was given my first overtime opportunity, which I readily accepted. That was followed by more overtime opportunities than I could handle, although I rarely ever turned an opportunity down. I had just purchased a used, but very nice, auburn colored, 2-door, 1977 Cutlass Calais, which like my move into Bill's home, was a major upgrade from the old Gremlin that I had been nursing along. Plus, while God had somehow helped me to meet all my monthly bills up till now, I was not making much of a dent in them, so the new job came at just the right moment. Consequently, I was either working, attending classes at Meramec, playing softball or, yes, attending church. While I certainly was not living a life that a Christian should live, I had come to recognize that even in this unfortunate spiral that my life had taken, I needed the balance of my Christian faith to keep me going. Unless I was working, I somehow found myself in the House of God each and every Sunday.

Upon moving in with Bonnie, I began to attend the First Assembly of God Church there in St. Charles. I liked the worship and the preaching but I never truly felt accepted. They did not have a ministry for the divorced people of their community and I kind of felt that the people, for the most part, were a little standoffish. But, I really did not know where else to go. Actually, New Covenant Fellowship was not that far from our place in St. Charles but there were just too many people who knew me and had known me in "a different light" still attending there; I knew going there would not be comfortable. I wasn't actually in hiding from all of my old Christian friends and acquaintances, but I wasn't exactly making it easy for them to find me if, in fact, they were looking. So, even though

Life Between Innings

it was a little bit of a drive from Bill's home in South St. Louis, each Sunday morning, unless I was working, I would point my car back into the direction of St. Charles to go to church.

It was during this time that I began to deal with something that I would have never thought possible in my religious existence. Even after Shirley was married and living some 700 miles away, the calls from her continued to come. I eventually became afraid to even answer the phone, as I did not want to get into it with her over money. In fact, the calls became so frequent and left me so agitated that I ordered a second phone line to be installed, which I dedicated strictly to her calls, and those from work. At this point, I was accepting overtime when offered while at work, but did not want to be bothered with it once I reached home. Consequently, when that phone rang, I just never answered it, as I did not want to hear from Shirley or work. However, by having the extra phone, it freed me up to take calls from friends, family and businesses I had given the number and from others whom I wanted to hear. And fortunately, I had set up my child support payments to go directly to a governmental agency that would receive my payments and then forward them on to her. I was regular as clockwork with those payments and really liked the idea that I did not have to personally communicate with Shirley over them. But, finally, it reached the point that I realized that I had actually come to "hate" this woman. Till then, I thought it was impossible for me to hate anyone as it just wasn't in my nature, at least I thought. But not now, even the mere thought of her made me cringe and the hatred for her grew day by day.

Finally, one night, driving back home to Affton from First Assembly in St. Charles, probably sometime around February or March of 1980, God broke my heart and shattered the hatred I had built up for her. I was driving south on Interstate 270, just approaching the bridge that runs over Marshall Road, when I

The Searching Years 1978-1982

finally prayed, for the very first time, asking God to forgive me for the part that I had played in the divorce. At that very moment all that hatred, all the bile, all that anger that had been building up over the months in my heart and spirit, broke and gushed out in the form of large sobs and tears. I'll never forget that experience. I have often traveled over that bridge, in that my apartment and the two homes I've purchased since, all are located in the Manchester area near that Marshall Road overpass. Even to this day, as I drive through that area, it is not unusual for me to silently think to myself that this is where God met me and broke me; and thankfully He did.

While Shirley and I have not always seen eye to eye since that time, I can honestly say that by God's grace I no longer hate her or even dislike her. In fact, not that I should receive any merit badges for it, but I have been able to pray asking God's favor on her through the years, and mean it. During a visit that she made to St. Louis several years following the Marshall Road bridge experience, we had the chance to mutually ask for forgiveness from each other for the part that we played in the dissolution of our marriage; I thank God for that opportunity. For the most part, we have been able to work out a variety of issues regarding the kids through the years in a very respectful manner, which I also greatly appreciate. To God be the thanks and glory and praise; Amen!!

By this time I was starting to really get into school. It was no longer just something to do to earn some extra dollars but I could actually see that an Associates Degree (AA) in Business was not that far fetched of an idea. In fact, I could see that if I stayed the course I could actually graduate sometime in 1980. I no longer was taking "throw away" courses but was meeting with the counselors to make sure that I was taking the classes that counted.

Life Between Innings

Though I had moved to Labadie, I continued to play softball for the Rush Island team. We continued to play at the Pevely complex through 1978 but there was a growing desire by most of the guys to start competing in the Union Electric Industrial League that was played at the renowned "UE Country Club" in Valley Park. The Company actually paid a full- and part-time staff to help maintain and prepare the field, which they did very nicely. With its short right field fence, and with me being a left-handed hitter, playing there was very appealing. The downside was that it was a much more competitive league than the one we had been playing in at the Pevely Complex. The fear that most of us shared was that we would simply get blown out of most games.

Before we made the final decision to move into the UE League we played our final season at Pevely under the banner of Syl's Cafe. Syl was the wife of Paul Huskey, Union Local 148's Vice-president, and the operator of a small Cafe in Arnold, Missouri. Craig Phillips was still managing our team, and with the new cash flow of having a sponsor, set out to purchase our new uniforms. Craig decided upon a full knit uniform with long pants and shirt; a really nice looking outfit. However, since we played like the *Bad News Bears*, it was often embarrassing to be playing in such nice duds.

One such occurrence happened in a pre-season double-elimination tourney held in Arnold. We showed up for our first game looking rather dapper in our new uniforms and found that the team we were to play was a rural team playing in jeans and, yes, bib overalls. In fact, several of the guys did not even have tennis shoes, let alone spikes, and were wearing nothing more than regular old boots. Our rural friends batted first and base hits were flying everywhere. Bill Dorner said he knew that we were in "serious trouble" when the runner on first base asked the umpire if the current hitter got to take a

304

The Searching Years 1978-1982

walk if "ball four" was called. How embarrassing. They didn't know the rules, they didn't look like softball players, and they didn't talk like softball players, yet they were kicking our collective asses. We were massacred!! Fortunately the mercy rule kicked in and we were able to get off the field quickly, but with our tails between our legs. What humiliation!!

Playing at Pevely created a lot of great memories for us, but not in the victory column. For a number of us we usually hit the local disco immediately after the game so I, like a few others, never wore a baseball hat; it would mess my hair, you know! There was also the problem of girl friends showing up uninvited to watch us play, such as in the case of Barry Sizemore, who had two show up unexpectedly at the same time. We also had to deal with the mouth on Randy Hyde's wife; she loved to come to the games but would never shut up. She was a very attractive looking lady with a boisterous, obnoxiously loud voice coupled with the most foul-mouth of any woman I have every met before or since. Even working with power plant guys, who create vulgar words and ways to use them on a daily basis, we were embarrassed for others to know she was rooting for us. None of us were too disappointed when Randy decided that his playing days were over after the 1978 season.

Then there was another pre-season game of note that we had with one of our rivals from the Festus/Crystal City area. On this particular day we were playing on one of the fields at the Festus Public Park located just across from the local Police Station. One of our opponents took exception to Bill Dorner running into one of their players in the base path and a brawl ensued. I was one of the first to come to Bill's aid and I immediately found myself on the bottom of a large heap of men. My arms were pinned down tightly and I found myself face to face with one of our combatants, who likewise had ended

Life Between Innings

up on the bottom of the pile. I was able to get one arm just free enough to where I could grab hold of this guy's cheek and give it a good squeeze and a pinch. Bob Meuth, a hulk of a guy, began moving bodies and pulled me out from under the pile. Bob quickly pulled me away and stood there just daring anyone to try to get at me. Thank goodness for Bob! Bob and I became very good friends from that day forward, in fact, very good friends. Funny how things work out. After the fight we would see these guys from time to time as they played in the same Pevely League that we did. They actually became good friends, often sharing a beer or two with us while we joked about our big fight in front of the police station.

We also had a problem in that Rush Island actually had enough people wanting to play that when the season began in 1980 there were more than enough to field two teams. By this time there were several of the guys that had become loyal to me and wanted to continue playing with me as the acting manager. These were the guys that were mostly competitive and more interested in competing than in just getting together around a game and drinking beer. So, we formed a new team called the *Islanders* that actually began to play a competitive game of softball. For the first year Tom Almany and Joe Kasmarzik played with us, but the following year they went back with the original Rush Island team. By this time I was firmly entrenched as the pitcher, Dave Bell was catching, Bill Dorner was at first, Burt Thompson at second, Jack Pritchard at short stop, Bob Meuth at third, Al Carron, Rich Boehm, Bob Lee, Vito Viviano and Mark Wilder playing the outfield. And, I, with each succeeding year, was actually getting better. With this particular group we did not win a championship but we were not slouches by any means. We knew that we were just a player or two away from having a championship caliber team but we did not know where we would find those players.

The Searching Years 1978-1982

In 1981, we decided to disassociate ourselves with Rush Island and the Islander team name as I had begun to recruit players who worked throughout the Union Electric system. Based on the fact that each of the plants was located on a river (Mississippi, Missouri and Meramec), we decided to become known as the *Rivermen*. We remained a competitive team but our best years were just ahead as those two or three players that we needed finally showed up.

As the winter of 1979 set in I was beginning to see my indebtedness decrease in measurable ways. In fact, in 1978, my last full year at Rush Island, I made $18,000. When I filed my taxes for 1979, and after working only 4 months at Labadie, I had doubled my wages to $36,000. In 1980, my first full year at Labadie, my wages increased to $52,000. Life was good, again. I was happy on all fronts.

After breaking it off with Sam in the early fall of 1979, I met an attractive young blonde at Meramec Junior College named Susan Schondelmeyer. We dated for only a few months as it was obvious we were going in two entirely different directions at this point in our lives. It was just after we stopped dating, however, that I entered into an agreement with myself that I would no longer date just one person at a time until I was fairly certain that I had found the person that I would likely settle down with. However, settling down, or at least marriage, was no longer a real interest to me. I had now been divorced for almost a year and was beginning to enjoy the single life and the independence that it afforded. The basis for my "agreement with myself" was that I had discovered in just two short relationships that what makes breaking away from an undesirable relationship difficult is that period of loneliness that immediately follows. It only stood to reason that if there were someone else with whom I could spend time with immediately following a "break-up," it would be much easier to break off an undesirable relationship. All I can say to the skeptics is that from that day until the day I became engaged in 1982, it worked for me.

From 1979 until 1982, when Tina and I became engaged, I was fortunate to date a number of really nice, very attractive women. To those who say that you cannot meet a really nice person in a bar, well, they are wrong. I met a number of nice ladies there and dated a few. Now, I would not advise this as a dating tactic or philosophy, I'm just saying that it did work OK for me. My philosophy was that I was not a "bad person" visiting a bar and thus it only stood to reason that there were most probably "some" good women that also visited a bar on occasion. Again, this is not good counseling; this is just the way it was for me.

On one such occasion in 1979, Bill and I had decided to go out together after a game and we stopped off at a local disco near the Dierbergs Center on Tesson Ferry Road. We were enjoying a drink and just watching others getting down on the dance floor when the DJ for the evening announced they were having a Hula Hoop Contest. Having performed with the Hula Hoop very well as a child, and of course with Bill's urging, I decided to enter. It was no contest. After a few rounds it was determined that I was the champ. With that, a table of girls began to pass by, then drop by, our table to offer congratulations. One of the ladies finally asked me if I would like to dance; I was more than willing to oblige. In the course of our dance I found that her name was Connie Lawrence, she worked at Maritz in their Business Travel Department, and that her mother's home was in Washington, Missouri, out by the Labadie Plant. She also volunteered, after discovering that I worked at the Labadie Plant, that her Dad had actually helped to build it; unfortunately, he had been killed on the job while doing so. She also admitted dating an acquaintance of

The Searching Years 1978-1982

mine for a short period that also worked at the Labadie Plant. Connie was a very attractive, blondish young lady with a nice laugh and a great smile. After a few more dances she offered me her telephone number.

On the way back to the house Bill began to question me if I intended to give Connie a call. I told him that I seriously doubted it, mainly because she had dated this acquaintance of mine and I thought that might be a little awkward. Bill called me an idiot and a few other names.

After several days I decided to give her call and she seemed genuinely glad to hear from me. We set a date and decided to go see the Bill Murray classic, *Caddy Shack*. I picked her up, we went to the movie and concluded the evening with dinner. By the end of the evening I found that I had just experienced the most wonderful, most fun-filled evening since my divorce. She and I soon became fast friends and began seeing each other two or three times a week. Working with Maritz Travel, she had to travel herself from time to time. Over the next two years she became the best friend that I had ever had up to this point in my life. She was the whole package. My family simply loved her. Her sense of humor fit so well with the family and her giving spirit made her a special lady. While she did not have a particularly strong faith in Christ, she did have a foundational Christian background. But, as Frank O' Pinion, a local radio personality likes to say, . . . in *life there is always a 'however.'* And, in this case, there was a *however.* I really cannot explain it but for whatever reason, regardless of the intimately wonderful and fun times we had just being together, regardless of the respect and love that I developed for her, it never developed into that special kind of "love" that needs to occur to translate into marriage. I had gone down that road in 1967; no way I was going to make that mistake a second time. Several days before Christmas in 1981, I broke it off. It was a very tearful parting and one of the toughest things that I have ever had to do!

Late in 1980 I met another attractive blonde at one of my favorite disco hangouts, Chio, out near the Lambert International Airport. It was a Halloween night and I had arrived about 8:00 PM following a day at work. I guess I had been sitting by myself for over an hour just watching the "talent" on the floor when this lady popped up in front of me and introduced herself as Linda Mues. Linda worked as a Shopper for *Lerner's*, a women's clothier, was a graduate from Missouri University and was obviously a very confident woman. She said that she had surmised that I was rather stuck on myself and therefore was not going to ask her to dance; so, she decided to ask me. We spent much of the remainder of the evening at the club with each other. As it came time to leave she handed me her card and suggested that I should call sometime.

Within a few days I called and we went out for dinner. We began to see each other on occasion, which was usually dependent on my odd work and school schedule and her travel. Like Connie, Linda was a very successful person in her own right, but much more daring and determined to tie me into a long-term relationship. With Connie traveling and no commitments between us, in fact I was very careful to keep that issue clear, the path was there to see where this relationship might take us. Linda did not have the patience that Connie had in allowing me the space I needed, or at least wanted, at this point in life. Sometime around Valentine's Day of 1981, Linda made it clear that she wanted to be the only person in my life and was going to work hard toward that end to make it happen. As much as I liked her and enjoyed her, I still was not ready to make such a commitment to her or anyone else. Shortly after that, without much fanfare, we decided to go our separate ways.

The Searching Years 1978-1982

Per my agreement with myself in 1979, I continued to put myself into position to meet a number of women, dating several off and on at the same time. Most of the women that I met and dated had marriage on their mind from day one, which sent me "exit, stage left," as quickly as I could get there. It was amazing to me how that after one or two dates I became the "boyfriend" and was scheduled to meet with the friends of these ladies immediately; this produced another quick exiting strategy for me. Quite frankly, had some of these ladies, such as Mel, Colleen and Dara, moved a little slower, I think one or two could have worked into a nice relationship, perhaps even one of some length. So, with few exceptions, most of the ladies I dated rarely got past the third or fourth date. The thing that I was most amazed at, and by this time I was no longer a prude, was how quickly many of these women wanted to shed their clothing. This will get a, "Yeah, right!," from the men in the audience, but it is the truth. While flattering on one hand, this often sent me running as well as I just wasn't comfortable moving that quickly from the batter's box to home plate; a slow slide into second would have been just fine. Such was life in 1979-1981. And then, I finally met Tina!!!!!

September had become my traditional month in which to make a move and September of 1980 was to be no different. In September of '78, I moved in with my sister Bonnie. In September of '79, I moved in with Bill Dorner. So, it was now September of '80 and it was time for me to move again. Bill Dorner and Patricia Kemlage had become engaged in the spring and had set a date for late August 1980 to get married. This time I decided I had had it with roommates and their penchant for getting married, so I decided to get my own place. Just like clockwork, one year from the date that I moved in with Bill, I moved into my new two-bedroom apartment at 1206-F Pinyon Drive in the Forest Lake East Apartment Complex in

Life Between Innings

Manchester, Missouri. This was a very exciting time for me as I gradually was able to buy all the furnishings that I needed to put a nice place together. My color scheme was very easy on the eyes as most everything was in earth tones. And, since I kept the place very neat, it was kind of a showcase for those who stopped by. In fact, many of the women who I dated that would come by were somewhat embarrassed to see how clean and neat my apartment was compared to their own. My mother once commented, as she made the tour, *My goodness, Leo, even your shoes are all lined up perfectly and in order.* I was glad she had not checked my refrigerator as all my Michelob Light was likewise lined up perfectly, the brand facing forward.

September 1980 also represented a significant milestone for me as I entered into my last semester, at least I thought, at Meramec Junior College. Upon completion of my last two courses I was scheduled to graduate with an Associate of Arts (AA) in Business in December. It was pretty cool. I finished the semester with a nice grade-point average and did in fact graduate that December of 1980. However, my counselor pointed out that I was just a few courses away from receiving another AA, this time in Communications, if I wanted to pursue it. By this time I was truly enjoying college and the decision was an easy one to make. I immediately re-enrolled and began to work on the new degree. In December of 1981, one year following my first degree, I was awarded the second Associates of Arts degree. Now, with the full wind of education in my sails, I enrolled at St. Louis University. St. Louis University took all the credits that they could from my junior college experience, leaving me about 18 months of dedicated study to receive my Bachelors Degree. The challenge was on!!

During the process of filling out my application for the apartment at Forest Lake I met Ginny Herbel, a dark haired, very darkly tanned lady who worked the desk in the office.

The Searching Years 1978-1982

Over the next month or two I would meet her as I would drop by to pay the rent. One day she stopped me and ask rather bluntly, *Are you dating anyone; that is, anyone special?* I replied that I was in fact dating a few women but no one that I would consider in the special category. She countered by stating, *Well, the reason I am asking, and I know that you will think I am just being prejudiced, but I have this beautiful, blonde daughter whose name is Tina that I think you should meet. I think you all probably have a lot in common. I see you jogging by the office from time to time and my daughter is also a runner. Would you like to meet her?*

I had enjoyed several blind dates over the past few months and actually found them intriguing, so I answered, *If she would like to meet, I think that would be great. But, be sure to tell her how old I am and that I am divorced with two children. If she still wants to meet, I will give her a call.* She stated that she would ask her daughter and see if it was alright to give me her phone number.

As I was out jogging a few days later Ginny came out of the office to meet me and gave me Tina's phone number. I am not sure why I waited, but it was several days before I decided to call. Upon calling, some lady, I guessed her roommate, answered the phone. I could hear people in the background talking but I could not hear what they were saying. The roommate politely responded that Tina was busy at the moment and perhaps I could call back at a later time. Several days later I called again; I got the same response.

A month or two passed and I dropped by the complex office to pay my rent. Ginny was there to receive the money and then proceeded to inquire if I had called Tina. I replied that I had called twice and "kinda got the brush off," so there was no purpose in calling further. I went on to say that I did not mean to sound egotistical, but getting dates was not a problem and I really had no reason, or quite frankly, any further desire to call her again. I went on to say that it was obvious to me that she

Life Between Innings

did not care to meet me, and that was OK. Ginny would have no part of this and insisted that she would have Tina call me, if that was OK. To end the conversation I said that it would be fine, and went on my way not really thinking any more about it.

It was now early in May of 1981 when I received a surprise call from Tina. I think her Mom was badgering her about me, primarily because she "hated" Jerry, Tina's current boyfriend. She had even offered to me at one point that she disliked this boyfriend so much that she was considering getting a "hit man" after him. I doubted that she was serious but nevertheless, who knew. Anyway, Tina had some tickets to the St. Louis Muny and she was calling inviting me to go. I explained that I had an important softball game (All softball games were important, even against the bad teams.) that night and could not go with her. As luck would have it, our game was rained out that very afternoon. As luck would further have it, I called Connie at work and asked if she would like to join me for supper at *People's Restaurant* at Highway 141 and Manchester Road. Little did I know that this was where Tina's mom liked to hang out with friends. Connie joined me for supper. Somewhere in the middle of our meal I noticed Tina's mother over on the far side of the restaurant. I played "dodge-em" with her for the remainder of the meal and got Connie and me out of there as quickly as possible.

A few days later in May I again encountered Ginny at the office and we went through the normal song-and-dance. She again insisted that I call and I promised I would. A few days later I called and for once actually got Tina on the telephone. We both decided that we would meet for a "5-minute date" at Gumba's, a popular club off Dorsett Road in the popular Westport area, and get this over with. The agreement was that we would meet, chat briefly, have a quick drink, and

The Searching Years 1978-1982

regardless of our initial impressions of each other, we would break it off after 5-minutes. This little date would then get her Mom off her back and mine. To be honest I was not expecting a whole lot as it was hard for me to imagine that Ginny, with her dark hair and dark complexion, could have an attractive blonde daughter anyway. The day for the big date came and I hurried home from work to get ready. However, this would prove to be another false alarm as Tina had left a voice mail on my recorder saying that something had come up and she would not be able to keep our date as scheduled. As far as I was concerned, this was now a dead issue.

But again, remember, in every life there is a "however," and mine came on Friday, May 15th, when I received a call from out of the blue from Tina asking if I would like to go with her and some friends to a Cardinal baseball game the next day. The Cardinals were playing the Los Angeles Dodgers and both Connie and Linda were out of town. Not having any plans, other than a mixed league softball game that afternoon, and with this sounding a little more definite than anything we had set up so far, I said, *Why not?* I told her that since I would be running a little late, as I would have to run home and clean-up after my game, I would rather just pick her up at her apartment and the two of us join her friends at the game. She agreed.

So, here it was, May 16, 1981, the date that Ginny had been scheming to arrange for nine months; our date was finally coming to fruition. Tina lived with two roommates in a very nice apartment complex, the Oxford, off Lindbergh Road out in the near North County area. I approached the door and knocked. Finally, the door opened and there standing in front of me was one attractive blonde female, the sight of which impressed me immensely. I was absolutely blown away. She invited me in and I was happy to find that she was not a roommate, but was in fact Tina, my date. She excused herself to go

Life Between Innings

finish getting ready while I became acquainted with her cat. This cat would eventually play a significant role in my not getting a first kiss for quite some time.

Finally, Tina was ready and we headed down Lindbergh Boulevard going south toward Highway 40 and then east to Busch Stadium. We had hardly gone a block or two when she sarcastically, but in a fun way, responded to something I said, and the ice was broken. We were about to embark on what would eventually be the best first date that I would ever have. It was also the last first date that I would ever have.

Upon reaching the ballpark we had obviously hit it off well and the conversation was flowing easily. We met up with her friends at the Musial Statue, and after a few pleasantries proceeded into the park. I took her hand as we walked along and told her, *Well, we might as well look like we know each other.* She did not object and away we went. For some reason our seats were not near her friends, in fact, our seats were only a row or two from the top of the nosebleed section along the first base side, high in the upper grandstands. However, we rarely watched the game as we sat and talked throughout. I think the Cardinals won something like 12-2, but who was counting? I was also impressed that she bought me a beer, something that most women would not have offered to do. I accepted.

Following the game we met up with Tina's friends at the Musial Statue, as planned. It became obvious to me, during the discussion that ensued, that they all wanted to go to a place called *Bogart's* in West County. It also seemed clear that Tina was not too anxious to go, and from what I could read between the lines, she knew that there was a good possibility of running into the "boyfriend," as this was a favorite hangout of his. Finally, I became a little tired, maybe silently irritated, at her friends for trying to put her, and quite frankly me, in that spot, so I offered that if she concurred I thought we would go

316

The Searching Years 1978-1982

somewhere else on our own. Tina readily agreed and we were off to our next adventure.

For some time one of my favorite hangout places was the Comedy Store over in Clayton. They featured a number of local stand-up comics, who were actually pretty good, plus they had a restaurant attached where we could have a fairly nice supper. We arrived and were seated and did, in fact, have a rather good meal. I noticed that Tina did not leave much on her plate and that she was not real shy about "packing it away." The conversation continued to flow easily and we were having a very good time. As it became time for the show to begin we were led to a front row table right smack in front of the stage.

The comedians were really on this night and we were laughing constantly. About midway through the show one of the comedians stopped right in front of us, and to make his point, he looked straight at us and said something like, ... *take this couple for instance; it is easy to see that they have known each other for a long time.* We lost it!

It was now about midnight and I started the drive back to her apartment. As we drove the conversation drifted into a religious vein. Tina revealed that she was Catholic and attended Mass regularly and had a keen interest in religious things beyond just the superficial. I did not reveal my "religious past," but I likewise confessed that I had a strong faith in Jesus Christ and that my Christianity had provided a tremendous balance in my life. As we reached her apartment I think we were both dismayed to find that Carol, one of her roommates, was up and doing her ironing. It was evident to both of us that we would have liked to continue the evening for a little while longer, but with Carol in the room it was not going to happen. I did not know at the time, but later discovered, that Tina had made her roommate promise to be there and to be awake when she got home just in case her date was a

Life Between Innings

psycho. Tina and I continued to date once or twice a week over the next few weeks. Soon after we met I found that she was planning on moving to California sometime in June to work in a doctor's clinic and that her long-term plans did not include a return to St. Louis.

The year of 1981 was continuing to be a very good year for me in all facets of life, but especially financially. Because of all the overtime work at Labadie, I was on a roll economically and my financial picture was becoming clearer every day. I had just purchased my first brand new car, a 1981 red Cutlass Supreme, and that very June, I paid off my very last bill, excluding my car payment. I could not believe how fortunate and blessed I had been. I had put in many overtime hours to help accomplish this, but nevertheless, accomplish it I had. When I sent in the check for my last bill the first of June, I would not work another overtime shift, by choice, for over 13 weeks. The next overtime shift that I worked was in September when I finally was "forced" on a day watch following my midnight shift. Those "mids" to "days" were ungodly to work and my love for overtime had bottomed out, at least momentarily. Finally, after working that forced double shift, I quickly got back into the groove and began to work my share once again. When I did my taxes for 1981, I was amazed to see that I had made over $60,000. I could not believe my blessings; from $18,000 to $60,000 in just 4 years. I was truly blessed again beyond deserving. For whatever reason, God was blessing me and I knew that it was nothing I merited or deserved; all I could do was simply say thanks to Him from whom all blessings flow!

As noted, Tina and I began to date with some regularity even though we knew that the relationship would be short term at best. Although I was a little leery about inviting women to any of my games, as women seemed prone to

The Searching Years 1978-1982

do the old "drop by" on occasion after that, often creating an embarrassing situation if another woman who had been invited, did come by. However, I decided to chance it and invited her to stop by the Country Club to watch a game. I was taken aback somewhat when she actually showed up; in fact, from the field I could not be certain it was she. I could see a blonde who kind of looked like her, but this blonde did not have the long flowing wavy hair that I had been telling the guys about; this blonde had hair but it was in the form of a tight bun. Don't get me wrong, she still looked really nice, even with the bun, but I strongly preferred the blonde that had the long flowing hair that looked so cool as it was blown carelessly in the breeze. Yes, it was a little superficial on my part but we did not have a true relationship going at this time, either. I never liked the bun and her father, Chuck, concurred. Chuck had long before me affectionately coined the phrase, *That Damn Bun,* and from time-to-time I borrowed this descriptive phrase from him.

I am guessing that over the few weeks remaining before her scheduled departure we had gotten together for about six or seven dates. We did just the casual things like dinner or a movie, our first movie being *On Golden Pond,* the old classic starring Henry Fonda, Jane Fonda and one of my favorites, Kathryn Hepburn; however, nothing was clicking romantically, or I should say, at least from the physical side. For whatever reason it did not seem to matter as I really enjoyed just spending time with her. But, on those occasions where a good night kiss seemed to be in order, something always happened to interfere with any legitimate attempt to make it happen. Even the cat conspired against me as she seemed to find her way into Tina's arms about the time I would be leaving. The cat made a fairly impenetrable shield that I just could not get through.

Life Between Innings

With my bills paid and school out for a few weeks, I decided that maybe I would accompany Tina in her move to California. Her parents liked me and they liked the idea that she would not be traveling that distance alone. The plan was to drive, starting on a Wednesday afternoon, reach Los Angeles by Friday night, help her find the home where she would be staying on Saturday and then fly back on Sunday. I decided to risk a little "sick leave" to accomplish this trek as I was leaving for vacation and Daytona Beach, Florida, the following Monday with Bob Meuth and Barry Sizemore. The year prior the three of us guys had taken a vacation to Daytona Beach together during the week of July 4th and had such a great time we had decided to do it again at the same time, same location.

The last week of June finally arrived and our plan was put into action. Tina stopped by my apartment and picked me up and away we went. She had a new Oldsmobile, a stick, which she had recently purchased but was too "cheap" or too poor to buy one with air conditioning. I was just hoping that when we crossed the desert it would be night or else we were going to be in serious trouble. Oh, and did I mention, she brought the cat?

We were barely 100 miles out of St. Louis when one of my cassette tapes became lodged in her player. Try as I might, it was not coming out. We were doomed, or blessed, as we were going to have to hold a conversation for the next 2000 miles. It actually turned out to be a blessing, plus we were able to finally get the radio to work at some point along the way.

Our first night we stayed at the Holiday Inn in Joplin, Missouri, with separate rooms. The second night we made it to Albuquerque, New Mexico, but it was kind of late when we arrived. We did not have a hotel reservation and our options were limited. We finally came upon a motel that looked rather safe, but soon found that all they had was one room with a double bed. We took it. She slept in her softball uniform and I slept in something similar as we remained nice and proper folks; she also remained un-kissed by me. On Friday we traveled through the day and fortunately did cross the desert during the PM hours. As we approached the outskirts of Los Angeles, it was very late and we were beat. We again found a room for the remainder of the night with pretty much the same sleeping arrangements as we had the night before.

The next morning we set out again on the Interstate to take the last 100 miles into Los Angeles. We really did not know at that point exactly where we were going to settle that night but we knew our trip was coming to an end as the sign loomed large ahead of us saying, *Interstate 10 Ends 1 Mile*. I'll never forget the awesome sight that we encountered as the road curved slightly to the right and through a small enclosed underpass to suddenly reveal an explosion of deep blues and bright whites as the sky, the Pacific Ocean and the glistening sandy beach jumped out to tantalize our eyes. It was an awesome sight that was hard to take in with all its beauty.

During our trip we had seen some other dazzling sights such as the awesome Grand Canyon, a small bit of the Petrified Forest and the beautiful earth tones of the snow-capped mountain ranges in New Mexico and Arizona, plus we discovered the Continental Divide. We also observed a cow walking beside the road in Arizona that happened to look up to gaze at us as we were driving by, only to trip like a real klutz, barely able to avoid falling down. This cow has forever become known to us as the *Arizona Cow* and comes up in conversations even today when one of us makes a klutzy move.

We used Saturday to kind of explore the area where Tina was to be staying and working. Both locations were very nice and certainly in a well-to-do part of town. Early that afternoon we found our hotel and checked in. By now we were

Life Between Innings

rather trusting of each other and took a double bed without any thought. We decided that it was now our time to relax after two and a half days of steady travel, so we donned our swimsuits and headed for the beach. The day was absolutely beautiful with clear blue skies and temperatures in the high 80's, but man, was that water cold. We forced ourselves to play for a little while in the water but finally the cold won out and we settled for lying out on the beach. I must say, the beach was beautiful but it was not the typical sandy beaches that I had grown accustomed to in Florida along the Atlantic or the Gulf of Mexico. But, the company was good and we were having a great time.

For the evening's entertainment, Tina had selected a Mexican restaurant that she had heard of that featured great peach margaritas. We dressed ourselves in casual attire, but Tina's casual was a sensuous red dress that was just stunning against her tanned features and flowing blonde hair. I had never seen her look so beautiful, a visual picture that I carry in my mind, even to this day.

We were never certain that we had found the right restaurant but the peach margaritas were superb and the meal was delicious. The sun was just starting to set so we decided to head back to the beach for an evening stroll. The sun was setting just beautifully, the waves were rolling in with an occasional loud crash against the shore and the sand was feeling cool beneath our bare feet. Slowly, and with a certain amount of grace and anticipation, I turned in toward her and embraced her for that long-awaited first kiss. It was absolutely perfect; I mean absolutely perfect!!!! Hollywood could not have set it up any better.

Sunday morning came, we said our goodbyes and promised to stay in touch; I grabbed the hotel shuttle back to the airport and began my trip back to St. Louis. It had been a wonderful

The Searching Years 1978-1982

trip filled with a lot of laughter and simply some good times. There were memories created on this trip that will last our lifetime.

I hardly dare say it but Connie met me back in St. Louis at Lambert International Airport. Her meeting me actually was not as bad as it sounds; first of all she asked if she could do it. I had kept my relationship with her above board, and while I did not come out and directly give her details and names of people that I was dating, she was very aware that I did occasionally date others. It was obvious to us both that I was not ready to make a commitment to anyone or have anyone make a commitment to me, and she seemed somewhat content with that.

As soon as I got home I unpacked and then repacked and promptly caught a flight the next morning with Bob Mueth and Barry Sizemore to Daytona Beach. Two Cincinnati girls that we had met the year before did not show up as we had hoped but it was another great vacation on the beach. I never did anything that I could not have written home about but we did meet a lot of women and did have a lot fun. We were shallow, I admit it, but memories are made of such vacations. One of the schemes we hatched was to take turns declaring it was our birthday each evening at supper. This way the attention would be focused on us above all others at the restaurant and invariably some ladies would come by to congratulate the "birthday boy." After that, it was easy to strike up a conversation with whomever and see where that might lead. On one particular evening we were invited to a "Toga Party" in our hotel, taken from that great movie classic, *Animal House*. We wrapped ourselves in sheets and the party began. As much as we would have loved to say that we were real Studs, the fact was that we were just three nice guys having fun, and that was it.

Life Between Innings

While in Daytona, Tina was still fresh on my mind so I did call her a couple of times. Each time she seemed very happy to hear from me. However, it sounded as if things were falling into place for her with her new jobs and so I did not anticipate that I would be seeing her anytime soon.

Late in the summer of 1981 I happened to be looking through the ads in the newspaper and stumbled across a small notice advising that a "Singles" group had been formed and was meeting at Hope Congregational Church in North St. Louis County on Brown Road. Oddly, as a teenager, I had played basketball on the outside courts of this church with my friends from the old Carsonville Full Gospel Tabernacle, which was only a few miles from Hope. I knew the church was not Pentecostal, but I liked the way the ad read and I was somehow drawn to it. I really was not enjoying First Assembly in St. Charles and felt more and more isolated by the people every Sunday. So, I decided, *What the heck, I think I will give it a shot.*

Hope Church had two services so I attended the early service, which I really enjoyed, and then stayed over to meet with the Singles Group during the Sunday School Hour. I'll never forget my first day. The group was made up of long-time singles, divorced singles, widowed singles, young adult singles, middle age singles and some folks that I would have considered as old singles. What an eclectic group! Yet, somehow, it seemed to click. From the very first moment that I stepped into the sanctuary, and again when I stepped into the adjoining chapel where the Singles Group met, there seemed to be a refreshing spirit in the air, something that had been totally missing at First Assembly.

I was one of three new people visiting the Group that morning. When it came time to introduce myself I made mention of how welcomed I had felt that morning and that I thought I had finally found my home! As I was about to be seated one

The Searching Years 1978-1982

of the ladies, and I might add, a fairly attractive lady at that, who was sitting toward the front commented loud enough for most everyone to hear, *Yes, you certainly have!!* WOW! That was pretty neat; I got both of her messages and I liked them both. Oh, and the sermon that morning by Pastor Don A. Miller in the service and the study given by Assistant Pastor, Don B. Miller, in the Singles Class, were both excellent; both were right on target!

So it was that I had finally found my home, my church, which I had been looking for since before Shirley and I were divorced. But God's timing is always perfect as this was to be the place that God would truly heal my spirit and my soul and restore me to His fellowship. But, I still had a struggle or two to go through and those struggles were right around the corner.

As I was beginning the process of renewing (restoring) my relationship with Christ, I also knew that there was some other business that I needed to take care of. After some thought and careful consideration, I decided to contact the home offices of the *Independent Assemblies of God (IAG)* and begin the process of withdrawing my ordination. I was certain that I was not called to be a minister and I had no desire, none, of returning to a pulpit ministry in any fashion. Consequently, I wrote to Dr. Rasmussen, the President of IAG, and expressed to him my desires and enclosed with the letter my ordination papers. Dr. Rasmussen wrote back to me a very gracious letter asking me to reconsider. However, I responded to him that my decision was final and did no longer believe I should hold such sacred documents.

The summer of 1981 had ended, which meant only that I changed from the summer semester at Meramec to the Fall Semester and that our Union Electric softball season had concluded and it was now time to gear up again for Fall Leagues at Johnny Mac's. It also signaled the beginning of some major

Life Between Innings

changes in my life as Tina abruptly left California and headed back to St. Louis. Things had not worked out as she had hoped with her new boss and at the clinic and without warning she packed her bags and her car and headed back home. My first inkling that she was back occurred in late August when I found a nice note attached to a 6-pack of Michelob Light on my doorstep.

After several attempts to make contact with her I finally tracked her down a few days later. We agreed to meet at *People's Restaurant* for a reunion of sorts. I could not believe how beautiful she looked as we met in the parking lot. Her hair was still long and wavy and appeared to be more golden than before, she was perfectly tanned and dressed in a white outfit that set off her attributes in a very positive way. I noticed that she had filled out a little, which is a compliment, and to be honest, she looked even better than ever. I could not help but to take her into an embrace and give her a kiss reminiscent of our first kiss on the beach in California.

But, as we now know, in every life there is a "however," and our "however" started almost immediately. At first I could not quite put my finger on it but there was obviously distance between us that did not exist prior to her departure to California. I soon connected most of the dots and came up with the answer, but certainly not the solution. The answer was simple; she had made contact with Jerry, the old boyfriend, and had been seeing him from the first day of her return. She obviously had the right to do; it also made it abundantly clear that I was not the main player in this "band."

Prior to making that discovery, I had invited her to play on our mixed softball team, which she accepted, that was playing in a Fall League at Johnny Mac's. And, furthermore, after making the "discovery," it was became increasingly hard to just write her out of my life as we had these occasions to be together

The Searching Years 1978-1982

once or twice a week at our games. And, there was the problem that I still enjoyed her company very much, but it was becoming vexing for me as she was there, yet like the elusive butterfly, she was not there. Since my brief relationship with Sue Schondelmeyer had ended back in 1979, I had always been the one in control of any relationships that I had formed. Suddenly, and without any warning, I was being sucked back into a relationship wherein I was not the controlling figure, she was, and I didn't handle it very well. Recognizing to some degree what was going on, I would try to put some distance between us, but then she would pop up unexpectedly from time to time, seem very happy to see me, and then disappear again for a few days, if not a week or two. The whole thing was frustrating.

Around the first of November, and I am really not sure to this day what actually transpired, but suddenly, and again, almost without warning, our relationship began to take a turn back to where it seemed to be going prior to her departure to California. It was not long, in fact it was just a matter of mere weeks, and I found that we were actually becoming an item and spending most of our free time together. Tina spent the Thanksgiving holiday with my family, getting to know them basically for the first time. Bonnie and Joe had invited the family to their beautiful home in West County and we had a good old-fashioned "Mooney Holiday," one of those where you laugh and eat till you hurt. Not surprisingly, the family really took to her, not the least of all my mother, as they quickly found that Tina could hand it out and she could take it, a prerequisite if you were to be accepted into the family.

It was at this Thanksgiving dinner with my family that several family stories developed that are often told and re-told at our family functions. First of all there was my sister Bonnie and Tina attempting to make coffee together. After some wait and no coffee appearing in our cups we found that the ladies

Life Between Innings

had put the grounds and the filter properly in place and had turned on the pot, only they forgot to add water.

Secondly, after a grand evening of fun and laughter, we were about to leave when my mother said to Tina, *It has been really nice meeting you; I hope we meet you again!* To this, Tina promptly replied, *I don't think so.* We were all kind of taken aback by Tina's comment but I could only ascertain that Tina had not truly heard mom's very proper goodbye; so I told mom, *I don't think she heard you.* Mom again repeated her goodbye by saying again, *I said, it has really been nice meeting you; I hope we will see you again.* Again Tina replied, *I don't think so.* This time, but with a chuckle, I said to Tina, *Do you understand what she is saying; she is saying she is glad to meet you and hopes to see you again.* With that, Tina burst out into embarrassed laughter as it was apparent that she had totally misunderstood. With that, she was officially welcomed to the family!!

But, almost as quickly as we had become an item, things fell apart again. It became obvious that Tina was still struggling with her relationship with Jerry and I was struggling with her relationship with Jerry. By this time I had pretty much ended all my other relationships, although I had not officially done so with Connie. I was willing to make some transitional moves with Tina, however, if she would quit being so "doggone" elusive. As the first two weeks of December drug along our relationship became rockier than ever; in fact, it was pretty much in shambles and I was beginning to look for a way out. This was a relationship going absolutely nowhere and now, at last, I wanted out and I wanted out right now.

Over the past couple months I had from time to time invited Tina to go to church with me and each time I had been rebuffed. At one point she had made it very clear that she would decide when, or if, she wanted to go to church and I did not need to keep after her about it. However, around noon on

The Searching Years 1978-1982

the Sunday of the Hope Church Christmas Cantata, I had casually thrown out the invitation to her that if she wanted to go with me to hear it, she was welcome; she of course rejected my offer. Actually, I was glad that she had rejected the offer as I had already begun to plot in my mind how on this very day this relationship needed to come to its rightful death. I had made up my mind that this relationship, if you could call it that, was over; I just simply did not need or want the continuing aggravation of dealing with her uncertainties. I had also reached a point, helped tremendously by the ministries of Hope Church, where I knew it was time that I get serious about restoring my relationship with Christ. Suddenly it seemed really clear to me that somehow, since her return from California, I had lost control of this whole relationship and it was past time for me to retake control over my emotions and my life. It was time to end this ridiculous and hopeless relationship with her and this was the day to do it. It actually felt good to have finally "come-to-myself" and realize just how wrong this whole thing had become.

My plans received a serious jolt when at about 4:00 PM on this particular Sunday, I received a call from Tina saying that she had changed her mind and would like to go to the Cantata. I must admit that I was not in a soul-winning mood and that I actually resented the fact that she was going. But, how do you tell someone who wants to go to church with you, "No?" There wasn't much conversation on the way to church and I certainly could not have anticipated what the Holy Spirit had in store. In my mind I still wanted to end this relationship today and this Cantata stood in the way of successfully completing the task. We took our place in the left middle section of the church about 4 rows back from the platform. Somewhere in the middle of the second or third song I noticed that Tina was beginning to cry. While I was not yet back to the place I

Life Between Innings

needed to be spiritually, I wasn't so spiritually dead to know that God was truly working on her heart. Her brokenness continued throughout the Cantata; I think at one point I actually took her hand to offer some comfort.

The car ride back was 180 degrees out from the one that we had endured on the way to church. We had the most intense discussion of spiritual things since the night of our first date some seven months back. The abrupt change in her was so dramatic that my plans for ending our relationship that night were put on hold. However, I was still not sold on the fact that this relationship had much fuel left in it as I was still fairly burned out from the struggles we had endured over the past several months.

New Year's passed and we were now heading into January of 1982. Tina's spiritual and personal metamorphous had continued and it was obvious that something had occurred in her heart and that I was the only man in her life. I too had resolved my issues with Connie and had broken off that relationship. Linda had decided several months back that she wanted me singularly or not at all. Since I was not ready to commit to anyone at that point, I had severed that relationship. So, for the first time in several years, the only person that I was seeing was Tina.

Part of the great change in Tina was exemplified by the fact that she immediately, following the Cantata experience, had decided that she would like to start attending the Singles Group with me as well as the Sunday services. Since I often attended the Sunday evening services as well, she likewise began to accompany me to that service. On the second Sunday in January we headed to Hope Church for the AM service, as was becoming our practice. Our relationship had rebounded tremendously since the Cantata and I was beginning to enjoy having her accompany me to church. On this particular

The Searching Years 1978-1982

Sunday, the Singles Group met as usual; however Pastor Don B. had brought a video to the class that he wanted to show featuring the dramatic story and testimony of Joni Erickson. Joni had been an athletic young lady that was tragically paralyzed from the neck down as the result of a diving accident when she was in her teens. Somehow, by God's immeasurable grace, she had fought through all the pain, mentally, physically and spiritually, found forgiveness in Christ and had now dedicated her life and ministry to His service.

Tina's spirit was greatly touched by Joni's story and testimony as it unfolded on the screen. Sensing that God was at work in the hearts of several in attendance, Pastor Don B., during the closing prayer, asked all those that would like to accept Jesus Christ as their personal Savior to pray along with him inviting Jesus Christ into their hearts and lives. Tina did not need any prodding. There in that very solemn moment, Christ took possession of her heart and changed her eternal destiny. At that precise moment God also changed our personal destiny. Amen!

At Hope Church, and later at Twin Oaks Presbyterian Church, I became more keenly aware of the "Sovereign" God of Scripture than I ever had previously. From this distant perch, as I now look back at Tina's conversion, her personal "Born-Again" experience, I am awed by God's sovereignty. In practical, human terms there is no reason that Tina should have or would have become a Christian. I do not dare try to explain it, because I cannot, but watch the bouncing ball; it is hard to deny that God was not involved from the very beginning in calling her to Himself:

> ... She did not come from a particularly religious family or at least one that openly practiced or espoused their faith.

Life Between Innings

... She attended Mass regularly on her own but never had encountered the living Christ; she admitted it was an empty experience, but she did not know what else to do or where else to turn.

... Prior to meeting me she was engaged to Brian, by all accounts a very nice man. I have no way of knowing if he is now a born-again-believer but at that time it is not believed that he was. Tina, although she admits she still cared for him, called the engagement off.

... Tina and I, by all practical reasoning, should have never met; yet due to the persistence of her mother it finally happened after a nine-month process.

... Tina had all the intentions of staying in California upon her move there in 1981.

... When Tina returned to St. Louis late in the summer of 1981, our relationship began rocky and stayed rocky. There is absolutely no reason that our relationship endured long enough to even make it to the Christmas Cantata or to January of the New Year when she finally accepted Christ as her Lord and Savior.

... The actual day that I planned to break up with Tina, God puts it in her heart for the first time to call and ask if she could go to church with me. My heart said to tell her "No," but even after saying "Yes," I was not too warm toward her as we traveled to church.

... "BUT GOD," a tremendous exclamation of God's intervention into the affairs of men, plucked her out of all these circumstances to call her to Himself. Truly (*as is true of us all that are Christ-followers*), Tina's salvation was and is a sovereign act of the only true God!! There is no other explanation.

January 1982 turned into February and February into March. By this time Tina had settled her personal issues and

The Searching Years 1978-1982

her personal faith in Christ was already growing by leaps and bounds. It was evident that Christ had done a work in her life and it was life-changing. I also felt for the first time since her return from California that I was in control of our relationship and not her. Both of these issues were important to me as our relationship was suddenly moving forward again. I did not realize how quickly it was moving until a certain Sunday early in March. Our routine had become for her to meet me at my apartment on Sunday morning, ride out to church together, go out to one of the nicer buffets in the area following the AM service, spend the afternoon together and head back to church for the evening if I was not working. On this particular Sunday we had decided to drive out to a buffet we had discovered in St. Charles. While in the process of eating our lunch our discussion turned to our relationship wherein Tina revealed very succinctly that, "... *I think I could make a very good wife!*"

I really wasn't quite prepared to hear her say that as I was now starting to coast a little in this relationship now that I was in control. She would not let the comment go unchallenged by me so she followed it up by saying, *Well, don't you think so?* I think I stumbled through some words of affirmation but I quickly moved the subject off into another area. But, from that day and over the next few weeks, those words rang in my ears, as I knew that her proposal was not hypothetical, but was in fact an invitation for me to consider. The more I thought about her proposition of marriage the more I began to think that she was correct; she could be a good wife, in fact she could be my wife!

By the end of March, those rocky days of our relationship were gone and had been replaced with much smoother ones. With instability now being replaced with stability, the joy that I had in being with Tina much earlier in our dating days had

Life Between Innings

returned. I was convinced that the rocky days were over and felt strongly that it was time to act on her proposition of marriage. Through the years I had become somewhat of a romantic but for whatever reason I did not put much effort into creating any kind of romantic setting to finally pop the question. In fact, other than the fact that she said, "Yes," the evening and setting of my proposal was so non-descript that I really have little recollection of it. I do recall that Tina made it clear that she wanted me to go to her Father, Chuck, and ask him for his permission, which I was glad to do. I knew with her mother already firmly in my corner, parental approval was not going to be an issue.

As I anticipated, Chuck and Ginny were both very accepting of the fact that we wanted to get married and both gave us their blessing. Chuck, in his understated way, offered me a ladder if it would help to speed up the process. We immediately decided that an October wedding would be ideal with nature's fall colors serving as our backdrop. We also knew that we wanted Pastor Don B. to officiate our wedding and we of course wanted it to be held at Hope Church. And lastly, because we had so many new friends from church and so many secular friends from our workplaces and our softball teams, we decided we would split the wedding festivities in two parts with our wedding service early on a Saturday afternoon with our Christian friends and then host a hum-dinger of a celebration with our family and our non-Christian friends, and some of our more liberal Christian friends who knew how to party, later in the evening. Admittedly, our rationale might not have been right on target but I have to say that when that day came, it worked out great!

March, obviously to all that know me, means March Madness, the annual celebration of the *Great Game*, the game of college basketball. Paul Helfrich and I had sent in our money

The Searching Years 1978-1982

for the random lottery to be held for selection of tickets to the Final Four at the Superdome in New Orleans many months prior, and had drawn the right to purchase a pair of tickets. Tina passed her first test with flying colors as she was not only agreeable to my going, as planned, she encouraged me to go. This would be a wonderful trait of hers that would follow our years of a successful and wonderful marriage. Her grandfather, Charlie Herbel, thought she was nuts letting me go to a place like New Orleans after just getting engaged, but his concern was more blubber than reality. The tournament is always held throughout March, culminating in the championship, or Final Four, the first weekend of April. Paul and I flew out on a Thursday evening to take up residence in our hotel and to enjoy a weekend of basketball and a little of famous Bourbon Street.

Paul could drink a little "better" than I could, but we both imbibed a few and took in the "scenery" along the famous avenue. There were coeds everywhere, but especially from North Carolina, Georgetown, Houston and Louisville, the four teams that had made it to the Final Four. Despite the wild reputation of New Orleans, we really did not see much of the wild side and certainly did not participate in it, if in fact it was there. Other than basketball, the major event that we witnessed was watching New Orleans' finest capture a thief. We were parked at a red light on Canal Street, a major thoroughfare running through town, the first car in line in the left lane. My attention was immediately drawn by a flash jetting past my window in the form of a slender black man running full tilt. The man immediately crossed over in front of our car heading to the curb with a white police officer in heavy pursuit. The unbelievable part of the story is that the white officer actually caught the black thief just as he got to the curb and began to quickly wrestle him to

Life Between Innings

the ground. From out of nowhere, police cars came flying from all directions blocking off the intersection. Several of the officers jumped out of their cars, assisted the first officer in subduing the thief, grabbed him and thrust him into a police car and then they all sped off. The light immediately turned green and we proceeded forward without a police officer or police car in sight. The whole thing could not have lasted more than 35-40 seconds. It was like we stopped at the red light, waited, the light turned green and we moved on. It was an unbelievable. Paul and I looked at each other and simultaneously asked, *What happened?* It was over just that quick!

In the semi-finals we watched from high, high above the floor, as North Carolina beat Houston 68-63 and Georgetown, with Patrick Ewing, beat Louisville 50-46; both were great games. It was here that a fan held up the infamous banner shown all over the nation, *Ewing, How Do You Spell IQ?* However, the championship game was one that memories are made of; this was the game that freshman player Michael Jordan was unleashed on the basketball world. James Worthy led the Tar Heels with 28 points, but Jordan scored 16 points, including the go-ahead sixteen footer with 15 seconds left. Georgetown had time to attempt a game-winning shot, but guard Freddy Brown, who thought he was passing to his teammate Eric Smith near mid-court, actually threw the ball to Worthy, sealing a 63-62 North Carolina win. What a game!

Upon returning home from New Orleans, the first thing on our plate was to go through the marital counseling program with Pastor Don B. I welcomed this process as it was woefully missing at the time Shirley and I were engaged. This involved some personal meetings with him, plus the taking of some compatibility tests. On our final day, when Pastor Don B. was to go over the results of our tests, he met with us in his office.

The Searching Years 1978-1982

At first he had a serious look on his face like he was going to recommend, perhaps, that these two people should not be joined together in holy matrimony. However, he finally broke into a smile and said, *Well guys, after looking at your tests, I am not going to tell you not to get married, but I am going to tell you it is going to be very interesting!* What a prophet!!

We weren't long into the process of planning our wedding when we both came to a meeting of the minds and decided that the October date just would not work for two people trying to live a Christian life. We both readily admitted that we were in "heat" and that it would be in our better interests as Christians to move the wedding up to something more reasonable, like July 24. Since it was already May when this decision was made, we had to make up some serious ground with our planning. Being the male in this planning process, I did not have remotely the issues to wrestle with that Tina did, but somehow it all came together. Other than getting my tux ordered, my attendants lined up, some minor work on the rehearsal dinner, giving my approval to our wedding colors (Peach & White or peaches-n-cream), picking out a few songs for the service, helping to scout out the live band for the reception and plan the honeymoon, I was fairly home free. Life was good!

Tina, on the other hand, did have her plate full. There were the many details of shopping for a dress, a veil, reception hall, coordinating the bridesmaids' dresses and all the other minute details that must be taken care of. While I was enjoying my final days as a single man without anyone to butt heads with, Tina was dealing with her mother, who can be strong-willed at times; OK, most of the time. Her only respite during this time was the fact that she was living with her grandparents, Charlie and Mildred Herbel, in south St. Louis, who made life tolerable, especially grandfather, with his unique, if not persistent, sense of humor.

Life Between Innings

In the middle of our planning and scurrying about we received a note from my mother saying that she and John (Pedersen) had eloped (Father's Day), deciding that they were tired of waiting for Tina and me to get married. My brother, Doug, an ordained minister, was to perform the ceremony and then the newlyweds were to be off to somewhere on their honeymoon. This was not a total surprise to us as they had been dating for seven years or more. They had met at the Post Office where mom worked and John was her boss. Upon retirement, she had succeeded him in the position of Maintenance Supervisor, the position she maintained until her retirement. She seemed to enjoy her job although she complained from time to time about the union and the grievances they would file.

With our wedding day fast approaching, Greg Maxwell, whom I had chosen to be my Best Man, came in on Thursday (July 22) for our rehearsal and the rehearsal dinner. The rehearsal was uneventful and went off smoothly. Following the rehearsal, we all joined together at the Herbel's home for the rehearsal dinner. Usually, the groom is responsible for this occasion but Ginny insisted that she wanted to do it. Ginny was a great planner and did a wonderful job of putting it all together; Ginny had the place looking festive and the food was outstanding.

On Friday evening, Greg and I got back together to revisit all that had been going on in our lives since we had last seen each other, which was plenty. Greg was still single, but still shopping, hoping to find that perfect gal. We had a nice relaxing meal at Robata of Japan, an interactive cooking and eating restaurant that had been the scene of several special occasions for the Mooney family. Little did I know that while I was relaxing comfortably with Greg and enjoying a restful evening, Tina was in considerable turmoil trying to work out final details with her mother.

The Searching Years 1978-1982

Finally the day of July 24, 1982, had arrived. I had encountered only one hitch so far and that was my son Marc's tux did not look like mine. Since our wedding was to be an early afternoon affair, I had chosen a light tan tuxedo with dark brown trim. And Marc, having just turned 10 two days earlier, really wanted to look like Dad. So, off to the Tux Rental Store we went and to my surprise they were able to outfit Marc in a tux identical to mine right there on the spot. Problem solved. Dionne, who would turn 12 in four more days, and who rarely wore a dress, was wearing a beautiful print dress that she seemed to like, so my only worry was to get to the church on time. Have I mentioned that Tina's day was not going so smoothly?

As I stated, Greg Maxwell, an old friend from my Full Gospel Tabernacle days and a pilot for Delta Airlines, was my Best Man and Bill Dorner, my great friend and old roommate, was my attendant. I really screwed that situation up, and have no good explanation for it, as Bill should have been my Best Man and Paul Helfrich my attendant. Paul and I had run together a lot over the previous three or four years and was a much closer friend than Greg. I simply screwed up with no reasonable explanation, except I think I was afraid I was going to hurt Paul's feelings if I asked Bill to be my Best Man over him. In retrospect, Paul wouldn't even had thought twice about it, he was just that kind of man and friend; so like I said, I screwed it up.

Tina had chosen Sue (Bernstein) Anderson, her life-long closest friend as her Bridesmaid and Denise Farhrig as her other attendant. Sue had been one of Tina's roommates at the time that Tina and I started dating. The fact is, had Sue opened the door at the apartment when I went to pick up Tina for our first date, I would have thought she was the girl that I was there to pick up. Sue looked much more like Tina's mother, being very slender with her dark hair and dark features, than

Life Between Innings

Tina did. Sue and Carol, Tina's roommates when we started dating, were both married during the short period of time that Tina and I dated prior to her leaving for California. One of the reasons that prompted Tina to decide to go to California was that all her roommates, just like mine, kept getting married and left her with no place to live (except with Mom and Dad, which was not an option, or her grandparents).

My sister, Bonnie, was the organist for the wedding and Dave Booker, a young man from Hope Church with an outstanding voice, was our soloist. Lindy Reynolds was our photographer; Lindy was a Christian friend of mine whom I had worked with at the Rush Island Plant who photographed weddings as a side job. He was also married to an unbelievably attractive woman. None of us could ever figure out how Lindy had managed to get her to marry him. (*Lindy was kind of heavy set and not very handsome by most critical observers. Of course they were both Christians and, as we know, sometimes Christian girls are a little forgiving on the "looks" if their potential partner is a genuine Christian. I concluded that must be the reason that she fell in love with him, plus he was just a great guy and genuinely funny.*). Of course, Rev. Don B. Miller officiated the wedding and he did a magnificent job. In fact, Lindy, who had worked a fair share of weddings, commented that he could really feel the Holy Spirit ministering during our ceremony and that he could not recall any other wedding that he had ever worked where this had been so. For Tina and me, we could not have asked for a better comment about our wedding as it was our goal from start to finish to have a God-centered, Holy Spirit driven wedding.

Suddenly I found myself marching out to the front of the congregation where Pastor Don B. was already standing. The church looked beautiful and there was a sizeable crowd, perhaps 200 or more people in attendance. The music began

The Searching Years 1978-1982

and the bridesmaids started their march to the front of the church. Then, the church stood in unison as Tina and her Father swung around the corner at the back of the church and began their slow walk toward the altar. I am not sure what Chuck was telling Tina as they marched toward the front, but whatever it was it was making her smile; that simple smile took the pressure off. Tina was stunning in her white gown with a flowing train. She was absolutely beautiful. She looked hot!! As Clark Gable once commented, and I paraphrase, *She looked like a woman who needed to be kissed hard and kissed often.*

We actually had fun throughout the ceremony. The only major goof was when I stuck out my right hand for Tina to put the ring on. Of course, my sister Bonnie and her husband Joe, were the only ones in the church to catch it, or at least to publicly ridicule me over it! When it came time for me to kiss the bride, I could sense a hint of fear in Tina's eyes as she had some doubt whether I would actually kiss her or lick the end of her nose, as I had threatened. This was no time for playing around; I kissed her.

The rest of the afternoon is a blur. I do recall that we were so very fortunate in that we had a sunny day with the temperatures hanging around 90 degrees. For a late July day in St. Louis, we were counting our blessings as near 100 degree weather with plenty of humidity would not have been unusual for that time of the year. Lindy did a great job in getting all our required pictures taken in short order and we were soon off to relax back at my new in-laws' home with the wedding party until our reception later that night.

Knowing the penchant of my friends for mischief, I decided to leave my car back at my (our) apartment so that it would not get trashed. Tina has ragged on me for years that she did not get to ride in a car with streamers and pithy statements written on the windows and the car's exterior. She really had wanted the car to be accessorized with those lovely, yet obligatory, tin cans strung along behind clanging joyously to all who were near that we had just gotten married. But, I still like my decision to hide the car; I am sure it saved me much elbow grease and grief. I am thinking that perhaps for our 50th anniversary, I will have the car decorated in the fashion she so much desired as an expression of my continuing love!

Our reception was held at the UAW Union Hall up on a hill overlooking the city of Fenton, Missouri. As we were arriving, it was easy to see that the place had filled with people ready to eat, drink and party. We had 300 people that had sent their RSVP indicating that they were coming; however, it was soon obvious that many of our friends that we had not invited had decided to crash their way in anyway. It made for a packed house and quite a reception as our friends were not strangers to the idea of partying long and partying hard. As I mentioned previously, these were not for the most part our new Protestant, church-going friends; these were our Catholic and non-churched friends from our work and our softball teams, plus family. This was the *Party Crowd*. It was definitely genius on our part to keep the two groups separated.

We had a nice buffet meal and quickly got the preliminaries out of the way so that the band could be introduced and the dancing (and serious drinking) could begin. We had personally gone out to interview the band and listen to them practice and knew they were good; and they were. Grandpa Herbel was the only one to complain as he was certain that the band was going to burst his eardrums. Tina and I were introduced to the crowd and we interlocked our arms in an embrace and began our first dance to the song of our choice, Billy Joel's '70's classic, *Just the Way You Are*.

Before our dance was fully completed others began to come on the floor, including Chuck and Ginny, both of whom could cut a pretty mean rug themselves. Most receptions have a lull at some point and the crowd begins to meander away. For whatever reason, such was not the case on this night as the band played strong all evening and the floor was packed, song after song. It was truly a great celebration and it was a joy for us both to see our friends having as much fun as they were. Of course on the dark side, I think several marriages were wrecked that evening, although they were probably on shaky ground before this party set sail.

The party continued to run strong, but this groom was anxious to sweep his bride away. As the clock rounded 10:30 pm and headed for 11:00, I began to make our exit. Tina, who enjoys parties and social events much more than I do, wasn't all that ready to leave but I finally convinced her that it would be a good thing for us to depart. Just before the clock struck 11:00 pm we were in the get away car driven by the Best Man and heading for the apartment to pick up our car and our luggage. From what we have been told, after we left, the party did not die, but in fact intensified. At some point, my father-in-law left to secure more beer as our ample supply had been tapped out; and the party "raged" on till way after 1:00 am.

Since we were to honeymoon in the quaint countryside of Nova Scotia, I thought it would be neat to stay our first night at the Henry VIII Hotel near Lambert International Airport. At that time, the Henry VIII was a "happening" place with a beautiful "Old English" style exterior and interior, including the rooms. Our room was the perfect honeymoon suite with a circular bed, a heart shaped Jacuzzi and all the other amenities that made it special. We tried to re-enact the "crime" on our 10th anniversary but we checked out as fast as we checked in; the hotel had really gone down in 10 years and was soon thereafter torn down to make room for a new runway at Lambert International Airport.

Life Between Innings

It had been an almost perfect day and it had been a truck-load of fun. Tina and I worked hard to make it so and we felt so fortunate to have been able to share it with so many of our friends and family. It was a great start to what has been a great marriage. Paying for most of the wedding ourselves, we both felt that it had been worth every penny; yet we had not been extravagant in our spending, just prudent, and it had worked out well. Praise God and Amen.

The morning of our first day as husband and wife was as bright and shiny as the day of our wedding. We awoke to our first breakfast together, a double-loaded continental breakfast served in our room and large enough to feed the two of us many times over. Our flight out to Boston, the first stop on our adventure, was to leave in the early afternoon, so it was nice not having to be hurried. We arrived in the late afternoon in Boston, picked up our rental car and headed for our hotel, the historic Boston Park Plaza Hotel and Towers, right in mid-town. The hotel was elegant and finely decorated. Our room was accented very nicely in the old English style, again fitting for our New England honeymoon theme. The tub even had the old style feet on it, perfectly made for two.

We had decided to stay in Boston two nights before heading across the narrow strait of the upper Atlantic Ocean and into Yarmouth, Nova Scotia. Our first day in Boston was spent seeing the many historic sites including the Old North Church, the Paul Revere Home, the USS Constitution and Museum, the historic site of the Boston Tea Party and the famous meeting and market place constructed in 1742, Faneuil Hall.

We had also been told that since we both had a passion for seafood, we needed to go to a restaurant buried deep in the wharf area called the *No Name Restaurant*. The bus driver dropped us off two blocks from where the restaurant was supposed to be, pointed us in the direction we should go and then

The Searching Years 1978-1982

left us to walk through a seedy, industrial area looking for a restaurant with no name. After some difficulty, and no small measure of fear, we saw a somewhat weathered sign indicating that the *No Name* was actually located behind some badly deteriorating walls that hid well any appearance of a restaurant. We ventured inside and to our delight and relief, there actually was a restaurant behind those weathered walls and the well-used door. In fact, it was filled with people no less, dining and laughing and enjoying themselves. Unfortunately, I had a great meal but Tina, being the adventurous one, had settled on some mussels that did not sit well. Almost immediately upon leaving the restaurant Tina became ill. Being the trooper she is, she gallantly attempted to fight off the effects of food poisoning, but she was to lose the fight as the afternoon turned into evening.

Tina battled the stomach issues for the rest of the afternoon but just could not shake it. But, as had been our plan, we went back to the hotel briefly and then headed over to Fenway Park, the hallowed and historic baseball home of the Boston Red Sox. For me it was such a rush to step inside this playground of many baseball greats, including Ted Williams, as well as future Hall of Famers, Boston's slugger Carl Yastrzemski and ace pitcher Dennis Eckersley. On this night, Yaz and Eck were both in the Red Sox line-up and Boston won 2-1 on a home run down the right field line that just curled inside the foul pole and over the short fence. However, the most significant moment came prior to the start of the game as we entered the concourse near our seats along the first baseline towards right field. Here, Tina finally deposited whatever it was that had been ailing her. Fortunately we had arrived early so the scene was neither too embarrassing nor observed by many onlookers. The wonderful husband and quick thinker that I am, held out my brand new Boston Red Sox coffee mug that I

Life Between Innings

had freshly purchased, and allowed her to gracefully barf in it. While it would not hold all that came up, it did allow that there was much less cleanup to be performed. I quickly cleaned up the mess and washed my mug and we went on to enjoy a great evening at the "Old Ball Park" (*Must be said in a true Bostonian accent for full effect*).

Being at Fenway took me back to that first game I attended at Busch Stadium with the group of Salem All-Stars in the late '50s. Through the years I have also enjoyed the great atmosphere found in the friendly confines of Wrigley Field in Chicago. All three parks hold great memories and offered unique character not found in many of the new stadiums. It would be hard to pick which one I enjoyed the most but I think I must give the nod to Wrigley Field, perhaps because of that great Cardinal-Cub rivalry, played out in front of my own eyes over the years.

We enjoyed Boston immensely, although we found that Bostonians, as a rule, quiet rude, if not just plain boorish. On one occasion, while sitting at a traffic light in the far right lane, a car came from my left and turned directly in front of me to the right. As I glanced over to my right my eyes met those of a cab driver parked at the curb. In the purest Bostonian accent he could muster he gave a hint of a smile and leaned out of the window to say, *Welcome to Boston!* On one other occasion we had stopped at a coffee shop inside our hotel that opened out to the street. It was a quaint place but filled with the bustle of many people. We found a place at the bar and ordered our coffee. When the coffee came Tina asked if she might have some cream? Well, you would have thought she had asked for the waitress's first born as she went on a rant explaining that Tina should have asked earlier, as she just did not have time to be running back and forth. The waitress was so abrupt and so rude as to actually be comical; so we laughed and went on our merry way.

The Searching Years 1978-1982

Our two days in Boston flew by but it was now time to board our Air Canada flight and head to our first stop in Nova Scotia, the seaport of Yarmouth. Upon landing at Yarmouth we were immediately captured by the politeness of the people, the slower pace of life and the vivid colors of the city, and later the villages and countryside. Nova Scotia would prove to be a garden of color and a place that would pull at our hearts for a lifetime.

At Yarmouth we picked up our car and headed for Digby, a small village about 50 miles north of Yarmouth right on the bay. Here we had reserved a small cabin that was too much like, well, a small cabin. So, the next day we checked out and checked in at the *Pines*, a beautiful rustic resort nestled on the edge of the bay. It was here on our second night, while sitting on the patio enjoying the night sounds along with an adult beverage, that we had one of those moments that means nothing to anyone else but ourselves. An older couple was seated nearby chatting quietly when off in the distance a train whistle gave a low, almost indistinct sound. In a very serious tone the elder lady noted to her husband, *That sounded like a boat in distress.* Here some 30 years later we often pipe up, *That sounds like a boat in distress,* when we hear that similar, somewhat haunting sound; we then smile at each other knowing that the sound carries with it a significant memory of a very special time in our life!

Over the next few days we continued our travels along the northern bay where the highest tides in the world occur daily, leaving the shore muddy and ships run aground only to be lifted high in the water only a few hours later. We then turned inward and south toward Halifax, the capital city, where we spent a day and night exploring its many delights. We left Halifax for Peggy's Cove, the most photographed location in the world, with its beautiful shoreline, colorfully painted

Life Between Innings

houses and an old lighthouse that now serves as a Post Office. We stopped for lunch and Tina enjoyed a big lobster dinner, rather inexpensive as it was, and a cool bottle of my new favorite ale, Blue Schooner.

From Peggy's Cove we headed to a small village along the southern coastline called Anchorage where we had reserved a nice cabin. After settling in we rented a small canopied pedal boat and headed out across the bay toward the ocean. Not realizing there had been a shift in the current we found ourselves at the edge of the bay and the ocean and we were losing ground quickly. After peddling frantically for a few minutes we were able to gain some ground and eventually were able to get back into the cove. The owner of the lodge where we were staying met us about half way in to inquire about our adventure, saying that he had become a little concerned when he saw that it was getting dark and we had not returned. Of course the whole incident is funny now, but for a few minutes it was more than a little scary as we were not sure if we could get the little boat back into shore or not against such a strong tide.

The next day we rented a fishing boat for a half a day and started out toward the open seas. The captain had asked if we minded if a couple of his friends came along to enjoy the ride; he assured us that they would not interfere with our fishing adventure. We readily agreed, although it became clear quickly that one young lady had unfortunately stayed at the bar a little too long the night before and the waves, small as they were, were starting to have an ill effect on her. The four-hour trip was probably much more than she bargained for but since we were paying we had no intention of returning early. We are not sure what happened with our little green friend but we never saw her again once we reached shore.

The Searching Years 1978-1982

Tina, of course, had to show off as she caught the most cod and the largest cod of our catch. I think one of the three that she caught weighed in over two and half pounds; I caught a cod too that was actually a nice size, plus a Red Fish that the captain chopped up for bait. It would be some 26 years later before I ventured out to fish again, this time in the beautiful waters of the Mediterranean Sea.

Later that afternoon we headed back to our starting point at Yarmouth on the western end of Nova Scotia where we stayed all night and boarded the huge ferry early the next morning for the 12-hour excursion to Portland, Maine, and the U.S. shoreline. While the ferry served to shuttle cars and trucks back and forth from Nova Scotia to the U.S., it also had a nice dining area, a casino and small private rooms where we could take a nap. We decided that since neither of us had ever been in a casino that we would take $25.00 and go play the slot machines. After a few minutes I hit a small jackpot, I think winning something like $11.00 in quarters; Tina immediately went into conservative mode displaying a brief moment of "panic." She decided that we should quit and take our winnings and use the quarters for the washing machines back at our apartment. I think I finally gently persuaded her that it was OK, we were not getting addicted and that we should enjoy ourselves. In the end we lost our "winnings" and our $25.00 stake but no evil ever came upon us.

After a night at the Holiday Inn in Portland, Maine, a nice breakfast in an empty restaurant except for some guys named Crosby, Stills and Nash (they and their band where huddled across the room enjoying a late breakfast), we boarded a very small plane back to Boston, connected with our TWA flight back to St. Louis and arrived at the airport about 4:45 PM. Having planned ahead, Tina drove the car while I changed into

Life Between Innings

my softball uniform and arrived at my game midway through the first inning.

Upon returning home from our honeymoon we settled back into life and our apartment on Pinyon Drive in Manchester, continuing with the things that we enjoyed most: church, school, work and softball. We were also caught up in the Cardinals run at the World Series that fall, which the Cardinals won in seven games against the Milwaukee Brewers, who at that time were members of the American League. On the evening of game seven, on a lark, we decided to invade downtown and see if we could get a cheap ticket from a scalper. Our cheap was much cheaper than what was being offered so we decided to head back toward home so as not to miss any of the game. Tina, never one to give up, kept asking individuals along the sidewalk as we returned to our car if they had any tickets they wanted to sell. Just as we had given up hope, two very young boys let us know that they had two tickets. The TV-news had cautioned fans about scalping tickets, so these boys were really scared, but anxious to sell. Tina, in negotiating mode, got them down to $35.00 per ticket and back to Busch Stadium we headed. With two great seats in the right-center field bleachers, fourth row back from the field, we watched as the Cards rallied for three runs in the sixth inning to overcome a 3-1 deficit to win by a final score of 6-3. Ace relief pitcher and future Hall of Famer, Bruce Sutter, took center stage as he shut down the powerful Brewers over the final two innings to win the game and the series. Life was good; life was very good!

The 7ᵗʰ Inning
THE UNION YEARS
1983-2002

In 1983 Ronald Reagan was into his third year as President of the United States; in 1984 he was reelected for a second term. The Republicans continued their stranglehold on Organized Labor and the plight of the workingman as Republican George H. Bush, Sr. was elected in 1988 to succeed President Reagan. In 1989 the Berlin Wall fell, re-uniting Germany. Fortunately for Democrats and the economy, Bill Clinton succeeded Bush as President in 1992 after only four years in office. Under President Clinton the economy thrived and he was reelected for a second term in 1996. Unfortunately, the nation, the President and our government became distracted when it was discovered that Clinton had a dalliance with a female intern, Monica Lewinski. Efforts to impeach President Clinton added to the legal circus surrounding his presidency while Republican zealots worked hard to prove a number of allegations against President Clinton and his wife Hillary in the high courts, dubbed the Whitewater Scandal. The President was not impeached and none of the charges pushed forward by the radical Republican leaders in the Whitewater probe were ever proven.

Several tragic events captured the headlines in the mid to late '90s. Former football star and Hall of Famer, O.J. Simpson, was charged in the murder of his ex-wife Nicole Brown Simpson and Ronald Coleman. In 1995, Simpson was acquitted, dividing the nation as blacks cheered

Life Between Innings

the decision while whites gasped in disbelief. In 1999, two teenage boys went on a rampage at Columbine High School in Colorado killing 13 students and injuring 24 others. Their actions spawned a number of copycat cases across America in schools and on industrial sites leading to a heated debate among Americans over the need for more stringent gun control laws. In 2000 George W. Bush, Jr., the son of former President, George H. Bush, Sr., was elected President. On September 11, 2001, terrorists hi-jacked four commercial planes and crashed two of them into the World Trade Center in New York City bringing both towers of the building down in a heap of burning rubble. Another plane crashed into the Pentagon Building in Washington, DC. On a fourth plane the hi-jackers were overcome by several of the passengers and the plane crashed in a field in Pennsylvania, killing all on board; the plane was rumored to have been headed to the White House. All in all over 3000 people were killed and another 6000 were left injured. Life in the U.S.A. has not been the same since. President George W. Bush immediately led the nation into war with Iraq looking for weapons of mass destruction, which were never found. This war set our nation into a financial tailspin from which it has never recovered.

In 1999 the city of St. Louis went crazy in their support of the football Rams as Kurt Warner and Marshall Faulk led the team to the Super Bowl and a 23-16 victory over the Tennessee Titans. The Rams returned to the Super Bowl in 1980 but were beaten back by the upstarts, the New England Patriots. In 2003, George W. Bush, Jr. was reelected as President over Democrat Al Gore in the closest election in our nation's history. The election was marred by claims of "hanging chad" in Florida, the home of President Bush's brother who was serving as Governor. With Bush winning Florida by less than 500 votes, the courts ruled Bush the winner with no recount options further available.

The St. Louis Cardinals won the World Series the previous season (1982) under the tutelage of Whitey Herzog; however, they floundered *over the next two seasons before recovering to win the National League title in 1985. In the World Series the Cardinals were up three games to two against cross-state rival, the Kansas City Royals, and up 1-0 in the ninth inning of game six when Don Denkinger, an American League umpire, missed badly a call at first base, giving the Royals an opportunity to come back, which they did, winning the game, 2-1. The Cardinals were so distraught over the call they never recovered and lost game seven by a score of 11-0. Also in '85, Lou Brock and Enos Slaughter were elected to the Baseball Hall of Fame. The Cardinals stumbled in '86 but rallied their forces to a World Series game seven against the Minnesota Twins in 1987, only to lose. In 1988, lights were added to Wrigley Field in Chicago, the last of the stadiums that offered only day baseball. In 1989, Red Schoendienst, the Cardinal's great second baseman, was elected to the Baseball Hall of Fame. In 1998 the baseball world became mesmerized by the home run race of the Cardinal's, Mark McGuire, and the Chicago Cubs, Sammy Sosa. Both men passed Roger Maris' record of 61 home runs in a season with McGuire finishing with 70 and Sosa with 66. In 2002, Ozzie Smith, the greatest shortstop that I ever saw play, was elected to the Baseball Hall of Fame.*

As we turned the corner into the new year of 1983, I had successfully completed all the credits I needed to graduate from St. Louis University. I had started this long journey way back in 1975, some eight years earlier, but with the goal in sight I had knocked out my remaining courses at St. Louis University (SLU) in an 18-month period. This was a remarkable feat considering that I was working about 64 hours a week, playing softball on two different teams, staying involved in my church and had recently gotten remarried. It felt really great to have finally reached this milestone. Looking back to December of 1978 (the time of my divorce), I could not have imagined that I would be debt free (except for a car payment), hold a really

Life Between Innings

good paying job, have my life restored with my Lord and Savior and have a Bachelor's Degree in my hand.

However, as my counselor and I were looking over my final transcript, she pointed out that I could graduate, but if I wanted to graduate with honors I needed one more class to be eligible. My grades were such that by taking one more three-credit course, I could graduate *Magna Cum Laude*, something that I really had not given much thought to. And, we discovered that my GI Bill account had just enough money left in it to cover one last class. But, I was not sure. I had really pushed hard at the end and had already resolved in my mind that I had finished; in fact, I was more concerned as to whether I should immediately pursue my Masters or not. I was pretty much ready to move on but Tina strongly encouraged me to take the class. She emphasized that if I did not, I was sure to regret it at some point down the road. In the end, her persuasion was pretty strong and I decided to go after it.

The month of May ushered in the various graduation ceremonies of which I was to participate. On the first Friday night in May, those of us graduating with a Business Degree had our own private ceremony on the SLU campus followed by the grand finale at the Checkerdome (previously the St. Louis Arena) near Forest Park on Saturday. For my graduation present I had traded in my 1981 Oldsmobile Supreme and had purchased a shiny red, 1983 Thunderbird. What a great car to drive with its wide-tracking suspension and just overall easy handling. I had been driving Highway T, a narrow, winding, hilly two-lane road back and forth from my apartment in Manchester to the Labadie Power Plant for some three years and this was the best handling car I had driven on that challenging span of highway.

Our graduation speaker, columnist Art Buchwold, did not linger long at the podium. Suddenly, it was my name and my

The Union Years 1983-2002

moment. Since we had actually received our diplomas the night before at our more intimate celebration, and since there were several thousand graduates at this particular exercise, we did not march forward. However, the grand moment came and I flipped my tassel from the right side to the left and it was now final. At long last I was finally a graduate of St. Louis University, graduating with honors; I was *Magna Cum Laude*!!

Tina and I were now closing in on our first anniversary (July 24) and it had been a really good year. One of the things we discovered early was that we should not try to change the person we had married from the person that we had married. In other words, prior to marriage I was working a lot, played a lot of softball, enjoyed going to school, stayed close and loyal to my previous friends, took trips to places such as the NCAA tournament, maintained my own checkbook and was involved in our church at Hope as the Singles Leader. Although we had been married for a year, the church leadership had decided that we should continue in the role that I had assumed prior to marriage, at least for the foreseeable future. We both were glad to do that, as the Singles Group Ministry was where most of our friends at Hope were still meeting for Bible Study and fellowship. Prior to marriage, Tina had also expressed interest in returning to school, loved to play softball, likewise had a groups of friends that she enjoyed, maintained her own checkbook and had a steady job at a doctor's office in Kirkwood. While those interests and others were basic, we intentionally set out not to change each other. Here some 30 years later, we continue to intentionally stay true to that decision. Outside of the grace of God and simply enjoying a Christian lifestyle, I think that this decision early on in our marriage has been the key to the fulfillment we each have found in each other and in our own lives.

For our big anniversary celebration I decided to take her someplace romantic and to a place somewhat reminiscent

Life Between Innings

of our honeymoon theme. That made the decision easy, as there was only one place that I knew of in the immediate St. Louis area that could offer such enticements and that was the Cheshire Inn. Consequently, I booked the bridal suite for us on the night of July 24 and we joyously reenacted our first night together as husband and wife. I blush!!

Several new opportunities were also starting to open up for me. Union Electric liked to run little articles in their company newspaper about their employees who had received degrees. Sometime toward the latter part of the summer, a little article appeared about me mentioning that I had recently received my Bachelor's Degree from SLU, graduating *Magna Cum Laude*. At the same time a group was forming within *Local 148 of the International Union of Operating Engineers* that were organizing behind a new young leader named Donald Giljum. Giljum had been the Chief Shop Steward at the Meramec Power Plant previously and had been a Business Representative of the Union for a short period as well during the term of former Business Manager "Red" Duckworth. This group was attempting to oust the current Business Manager, Jim Snipes, an Operations man that I was familiar with from working at the Venice Power Plant. Duckworth and Snipes had alternatively held office for three-year terms over the past 12 years, which had created some instability within the Union; consequently the Giljum candidacy.

During the fall of 1983 I received a call at work from my former Chief Steward at Rush Island, Carman LaPresta, who, like me, was an Operations man. He inquired as to where I sat politically with Duckworth and Snipes and asked if I might be willing to support a new candidate? He also mentioned that he had seen the article in the UE newspaper and thought I might be a good candidate to run on the ticket with Don Giljum, as Giljum was a proponent of bringing in some new guys to the Union office that had a good educational background. He also

356

The Union Years 1983-2002

noted that I had left a solid reputation back at Rush Island as a good Shop Steward and that my Operational experience would be a plus since they had some good Maintenance types already lined up to represent those groups across the system. Finally, he asked if I might be willing to meet with Mr. Giljum in the near future so that Giljum might evaluate my viability as a Business Representative of the Union, should he offer and should I, after our discussion, be interested. I gave him my permission to set up such a meeting.

A few days later Mr. Giljum called and asked if I might meet him at a McDonald's Restaurant in Arnold, Missouri, the following Saturday morning. My work schedule was such that I happened to be off that morning so we agreed to meet. When we first met I was kind of taken aback by his soft-spoken nature and kind of laid back attitude. He certainly did not look like what I would have anticipated a strong Union official to look like and to act, but I was impressed with his ideas and thoughts regarding how to make our Union stronger and more effective. Likewise, he seemed impressed by my "credentials," especially the fact that I had recently graduated from SLU, had been the Shop Steward at Rush Island and had been the Shop Steward for Labadie Operations almost since my arrival, and had never lost an election. Ironically, I had taken over for Paul Helfrich, my good buddy, soon after coming on line at Labadie. We talked quite a bit about what the Business Rep job entailed and then asked if I might be interested, should he make an offer. I indicated that certainly I would be interested, should he offer, at which point he indicated that he thought I was just the right guy that he needed. He stated that he would get back to me in the near future so that I could meet up with the rest of his core support group.

Simultaneously, the Company posted a bid for a position within their Power Operations Department, ironically one

357

Life Between Innings

of the two management groups within Union Electric (UE), the other being Industrial Relations, that I would do most of my grievance, discipline and contract negotiations with if I became a Business Representative for the Union. And, the current head of Power Operations was Mr. Ernie Kohlenberger, the former Superintendent of Operations at the Venice Power Plant, a man with whom I had established a very good relationship and had developed a good measure of respect. I did not want to blow my chances with the Union, but this was the job I had been aiming at for some time, and one for which I felt that I was very qualified. Should I get the job, my career path within UE would be set and could be one that I could have only dreamed of just months before. So, I decided to risk it and sent in my resume to the Union Electric personnel department and petitioned for an employment interview. Obviously the company had no knowledge that I had been approached by the Union and the Union had no idea that I was approaching the company about their job opening. The funny part about this scenario is that regardless of which job offer I would take, I would be sitting at the same table, the exact same table, and the only thing to be determined would be which side of the table I would be seated.

A few days later Mr. Giljum called and asked if I could meet with him and several of his key supporters the following Sunday afternoon at the Holiday Inn near the campus of SIU-E in Edwardsville, Illinois; I agreed to do so. It was here that I met for the first time the key men who were working with Giljum in organizing his campaign. It also began to become clear who the men were that would be taking on the other Business Representative positions in the Union Office should Giljum be elected. Obviously, Giljum would be the boss and fill the Business Manager's seat, I would be the representative for the Union Electric Fossil Fuel Operations and Carmen LaPresta

The Union Years 1983-2002

would take on the responsibilities for the Callaway Nuclear Plant and the hydro plants at Taum Sauk, Osage Beach/Lake Ozarks and in Keokuk, Iowa, all of which were UE plants. In Keokuk there was also a smelter plant that had been organized by Local 148 some time back that would fall into LaPresta's area of responsibility. It was still undetermined who would be the UE Maintenance representative for the fossil fuel plants, although by the end of the meeting it became clear that Joe Bauer, the current Chief Steward at the Labadie Plant, was the key choice if he would be willing to accept. The representative for the four power plants within the CIPS (*Central Illinois Power Service*) and EEI (*Electric Energy, Inc.*) systems was to be John Snyder, a former Local 148 Business Representative (worked for former Business Manager Red Duckworth) working at the EEI plant in Joppa, Illinois, near Paducah, Kentucky. The final position was the Union's Health and Welfare representative that would be filled by Keith Linderer, the current Chief Steward at the Meramec Plant. Of these men, only LaPresta and Bauer were men that I knew and both would obviously make exceptional Business Representatives.

Within days I received a call from Personnel at UE wanting to schedule a meeting for me with Mr. Kohlenberger, who would be interviewing me for the Company position. By this time I was becoming very excited about the possibilities with the Union, although I realized that we still needed to be elected before I would get the position. My meeting with Kohlenberger went well. It was obvious that he liked me; what I did not know was whether this whole process was a charade, and they already knew who they wanted in this job, or if I truly had a shot at getting it. The only stumbling block in the interview came when Kohlenberger asked what salary I would expect should I be named to the position. I commented that I thought it should be at least commensurate with what

Life Between Innings

a Union Business Representative makes since that would be with whom I would most often be meeting. I was not sure how that part of the interview actually went.

Within a few weeks the Company announced the name of their new employee, Mr. Darrell Rose, and it was a name that I would have expected to get the job; I was not overly disappointed. In fact, I was kind of relieved as I was becoming more and more excited about the prospect of working within the Union.

As 1984 approached, the campaign for the Union election, scheduled for July, began to pick up speed. Several of Giljum's core group, along with me, would accompany him to various locations around the system to meet with members and to seek their vote. By this time, Joe Bauer had agreed to be the UE Maintenance Rep, which gave us a really solid team. My only concern was this Keith Linderer fellow, as he seemed more interested in drinking and partying than he was in helping out with some of the campaign work. Finally, I approached Mr. Giljum and told him quite bluntly about my concerns regarding Keith, asking him if he was certain that Keith was the right man for this job? With a big smile, Mr. Giljum replied, *I think you will see that Keith is immensely qualified once you get to know him.* No words could have been truer spoken as Keith proved not only to be good, he was the best at what he does. He became a great friend, and came along side of me in negotiations a number of times through the years when I really needed the help, and he did it without being asked or without it being expected. Keith's loyalty was his strong suit and proved over and over again his dedication to the cause. Other unions and various companies tried to steal him away, but Keith held true. I had definitely been wrong on this one!

It was now August, the election was finally over and the ballots were being counted. Our opponent was the incumbent

The Union Years 1983-2002

Business Manager, Jim Snipes, and Jim and his team were very confident that they would easily beat this upstart, Donald Giljum. However, it was not too far into the ballot count that a clear trend was starting to emerge and that was that Giljum and the candidates that he had been pushing for other key Union offices were going to win, or make it very close. When the votes were finally counted, Giljum had won by more than a 2-1 margin and two other key Giljum supporters, Don Nash and Tom Alexander, had won the offices of Union Vice-President and Union Treasurer respectively. Ted Antoff, the current Union President, and Carl Jordan, the current Recording Secretary, barely retained their offices, demonstrating to them that they needed to get on board with Giljum quickly or they would most likely lose those positions at the next election. Both men quickly became strong supporters of our regime, although Jordan would waffle time and time again. Invariably, after a period of waffling with his support, he would come back and apologize and get back on board again. Despite his wishy-washiness, none of us could stay mad at Carl for any length of time as his heart and emotions were solidly in the Union; he was certainly a unique guy who remained one of my most solid supporters and allies to the very end.

On September 10, 1984, the Giljum team took office for what would be an extended period of time, bringing stability to Local 148 like it had not seen since its first Business Manager, Leo Bachinski, had been in office. Leo had served as the Business Manager for 20 years before he retired in the early '70s. Jim Snipes and his Team were actually very gracious in defeat and helped to make our transition into office as easy as they could. On the night the transition was made official, we were handed the keys to the office (148 Wilma Drive, Maryville, Illinois) and to the Union's automobiles and we were off and running.

Life Between Innings

My car was a big, light-blue 1982 Oldsmobile diesel that was great to drive, but much more car than I needed. Giljum did not want us driving the big cars that Union officials were so often associated with, due in part to his desire to present in fact and appearance, a more frugal Union than what our membership had become accustomed. Within months of taking office, Giljum had us in smaller Oldsmobiles and Ford Tauruses, and would probably have had us in something even smaller, if we had not protested loudly and in unison. Being out on the road as much as we would be, none of us looked forward to being cramped in a really small car day in and day out.

For Don, Carmen and Keith, they hit the ground running. The smelter plant in Keokuk, Iowa, was preparing for negotiations and the boys up there were not too happy. They had not had a raise in the past three contracts and it appeared that the Company was going to try and stiff them again with another contract package with no raises. These may have been rural, somewhat uneducated men, but they were tired of doing the hard and dangerous work that they were required to perform daily without any substantial recognition for it in their paycheck. After several months of negotiations, the Company insisted that the Union take back a package to the membership for a vote without the pay increase that the membership had demanded. Giljum explained to the men that it was not a good package but that it was probably all they could hope for. He also told the men that if they voted the package down, the Company most likely would not agree to come back to the table and resume negotiations. In fact, it was his prediction that the Company would most likely lock them out and hire permanent replacements to fill their jobs. Therefore, a NO vote on the contract meant a YES vote to STRIKE.

The Bargaining Unit was not very large, probably about 75-100 men and women. It finally came time to vote and

The Union Years 1983-2002

each of those present cast his vote understanding that if the package was not approved, they were most likely on strike or locked out and permanently replaced. When the votes were counted it was found that the package had failed by four votes. Giljum addressed the crowd and tried to convince them that with the vote so close, they should allow him to contact the Company and see if they would be willing to continue negotiations and perhaps give them a concession or two that the men could hang their hats on. However a large, vocal contingent of the group let it clearly be known that they did not want any part of that. When Giljum tried to reason with them again, this time he found himself staring down the barrel of a gun. One of their spokesmen made the point clear, *Giljum, we are going to strike; do you understand this?* He did! And, as Giljum had predicted, the work force was locked out and permanent replacement workers (thanks to good old Ronald Reagan) were hired almost immediately, breaking the Union. Some of the men, unfortunately, were willing to put their well being on the line and eventually crossed the picket line. Those men had many restless and sleepless nights as they faced the taunts of those who honored the pickets at the expense of their jobs. It was hard for them to show their faces in town and as a result, long-standing friendships, and even families, were torn apart. It is not a good idea to cross a picket line, ever!

My first couple of months in the office were very busy; in fact it was busy for all of us as we played catch-up to all the business that had been put on hold by the previous administration once they had lost the election. In fact, for the first six months it was not uncommon to be working a minimum of six days a week, sometimes seven, with those workdays running 12-14 hours each. None of us complained as we thought that eventually things would settle down and we would once again have a life. After about a year, the pace was still hectic but

Life Between Innings

some of us had families and we were determined not to lose them. Consequently, we gave as much as we could through the week, but come Saturday, and especially Sunday, we took time away. For guys like Keith and me it did not make sense to be fighting for an 8-hour day, 40-hour week, for the men in the plants and then put in all the hours that we were. Over Giljum's objection, we stuck to our guns and finally it became a non-issue. We also got the job done and done well.

My first indication that my relationship with many of my friends back in the power plants was changing occurred about six months into the job. At the time that Giljum appointed me as a Business Representative, I was serving as the Shop Steward for the Operations guys in Control Rooms #3 and #4 at the Labadie Power Plant. Labadie is a very large coal-fired four-unit plant that is one of the workhorses in the Union Electric system. At one time it was the seventh largest producer of electricity in the world. As I was preparing to depart and move to the Union Office, the men gave me a beautiful leather briefcase, a nice pen set and a gift certificate in thanks for the representation that I had given them over the past five years or so. Several also had noted that I had given them the best representation that they had ever received; it was a really nice send-off and I appreciated their sentiments.

However, as I began to represent the Operational forces I often had to make decisions that impacted all of Operations throughout the Union Electric system and these decisions, while perhaps good collectively, were not always what the Labadie guys themselves would have desired. One night at one of the union meetings one of the guys from Labadie Operations stood on the floor and in exasperation said, *Mooney, you bastard, you have already forgotten what it is like to be a worker out here!* Of course that kind of hurt my feelings a little bit but I had to recognize that it was hard for the guys to understand

The Union Years 1983-2002

that not only did I represent them, but I also represented all of UE Operations around the system; thus, I was working for Operations collectively and not just the individual group as I once did. What might be good or ideal for an individual group may not be good or ideal or represent the wishes of the men system wide. It was a good lesson to learn but it was never easy disappointing the guys that had helped me to get into the position that I was now working; all I could do was keep doing what I felt was best for the majority overall and hope that the majority would see it and appreciate it.

The year 1984 was also a landmark year for us as we decided to buy our first home. After several weeks of shopping with our realtor and not finding anything in our price range in the area that we wanted to live, we finally happened on a home not too far from our apartment located at 812 Wild Hickory Lane in unincorporated St. Louis County. We loved the house with its three bedrooms, basement and a Japanese-styled rock garden in the front yard. It had a big level fenced back yard that backed right up to the Parkway South High School gymnasium. The area was safe and close to most of the things we did except church. We knew that eventually we might have to leave our beloved Hope Church and find something closer, but that was something for another day.

We had not been long in our new home when we received a call from Shirley saying that Dionne, now 14 years old, had run away from their Macon, Georgia home. No one knew where she was or where to start looking for her. Obviously the authorities had been contacted and they gave us whatever assurances they could. Several days had passed when a call came from her grandfather, Henry Redman, saying that Dionne had called from someplace in Utah and that he was on his way to pick her up. I thought it interesting that I had not been given that option; nevertheless that was how Henry

Life Between Innings

worked. He did not always ask permission, he just did stuff. Apparently Dionne had become distraught over a number of issues at home, much of which did not come to my attention until several years later; consequently she hit the highways hitchhiking across the country in an attempt to get as far away from Georgia as she could.

Just prior to this I had been negotiating with Shirley to see if she would allow Marc, now age 12, to come and live with us as he had indicated a desire to do so during the summer of '83. It was clear that she was having difficulty with both kids, and from what little the kids would tell me, she was having troubles in her marriage as well. At the same time Shirley continued to exert pressure on me for more child support and threatened to take me back to court if I was not willing to ante up. I was not willing to ante up so she continued to badger me; thus we continued to do this dance year in and year out. I had to believe that a lot of her antics were due to pressure she was receiving from her husband, Dave, a retired UPS employee who now owned his own TV satellite company. They were living in a very nice home in a very nice subdivision in Macon with all the amenities that you could ask for, including a pool, so I was never really sure what they needed with an increase in child support pay. My payments were more than fair when they started in 1979 and I was confident that they remained fair here in 1984. So, it was with this backdrop that we now had to deal with Dionne.

Dionne was finally returned to her home in Macon, but not in very good condition. It seems that a number of disturbing things had happened to her before she hit the road and even more disturbing things had happened to her while out on the road. At the recommendation of a psychologist, it was finally decided to put Dionne into an adolescent behavioral rehab program. Fortunately for me, my medical insurance covered

The Union Years 1983-2002

most of the cost, although the remaining 20% of the bill still hit our pocketbook pretty hard.

After about a month, Dionne was released and seemed to do better for a short period of time. However, tragedy seemed to follow her wherever she went. One night while driving back from a concert in Atlanta, she and a boy friend just missed being killed when the car they were riding ended up underneath a tractor-trailer. Not long after that her boyfriend was tragically killed in a car accident when his souped-up car went out of control; the young man was actually decapitated in the accident. And these issues only represented a couple of the many other issues going on in her life. It was not long until I received a call from Shirley saying that they had readmitted her into the rehab center, although a different one than she was in previously. While Dionne's mental and health issues were of the utmost importance and priority, it was starting to get old writing out large checks to such programs.

Not all the news in 1984 was bad. Shortly before Christmas, Tina revealed to me that she was pregnant and that the baby was due sometime in late August of '85. I had promised her before we got married that we would have at least one child of our own and we had been working on making that promise come true.

It was also a time when the basketball Billikens of St. Louis University were starting to improve under new coach Rich Grawer. We had been attending games regularly so we decided that perhaps we should invest in purchasing our first season tickets, ensuring that we would have our regular seats at each game sitting among the fans surrounding us we were getting to know. At the time, the Billikens were playing in the 9,000-seat Kiel Auditorium in downtown St. Louis and our prized seats were right behind the SLU bench and just off to the left; perfect seats to watch a game and the coaching

Life Between Innings

on the sidelines. This was the era of Roland Gray and Monroe Douglas with Anthony Bonner to follow. Grawer had the program going great guns until the university screwed up his recruiting of Beaumont grad, Craig Upchurch. After signing a Letter of Intent to come to SLU, the university first agreed that he could come, but later rejected him for alleged academic reasons, reasons that have never been fully explained to the fan base. Upchurch eventually went on to play with the Houston Cougars and had a stellar four-year career. Once Bonner graduated, the team fell back into mediocrity until coach and fan favorite, Charlie Spoonhaur, came on board and reestablished a winning program with recruits brought in by Grawer. Grawer was a first class guy and I hated to see him go; but, if he had to go, Spoon was an excellent choice to bring in behind him.

As May of 1985 rolled in, it was time to begin our first contract negotiations with Union Electric. I had never participated in such before so I was anxious, and somewhat nervous, to see how this whole process worked. The Company's primary spokesman was a gentleman by the name of Bill Sanford and he appeared to be a fairly reasonable guy. Nothing throughout the negotiations ever changed that impression. While certainly not a pushover by any stretch, he was fair. His trademark was the wearing of shoes with holes in them to negotiations to demonstrate how broke the company was. However, I was mostly impressed with Donald Giljum and his preparedness at the table and the knowledge that he possessed regarding this whole contract bargaining process. The man did not miss a thing and always seemed to possess the uncanny ability to anticipate correctly what the Company was going to do.

Contract negotiations always produce innumerable stories that must be told time and again. Perhaps the best in this one occurred during a difficult day that we were having toward the end of negotiations. The issue that was on the table was

The Union Years 1983-2002

basically a deal breaker and was one from which neither side dare back down. Consequently, both Giljum and Sanford knew that if they responded to the question on the table, we were probably stalemated and that can never be good. So, we all just sat. No one talked. In fact, no one talked even to those on their own side of the table. One hour went by. Two hours went by. Three hours went by. Several of us got up quietly and went to the restroom and hurried right back, but the two negotiators just kept sitting there saying nothing. Finally, Sanford broke the ice and stated that he needed to go home. We all said, OK, packed up our stuff and went home; well, actually, to the local bar to discuss the non-events of the day. Several days later the two negotiators agreed on a new date to meet. When that day arrived Mr. Sanford appeared to be pretty ticked off from the get-go. He stated that he had heard that the Union had circulated a rumor that he had walked out of the last negotiations feigning a headache. In an emphatic tone he said, *I want to make it very clear, I did not and do not have a headache!* Without even batting an eye, Carl Jordan, our Recording Secretary, replied, *Then I guess that means that we can f#*k!* With that, the whole room erupted in laughter and the tension was broken. Negotiations proceeded and we reached our first contract with Union Electric without too much trouble.

In June of 1985, Shirley made a very difficult decision, one that I truly give her credit for making, allowing Marc to come to St. Louis to live with us. I know for a mother that this decision had to be most difficult, but I was thrilled that I would have my son back home with me. We immediately put Marc into the Parkway Junior High School and he seemed to thrive as his grades were good, his behavior was excellent and he seemed to be making quality friends at school. He also became involved in the band playing a Jazz Saxophone and actually did fairly well with it. We also got him involved in the

Life Between Innings

Manchester Baseball League and I eventually signed him up at my old alma mater, the Boys' Club of St. Louis, in the hopes that he could play basketball and experience what I had at the Club when I was growing up. In all honesty, Marc did not get much of a fair shake playing baseball on his Manchester team as his coach rarely let him play. However, when he did, he performed well. After one season at the Boys' Club, for whatever reason, his interest was not strongly kindled and he gave little indication that he wanted to continue.

As August approached we were getting anxious for the big day when the baby would arrive. We had enjoyed ourselves during the pregnancy as there were so many dances and parties to go to in my new role of Business Representative. Yes, there was a lot of work to be done but, Union guys also know how to party. Because this had been such a happy time for us, we were convinced that when the baby was born, it would be a baby that loved to have fun, love to dance, be generally happy and have red hair, as Tina had indulged in eating massive amounts of strawberries throughout the past nine months. I am not sure that our good times made the difference, but we sure were correct as that has been the history of our little bundle over her life, that is, except for the red hair.

On August 28th we decided to do something different. We kind of figured that the baby would be coming on this date, or perhaps at the latest the 29th. So, we made reservations at the restaurant at Fairmount Park, the local horseracing track in Collinsville, Illinois, only a couple miles from my office. I hadn't been there since a date in high school and Tina had never been. However, about mid morning Tina began to have contractions, but they were irregular at best and not all that close together. We contacted the doctor, but the doctor did not feel that a birth was imminent. He gave us some instructions on what to look for and assured us that everything would be

OK, just be prepared to come in when her contractions began to be two-minutes apart.

With those instructions we headed to the racetrack for a delicious meal and a few two-dollar bets on horses that we knew nothing about. We actually ended the evening up $50, which paid for our meal. At our neighboring table was a young black doctor and his wife. We engaged them in conversation, so they soon became aware of our "blessed" plight. When Tina told him that her contractions were now coming about every 10-minutes his eyes lit up like saucers. He advised us that it might be best that we start back toward St. Louis as it was his opinion that the moment might be sooner than we think. Taking the advice of the good doctor we headed home. It was now close to 11:30 PM and nothing much had changed, so we decided to go ahead and go to bed and wait. Wait we did not, as her contractions suddenly began to pick up with some regularity just as I dozed off. We jumped out of bed and she began to try to put on a pair of pants, but the contractions were such that each attempt to put in a leg was accompanied by a contraction; well, the dressing part was not going well. We finally got her presentable, I called the doctor to alert him that we were on our way, got her in the car, but with some effort, and off to St. John's Medical Hospital we went. At the Emergency Room I accompanied her inside and then left to quickly park the car. By the time I got inside, the nurse was telling me that she was ready to deliver, but they were waiting on the doctor.

About a half-hour passed and the doctor finally showed up. After checking over the situation he commented that this baby could have come earlier but he didn't think the nurses were that serious. About 20 minutes later, somewhere around 1:20 AM, and without pain medication, the baby began to push its little head through. At that the doctor commented that he sure hoped that it was a girl as he would hate to waste all that

Life Between Innings

dark hair on a boy. Then, at the last moment, there she was, a girl-little Whitney-in all her glory. Suddenly I heard the doctor exclaim, *Damn; she just shit on my shoe!* I think it was Whitney's revenge for having to wait so long on him to arrive. When I was allowed to hold her she looked so beautiful. She had a cute little pug nose, so we immediately dubbed her *Maggo*. It stuck.

Other than Tina and I, my mother was the only one there to experience the evening with us; mom wouldn't have missed this moment for anything. We had left Marc at home alone asleep, so after a few moments of celebration, I escorted mom to her car and we left. The next night Tina and I had a beautiful candlelight dinner at the hospital, just the two of us, which was a great touch to end our great and joyous weekend.

A day later, Marc and I decorated the house with streamers and placed a *Welcome Home* sign in the yard and then we were off to the hospital to pick up our new roommate. Marc and baby Whitney hit it off well, and especially so as she grew older; he seemed to take great pride in her and unabashedly would show her off to his friends at school. Except for Dionne's plight, 1985 was turning into a great year for us.

Along about November, I traded in the '83 Thunderbird and bought the most beautiful car that we have ever owned, a 1986 red Mercury Cougar. Since I was driving my new Union car, this became Tina's car with the talking voice that often reminded us, *The Door is Ajar.* We nicknamed the voice, *Barrington.*

We had also made arrangements with Rev. Don B. Miller to come to their special Thanksgiving Service at Grace Chapel in St. Peters and have Whitney dedicated. Grace Chapel was the new church plant of Hope Church and Don was the founding pastor. Tina had Whitney dressed in her finest and she obviously looked so beautiful. It was our joy to hear Don charge

The Union Years 1983-2002

us as parents to bring her up in a godly fashion and in a godly home, and then offer up a prayer for her that God would keep His hands of grace upon her for a lifetime. Amen!! We took the charge seriously and began immediately to pray regularly that God would bless her life and would begin to form, even then, a strong Christian man that would come into her life at the appropriate time.

In 1986, Dionne continued to struggle with Dave and Shirley's parenting and alleged physical and mental abuse, so it was agreed that Dionne would come and live with us. We knew that we were not aware of all of Dionne's issues but we felt confident that Dionne would quickly feel welcomed and safe and at home. We enrolled her at Parkway South High School, right next door, and for a few days things seemed to be going OK. A week, maybe two, after her arrival and starting school, I was watching through the kitchen window one day as she walked over to the school and then disappeared around the corner of the gymnasium wall. As she disappeared from sight I remember thinking, *She sure is a pretty girl; I hope she makes it!* Little did I know that this fleeting glimpse would literally be my final glimpse of her for some time.

As the evening of that day wore on, it became evident that Dionne was not coming home. I notified Shirley in Macon and then the police. They were not too encouraging. We later heard from two sources that they had thought they had seen her at the intersection of Highway 141 and I-44, near our home, hitchhiking, but had quickly dismissed the idea. At least a week went by before we finally got word that she had hitched a ride back to the East Coast and was staying at the home of a truck driver she had met on the road and his family. To this day, I do not know the truth or the full story. Eventually, Dionne returned to Macon and for a third time was placed in an adolescent rehab center. I have to admit that I was not too thrilled about this, but I couldn't really blame Shirley and Dave as I was sure they didn't know what to do either. After leaving the center Dionne headed out again, this time ending up in Jacksonville, Florida, where she lived homeless on the streets or, at times, in a Salvation Army center. I really did not hear much from Dionne again, although we prayed for her daily, until Shirley's marriage ended in divorce. Following the divorce, Shirley moved to Oklahoma to live closer to her mother; at some point Dionne surfaced and joined her.

In March of 1987, I began what became a tradition that lasted for about 21 years and still continues. The St. Louis University basketball program was on a nice roll with Gray, Douglas, and Bonner and later with Highmark, Claggett and Waldman. In '87 the Billikens were playing in the Metro Collegiate Conference (MCC), affectionately known as the Mostly Catholic Conference, as the majority of the schools were Jesuit. The finals of the season-ending conference tourney were being played in Indianapolis, a short three and half hour drive, so Marc and I took off to watch the championship game between St. Louis and arch rival, Xavier. The winner was to receive the automatic birth in the NCAA Tournament. It was a tight game but the Bills lost; however, I was hooked. The Bills did play in the NIT (*National Invitational Tournament, a secondary tournament for good teams that did not make the bigger, more prestigious NCAA tournament*) finals that year and the next, thanks to the efforts of Anthony Bonner, but it would be several more seasons before the team actually made it into the NCAA tournament.

From this time forward through 2007 I traveled to wherever the league season-ending tournament was held. This was a time of considerable NCAA conference changes and

The Union Years 1983-2002

realignments by schools and the Bills were no exception, jumping from the MCC to the Great Midwest and ultimately to Conference USA. This worked well as all the affiliated schools were in the Midwest and in easy driving distance. To fund my trips I would throw my change into a coin jar at the end of each day and by the next tournament I would have several hundred dollars saved to help provide a nice hotel in which to stay. The Bills joined the Atlantic 10 Conference beginning with the 2006/2007 season. The first tournament was held in Cincinnati, but was moved to Atlantic City, New Jersey, for the 2007/2008 games and for the foreseeable future. At that juncture, with the team in a rebuilding mold, moving from the Brad Soderberg regime to that of Rick Majerius, and the games no longer in driving distance, I decided to take a pass for a few years.

It was around this same time that we began to see evidence of Marc developing issues of his own as he was starting to hang around some unsavory characters. His grades began to fall off and we noticed that he was having a heck-of-a-time staying awake in church (and probably school, we just didn't know it). One evening, after everyone was in bed, I went into Marc's room for some reason only to find a nice roll of pillows impersonating a person in his bed and the window to his room slightly ajar. I sat up "shop" in his bedroom waiting for his return. Sometime much later the next morning he did return and was obviously startled to find his Dad in the room.

As the days and weeks went on this pattern continued, despite our best efforts. Eventually, I placed steel bars on the windows and hid the screwdrivers, but to no avail; it was evident we were not going to be able to stop him.

One day while at work I received a call from Tina and it was obvious that she was agitated and upset. We had been house-sitting for our neighbors and they had just returned from their

Life Between Innings

vacation. It seems that our neighbor had found a note in his bright red Porsche that he kept in their garage that appeared to belong to Marc. He then noticed that the odometer had more miles on it than when he had left to go out of town. After making this discovery, the family noticed that other things around the house were not as they should be. I hated to go home; what an embarrassing situation to be entrusted by your neighbors with the keys to their home and personal effects and then be betrayed by your own son.

I met with the neighbor and apologized. There wasn't much else we could do. He could have, and probably should have, called the police and reported "the break-in," but out of kindness for us, he didn't. Our relationship with them, however, was strained and never quite the same; within a year they moved.

Somewhere in the timeframe of 1986, I was beginning to get my feet on the ground as a Labor Representative and starting to enjoy the job. I was beginning to feel confident that I had what it takes to be a good Business Representative and my confidence was growing at a steady pace. The stack of grievances that had been left me by my predecessor had greatly diminished and my relationship with both the men in the plants and with the various plants' management began to solidify, including with those working in the company's executive offices. It was at this time that one of the more momentous events in my career occurred, one that truly set my course on how I would do business for the remainder of my career in Organized Labor. I was sitting in a waiting room in the Union Electric headquarters building in downtown St. Louis attending an arbitration case where I was being sequestered as a potential witness along with Tom Kraus, the Business Manager for IBEW Local 1439, one of our sister unions on the Union Electric property. Tom was a short, stocky man,

The Union Years 1983-2002

perhaps in his early 50s at the time, kind of an old crusty guy that looked uncomfortable in a suit. As he and I sat there solving the world's problems our conversation drifted into spiritual things. As our conversation continued he stopped, stared right at me with those hardened eyes of experience, pointed a chubby finger at me and said, *Mooney, if you think you can go into these meetings with the Company day after day and not take God with you, you have made a grave error, my friend!* I do not remember anything else about the conversation, the arbitration, or anything else about that day, but I never forgot those very poignant words.

As I milled over the words that Tom had so emphatically spoken, I began to think that if this was true for Old Tom, a man whom I would not have thought, up till now, had any relationship with God, then certainly, for me, a Christian, a born-again believer, I should take these words seriously. From that day forward I cannot recall any grievance meeting, any arbitration, any contract negotiation or any disciplinary case that I was handling, where I went in without first praying and asking God to help guide me though the meeting and give me wisdom in how to handle each matter. I am sure somewhere, sometime, I forgot to pray, but as a rule, I never failed to pray . . . and I have very little doubt that this is why God blessed the efforts over the 18 years that I served. I never asked God to let me win a case or a grievance, I just simply asked that he intervene in my deliberations and bless the efforts; and He did.

Much later in my career when I started handling contract negotiations for CIPS and EEI, I often found myself in prayer asking for God's intervention. In reality, what did I have to offer these company representatives that I was negotiating with? What could I say that would make them want to share the wealth of their companies with the men that I represented? I had nothing to offer, but God's grace that He had fully extended

Life Between Innings

to me; absolutely nothing. This often reminded me of a saying that Bob Mumford, a teacher/preacher used to say, *You don't get spiritual because you want to, you get spiritual because you have to.* Well, that described me and this job; this job that seemed so wrong for me by most human and spiritual standards, yet it was this job that kept me on my knees, not because I wanted to be spiritual, but because I needed His grace and His favor to succeed. It was truly in my weakness that I found God's strength, a lesson I continue to learn even today!

For years Tina had wanted to become a Registered Nurse so this seemed to be the right time for her to pursue that dream. During the spring and fall of 1986 she began to investigate the various nursing schools to see where she might be accepted and get started. We were both thrilled when a slot opened up for her at Meramec Junior College. Meramec offered a two-year program whereby she could receive her Associate Degree in Nursing and then be eligible to take the tests for a Missouri State Nurses' License. She began her studies in January of 1987, graduating at the end of the fall semester of '88. I rented a limousine to escort her to the graduation ceremonies at the college and then on to Balaban's Restaurant in the eclectic Central West End. Here she was joined by a number of friends and family who had gathered to surprise her and to celebrate her accomplishment over a great meal and refreshments. What a great night of celebration this was for her as she was finally realizing her dream. A few weeks later, she journeyed through ice and snow to Springfield, Missouri, to take her state test, which she passed on the first attempt. She had already secured a nursing position as an RN (Registered Nurse) based on her pending test scores at St. Joseph Hospital in Kirkwood (later built anew and renamed St. Claire Hospital in Fenton, Missouri), where she has continued to work for some 22 years.

The Union Years 1983-2002

In the summer of 1987, the Giljum Team faced its first reelection. Our first three years had gone so quickly and I was hopeful that we would be returned to office as I had my area of responsibility in excellent shape and had key people working at my various UE locations that were making things click along. The election was not even close as the Giljum team won by even a greater margin than in '84.

With the election behind us, Giljum decided, following a week-end meeting with the full team, that the issues at Callaway Plant were subsiding to such a degree that perhaps it would be good to realign our areas of responsibility for better utilization of our manpower. One of the things that Giljum had wanted to do was to start an internal EAP (Employee Assistance Program) within the Union to address the growing drug and alcohol problem within our membership, plus develop our own PAC (Political Action Committee). He also wanted to get involved in union organizing. As junior man on the staff, and with no one else volunteering to do this work, Giljum asked me to develop the EAP and PAC programs. Once I had both of these programs up and running, he wanted me to start working on some union organizing activities (the process of soliciting employees from a specific company asking them to request representation by Local 148 as their bargaining unit through a process set up by the National Labor Relations Board).

In recent months we had arbitrated several employee dismissal cases and had won each of them. However, it was Giljum's belief that we were, in reality, just wasting money on these cases, as we were not addressing the real problems and issues that had gotten these employees fired in the first place. He obviously was right. The various companies would build a case against an employee based on such issues as absenteeism, tardiness and job performance, which we could beat in

Life Between Innings

arbitration, as the Company had not yet learned how to maintain a good paper trail. But, we knew that the underlying issue in almost every one of these cases was drugs and alcohol. We also knew that until we addressed those issues, we could win all the arbitrations we wanted but these employees, our members, would still find a way to "fire themselves" again in short order.

Knowing that I had been working through similar issues with my own daughter and son, junior man or not, Giljum thought I was probably the man on staff to build the Union's EAP and develop the PAC. He then gave LaPresta my area of jurisdiction, since he had more seniority. I was not too thrilled about the changes as it had taken me three years to clean up the mess left me by my predecessor and I was just starting to enjoy the fruits of my labor. However, I really did not have much choice in the matter. The changes were to take effect as we rolled into 1988. Once into the new calendar year, Giljum totally freed up my schedule so that I could fully concentrate on the job of developing the EAP and PAC. The PAC was easy to work on but the EAP would take some time as I would need to get myself familiarized with the substance abuse field in general and the organizations that could help us, specifically.

As I began the process it was actually pretty cool as I was meeting a lot of new people, attending some really informative seminars and being schmoozed by a number of agencies that wanted our business and our referrals. It was also a job with much less pressure than the one I had working grievances and handling the various disputes and negotiations that were continuously occurring in the plants. I soon found that I was really enjoying the job; however, some of my peers, namely Joe Bauer and John Snyder, were somewhat resentful that I was drawing the same Business Rep pay as everyone else but was not handling the same level of responsibility that they were. Evidently

The Union Years 1983-2002

they took their resentment to Giljum and strongly voiced their displeasure behind my back. The fact that it was at no fault of my own must have escaped them both, plus Bauer was part of the team that met with Giljum that had resulted in my being forced (asked) to take on this particular job in the first place. A strong rift developed between Bauer and me and for the next three years we rarely talked. I later found that he had tried hard to get me fired and that incensed me even further, but Giljum had remained loyal. From an extremely tight team that worked hard together and worked hard to protect each other those first three years, following the jurisdictional change, that cohesiveness was gone. It was an unnecessary shame.

Joe Bauer had been my Chief Steward at the Labadie Plant while I was serving as Operations Steward. Joe and I had gotten along great and I had been a strong supporter of his and had worked to get him elected. During our first three years in office we continued to have a good working relationship, although Joe did his business much differently than I did mine. In fact, all of us reps had been very successful in Union affairs prior to coming into office even though we all had different personalities and different ways of getting the job done. It was somewhat ironic that Giljum was the only one who had ever lost an election; none of us on staff ever had.

Despite the strong tensions in the air I had Giljum's assurance that I was doing what he wanted. Consequently, I continued to endeavor to put the EAP program together and develop a team at each of the individual UE plants to work with me. Taking a cue from the United Way and their First-Step Program, we named our program the *Local 148 First- Step Assistance Program*. We began to have success almost immediately and began to receive recognition and assistance from Union Electric's management. By 1990-91 the program was starting to receive national recognition and the program was

Life Between Innings

expanding from just a drug-and-alcohol program to one that embraced mental health, finances, children's issue, etc.

Putting the PAC program together was fairly easy, as it required a couple meetings with the attorneys to get the paper work in order and then form a system wide committee to develop the program at their individual plants and work locations. However, being a Union Organizer was and is a whole different world, but it is where I quickly and clearly learned about the under belly of doing union work as I found the playing field of Management and Organized Labor unfairly tilted (did I say unfairly tilted?) in favor of Management.

One of my first leads was at E.F. Trucking, a small hauling firm, located near Lebanon, Illinois. Their primary customer was the *Wall Street Journal* that was published nearby. The guys would pick up their load of newspapers and drive all over the Midwest each night in order to have the papers ready for delivery bright and early that day in Hometown, USA. Obviously, the company was not interested in a union being on the property and they fought hard against our efforts to organize. I had three key individuals from the firm that were helping me to get *Union Authorization Cards* signed petitioning the *National Labor Relations Board (NLRB)* to hold a secret ballot election. The company pulled the usual anti-labor tactics to put fear into the hearts of the employees, like threatening to close down the operation, threatening to fire employees and putting out highly slanted anti-labor printed materials. They would also hold meetings with employees appealing to their sense of loyalty to the company and insisting that their door was always open to hear their grievances and issues without the involvement of an outside third party. And, of course they talked incessantly about the fact that employees would be required to pay union dues even if they did not vote for the union. Then the inevitable came as they would find the weakest link, the employee with the poorest work record, and fire him or her. Of course they were always certain to fire the employee for poor job performance, although everyone knew it was due to that employee's involvement in the organizing drive. Firing an employee for being involved in a union-organizing drive is illegal and a violation of the *National Labor Relations Act.* However, cases that are pursued usually take up to two years to resolve. And, even if the Union prevails, all the employee gets is his job back and is made whole for wages lost. The definition of *wages lost* means taking the total of what the employee would have earned if not unfairly fired, minus the wages he earned elsewhere trying to keep the bills paid prior to being reinstated. The companies know that most employees will have lost interest long before the process is complete so firing an employee, even illegally, is not a detriment to them.

After a couple months we had the necessary authorization cards signed and we gave them to the NLRB and petitioned for an election. We knew that the election would be close. Compounding our problem was that management had insisted that two of their management employees were truly not management employees and asked that the NLRB allow them to vote. The Board agreed that they could vote but that their ballots would be held in abeyance, uncounted, pending the outcome of the election. Should the election be within two votes, the NLRB would then rule on whether or not their votes should legally be counted in with the bargaining unit employees.

The day of the election arrived and the Union won by a two-vote margin. The margin of victory was such that the NLRB then met to decide whether the two outstanding votes from the "management" employees should count. Of course it was their determination that they "really" weren't management employees, therefore their votes would be counted. As

Life Between Innings

we all surmised, the two votes were against the union creating a tie vote. A tie vote in a union representation election goes to the company and the union was therefore not allowed to come in and represent the employees. Following the election the company made life pretty miserable for those who supported the campaign and eventually most of those who had worked to try to get the union in were either "persuaded" to leave or resigned.

I was involved in two other organizing drives, one that ended in defeat and one that we won. I always resolved to be very honest with those employees that attempted to start organizing drives so that they would be keenly aware of what was in store for them and their families. Organizing is probably the dirtiest, most heart-rending activity that I was involved with in working for the union. It is obviously a very needed function of what we do, but the tactics used by companies and their high-powered union-busting attorneys are so disgusting, so inhumane, so unfair, as to be simply laughable. But, with strong Republican leadership in Washington since the mid '60s, labor laws are rarely changed in favor of helping the worker. Or, as in the Ronald Reagan administration, the government would simply under-fund those agencies that are the watchdogs of these types of irregularities so that management's unscrupulous tactics would go unchecked due to a lack of manpower to oversee the operation.

By now Marc had become totally out of control and was finally picked up on car theft. I got him the best lawyer I could find, a highly recognized attorney from Belleville through some connections within the Union. He did not come cheap. We met with Marc at the Juvenile Center in Clayton, Missouri, and then later at a hearing. It was here that I told Marc that this was the last attorney that I would ever retain for him and that any future problems, should he continue in this vein, he

The Union Years 1983-2002

would face on his own. Marc continued to get in trouble with the law and that was the last time I ever paid for an attorney and I never paid for bail. I absolutely refused to waste my money on such irresponsible behavior once the ground rules were clearly defined. I did not receive much support for my stance from family or the courts, but Tina stood steadfastly by me and she walked this dark path with me from start to finish.

Marc's 17 birthday came and I was tired of our little family having to live with police coming to the door regularly, like this was something normal. A few months after his birthday another criminal incident, following a number of other criminal incidents, occurred so I kicked him out of the house. He stayed for a few weeks with the "loving" family of one of his criminal peers. Finally, an opportunity came for him to move to Minnesota with another one of his peers. He did stay in contact while there but soon became engaged in more trouble, landing him in a Minneapolis jail.

The list goes on and on. He had a number of opportunities to right himself but just couldn't or wouldn't do it. One of my contacts offered to take Marc into a long-term rehab center in the heart of Manhattan, New York, and would only charge me what the insurance would pay. I decided that it would not hurt so we put him on an Amtrak Train and sent him on his way. Marc did very well in this program, as he would do in all similar programs that he would be thrust into over the years; he learned to play this game very well. I had the opportunity to visit with him one weekend while he was there and it was actually one of the hi-light events of our Father and Son relationship. He showed me around Manhattan during the day, along with a very cute female friend of his from the center, and we visited the Statue of Liberty among other things. But, not long after his release he was back into trouble again and, as usual, it was alcohol related.

The kids and their alcohol related issues pretty much destroyed any semblance of the joy and laughter that we had enjoyed around the holidays when we were kids growing up. As the kids later admitted, they were there for the presents and the dinner and then *get the hell out of Dodge*, to go wherever they could find some beer or drugs.

Aside from the trials that Dionne and Marc were putting us through, our lives, were being blessed in unbelievable ways. In fact, throughout our marriage we have rarely fought with each other, or had harsh words; we just didn't. Our home was and is basically characterized by considerable peace and quite except for outbursts of laughter and/or loud cheers or groans while watching a sporting event. But, if we did, it was usually the result of how Tina let phone calls from her parents involving a variety of issues, often coming at odd hours, bother her for days on end. These conversations, which were usually one-sided and lengthy and containing unfounded accusations of varying degrees, often over issues we did not even know existed, well, I had no tolerance for it and would strongly suggest that she simply hang up and not further the discussion. To protect our marriage and our sanity, we mutually decided that hence forth such calls would only rarely be answered after 7:00 PM. That said, our relationship with my in-laws for the most part is a good one. In fact, I think I can safely say that from the beginning till now, my mother-in law, in particular, is perhaps one of my biggest fans.

In 1989 we started a tradition that became the setting for our most favorite memories as a family (Tina, Whitney and me), that being annual vacations to the beach in Florida. Early that summer we had decided to take a little vacation so Tina had connected with a travel agent who put together a four-day

The Union Years 1983-2002

trip for us to Marco Island, Florida. Whitney was now four-years old and learned to love the beach immediately, but loved the pool even more. As a compromise, we would go to the beach in the morning, and then after Whitney and I had our nap, we would go to the pool in the afternoon.

In 1990 we took another four-day vacation, although this time to South Padre Island near Brownsville, Texas. This was only our second vacation but we were already getting spoiled and quickly ascertained that four days was just not enough. It was here at Padre Island that I was stung by a jellyfish. It felt like somebody had hit my foot with a hammer. By soaking my foot in hot water for several hours, the pain went away without any repercussions.

The year of 1990 meant it was time for the Union's election again. As in '84 and '87, the Giljum Team won by a large margin, even greater in fact than in the two previous elections. While our team was not as cohesive as it was in '84-'87, we were still a very effective group and the membership, as a whole, recognized that.

We had also started looking for a new church as Pastor Don A. Miller had retired and Pastor B's church in St. Peters was just too far to drive. We attended the West County Christian Church in Chesterfield for about a year. It was interesting in that our first Sunday there, the Pastor resigned. The Youth Pastor then took the pulpit and we really liked him. We were about to join the church but he called and asked to meet with us, the purpose being to tell us he was taking a church near Chicago and thought we should know before we became members. We did stay for a while after a new pastor came, but after about three months and never hearing the name of Jesus spoken from the pulpit, we knew this was not for us.

It was February of 1991 when I came upon a front-page article on the sports page of the *St. Louis Post-Dispatch* regarding

Life Between Innings

a St. Louis University basketball recruit from Parkway West High School named Scott Highmark. In the article it talked about this young man's faith in Christ and that he and his parents were attending Twin Oaks Presbyterian Church, now meeting in the Parkway South High School auditorium, right next door to us. On the second Saturday in March, Scott's Parkway team had won the State Championship, a game that I had watched on television. I thought it might be interesting to drop in for the church service that following Sunday morning at the school to see what it was like and also see if they might make some mention of Scott and the State Championship. I also reasoned that if this was a good place for a young man to experience growth in his faith, just maybe this was the church that we were looking for as we wanted Whitney in a church with other children her age that lived in the community.

Tina was working that Sunday so Whitney and I drove over (which took about 20 seconds, once we were in the car) and was greeted by a host of people as we entered. I also quickly noticed that there were a lot of small children here. As we were being seated, a man introduced himself as Dave Bias and likewise welcomed us. I was blown away by the worship service; the Holy Spirit was truly at work and the refreshing atmosphere of God's presence was so real. Finally, the pastor, Rodney Stortz, began the message. I have had the great privilege to sit under the ministry of a number of great preachers and expositors in my life, but without a doubt Rodney was the best, or at a minimum tied for first, that I have ever heard; he presented the Word so powerfully and so clearly. As I sat there and bathed in the worship and the Word, I knew that we had found our home.

I could not wait to tell Tina about the new church that I had found. Tina was not one who wanted to church hop so she patiently listened but still wanted to go back to West County for the evening service, which we did. Not surprisingly, it was another Christless message that was as hollow as an old reed. It was easy to get her to agree to go with me to Twin Oaks the next Sunday morning.

Just as I had been the previous Sunday, Tina was likewise blown away by the worship and the Word and the friendly people. It was also not lost on her the number of small children running around. It was evident that this was a family church. We also ran into a young man, JG Porwoll, who was in charge of their World Missions ministry. In fact, the Sunday before my first visit was the first World Missions Conference of Twin Oaks Church. Tina and I talked about our passion for foreign missions with JG and he invited us to a dinner that the church hosted for visitors following every Sunday AM services. Here we met more of the Twin Oaks people and were made to feel welcome immediately. Needless to say, we never returned to West County Christian.

It did not take long for us to realize that we wanted to be part of this vibrant work going on right in our backyard. And better yet, we found that they were going to build their new church just a mile or two from the house. This was perfect. Without much debate we started attending their Inquirers Class. The introduction was taught by Pastor Stortz wherein he explained that Twin Oaks was basically a church plant of Covenant Presbyterian Church located in the city of Town and Country. Twin Oaks was part of a conservative denomination called the PCA, or the Presbyterian Church in America, and taught what they called, "Reformed Theology." However, the most interesting subject that was taught was the issue of "predestination." About 20 years earlier this denomination had begun as a result of a split within the Presbyterian Church in the United States of America, or PCUSA, which had gone very liberal in their teachings and practices.

Life Between Innings

We were introduced to a white haired gentleman, Charlie Johnson, who was to take us through the subject of predestination and the other teachings of the PCA doctrines and sacraments. Obviously, this first subject was a controversial issue for some in the class and eventually a number of them left as they just could not accept that God would choose those whom He desires to save and rejects those that He desires to reject. I had been in Christendom all my life and had graduated from Bible College, but I had never heard this subject taught with such clarity. In fact, I had to admit that for the most part those that I had heard teach on this subject had tried to either talk around it or bring in other scriptures to try to make it say what they wanted it to say. For me, for the first time in my life, the Scriptures actually came together and the teacher was making no apology for it saying exactly what it was saying.

Charlie took us through the foundational verses, although the Bible is replete with others, regarding predestination found in Romans 8:28-31 (NIV):

28. *And we know that in all things God works for the good of those who love him, who have been called according to his purpose.*

29. *For those God foreknew he also predestined to be conformed to the likeness of his Son, that he might be the firstborn among many brothers.*

30. *And those he predestined, he also called; those he called, he also justified; those he justified, he also glorified.*

31. *What, then, shall we say in response to this? If God is for us, who can be against us?*

Then, from Romans 9:11-24 (NIV), Paul even makes it further clear as to exactly what he is saying:

11. *Yet, before the twins were born or had done anything good or bad – in order that God's purpose in election might stand:*

The Union Years 1983-2002

12. not by works but by him who calls—she was told. The older will serve the younger.
13. Just as it is written: "Jacob I loved, but Esau I hated."
14. What then shall we say? Is God unjust? Not at all?
15. For he says to Moses, "I will have mercy on whom I have mercy, and I will have compassion on whom I have compassion."
16. It does not, therefore, depend on man's desire or effort, but on God's mercy.
17. For the Scripture says to Pharaoh: "I raised you up for this very purpose, that I might display my power in you and that my name might be proclaimed in all the earth."
18. Therefore God has mercy on whom he wants to have mercy, and he hardens whom he wants to harden.
19. One of you will say to me: "Then why does God still blame us? For who resists his will?"
20. But who are you, O man, to talk back to God? "Shall what is formed say to him who formed it, 'Why did you make me like this?'"
21. Does not the potter have the right to make out of the same lump of clay some pottery for noble purposes and some for common use?
22. What if God, choosing to show his wrath and make his power known, bore with great patience the objects of his wrath – prepared for destruction?
23. What if he did this to make the riches of his glory known to the objects of his mercy, whom he prepared in advance for glory –
24. even us, whom he also called, not only from the Jews but also from the Gentiles?

At the conclusion of the two-month long course, I told Tina that I really needed to go through it again to make sure I was understanding what I thought I was understanding as this was actually revolutionary in contrast to what I had been taught my whole lifetime. We did go through it a second time and it

Life Between Innings

was more convincing for us both than it was the first time. Wow, just to think, the Bible actually meaning what it says; now that is revolutionary!

In less than a year the church moved into its new building at Highway 141 and Big Bend Road in the small village of Twin Oaks. It had been so exciting to watch the church go up and then for that final piece, the tall steeple, to be lifted into place. The men who had the vision for building this church had thought they were thinking big as they labored over the blueprints, as the sanctuary would seat 800. Our attendance at the school by this time was running somewhere in the neighborhood of 300 or so. That first Sunday, with some, but not a lot of advertising, the place was packed and overflowing. We soon went to two services but we still needed more room. Finally the balcony was finished and it was still a tight fit to get everyone in. At the peak, our attendance was hovering around 1700 on a Sunday morning. But, the most important thing was to see people being saved and God bringing into our midst those who He had foreordained to be His son or daughter. This was certainly a spiritual high, a glorious mountaintop if you would, and God continued to bless.

Soon after arriving at the new church, JG Porwoll, the Twin Oaks Missions Director, gave Tina and me both an invitation to come and be a part of the World Missions Committee and ministry. We were excited to be part of this ministry and readily accepted his offer. This began a 19-year commitment of service for us both with this wonderful, and very impactful ministry. I was blessed and fortunate to have served as a member, as Elder Oversight, Chairman and finally Director. Working in this ministry was one of the true joys and passions of my Christian life and spiritual endeavors; I truly considered it to be a high-calling.

The Union Years 1983-2002

Even though I had left the power plants in 1984 and was now working out of the Local 148 Union Office, I was still technically a Union Electric employee. Consequently, I was allowed to continue my participation with the Rivermen softball team as captain/coach. Giljum also thought it was a good idea for me to continue to play as it would keep me connected in a positive way with the men from the various power plants that we represented. With the pressures of the union job and the added pressures of misguided teenagers bent on destroying their lives, this was a great place to release my frustrations and to enjoy the comradeship that can only come from being part of a great team of guys. Again, I was fortunate in that our team was not made up of a bunch of jocks, but just some really good men who, together, were beginning to play a good brand of softball.

In 1987, those two, three or four pieces that we were missing that would take us from being a good team to an exceptional team showed up. These pieces came to us in the in the form of Tom Haegele and Mark Koehler soon followed by my nephew, Steve Mooney, who I was able to help get hired on at Union Electric, plus Frank Zoellner. In fact, Zoellner, Mooney and Haegele took up the first three spots in our batting order. Frank was a slightly built man with flowing blonde locks that could run like the wind, play an exciting and exceptional outfield and swing an awesome bat. Steve, well, he is the best softball player that I have ever played with. While small of stature, he too could run extremely well and field his position, infield or outfield, with the same adeptness. But, the important ingredient was his hitting. Steve had wrists that I would equate with the great Hank Aaron that could generate unbelievable power. With his speed and power, rarely did we see Steve at first; most often he was at second base or beyond. Then, there was Tom Haegle, a total gift of God. One night at

Life Between Innings

our practice he showed up to sign on with a team from his workplace. However, due to some miscommunication, that team never showed. We invited Tom to practice with us and he took a liking to our team and the quality of players that we had; on the spot, he decided to play with us. Tom not only could field both in the infield and outfield, but he became immediately one of the top sluggers in the league. With all the other good men that we had in place, we were now ready to challenge for the championship, and we did, each year from 1987 through 1995.

Before my retirement from softball in April of 1997 (at age 49), we won two championships, and as stated, were in the mix every other year. Our final championship came in 1995 against the Woodpeckers, our chief rival. However, the most exciting was the first one that we won in 1993 against those same "Peckers." They were an impressive team with a lot of power. Bill Dorner and I knew that if we tried to play them straight up, most likely they would kill us. Since we had a loss coming into the championship round, it was necessary that we beat the Woodpeckers two straight games, they being undefeated. It was with that backdrop that we decided to walk their #3-hitter, who was undoubtedly the most feared player in the league, every time he came to the plate, regardless of circumstance. With one exception (and we got him out reaching for a really bad pitch as he was overly anxious to hit), we did this for both games. With every walk, the more frustrated our opponents became; we had gotten into their head, which was an advantage that we needed if we wanted to prevail. The fans in the stands were on us mercilessly, but many later complimented us on our strategy. With these walks, the #4-hitter, a good player in his own right, went zero for 8 that evening, playing into our hands as we had hoped. With that, we won the first game 11-3 and the second game 11-5 to secure our first championship. As we looked back to that time, just a few years previously, when playing for Syl's Café we had gotten our brains beat in by a team with bib overalls and combat boats, we realized we had come quite a ways; and it felt really good.

In 1995, we captured our final championship with relative ease, blowing out our opposition in the league and in the championship game. The championship game was called after four and a half innings due to the mercy rule as we were already up by some 11 or 12 runs.

I was also on a championship team in 1996, my last full season, but not with the Rivermen. I had disbanded the Rivermen following our championship in 1995 at the end of the season as it was obvious I was getting too old to play without pain and my travels working for the Union were making it much more difficult to get back in town for each game. It was also becoming increasingly hard for me to keep up the necessary communications with the guys, especially since they were employed at a number of locations throughout the region. The Woodpeckers asked me to pitch for them in '96 and I agreed, knowing that all I had to do was show up at games and that was it. We all admitted it was much more fun when we were rivals and "hated" each other, but it was nice to get one more title under my belt.

I returned to play with them again in 1997. However, upon returning home from the first game, I was so sore that I could barely crawl up the steps to our bedroom. Tina, always the fan but not too sympathetic (more like just being sarcastic), said, *Well idiot, go look in the mirror and see what color your hair is; maybe that is a clue.* She was right; it was time to hang up the glove and the spikes from the game I had loved so much. They always say that you will know when it is time to quit; and I knew it. That was my last game. And, I was OK with that.

Life Between Innings

Early in May of 1991, John Snyder, the Business Rep handling the contracts of the four CIPS plants and the EEI plant, had a heart attack. This was going to obviously tie John up for awhile so Giljum asked me to accompany him to Paducah, Kentucky as EEI contract negotiations were just starting up. I had only been to the Joppa Plant (EEI) one other time, and that was back in '84 when we were first campaigning. Consequently, I did not know the people, nor did I know their contract. But, no problem, I was only there to give Don moral support and to take the minute notes. My reputation for note taking had become well known as I had the uncanny ability to often remember verbatim conversations and would go back to the hotel or office or at home and then reduce my recollections to writing. These notes proved very helpful during the term of agreement when issues over contract interpretation or intent would arise, as well as in arbitrations over contractual issues.

It was while in the early stages of the negotiations that I received a call from Tina saying that I needed to return home quickly as her oldest brother, Lee, was dying and they did not expect him to hold on much longer. I immediately jumped in the car to return home but, by the time I reached St. Louis, Lee had passed away. Lee had contracted Leukemia several years earlier and had been able to get it into remission. However, he soon went back to work and under the pressure of mounting bills began to push himself hard and the cancer returned. It became necessary at some point that he be given a blood transfusion. Unfortunately, blood was not tested to the degree it is today; consequently, Lee received blood that contained the HIV virus. In the end, it was not the cancer that killed him, it was the AIDS virus. This was a difficult period for the whole family but Tina hung in with him, nursed him, loved on him and shared her faith in Christ with him. We never really knew

The Union Years 1983-2002

if Lee fully trusted in Christ as his Savior, although there were some positive reasons to believe that he had.

One Saturday in June, Giljum called me to say that he would not be going back to the contract negotiations at EEI and that he needed me to take the negotiations. I had been observing him for these past seven years but had never handled negotiations at this level before. That Sunday following I traveled to Paducah and checked in at the Pear Tree Hotel and began to ponder as to what I should do. I had seen Giljum write up proposals and counter-proposals before, and writing was kind of my forte; so, as I sat alone, kind of fearful of what tomorrow might hold, I decided to look at some of the proposals on the table and see if there were some simple ones I could respond to. I prepared three counter-offers and took them to breakfast the next morning and showed them to the committee. They were obviously a little, if not greatly, disappointed that Giljum was not going to be there, but, they were OK with the counters that I had drafted.

Negotiations that day and over the next few days actually went pretty well. The Company's chief negotiator was the vice-president of EEI, Mr. Robert "Bob" Powers. Bob was not real fond of Local 148, John Snyder or Don Giljum and the word on the street was that he wanted to break the Union and get them out of his hair. He had felt that Snyder especially, and Giljum to a great degree, had lied to him about some past issues and the committee was fearful that Powers might try to force a strike and then lock them out, thus breaking the Union. EEI as a company was also experiencing some difficult days through previous mismanagement and currently had two of their six units sitting in cold steel (not operating). Bob was determined to bring this plant back to life and if the Union got in his way, well they shouldn't have.

Life Between Innings

Somewhere along the first week of July we were working on a contract extension, the original contract expiring at midnight on July 1. We had been holding our negotiations at the Executive Inn Hotel in Paducah, Kentucky; however, on this given day a large convention was in town and all the rooms that we normally could use for negotiations were being utilized. Someone from the Company had secured several rooms in a nice sized Methodist Church on the main street of town for our use that day and the remainder of the week. We were about an hour into negotiations when one of the guys on my committee responded to something that Mr. Powers had said by stating that one of the foreman at the plant was a 'liar." Mr. Powers did not take kindly to the remark and demanded that the committeeman cease saying such things. The committeeman, not being intimidated, responded back that in fact the foreman was a "liar." At this time it looked to me like Mr. Powers was about to come across the table at my guy, his anger building in intensity. With that, I slammed my negotiating book closed, stood up, and forcibly stated, *We are out of here!!*

I turned to leave and my whole committee grabbed their stuff and followed and out the door we went. Word spread quickly on the street that the Union had walked out of negotiations and was going on strike. Powers did not know me well and certainly did not know how I was going to respond or what I was going to do. I took the men to lunch and word finally reached me that Powers would like to see me back at the church as soon as I could get there. We finished our lunch and headed back with the whole committee in tow. Seeing Mr. Powers I went on ahead and he asked very politely if we could meet and talk. I assured him that I was willing to talk but he was going to have to remain calm or else I would not

The Union Years 1983-2002

continue. He did not respond but he did give me the famous Powers' glare.

We started walking around looking for a private room in which to meet, but all we could find was a Sunday School room with those really small toddler sized chairs. We went in and took a seat. The absurdity of this picture makes me laugh even today. Here is the vice president of a large utility and the chief negotiator of a powerful Union sitting together in a Sunday School classroom on very small toddler chairs talking about contract negotiations. I think this scene is hilarious!

For about the first 20 minutes or so we just talked about things in general, just kind of getting to know each other. At some point in the discussion something was mentioned that caused us to question each other regarding our "faith." It did not take too much prodding until we both found that we were Christians and that our goals for the guys and the contract were actually mutual. Just how we would get to that final agreement with something that we both could accept, well, that was the question. After about an hour or more we decided to have a time of prayer. This was unbelievable. Finally, we both walked out together, we collected our committees and proceeded with negotiations. I negotiated across the table from Mr. Powers for the next nine years. This would prove to be the earliest contract resolution that we would ever enjoy. I must admit that when it was over, I knew that Powers had won these negotiations. However, all in all I was pleased in that with me at the helm we did keep the bargaining unit from a lock out or strike. We had also secured a bonus and a three-year contract and incremental raises throughout with a 4% increase in that final year. However, my turn (for a win) would come three years later.

With negotiations settled much earlier than was antici-pated, Tina, Whitney and I organized a quick vacation to

Clearwater, Florida, on Sand Key Island. We had a good time but it was probably the least favorite of the vacations that we would ever take. For one thing we had to cross over the highway to get to the ocean. Like I said, we were starting to get spoiled!

Other changes were developing for us as we rolled into the '90s, especially as it involved our relationship with my two older children. I had promised Marc in the mid '80s that I would never spend another nickel on an attorney for him following my initial expenditures on his juvenile car theft case. I have never backed off that promise despite multiple opportunities scattered over 15 –20 years or more. As Marc's criminal issues mounted, I refused to offer bail money or money for attorneys, often over the strong objection of family and the courts. While grandparents, especially, have contributed, we have not. This was likewise true with Dionne, although her issues were not generally the result of crimes, just bad decisions piled on top of bad decisions. As a result, Tina and I made a conscious decision that we could not throw enough money at their issues to ever make a difference, and we couldn't, and we haven't. With very, very few exceptions, from that time forward we have not invested a dime in the results of their folly, directly or indirectly. Instead, we promised both that we would stand on the sidelines and cheer (translated pray) as hard as we could for them and certainly not take credit for any of their successes or their failures. However, it was time for us to move on with our lives (including Whitney) and spend our money on more positive and meaningful things. We still believe this to have been a good decision, although as parents, we do hurt for them and hurt often. Our commitment to prayer was genuine and rarely is there a night that we do not place them both before the Lord asking Him to make their paths straight, heal their hearts and their lives, and as God, draw close to them in a personal way.

The Union Years 1983-2002

With negotiations completed and Snyder's health not coming around as well as everyone had hoped, Snyder announced his retirement. Within a few days Giljum approached me about the CIPS/EEI job and asked if I would be interested in taking over that jurisdiction. The four CIPS plants were scattered throughout Southern Illinois in Grand Tower, on the Mississippi River near Cape Girardeau, Missouri; Hutsonville, on the Wabash River near Terre Haute, Indiana; Coffeen, located in Coffeen on Coffeen Lake, near Hillsboro, Illinois; and Meredosia, located on the Illinois River near Jacksonville, Illinois. Of course the EEI plant was located on the Ohio River near Paducah. Having just come out of negotiations at EEI, my juices were flowing again and I was anxious to get back into the nuts and bolts of Union work and immediately responded, "Yes." A number of folks, including Giljum, were surprised by my decision but Giljum said, "Go," and so I did.

From September of 1991 through December of 2001, this remained my jurisdiction. It also provided for me the best experiences that I would ever enjoy in Union work. I was soon accepted by the men and leaders within CIPS and EEI. The EEI bargaining unit was already impressed seeing how I had reacted to the pressures of our recent negotiations and the fact that I was one of a very, very few that could actually work with Mr. Powers and do so effectively. As I quickly adapted to my new role, it became evident that the First-Step Assistance Program had grown too large for me to maintain and do my current job. I very reluctantly turned the program over, at the urging of Giljum, to Mike Nanny, who was the current Union President. I knew that Mike just did not have the personality that was needed to take on such a role as the job did require a lot of compassion and some spirituality, traits that Mike did not necessarily have. My fears would later prove to be correct.

401

Life Between Innings

In 1992, we began my first round of contract negotiations with CIPS. The representatives of CIPS did not like to meet in Springfield, Illinois, their home base, so we met in Effingham, Illinois, a two-hour drive from the house. As at EEI, the committee liked having Giljum at the table but I could already see the handwriting on the wall. While he did show from time to time, for the most part, until deal closing time, he would find excuses not to be there. The fact was that it was easier for me to run negotiations without him than with him popping in from time to time. Eventually, I told him so; I told him that I knew the guys liked to have him there, but in reality only if he was there all the time. Gradually, the committee, just as at EEI, grew to have confidence in my leadership and they too saw that negotiations often went backward when Giljum showed up.

The CIPS negotiations in 1992 also marked the beginning of a new project for me. Pastor Stortz had been encouraging the members of our congregation to read through the Bible every two years. He had drafted a small pamphlet that easily fit into my Bible marking out the chapters that needed to be read each day to accomplish the task. I hate to admit it but I had been a Christian most of my life, even graduated from Bible College, yet I had never read the Book from cover to cover. In Effingham I usually had some free time at the end of the day so I quickly got caught up to where I should be for the year and continued my daily reading as prescribed. At last count I have now read though the Bible cover to cover six times and am nearing the completion of my seventh. I am sure I will not receive any gold stars in heaven for this, but this discipline has been invaluable to my Christian walk.

It was in Effingham in 1992 that my career as a Labor Representative almost came to an abrupt end. It was one of those days that Giljum had decided not to show so I was

The Union Years 1983-2002

the lead spokesman for our side of the table. I was still fairly new at negotiations at this level and was obviously feeling some stress. I was extremely fortunate to have a great committee working with me, men that through the process of time became real friends and men who "took" the bullet for me on a number of occasions. The team was made up of: Phil Koppelman (Meredosia); Shelby Slusher (Grand Tower); Pat Sparks (Hutsonville); Dan Sweet (Coffeen); Paul Golden (Coffeen); Bob Henson (Grand Tower); Larry Ledermann (Hutsonville). However, there was one guy, Jack Gregory (Meredosia), the vice-president for the Union at the Meredosia Power Plant, who was not a bad guy, but he could get under my skin quicker than anyone. He is one of those guys who always seems to be nipping at you, day in and day out. During negotiations, schedules get to be rather hectic and it was hard to keep up with normal plant matters at the CIPS plants as well at EEI and conduct contract negotiations for three or four days in any given week. Consequently, it was not unusual for grievance meetings to be put on hold during this time as that was not the highest priority or greatest concern with all that was going on. All the leaders understood this, that is except Jack. Jack was always after (pestering) me about getting a date on the calendar and I kept putting him off explaining, with some patience, that there just weren't enough days on the calendar for me to prep and to squeeze in a meeting.

On this day we were sitting in the caucus room in Effingham working on a variety of contract issues when out of nowhere Jack asked me if I could give him some dates for a grievance meeting. Needless to say, I lost it!! After giving Jack a piece of my mind I stormed out of the room and left the building. In fact, I was so angry that I was actually heading for my car; I was done, I was quitting, I was going home. Unfortunately, or fortunately, as the case may be, I had left my car keys on the

Life Between Innings

table. I wasn't about to go back in, as my pride was at stake, so I walked over to a nearby restaurant and spent the remainder of the day drinking coffee and reading the newspaper. I was told that the guys looked all over for me but, of course, I could not be found. Keith Linderer, the other Labor Rep attending the meetings, took over for me that afternoon; not much got accomplished. Afterwards, after the dust had settled, we all had a good laugh, at my expense, and we went back to work.

In the fall of 1992, Tina finally convinced me that we needed to enroll Whitney in Twin Oaks Christian School. Whitney had attended Kindergarten in the Parkway School District and Tina was not too pleased with all that she saw. The tuition at Twin Oaks was almost $3,000 annually and it seemed to me that we were paying good taxes to a good school district, why not use it? However, I finally gave in and we signed Whitney up. Almost from day one we saw what a great decision this was. Whitney loved it and all of her classes were taught from a Christian, biblical viewpoint. When I tally up all my receipts at the end of life, putting Whitney into Twin Oaks and ultimately Westminster Christian Academy, this will easily be the best money that we have ever spent.

One day late in '92, Giljum and I happened to be in Paducah together meeting with the Company. Following the meeting I approached him about the First-Step Assistance Program and my fears that it was going backward under Mike Nanny's leadership and told him I would like to have it back. I knew that it would be a big load on my plate but the program was "my baby" and I couldn't just stand by and watch it fall apart. Giljum reluctantly agreed.

About this time Joe Bauer, who was slowly coming back around (in support of me) again after the work I had done at EEI and had already accomplished at CIPS in the short time that I had taken over the reigns, suggested that I meet a guy

404

The Union Years 1983-2002

named Gary Randle, a Black employee at Labadie, and see if he might be willing to help me out with the EAP program. I knew Gary from playing in a UE Basketball League back in 1980 where he and I had played on the same Labadie team. I knew him to be a pretty straight shooter, no pun intended. That does bring up a point, however, in that when we did play basketball together, we were both guards. Somehow it seemed I was always the one taking the ball out of bounds and passing it in to him, never to see it again!

I gave Gary a call and we met and discussed the status of the program and that I needed some help. Through life experiences and maturity, Gary had a bond with the workers that few men had. He was trusted by management and labor alike, as well as the Blacks, whites, Hispanics, and both genders. He had a layer of compassion that was genuine and was truly a spiritual man. The more we talked the more I was becoming convinced that this was the man we needed to fill the leadership role of the EAP Program. I invited Gary to one of our quarterly meetings and introduced him to our First-Step Assistance Committee formed by the reps I had put in place in the plants. He and I soon met again and he agreed to take over the leadership of the program.

It was not long after that Giljum met with UE management to tell them of Gary's appointment and new role. He also convinced them to allow Gary to be our rep, yet be on their payroll. As a result, at the start of 1993, Gary officially became the new head of the Union's EAP and he promptly renamed it the RAP Program (*Referral and Assistance Program*). From day one Randle took the program and ran with it. He had the personality and spirituality that connected with all those he needed to work with, both within the Union and the Company. In just a few short months he had established relationships within the plants and with the various agencies that we were

405

Life Between Innings

working with. I got him involved in the St. Louis Area Union/ Management EAP and he took it from there. In just a few short months Gary had taken the program far beyond what I was capable of doing. For a period of time, he actually became the President of the St. Louis area-wide EAP Program, leading management and union counselors at the highest level. Gary remained in this union role for some 16 years before leaving the company to become the Assistant Labor Representative of the United Way of St. Louis, quite a well-deserved promotion. Gary became one of my best (*if not the best, and most loyal*) friend and remains so till today.

However, 1993 had quickly rolled around and we still did not have a contract with CIPS. In fact, I spent a lot of time in Effingham, Illinois, that winter, spring and summer and early fall as we worked on the contract. While some of the events we faced that year, especially that summer, were tragic, we also had a lot of fun, or at the least, a lot of funny stories. The Committee, as noted previously, was a collection of really great guys and several were just out-right funny; they could keep you laughing, even when they weren't trying. But, since we did spend so much time together, and we all lived too far away to go home at night and be back ready and prepped for negotiations the next day, the team would stay at one of the hotels in the area. Here we could work and prep for meetings, but we also could get in a couple games of golf each week. And, it was on the golf course that summer that a number of memorable events occurred.

My favorite story occurred while playing golf with my best buddy, Shelby Slusher, and Pat Sparks. We were standing on a green, which was situated high above a bunker (sand trap) from which Shelby was trying to eradicate himself. We could not see him, the bunker being so low and close to the green,

The Union Years 1983-2002

but we did see several whiffs of sand fly up, but no ball. After three such whiffs of sand we saw the ball go up in the air and then the head of the club hit at it like you would if you threw a baseball up and tried to hit it with a bat, which in fact did place the ball back on the fairway, but certainly not on the green. Then we began to hear mutterings such as, *If people would rake their tracks out of the sand, one would not have so much trouble hitting it out!* That was immediately followed by some colorful language with the final comment, *I see you guys over there laughing and it's not funny!* Well, it was funny; it was hysterically funny to us, and we laughed till our sides hurt. He forgave us later over dinner.

Another golfing event again occurred with my good friend Shelby. He actually had a decent game going when on about the fourth hole his ball landed just off the fairway with a tree standing in the way of his ball and a clear shot at the green. Shelby, who would best be described as short and kind of chunky, lined up his shot and fired. The ball hit the tree squarely in the middle and shot right back at him at a terrific speed and in a micro of a second. All we saw was Shelby swing and then instantly hit the ground, laid out on all fours face down, thanking God for his life. My sides still hurt from laughing at my good friend rolling on the ground in front of me. Not to be outdone, after I found my composure, I lined up my shot which was on the fairway, but it kind of hooked sharply to the right and headed literally for the broad side of a red barn where two workers were raking and doing some clean-up. I heard them yell and then they quickly fell to the ground in a life-preserving maneuver, narrowly escaping with their lives and with clean shorts. Our game that day never got better; we endangered a lot of living things, but it was a memorable day!

But perhaps the most memorable of all the side issues that occurred during these negotiations actually began in

Life Between Innings

preparation for negotiations. The Committee had gathered for their initial meeting at the Union Hall in Maryville, Illinois, to meet with Business Manager Giljum to discuss our demands and to get acquainted with each other. One of the new guys was Larry Ledermann, a great guy who we all later grew to appreciate, but on this day got off on the wrong foot with Giljum. Larry had never dealt much with Mr. Giljum and this was his first opportunity to serve on a negotiating committee. As such, Larry was anxious to get after it and let Giljum and the rest of us know that he was there to do business.

The conversation at some point got around to health care and the associated costs, an issue near and dear to Larry. At this point he decided to challenge Giljum and our Benefits Representative Keith Linderer about what he assumed had been a less-than-aggressive approach to negotiating these benefits in the past. The conversation went something like this:

Larry: *You guys should grow some balls and let management know this is what we have to have. In the past, you guys haven't gotten us much of an improvement!*

Giljum: *Balls* (long pause), *balls* (another long pregnant pause), *you want balls. Let me tell you something you f**ker, I got balls as big as basketballs; in fact, I got balls as big as elephants. You want to see balls. I got balls"* And on and on it went until Larry had been humbled, if not humiliated.

Later, when enough time had passed (weeks) that the story was now funny, Larry was quick to say, *You know, those words were barely off my lips when I realized I had said the wrong thing.* And he had.

This is similar to another story involving Giljum that occurred about two or three years previously while presenting a contract to the Meredosia membership. It was getting late in the tour of the plants with Giljum presenting a new contract to the membership for their vote and/or consideration. Giljum

408

had given the same speech over and over, answering a myriad of questions, some good, and some really stupid. On this occasion one of the stupid questions was raised and Giljum went off on the guy with his usual barrage of colorful language. About midway through his "attack" on the poor questioner, a Black man from the plant came in and sat down on the front row. When Giljum had finally finished and gained some composure, the Black brother raised his hand and politely asked, *Mr. Giljum, could you tell me what the question was that you were responding to because I never ever want to ask that question?* The ice was broken, everyone had a good laugh, and the meeting proceeded without further incident.

But on the negotiating front in 1993, there were several things going on that we just were not comfortable with. On a Saturday late in the winter or very early spring, the Company had called and asked to meet us at the Collinsville, Illinois, Holiday Inn; they stated that they felt they had a proposal for us on medical that we had been waiting on. The medical plan changes and costs were the last remaining obstacles in our way of getting a contract so we were anxious to see what they had. Since the negotiations had begun, they had been trying to convince us to leave the medical plan that we had and to join with them in the management plan. The tables that they provided indicated a much higher cost for our members if they stayed in the current plan and a much, much lower cost for those in management, and us, if we would agree to come in with them. Keith Linderer, our expert on such matters, could not put his finger on it but something just did not jive with the figures that they gave us. As the end of the day drew near, those first-year costs of the plan looked good but they still could not give us the actual cost associated with the plan; they just wanted us to trust them.

Life Between Innings

It was really tempting, but as Giljum said, it was like buying a used car, signing on the dotted line agreeing to take it, but letting the salesman fill in the price somewhere down the road. The Company was pretty disgusted with us, but we refused to budge so negotiations ended for the day.

However, just a few short days following, a phone call came saying that CIPS negotiators needed to meet with us in Effingham, Illinois, ASAP. Keith had gotten a tip from an insider at the Company's Springfield offices that some irregularities had been discovered in the medical plan that they were proposing, serious irregularities, so we needed to talk and needed to talk soon. In a speech that I will forever remember, the CIPS management negotiating team, led by Mr. Chuck Baughman, sporting a very solemn and sober face, stated that they were *coming to us with their hat in their hand*. It had been discovered that Mr. Grant, the Company's chief negotiator up until this day, had schemed, along with others within the Company, to artificially raise the union's medical plan rates so as to offset, in other words, to lower, the rates that the management employees were already enjoying. This scheme had already cost the bargaining unit members in premiums alone over $1 million dollars. What a mess!!

Obviously the trust between the parties was shattered. One of the other unions that represented CIPS Linemen and other outside crews, had already bought into the plan, presented it to their membership and had subsequently voted it in. To say the least, they were furious and filed a lawsuit to immediately have their contract disqualified.

The Company, however, in their arrogance made it clear that although their actions were egregious we should not expect that they would bend over backwards to meet our wants and desires. Sometime early in May, with the help of Federal Mediation, it finally appeared that we were going to get

The Union Years 1983-2002

a contract, despite all the distractions. In fact, the Company, knowing that we were not prepared to stay overnight, as we often did to continue negotiations the following day, asked us to please stay so that we could hopefully get signed off on this thing first thing in the morning; we agreed to do so. Saturday morning came and we all gathered together again, including the Mediator, to see what the Company was going to come back with. When they presented their offer, it was the same one that they had given us the night before; even the Mediator was taken aback and indicated to us that he felt something was amiss. At long last, it was evident that a contract was not forthcoming after all, so about noon we headed home.

Two days later, somewhere around 4:00 AM on Sunday morning, my telephone started ringing; it was my buddy and Chief Steward from the Grand Tower Plant. With my head still groggy, I could hear Shelby Slusher saying, *Leo, those Sons of Bitches are locking us out. They have just marched all of us out of the plant like a herd of cattle. They won't tell us anything except that we are locked out. They wouldn't even let me make this phone call to you; I had to make it after I was out of the plant!* I couldn't believe it. I immediately called Giljum, who was much more calm, but clearly agitated, to give him the news. We discussed what needed to be done and determined that he would go to the office and man the situation from there and that I would hit the road making the rounds at the individual plants to help keep the members, who would now be on picket lines, informed and hopefully calm.

As it turned out it was not us that the Company truly wanted to lock out, but our sister union, the IBEW, who it was alleged was causing some major disruptions along the power line system as a protest against the medical fiscal. Since they had filed a lawsuit against the Company in an attempt to disqualify their current contract, evidence of sabotage and

Life Between Innings

other work stoppage situations were occurring. The Company had feared giving us a contract, believing that we might use the fact that we were still inside the plants working to help further aid the IBEW by sabotaging equipment. So, they just decided to lock everybody out to avoid any potential problems. The fallacy in their argument is that they knew fair well that if they locked the IBEW out, we would not have crossed their picket lines and would have stayed out in sympathy support. Consequently, our opportunities to enact any sabotage inside the plant, even with a contract, would have been negated.

May was proving not to be a good month. One evening, about bedtime, I received a call from Steve Toliusis, Dionne's husband. Dionne and Steve had recently had a baby boy named Michael and were not living too far from us. Steve began to tell us that it appeared that Dionne had suffered a stroke and that she was at St. John's Medical Hospital. He said that she had gone into a Food Mart to buy some cigarettes and just suddenly flipped out and fell to the floor. We rushed over to the hospital and the report that we got was not encouraging. The doctor told us that she very likely would not make it as she had, in fact, suffered a major stroke, probably due to a combination of just having a baby, going back on birth control and restarting her smoking habit again. He said that it was not uncommon for women in that situation to have such a stroke. He told us that if she could make it through the next 48-72 hours, she might have a chance, but all we could do would be hope and pray.

At the time we were living in the Stone Gate Apartments with two bedrooms as we had just sold our house and were building a new one in the Big Bend Station Subdivision. Helen Redman, my former mother-in-law and Dionne's grandmother, came immediately from Oklahoma to help care for Dionne, so we invited her to stay with us. It was crowded, but proved to

The Union Years 1983-2002

be a beneficial time as Tina and Helen clicked as if she was still my mother-in-law. In fact, a few years later, Tina went with Helen on a mission trip to Haiti resulting in a friendship that remains today.

Dionne did gradually recover over the following year. She had suffered permanent brain damage but the doctor assured us that her brain was like a computer that had developed a bad circuit; however, in this case the brain would continue to seek to develop ways to re-circuit itself and that she would eventually be close to 100% again. Out of this near-tragedy, Dionne's life turned unbelievably upside down, but this time the right way. She led her husband Steve to Christ, they joined the Ballwin Baptist Church and attended faithfully. Dionne began to play her horn in the church's brass band; I didn't even know she knew how to play the horn. It was not uncommon for her to call and see if we might go to church with her or attend one of the church functions. It was great to see her doing so well after all the pain that she had gone through. Unfortunately, three years down the road she inexplicably made another one of those monumentally bad decisions, which was becoming an unfortunate life pattern for her, that would spin her life out of control, a decision that almost cost her life.

While the lockout was ongoing we were also involved in the next election campaign, as the ballots would go out in July, 1993. Giljum was still highly admired by most of the membership system wide and the Team easily won its fourth-consecutive 3-year term.

I continued to be on the road visiting the troops on the picket lines. Most of the guys stayed upbeat, but for many the lockout was costly and greatly damaged them financially and ruined a few marriages. It was hard to watch. It took 101 days before this nightmare came to an end. This incident changed my life forever in regard to my relationship with management

Life Between Innings

at any level and Big Business in general. I haven't trusted them since and probably never will. The way they screwed over lives with the medical plan and then screwed over them again because of their own incompetence was, and is, inexcusable. I can count on one hand the number of management personnel from that day forward I could trust. And over time, they didn't let me down; they continued to prove themselves untrustworthy, time and again.

On the weekend just prior to the Company lifting the lockout, Tina and I had been invited by the Hutsonville membership to come and celebrate a Labor Day picnic with them at a local park. With an air of hope that the long nightmare was coming to an end, everyone was upbeat and enjoying themselves. We were about an hour into the party when Whitney somehow got her arm stuck in a little merry-go-round and it appeared that her arm might be broken. So, we left the party and took her to the emergency room where they confirmed that she had a "green twig" break, meaning it was not broken, but the bone had that frayed appearance like a green twig that someone had tried to snap, but it wouldn't.

The lifting of the lockout ushered in an era of endless lawsuits and Unfair Labor Practice (ULP) charges against CIPS. Some of the lawsuits and ULP charges went all the way to the Supreme Court with the final case finally resolved sometime in 2004. Mr. Grant, the Company's Chief Negotiator and in on the scheme to defraud the union, was not initially fired, only transferred. However, several years later he was let go. Our informant from the Company side regarding the irregularities committed suicide. Bargaining Unit lives were impacted in many ways and the pain and scars of this experience still remain. Ask me why I loved my job? It was a real privilege to come up against this scum everyday from that point forward until I retired. Bitter? I guess so! The Company could have

The Union Years 1983-2002

stopped this fight at innumerable places along the road, paid a few thousand dollars, and restored some of their integrity and begun the process of rebuilding trust and good faith. Instead, they continued to fight the Union on these issues until the last issue finally died, some ten years later in the Supreme Court, showing their arrogance from start to finish. That demonstrated all that needed to be said by them about how they felt about us; they said it loud and clear and I heard them!

As January of 1994 was peeking its head around the corner, Tina informed me that she had signed me up to coach intramural basketball at Twin Oaks School to second and third graders. I really am not good with small children, my own children excluded, so I was not too thrilled and complained to her about it, which probably sounded more like whining. She knew I was busy and that I did not have time to teach second and third graders anything, including basketball. The appointed day came and I showed up somewhat apprehensive. Mrs. Debbie Mosley had volunteered to assist me so we gave it a valiant attempt and the kids seemed to enjoy themselves. As it turned out, it was actually a lot of fun and gave me some time to be with Whitney, which I enjoyed. In the end, I agreed to do it again the following year.

In my job as Business Representative it seemed as if time truly did fly. It is amazing how that happens when you are literally living by the calendar. It was now April of 1994 and time to restart contract negotiations with EEI, our contract expiring on July 1. Over the past three years Mr. Powers and I had actually developed a very good working relationship. I think most everyone, especially my peers from the Union Hall, were impressed, if not amazed. I had learned a lot over the past three years about negotiations and I still had that horrible taste of CIPS in my mouth. Powers reminded me on numerous occasions that at some point I had to get over it and put it

Life Between Innings

behind me. I am not sure that it is possible; for me it became the fuel that drove me till the day I retired.

We knew that Powers would be pushing hard for more concessions, especially in the area of cross-training and work-force utilization. I was not personally opposed to some of the things he was asking for, as our work practices were archaic, but the membership was up in arms. Their view of things was quite naturally very narrow and it was my job, within certain parameters, to help them broaden their view somewhat. Of course I knew Powers would assist as he loved to take center stage in negotiations with slides, power point and newspaper and magazine clippings.

As expected, Powers came on hard trying to convince us that the job changes and flexibility that he was demanding was what he needed for the plant to continue to thrive and be even more competitive. His big argument was that de-regulation (good old Ronald Reagan again) of the electrical industry was now a reality and in order to compete with the big boys, like Enron, he had to have changes and he had to have them now. In a number of sidebars I told him we could work on some of the things he needed but I needed a few trophies to take back to the committee as well if he expected us to capitulate on his demands.

I had a very strong and hard-working committee and we worked diligently on the Company's demands and in the creation of a few of our own. Negotiations were slow but over time we were able to work out a number of good agreements and the end was in sight. Sometime around the Martin Luther King Holiday, we finally reached a tentative agreement. I liked it, all things considered, but Powers did not. Finally, the evening came and we had the tentative agreement and financial package before us that we as a committee were willing to take back to the membership with a recommendation to accept. I could not help but recall 1991 when Powers sat so arrogantly across the table after reaching our tentative agreement (TA) giving a speech about how proud I should be of my committee and the hard work that we had accomplished. The whole time he was talking I had my head slightly bent as I knew that it wasn't a bad contract, especially for my first one, but that in reality he had beaten me.

However, this time, the tables were turned. It was my turn to sit uprightly and speak with an air of confidence and tell him how proud he should be of his committee and the hard work that they had put into this thing. And, it was his turn to listen with his head slightly lowered as he knew, as I did, that this time I won! It felt good!! It felt real good!!

However the feeling did not last long as the ink was barely dry on the contract before Powers was already trying to find ways to weasel out of key provisions. This time I was incensed as he was trying to steal back from us what we had earned in negotiations. The easiest way for a company to steal back contract provisions is to just violate them and let the union file grievances regarding the infractions. I hate arbitration because even if you win, you only win the one grievance and not necessarily the issue; you never truly win the battle with a company in arbitration. However, since Unions no longer threaten company officials at the point of a gun or threaten to burn down their houses and harass their children, all that is left is the legal system. I should quickly say that I do not espouse those things just mentioned above, I am just saying that once the threat of violence was removed from the vocabulary of the union, it quickly began to lose its power.

Consequently, Powers violated the contract and we filed grievances. He violated more areas of the contract and our stipulations and we filed more grievances. Looking over the many cases that we had pending arbitration we selected two

Life Between Innings

to arbitrate. Our first case came before an arbitrator who was a professor at Southern Illinois University-Carbondale. Unfortunately, the Company's attorney was from Carbondale and his assistant was a graduate from Carbondale. You draw your own conclusion but when we received his award, with every bone of honesty in me, it was the most biased, most tightly written award I have ever read or seen in favor of any party, but in this case the Company. It truly made all us of feel that the process was nothing more than a sham. And it was!

The arbitrator in the second case emphatically told us that the award given by the previous arbitrator would not sway him, and then, inexplicably, he provided numerous direct quotes from the first award explaining why he too was ruling in favor of the Company and against the Union. It was at this point that I truly appreciated the loyalty and support that Giljum had given me, as I really wanted to continue the fight a little longer. I was not naïve to the fact that our chances, after two defeats, were not good. But I also knew, as did the negotiating committee, that Powers was stealing from us and was using the system to do it. If we couldn't stop him, short of violence and sabotage, then at least we wanted to make his life miserable, and we did.

The third arbitration at least gave us some vindication, although we did not gain a victory. As usual, Powers put on his grand show in front of the arbitrator talking about de-regulation, talking about how these negotiations were geared to flexibility issues and work rules changes that he needed in order to stay competitive and stay in business. And, as usual, he brought along his slides and power point, the process that we had long started calling *his dog and pony show*; it was all a grand production for the arbitrator to see and quiet frankly made us sick. There was never a man like him in this regard; he was the most prepared man in any meeting that I

The Union Years 1983-2002

ever attended and he absolutely hated it if one of his subordinates had not produced or found the information that he needed for a grievance meeting, an arbitration or a contract negotiation. In fact, I often accused him of having boxes of old paper and an old typewriter hidden away somewhere, as he would come up with some of the most obscure documents that could ever be imagined to support his case. When I would make this accusation, it was one of the few times that you might actually see him smile. Interesting! However, as he continued his marathon testimony he then got into the issues of negotiations that were actually germane to the issue.

When it was time for my rebuttal testimony our attorney, Mark Waldemer, asked me if a certain portion of Mr. Powers' testimony was correct. Under oath I testified that, *Either Mr. Powers does not remember our agreement correctly, or he misunderstood his attorney's question and was not replying to our issue or he lied.* The arbitrator turned to the court reporter and said matter-of-factly, *Well, he couldn't be clearer than that!* You would have thought someone had put a fire under Powers as he turned as red as the proverbial beet, demanding that his attorneys ask for a recess.

My side was loving it. His side wasn't sure what to do, as Powers was livid. I was asked by the arbitrator not to leave the room so that my further testimony would not be tainted, but the attorneys did a sidebar in the hall to discuss the matter. After some time, Mr. Waldemer came back and said to me that the Company's attorney wanted to know if I would be willing to go back on the stand and offer a clarification saying that I did not mean to imply that Mr. Powers was a liar. I refused to do so. For about 30 minutes the Company's attorney worked feverishly to come up with some kind of verbiage for me to say to try and defuse the situation and help to get Powers off the hook. Finally, after considerable work by both attorneys,

Life Between Innings

some acceptable verbiage was worked out where my testimony stood but allowed Powers to achieve some face. I went back on the stand and approved the statement that had been worked out, but, I never backed off my testimony and Powers knew that it would forever be part of the record.

As expected, we lost this arbitration as well, and the next, as the die had already been set by the two previous cases. While the first award sure looked like a fraud, it was the second arbitration that was a killer to us as the arbitrator went back on his word and used the first case as the basis for his award, even though he promised he wouldn't. Despite all our issues, EEI continued to make money, as did my guys. At the end of the day, maybe that is all that matters.

Life for Tina and Whitney and me continued to remain good. We had a great church, we both had great jobs that we enjoyed, we were in our new home and Whitney was making new friends and really enjoying her school. When the fall of 1995 rolled around Whitney was in the fourth grade at Twin Oaks Christian School and announced to us that she wanted to play on the Twin Oaks soccer team. Jim Boyd, the father of one of her best friends, Meredith Boyd, had agreed to coach the team, a combined team of third and fourth graders, and had asked me to assist him. I knew nothing about soccer but I figured I could learn right along with the girls. However, before the first practice and after we had paid the $50 fee, Whitney decided that she didn't want to play. After some negotiating with her I established that she did not have to play but she had to find a way to pay me back the $50. I also agreed with her that for each practice she attended, I would deduct $5 from the total. She wasn't happy with the deal but, hey, I was the parent so she had to go to at least the first practice.

Upon arriving home from work, and following her first practice, I discovered that I had a new soccer fan on my hands;

The Union Years 1983-2002

she loved it! Jim Boyd was a former Marine and he conducted fourth grade soccer practices like the girls were "a few good men." The parents thought Jim a little weird and perhaps a little too tough, but the girls responded to him and played well. On the last day of the season the team had a doubleheader; a game in the morning followed by another game later in the afternoon. Should the team by chance win both games they were the Champs. Now I realize it was just fourth grade soccer but the girls won both games for the title in their very first year. What a difference great coaching can make!! This tandem of Boyd and Mooney continued for five years total as I would assist him in soccer and he would assist me as I coached girls' basketball.

This was the inaugural year for Twin Oaks to participate in competitive sports with outside teams. Whitney has already made two breakthroughs finding that she loved soccer and bowling. We already knew she liked basketball as she had been playing "small ball" with me since she was about three. Without much prodding, I willingly took on the title of Coach for Whitney's fourth grade basketball team. In our first competitive basketball game we came up against St. Girard with my friend Dale Dietrich coaching their team and their daughter, Ashley. Ashley and Whitney had become friends at St. Joseph's Day School when they were about four years of age. We became friends with both Dale and April, the parents, and had gone with the Dietrichs to Colorado a couple times for skiing at Breckenridge. However, neither of us knew that the other was coaching their daughters until we showed up for the game. In a defensive struggle, Twin Oaks prevailed by a score of 9-6. At one point, late in the game, Corey Chapell, the daughter of the President of Covenant Seminary, muttered those now infamous words that I have used with all my teams

Life Between Innings

since, *Mr. Mooney, if we play good defense the rest of the way, will we win this game?*

Twin Oaks did win that game and the next nine in a row to win their league with a 10-0 record; who would have thought I was such a great coach? We were placed in the County championship series with about 40 other teams and were knocked out early, losing both of our first two by close scores. But, I had suddenly found something I had been missing for a long time and that was coaching; I discovered I had the passion and desire to do it as long as I was able. In the end, I was surprised at how long that was to be.

Through Whitney's basketball and soccer activities, she and I were able to bond as father and daughter even beyond that which we had previously, which was already good. Under the Boyd/Mooney and Mooney/Boyd tandem our girls did very well every season in soccer and basketball. Whitney went on to play for a select basketball team, the Reds, which was primarily a group of girls headed to Visitation Academy, a girls' school known for their basketball prowess. Arguably the team's best player was Katie Dierdorf, the daughter of Hall of Fame St. Louis Football Cardinal, Dan Dierdorf, who went on to play at Michigan following in her dad's footsteps. Since Whitney was not Catholic and not headed to Visitation, she was let go following her seventh grade season. The majority of the team did go on to play at Viz and were consistently in the hunt for district, regional and a state championship.

I also formed a club team called the Blue Katz so that Whitney and my girls could gain some valuable experience. We entered into various leagues around the city for three seasons, including the Mathews-Dickey Boys' & Girls' Club, where it is said that, *All girls' basketball in St. Louis goes through Mathews- Dickey."* This was pretty much the truth as this club was in a tough area of the city and the basketball here was

The Union Years 1983-2002

very physical. If a girl could play here, she probably could play most anywhere. Since we were primarily a school team, it was tough to compete against these all-star select teams; consequently, we did not win as much as we used to but the games helped the girls mature into competitive young ladies while being exposed to an inner-city culture that they would not have otherwise experienced.

We had great support from a group of great parents and I was privileged to coach some of these girls well into their high school years. Several, such as Kathryn Fanchi, Rachael Greenplate, Lindsay McClure and Megan Jones, and their parents, have remained close friends, even unto today.

The whirl of the calendar continued and it was 1996 and an election year again. Giljum's popularity was still strong within the membership but cracks were starting to form, as would be expected, after being in office for 12 years. While the election was a little closer than previous ones, mainly because those who were in our corner were becoming somewhat complacent and did not always get their ballots cast; still the margin was better than 2-1.

Soon after Thanksgiving of '96, Fred Bendick, the Director of World Missions at Twin Oaks Church, approached me and asked if I would be willing to take a vision trip to Juarez, Mexico, and see what kind of impression I might get from a MTW border ministry that he had just visited named BEAMM (*Border Evangelism and Mercy Ministries*). Fred was anxious to get our committee involved in "deed" ministry as we were supporting pretty much "Word" only ministries, meaning mostly church planting endeavors. He had come back less than impressed but was wise enough to realize that maybe he just did not get it.

Two weeks before Christmas, good friend Ron Haynes, also a member of the World Missions Committee accompanied me

Life Between Innings

to El Paso and Juarez to meet with Moses Zapata, the Director of BEAMM. Moses was bringing in a number of pastors and lay leaders interested in mission work for a vision trip wherein we would spend three days with his team looking at the work they had accomplished, the work they were doing and then hopefully catch the vision of where they wanted to go.

BEAMM, a mission supported by the Presbyterian Church in America missions arm called Mission to the World (MTW), had actually been in existence for seven years. The border had proven to be a tough place for the advancement of reformed theology so Moses and MTW were prepared to embark on a new strategy. This strategy basically was a long-term approach by first moving the team into Juarez. Once there, the team members and visiting short-term teams would help them to become involved in the schools and the community by helping to build parks, school buildings, basketball courts, plant trees and hold Vacation Bible Schools and craft fairs in the parks. They had also managed to start three churches. The first one was pastored by Josue Mayo, and his lovely wife, Martha, who have both become good friends. Josue, a national, is an excellent preacher and pastor. The second church was pastored by Dan Young (and his wife, Becky and their four children), who likewise became very good friends over the years. The third church had a new national pastor who was just moving into the community and currently had a regular Bible Study with seven women. Basically, the BEAMM ministry was a version of friendship evangelism wherein the work originally is slow as the team works first to build lasting relationships in the community. This plan seemed to Ron and me to be working.

We were not sure what Fred had seen or not seen but we were blown away with this model of evangelism and church planting. We came back with a positive report and I immediately began to form teams from Twin Oaks to take back during

The Union Years 1983-2002

July of each year. It was a real joy to bring in a team each year to teach English Camp, run a Vacation Bible School and provide some work crews to help paint and do fix-up work in the community. I led the first three teams into Juarez and then turned it over to Dave Glass, a member of the World Missions Committee, who led it for several more years.

This represented the beginning of regular short-term missions teams going out from Twin Oaks Church each year. After getting Dave Glass placed into leadership, I moved on to lead a team to Velingrad, Bulgaria, a beautiful village about 150 miles from the capital city of Sofia. It was my job within the committee to get the mission established, so to speak, and then turn it over to a new leader and then seek out the next place that God might want us to begin partnering. Good friend, Dave Hoefakker, picked up the reigns for the next trip into Bulgaria and I began to look to see where God might lead us next.

In 1997, I began my third contract negotiation with EEI and Bob Powers. I was actually looking forward to it as I enjoyed taking on the Big Man from across the table. Over the six years we had been dealing with each other he had become convinced that, as a Christian, I would do nothing to hurt his company and would handle negotiations honorably. On the other hand, he knew from our battles that I strongly believed in what I was doing and in the cause in which I was working; but, he wasn't real sure how much control I had over my men. I used that fear to my advantage as often as I could because beyond the element of fear, what incentive did he have to share his company's newfound wealth with the workers? Bob was as committed to giving us as little as he could as I was committed to getting, at a minimum, what I thought we should have. Therefore, from that basis of "mutual respect," we plunged into another epic battle at the table.

Life Between Innings

Again, I was fortunate to have a very good committee working with me led by Dan Mizell, the Union's Vice-President at the plant and a Certified Welder. For months when I would visit the EEI plant, Mizell would in good nature, but with a bite of sarcasm, rag on me about his seniority, or lack of, and how the current seniority system was unfair. Seniority in all Unions is the backbone to receiving and enjoying negotiated benefits and other preferences in the workplace. I finally convinced him that the best way to get his seniority issues resolved was to run for office and get involved. To his credit, Mizell did just that and was elected Vice-President just in time to lead the committee with me into negotiations. Dan became my closest ally throughout the negotiations and was not afraid to take the heat from the membership when it was necessary. He didn't like it, but he handled it well. Dan had my back, and I knew it, and he proved this more often than I can express in words.

At the very beginning of the negotiations Powers threw out a challenge to us that he did not expect us to bite on, but we did. In these negotiations Bob wanted to go after the whole pie with regards to job flexibility, work rule changes, job descriptions, etc. After some consideration we told him we were willing to look at it but he should know up front that we wanted money for these changes and we were not talking about pennies and nickels. We also reminded him that should we make proposals, knowing that the monetary package is not discussed until the very end, should he not come across with the dollars we needed to sell these major changes he was asking for, all bets were off and we would withdraw every proposal and start all over again. He indicated that he understood and understood it clearly.

The fact was that since the concessions we had made in 1991 and again in 1994, the EEI Power Plant had not only

The Union Years 1983-2002

survived a shutdown, it had become the fourth most cost-effective power plant in the nation, and two of those ahead of us were hydro plants with a free source of energy. That recognition alone was not just a feather in the Company's hat, but it was also a huge feather in the Union's hat as we had helped save jobs, and even a company, while maintaining good wages and benefits. I was not going to let Powers think for a moment that he had done this alone. While I was happy for the success of EEI, I also wanted my guys to enjoy some of the fruits of their sacrifices and labors.

As before, my committee worked extremely hard to write and rewrite hundreds of job descriptions, work rules and so on and the negotiations began to drag. However, it was not because we were dragging our feet, but Powers; he would spend endless hours addressing the committee with his power point graphs, charts and clippings, basically trying to brainwash us over the period of months; but the guys did not bite. In fact, over time, they were becoming infuriated with Powers and his ability to waste time, precious time.

As February of '98 approached we were long past the July 1 contract deadline and working on extension after extension. However, finally, after 10 months of negotiations we were down to talking money. Prior to receiving the first monetary pass from Powers I had implored the guys not to take offense at what they saw as it was normal for the Company to low ball on the first pass. However, I must admit, even I was "impressed" at how low the low-ball offer was. My guys were not happy but they had been forewarned and they handled themselves well.

However, following the second pass it was obvious that Powers was not going to live up to his part of the bargain and now I was furious. After all these months and after all of these stalling tactics, he was going to force us to withdraw and start all over. I took a sidebar with Powers prior to what he said was

Life Between Innings

going to be his final offer and warned him what was going to happen if he did not come through as he had indicated he would back in May of '97. I went back into the negotiating room while he took a brief caucus with his committee. In short order Mr. Powers came back and gave us his final.

In the final offer he had not addressed over 10 of the major items we had on the table. In the final offer the new money that we were seeking was not even in the ballpark. Giljum had come down for this day and Giljum, as were all of us, was beside himself. I will never know what was going on in Powers' mind, but Mizell and I often thought that Powers' hatred for Giljum was so intense that when Giljum showed up, he just decided to screw it and screw us. In retrospect, I think it was probably a little of the latter but it was mainly Bob Powers being Bob Powers. He was a strong and powerful man but he had long lost the integrity of dealing at the table. Why should this surprise me; I was still living the effects of the CIPS debacle?

Powers again caucused with his committee and then invited us all back into the negotiating room. In very terse words he announced that he was implementing the contract effective March 1 with the new wages that he had proposed and all the new language that we had worked on, but had never agreed to. If there had been guns in the room, Powers would no longer be among the living.

I immediately left Paducah for St. Louis to confer with our attorneys. The next day I met with a representative of the National Labor Relations Board (NLRB) and filed several Unfair Labor Practice (ULP) charges. The membership also chipped in several hundred dollars and we purchased a large billboard on the main thoroughfare that comes through the city of Metropolis (yes, the home of Superman) and then on to the EEI plant, a road probably 65% or more of the employees working at EEI had to travel daily to get to work, including Powers. The

The Union Years 1983-2002

sign was a major source of irritation to Powers as the billboard addressed the need of a negotiated contract, not a unilateral implemented contract, and it was there for all the world to see. We also purchased temporary signs to notify the public of the unfair labor practices instituted by the management of EEI and placed them strategically all over the area.

I began to step up the publication of the *Union Brief*, a monthly newspaper that I had started for EEI members many years prior, keeping them updated on negotiations and meetings with the Company. Powers hated this newspaper, as I was not shy at reporting it just as it happened. At one time he forbade his supervisors and management people to read it for fear that it might influence their thinking. However, a number of the foremen and supervisors were our best customers. We were confident that Powers had a copy on his desk first thing each morning on the date of release, even though he was not on our "mailing list." The fact was I wanted Powers to read it, I wanted him to know what I was saying about him and his negotiating tactics and I wanted the membership, his employees, to know what we were dealing with. I also wanted them to be aware of his unfair labor practices and I wanted them to be documented. Powers knew that what I wrote was the truth or he would have sued the Union's pants off. It was fact that his attorneys got a regular copy of the paper and they hated me about as much as Powers did. I have to admit it; I loved it. I never felt so much a part of the cause for the workingman and against Big Business scoundrels as I did during my service with CIPS and EEI. But, with Powers, the guidelines for engagement were always clear. He was going to try to cheat the union and me every chance he could, so I never had to feel bad about anything I did or said. Ever! He was the poster child for the saying, *The end justifies the means.*

Life Between Innings

Word began to filter across the Local 148 Union system about the tyrant holding our contract hostage at EEI. I did have two men approach me about doing away with Powers; all I had to do was give the word. I obviously declined their "gracious" offer but I was confident that in the end God was still working with me, a Christian, in this most unusual circumstance.

By implementing the contract and stopping dues collections (payroll check-off) through the company's payroll, Powers really thought he could wear us down, perhaps even destroy us. However, his actions actually galvanized the union, especially at EEI, and they became one solid group working to help me win the fight. Because the men were united and angry, Powers became more concerned than normal about his own safety and my ability to control the men. He took to driving his car to a dealership in Paducah, dropping it off and picking up another and driving it to another dealership, and then repeat the process several times until he was able to get to work. I will have to admit that his fears had some basis. I would never ask the guys to do anything illegal, but from time to time I would mention to the Solidarity Committee that I could use some help, and in a few days I would get a call from Powers saying that he knew I had not authorized it but that he felt certain, although he could not prove it, that the guys were sabotaging things at the plant. A lot of what he thought was sabotage was nothing more than his own mind playing tricks on him as he truly was paranoid, and probably with some justification. Finally, the local police told him to quit calling as they could never verify any of his claims or allegations and they began to think he was "wacko." We knew he was!

The National Labor Relations Board ruled in our favor on the ULP that I had filed and forced Powers to come back to the table. Seven of the 10 major issues that had been on the table at the time he implemented the contract were resolved

The Union Years 1983-2002

and a contract was finally ratified. But even that took the assistance of a Federal Mediator. After a couple meetings, all the Federal Mediator could say was, *Boys, I never met a man like this in all the years I have been a Mediator. Bob, well, he kind of views himself of, how do I say this, as the shepherd of the sheep, willing to do anything within his ability to protect them and to take care of them. He truly believes that what he has done is in the best interest of 'his' sheep.*

But still, justice was not served, even though we did eventually ratify the contract, as we really had no choice as Powers was allowed to maintain all the work rules, job descriptions and job flexibility changes that we had worked on but on which we had never reached agreement. Labor Laws are not set up to be fair; they are set up to aid Big Business in their all out pursuit of profit, and hell be damned if the working guy gets in the way. In reality, Powers stole the contract; he got what he wanted, but he had to cheat and lie to get it. In the end I could not have been more proud of my guys. They had stood with me through thick and thin and these ole country boys will forever hold a special place in my heart.

Following the ratification of the EEI contract in 1998, life resumed again. Tina and I went back to Juarez in March, this time for leadership training, and then led a large team back in July. By this time we were firmly entrenched in taking two weeks of vacation to Sanibel Island, Florida. So, in late summer we flew south and received our beach fix. Whitney graduated from Twin Oaks Christian School in May and began seventh grade at Westminster Christian Academy that following August.

My basketball coaching experience received an unexpected extension that fall when the Westminster Christian Academy seventh grade girls' basketball coach stepped down voluntarily and I was allowed to step into his place as the head

431

Life Between Innings

coach of the "A" team, the team on which Whitney would play. There were a lot of familiar faces on that team as a third or half of the girls were girls that I had already been coaching at Twin Oaks, or had joined us for one of our seasons of club ball from Central Presbyterian Christian School and Kirk of the Hills Christian School. Ironically, the Twin Oaks' sixth grade team had gone all the way to the championship game the previous year before losing, taking second out of 40 teams. Our Westminster seventh grade girls did exactly the same, again taking second place out of a field of 40.

The school shortened the season the following eight grade year and out of protest I did not take the head-coaching job, but did remain on as the assistant to Josh Hendricks, a good friend.

The year 1999 would also serve as my last union election campaign as the next election would be in the summer of 2002. And, if we were reelected this time, I planned to retire in June of '02 as it would not really make much sense to keep working with the two excellent pensions that I had coming. In 2002, I would be 55 and would have a 28-year pension with AmerenUE (previously Union Electric) and an 18-year pension with the *International Union of Operating Engineers*. Although I had actually worked for Union Electric (AmerenUE) for only ten years, someone long before we came into office had negotiated that UE employees who were elected to a Local 148 union office position would continue to build seniority and pension accrual just as if they were still working. The basic idea was to protect the job of those who went to work for the Union, as they usually were only able to maintain that position for a short time. In fact, when Joe Bauer and Carmen LaPresta retired from the union office in 1996, they were the first ever Local 148 Business Representatives to actually draw a pension from the International. A Business Rep had to work

The Union Years 1983-2002

a minimum of 9 years in the union office to draw a pension from the International and obviously no one had ever held office that long until our team. The Company had never protested this negotiated benefit so I was not going to look a gift horse in the mouth.

The Giljum team had a surprise opponent in this election in that Al Dion, the Chief Steward at the Labadie Plant, had been led to believe that he had a good shot at ending the Giljum regime. For the most part, Al had been a little bit of a thorn in the side of some of the reps, although Al and I got along well and worked well together. However, all said, he was more friend than foe and he too was already looking to retire. Carl Jordan had been one of the major pushers of Al's candidacy and was the primary influence in getting him to run. But, as had been the vote every year since 1984, Giljum won and won by an even greater margin than he had over some lesser lights in previous campaigns. It actually turned out to be a little embarrassing for Al and for Carl Jordan. Carl, as typical throughout the years, came back to us explaining that he meant no harm and was just trying to give the Union a choice. You would have thought we were a church, considering the number of times we forgave him and let him back into the fold.

In 2000, I received another great surprise in that I was hired to be the Head Girls' Junior Varsity Coach at Westminster. The previous head coach had resigned and Doug Butte, a teacher at the school, had been named to succeed him. My interest began to pique when August rolled around and no one had been named, or even applied as far as I knew, to the position of Junior Varsity Coach. With this being Whitney's first year to play high school ball, I was not content to let them name just anybody to the post, so I applied. After an interview with Doug and his assistant, Sue Tammeling, I was named to the job. I could not believe it!

433

Life Between Innings

Coaching at the high school level was a dream come true. This was part of the dream that I had back in high school when I drew up my plans to attend Southeast Missouri State. I obviously never made it there, as I took a different road in life, but now, here late in my life, I was being given this opportunity. Don Giljum was not opposed to me taking on this job as long as it did not interfere with my work with the Union. Since I controlled my own schedule, I knew there would be few, if any, scheduling conflicts.

Whitney made the varsity team as a freshman for the 2000/2001 season. As the Junior Varsity Coach, part of my duties was to be one of the two Assistant Coaches for the Varsity Team meaning that I would get to watch her games sitting right there on the bench. However, except for the two seasons she played for the Reds, this would be the first time that I was not her basketball coach. This was good in that it was past time for her, and some of the others that I had been coaching since the fourth grade, to hear a different voice. Whitney started out doing very well, often times scoring in double digits. For a short lady, she had developed a nice high arching shot, which she knocked down with some consistency. She was an even better free throw shooter and, in fact, set a school record with the highest free throw shooting percentage for a season when she was a sophomore.

From a Dad's perspective it was great being able to coach and be around my own daughter while she played high school ball. The fact that she was pretty good made it even better. Unfortunately, Whitney had suffered a major injury to her left shoulder close to the end of her eighth grade season when a very large girl fell on her arm while it was fully extended as she reached for a loose ball. The shoulder was completely detached and it really looked bad. The doctors told us that if she could withstand the pain it would not hurt her to keep

The Union Years 1983-2002

playing but that her body was not mature enough to have the surgery necessary to repair it. So, for her freshman and sophomore seasons she played with basically a dislocated shoulder. It was not uncommon for her to get hit on the shoulder, especially on a break-a-way lay-up, and the arm would pop out of joint. She would then jog over to the wall and jam it back in and keep playing.

Finally, we found a surgeon who had previously worked for the U.S. Olympic Team. He looked her over and decided that here, at the end of her sophomore season, her body was mature enough for the surgery. The day following the last day of the 2001/2002 season she went in and had a very successful surgery. She was dedicated to her rehab and by late summer her left arm was actually stronger than her uninjured right shoulder. The only problem was that she could only lift the left arm to about 80% of what she previously could, which impacted her shooting dramatically

Christmas and New Year Eve of 2000 had been good holidays for us. Many of the family issues that had troubled us, especially those with the kids, seemed to have passed, at least to some degree. My mother had come to have dinner with us and to play Scrabble on one of the days between the two holidays. As the evening was ending, Dionne, who had come by to enjoy the evening with us, walked Grandma out to her car to help her through some of the ice that was still on the drive from a recent storm. This was the last time we would enjoy mom's charm and grace and that dry subtle wit that she would spring on us from time to time.

It was Friday, January 5, 2001, and I was attending the monthly Executive Board Meeting of the Union at our Maryville offices. Steve Mooney, my nephew and the Union's vice-President, said that his dad was on the phone and needed to talk with me right away. I picked up the phone to hear Doug say,

Life Between Innings

Leo, I think we have lost her. The ambulance has just taken mom to St. Anthony's Hospital; you need to come right away.

I told Steve what was going on and rushed on over to the hospital. When I arrived, Doug met me in the waiting room and gave me the news; Mom had just passed away. The doctor invited us into her room to allow us a brief moment to say goodbye. I touched her gray head and brow and it was still warm; I was so glad that my last touch was "warm!"

I received the tough assignment of calling Bonnie, my sister, who was living outside of Pensacola, Florida, at the time. Somehow I made it through, but I am sure it was short as it was too difficult to hold back the tears and heavy sobs.

Westminster was playing a basketball game that evening at Orchard Farm, Missouri. It was way on the other side of St. Charles and I knew that I would most likely miss my game. So, I contacted assistant coach, Sue Tammeling, and asked her to take over for me that evening and to tell the team and Whitney that an emergency had come up, but not to tell Whitney what had happened; we would then pick her up at the game and tell her on the way home. That was a tough ride home as Whitney, like all the grandkids, loved Grandma (Mooney) Pedersen.

Mother had always said that when she died there better be a lot of people at the funeral and they better be crying. She got her wish on both counts. The church that she and John had worshipped in for years, Southside Nazarene, had recently moved, but the new owners of the old church allowed us to hold the funeral there. The place was packed and people were crying; it was a really good service. Somehow, God had given me the grace to be able to give the eulogy, an honor that I will always treasure. We laid her to rest at the *Jefferson Barracks National Cemetery*, sharing the gravesite with John, who had passed on just three years prior.

The Union Years 1983-2002

Mom had left me as the Executor of her will so Tina and I set about cleaning out her house and getting all of her possessions to the right people. No one complained, that I am aware of, of the work we did, so I guess it went well. Mom's will was pretty straightforward so there was not much to argue about should anyone have been inclined. I guess more than anything we were worried how John's children would react as most everything was left to us kids. But, there were never any issues and my job was, for the most part, fairly easy.

Later in 2001, Oliver Claussen, the Pastor of World Missions at Twin Oaks, invited the Youth Pastor, Chris Polski, and me to go with him to Ecuador and Peru on a vision trip. We had several missionaries in these countries that were working primarily with the Quechua Indians, descendents of the Inca Indians. This area is commonly called the Hinterlands and it comprises the Andes Mountains regions of Peru, Ecuador and Bolivia. I was to be looking for short-term ministry opportunities for the adults at Twin Oaks while Chris was looking for opportunities for the Youth.

In Miami, we met up with MTW regional director for the Hinterlands, Don Gahagen, and continued on to our first stop in Quito. Quito is the capital city of Ecuador, which sits between several mountain ranges near an active volcano. Here, we were wonderfully and graciously hosted by missionaries at the famous World Radio HCJB headquarters. While in Quito, we toured this beautiful city and several of the reformed Quechuan churches. We also stopped at a national park through which the equator crosses; we performed the traditional custom of standing with one foot on the Northern Hemisphere and one foot in the Southern Hemisphere. Oddly, when you think of being on the equator you think of being warm; we were freezing!

437

Life Between Innings

On the second morning we left Quito with MTW missionaries Don Williams and Keith Powlison. We traveled along the Pan American Highway enroute to Riobamba, the city were Don Williams and his wife were working. Riobamba was about a four-hour drive, and with Don driving, it was quite the adventure. I was sitting in the middle of the back seat of the car so I had the perfect view of what lay before us. It was actually like playing a video game wherein we would try to see what obstacle we should try to miss first. We certainly had our options as we missed cattle on several occasions, pedestrians, large potholes, which were created by striking teachers who would burn car tires right in the middle of the road to disrupt traffic, cars and trucks coming from either side of the road, landsides, large rocks and trees. That was exciting, but the most exciting part was having absolutely no control over the fact that Don loved to pass cars and trucks on the tight curves along the hills without any way of knowing if a car was coming at us or not. Somehow, we were always able to stop and get over before we were run over. After awhile, all you could do was sit there and grin and watch it all happen. It was amazing!

We stayed two nights in Riobamba and visited with some of the church people, had a great Ecuadorian dinner and listened to some Quechuan musicians who played flutes unique to this region of the world. They had just made a new Christian music CD and were very pleased to sell us each one.

One of the things that Don wanted to show us was property in two different locations that he was wanting to buy to use for a training center. At the training center they would teach theological studies to their pastors and leaders, plus use it to teach the pastors a trade. Pastors here did not live off the tithe of the church as most of those who worshipped at the Quechuan churches were very poor. At best, they might be able to offer their pastor some grain or vegetables. One piece

The Union Years 1983-2002

of property sat on a beautiful hillside right next to a volcano that was belching ash all over the place and all over us. Their so-called experts had advised that this volcano would soon become dormant and, if so, this would be a great piece of property. In unison we advised Don to look elsewhere.

After another eventful drive back to Quito we boarded our plane to Lima, Peru. At Lima, we said goodbye to Chris Polski who had to return home to prepare for his upcoming ordination. Here in Lima we again stayed overnight in a hotel that regularly hosted Christian workers visiting in the area. It was still dark when we rose in the morning to leave for the airport. I am not sure what I was thinking but I saw Don Gahagen plug in his hair dryer, so I decided it would be OK to plug in mine. The only difference was that Don's was wired for 240 while mine was wired for 120, such as in the States. Immediately the lights went off and all the circuits in the house were tripped. I looked outside and all the lights in the immediate area were also off. I did not dare tell anyone, at least immediately, how much of an idiot I was, but we dressed in the dark, caught our cab, which thankfully had been arranged the night before, and headed through the darkness several miles and on to the airport.

The rest of the morning was uneventful as we boarded our flight to Cusco, Peru. In Cusco, we were picked up by Ruth, the wife of Keith Powlison, and taken out to their home just beyond the edge of this sprawling city. It is here that Keith and Ruth were already in the process of building a training center like Don Williams had envisioned. The following day Keith took us touring over many hills and through the dales where we saw some of the most awesome country and cultural sites that you could imagine. At one place we stopped and purchased a wheel of cheese and ate quite a bit of it before we returned to the house. He also drove us up one mountain that took us up above the tree line, something like 13,500 feet. We watched as old ladies would dig their potatoes at this high level, place them in sacks and then begin the long walk down the mountain to Cusco where they would hopefully sell them. Keith allowed the ladies to pile into the back of the truck with their heavy sacks and ride all the way down the hill and back to town. I do not know how they would have ever gotten those sacks to market if Keith had not come along. I helped one of the ladies put a sack in the truck and it was all that I could do to hoist it up and in. I can only guess that they stay by the road and hope someone will come by who will provide them a lift.

We enjoyed staying in a beautiful hotel in the city. There was no way to know that such a beautiful hotel was behind the plain, barren walls that surrounded it. We drove up a tight cobblestone street in midtown, just room enough for one car, to find this treasure. It was pretty cool.

The following day we enjoyed worshipping with the saints at the primary Presbyterian Church in Cusco, obviously understanding nothing but recognizing the melody to a few familiar sacred hymns. The people were warm and welcoming but it was hot and hard to stay awake as the service was not a short one

Upon returning to St. Louis, in just a matter of days, I became very sick. A visit to the doctor revealed that I had picked up a bacteria called campylobacter. The doctor said that I would probably recover in about 10 days; however, in some cases the symptoms do not go away for seven weeks or so. Lucky me, I got the seven-week variety and was quarantined by the St. Louis County Health Department for the next few days.

For some time the Elders of the church, including our Pastor, Rodney Stortz, had been after me to seek a leadership role in the church. Three times I had started the training for a Deacon or Ruling Elder (Ruling Elders in the Presbyterian

The Union Years 1983-2002

Church make up the Session, the equivalent to "the Board" in most churches.) and twice had actually completed it, only to decide that my schedule was just too full. Finally, in September of 2001, I finished the nine-month training class (again) and was elected by the membership of Twin Oaks as a Ruling Elder. Other than doing missions work, this was the first time since the '70s that I had held an office in the church. I guess God thought it was time for me to get back to work.

When Giljum had freed up my schedule in '88 to acquaint myself with the various agencies and organizations in the community that offered benefits that our members might need, the very first organization that I became familiar with was the United Way. Labor had ties to United Way nationally; in fact, the AFL-CIO is one of their biggest supporters. Union Electric, being a public utility, was likewise a big supporter and twice, during my tenure with the Union, had allowed two of their Company CEOs to act as the area Chairman of the annual *United Way of Greater St. Louis Campaign*. Union Electric, knowing of my current role with the Union and my role in developing our acclaimed EAP program, began to ask me to participate in their rallies around the system. I was a product of the United Way in that the Boys' Club of St. Louis received support from them; consequently it was easy for me to speak with passion regarding this important cause.

As my reputation spread as a Labor Leader speaking strongly in support of the United Way effort, I was annually asked by various organization to come and speak. Union Electric asked me on several occasions to be the Labor Chair for their annual drive, which I readily accepted, and I would participate in this lead role usually with one of their key vice-presidents. I had also been asked to sit on the Board of the Tri-Cities Area United Way (Illinois) and later to be the Labor Chair in their campaign. It became common for me to appear

Life Between Innings

in various videos put out by Union Electric to use during campaigns and once appeared on television in Paducah, Kentucky, as the Labor Chair for their campaign. I am guessing it was a slow news day! My first ever speech to the membership of EEI was at a United Way rally held at the plant.

It was with this backdrop that on September 11, 2001, I was appearing at two early morning United Way rallies at the Grand Tower Plant. Over the previous week, CIPS management had scheduled me to speak at the Meredosia, Hutsonsville and Coffeen plants, as well as at their headquarters building in Springfield, Illinois. I had arrived early so that I could speak to both the bargaining unit members and management personnel that were coming off the midnight shift and then stay over and speak to those coming in on the AM shift.

At about 9:15 AM I finished my last speech and began the two-hour drive back to my office in Maryville. As was my custom, I tried to dial in my favorite morning radio show hosted by the "notorious" J.C. Corcoran. Through the heavy static I was able to tell that something was amiss, but I could not immediately put the pieces together. Finally, I reached a spot on the road where the signal came in clear enough for me to hear J.C. say, *Did you see that? Another plane has just hit the other tower of the World Trade Center. Folks, this is much more than just a coincidence!!!*

J.C. and his radio partners did a great job that day of keeping me informed of what was going on. Being an *Old Time Radio* buff, my first thought was that this was a real life version of the *War of the Worlds*, the old Orson Wells radio drama, broadcast on Halloween back in the '30s. That broadcast caused a lot of hysteria, especially for those who had tuned in late and did not realize that the news reports of an invasion from Mars were nothing more than a radio drama. I drove slowly back to the office in disbelief at what I was hearing. Not long after,

442

The Union Years 1983-2002

it was reported that a plane had crashed into the Pentagon Building and that another plane was suspected to have been hi-jacked and believed to be headed toward Washington D.C. and most likely the White House. It was later confirmed that the passengers of this plane, having heard reports of what was happening elsewhere from family and friends on their cell phones, overcame the terrorist and forced the plane to crash, killing everyone, in an open field in Pennsylvania. About 10:30 AM it was reported that the FAA had closed every runway in the nation and all flights were cancelled until the government could ascertain what was happening. In total, over 3000 lives were lost that day and America, as we knew it, has not been the same. The U.S. government soon thereafter placed the blame on an illusive Al Qaeda leader, Osama Bin Laden, as the mastermind behind the attacks.

President George W. Bush, Jr. tried to draw the net around Bin Laden for capture but was never successful. He did, however, turn his attention to Iraq and Saddam Hussein, a notorious dictator that was thought to be storing weapons of mass destruction for an eventual attack on the U.S. or Israel. Consequently, Bush ordered an invasion of Iraq. The military authored what was termed a *Shock & Awe* campaign destroying much of the infrastructure of Baghdad, the capital city, as well as other major cities across Iraq. Eventually, almost by accident, Saddam was captured, tried, convicted and hanged, but no weapons of mass destruction were ever found. To fund the war the government began printing money like never before, eventually leading to a recession with banks, big businesses, the housing market and Wall Street toppling over like dominoes. In the end, Iraq became another Korea and Viet Nam for us, an albatross around our necks that brought our country into great disfavor around the world and to our knees financially. Although Bush would go on to win a second term, he

Life Between Innings

would go down as having the worst approval rating in history of any president leaving office. He was also, in my opinion, the worst President of my lifetime, squeezing past Ronald Reagan as the President that enacted policies that totally destroyed the fabric of the nation, but particularly the middle class. Bush's claim that he was a Pro-Life, born-again Christian helped him to retain the acclaim of most of the Conservative Right, but they too began to tire of his ineptness as his second tour came to a close.

Whitney enjoyed her 16th birthday on July 29, of 2001 and so began the process of getting her driver's license. Tina did the bulk share of teaching her, although I got the "joy" of handling the parallel parking chore. Actually, teaching her was a lot of fun. We would go to the Twin Oaks School back parking lot where I would sit up some orange cones that we had used for soccer practices back in the day. It wasn't long before she began to do an acceptable job. Upon obtaining her license, and ultimately the purchase of an older, but still shiny red Pontiac Grand Am, we allowed her to start driving to school with all the trepidation that parents have in these circumstances. I remember her coming to me one day and commenting that she was sure that after lugging her and her friends around to all their practices, all their games, all their many activities for lo these many years, I was probably glad that she could now drive and I would no longer have this duty. It was one of those moments for me as, I explained with little tear drops welling up in my eyes, that, *No, it's just the contrary. I enjoyed all those trips, all those days of taking you and your friends to games and events. Each one of those trips allowed me to enjoy you even more and was part of being your dad; and, I really enjoy being your dad!* I think she got it!

With my plans for retirement in 2002 widely known, Giljum decided that he would like for me to relinquish my CIPS and

The Union Years 1983-2002

EEI jurisdictions to Dan Sweet, a former CIPS employee and Chief Steward at the Coffeen Plant, that he had appointed as a Business Representative soon after John Snyder had retired back in the early 90s. Giljum asked me if I would take on some organizing responsibilities for my final year, which would allow Sweet to become familiar with the workers and the contract at EEI, as well as with Mr. Powers, prior to new contract negotiations starting in May of 2002. I was very, very reluctant to make the switch, as I really wanted to retire in the saddle representing both CIPS and EEI, but especially the EEI membership. My work with these men and women in opposition to the unscrupulous tactics of EEI management, and especially Mr. Powers, was the hi-light of my career in Organized Labor and I was not ready to give up that role. However, Giljum's arguments for making the switch made sense, so I reluctantly gave in.

After serving in the Union Organizer role for a few months, a role that I had taken on for several years as part of my duties back in 1987, I was miserable and simply not happy, as I was not able to get my mind wrapped around the organizing assignments as I had back in the late 80s and early 90s. Consequently, I was seriously considering resigning and returning to the Labadie Plant for my final few months. Word of this got back to Giljum and he offered to have me take over the entire grievance and arbitration procedure for AmerenUE, AmerenCIPS (Union Electric had merged with CIPS in the late '90s and their corporation's new name was AmerenCIPS.) and EEI. This was a role that I relished and immediately went to work cleaning up the pile of grievances that had gotten backlogged in the Ameren system and began scheduling and conducting all the third step grievance meetings systemwide. By the time I retired, I had the backlog cleared and the files back in shape. I truly enjoyed this role and it provided me a great

Life Between Innings

opportunity for closing out my career and maintaining contact with old friends across the entire Local 148 system as I said goodbye.

For several years our beloved Senior Pastor, Rodney Stortz, had battled liver cancer. He had valiantly fought the disease while undergoing several series of chemotherapy treatment and enduring a number of operations. In March of 2002, Pastor Stortz's long battle ended as God took him home to glory. Rodney was an amazing man continuing his radio and pulpit schedule without missing a step. At times it was painful to watch, but he refused to leave the pulpit till God called him home.

Because of his radio work at KSIV in St. Louis, Rodney came to know Carole Buck, the wife of Hall of Fame Broadcaster, Jack Buck, who also had her own radio show. Carole was a Christian and a strong pro-life advocate, as was Rodney; consequently her friendship with Rodney was cemented. Carole insisted that she be allowed to introduce her husband to Rodney, which she did, and they soon became good friends. From time to time Jack would have Rodney, who was a great sports fan, and especially a Cardinal fan, accompany him to NFL games that he was broadcasting or to be his guest at Cardinal games. Rodney even convinced Jack once to MC our Youth Missions Auction, which was a great success. Rodney, ever so determined, would witness to Jack and question him whether he had the assurance of salvation? However, Jack, a devout Catholic, would not confess Christ as his Lord and Savior regardless of the efforts Rodney put forth. However, in 2001, Jack became very sick and was hospitalized and it soon became apparent that he was not going to make it. In those final few days Rodney stayed at Jack's side as a friend, but also as God's servant. Finally, one evening Rodney again presented the gospel and then asked Jack if he would like to receive Jesus as his Lord and Savior.

This time Jack said, "Yes!" Rodney continued to question him to make sure that Jack understood clearly what he was doing, and Jack confirmed that he did. Within a few days Jack passed on to be with His Lord and Savior, Jesus Christ. Rodney preached Jack's funeral to an overflowing crowd at Twin Oaks and by radio through the mighty voice of KMOX. The church was packed with dignitaries from all walks of life as Jack's life had impacted many through his broadcasting career and charitable work. Rodney, true to his calling, preached an outstanding message painting clearly the way to salvation. He closed his sermon borrowing one of Jack's trademark phases, *So long for just a while!*

Rodney's words were prophetic as he too passed on to glory in March of 2002. Again the church was full to overflowing for this beloved preacher and teacher of the Word. The Manchester and St. Louis County police that arranged for the motorcade said that they had never seen a processional this long as cars literally stretched for two miles or more.

Because Giljum was not willing to pay for vacation not used, I began to plot out my exit strategy from the Union. Officially, my retirement date was June 1, 2002. Since I had so much vacation stored-up I was pretty much through working at the start of April, leaving one week to work at the end of May so as to get out to the various locations and meetings to say my goodbyes and offer my thanks to the many guys that had helped me obtain a certain level of success. The fact was, and I made this clear in all my closing speeches and news articles, that my success was nothing more than putting good men around me who knew what was needed to be done and got it done. I teared up only briefly at my last Executive Board meeting, as I was asked to say a few words. However, when I got into my car and left the office for the final time, I left without any tears but with a tremendous amount of appreciation

Life Between Innings

for the opportunity that Giljum had given me and for the great men and women that I had served with. I had come into the office in 1984, admittedly without a strong appreciation for what the Union stood for. Here I was leaving some 18 years later, totally and unabashedly a union guy, a strong advocate for Labor and for the cause we represent; no apologizes!! I had been blessed in my service, blessed beyond deserving; life was good! To God be the Glory!!

The 8ᵗʰ Inning

THE RETIREMENT YEARS
2002-Beyond

As 2002 began, the war in Iraq was heating up and was the lead story on the evening news. President George W. Bush, Jr. continued to persuade the American public that the war was necessary as Iraq, led by the notorious dictator, Saddam Hussein, was developing and hiding weapons of mass destruction, jeopardizing our safety and American freedoms. As the war escalated and more and more American dollars were poured into the effort, it soon became clear that Bush's intelligence sources were wrong and that there were no hidden weapons of mass destruction. The war kept the government and the American people distracted while the instigator of the September 11, 2001 attacks on the World Trade Center and other American institutions, Osama Bin Laden, became, at times, an afterthought to the ongoing losses of men/women, money and national morale created by the Iraq War. President Bush, despite very low approval ratings, ran successfully against the Democratic candidate, John Kerry, and his very liberal agenda in the 2004 presidential election securing a second term. Pro-abortion and gay rights issues dominated the anti-Kerry campaign and the election became more about morals than the ongoing war in Iraq or the economy. In 2005, Hurricane Katrina, hit the city of New Orleans broadside killing 1836 people and causing over 81 billion dollars in damage. This was the costliest natural disaster in U.S. history.

The St. Louis Rams Super Bowl era, with its "Greatest Show on Turf" mantra, was long gone and a new era of ineptness took over the team's front office and on the field. The hockey Blues still had not recovered from a lock-out of the players in 2004 and a recent ownership change, but good drafting and a new solid ownership group was beginning to stir the hopes of the faithful once again. The baseball Cardinals continued to compete within their division and made a strong run at another World Series ring against the Boston Red Sox in 2002, only to be swept in 4 games. However, in 2006 they limped into the wildcard spot, but caught fire through the National League playoffs, finally winning out in 5 games over the Detroit Tigers for a World Series win. The Mizzou Tigers struck gold under football coach Gary Pinkel turning in consecutive 10 win seasons in 2008, 2009 and 2010. The roar was finally restored at Missouri University after some 20 years. And, the St. Louis University Billikens hired Rick Majerius away from ESPN in the spring of 2007 to lead the Bills into their new, on-campus arena, opening to rave reviews for the 2008/2009 season. Under Majerius the recruiting began to improve immediately and the prospects for a great future began to materialize. In 2009, tragic news came to pop fans around the world with the announcement that Michael Jackson had passed away from the overuse of prescription drugs given to him by his personal doctor to help him sleep.

The year 2008 marked a significant moment in American history when a U.S. Senator from Illinois, Barack Hussein Obama, became the first black President of the United States. The Republican challenger, Arizona Senator John McCain, could not distance himself from the ineptness of former Republican President George W. Bush, Jr. and his failed military and economic policies and his fate was sealed. McCain selected the Governor of Alaska as his running mate, Sarah Palin, who created quite a stir. She was a very attractive lady but hardly had a resume to be considered. After a brief honeymoon with the American public, her popularity fell off dramatically, except within the very conservative Pro-Life, far-right crowd, after performing very badly in a

The Retirement Years 2002-beyond

series of televised interviews and a debate. It was my opinion that this was the most dangerous, most irresponsible selection of a vice-presidential candidate in my lifetime, even out-distancing George W. Bush, Sr.'s selection of Dan Quail.

June 1, 2002, came and went and I was finally retired from my labors as a Business Representative *of Local 148 of the International Union of Operating Engineers (Stationary)*. With my 28 year pension from AmerenUE and my International pension of 18 years from the Operating Engineers, I was sitting pretty good. Unless something should go horrifically wrong on Wall Street, these pension plans should secure me financially to the end of my life, and provide a nice monthly sum for Tina upon my death, as both plans are guaranteed at 100% for her lifetime. Both plans are called Defined Pensions, meaning that they are not [necessarily] tied to the fluctuation of the stock market like 401-Ks.

Ameren had also guaranteed me a lifetime cap on my major medical plan wherein I would never have to pay more than $150 a month for life for both Tina and me. However, that guarantee lasted all of four months when President and CEO of Ameren, Mr. Gary Rainwater, announced that the premiums to our plans would start rising yearly over the next six years until reaching a level close to $800 a month for a family plan. While the Union cannot bargain over Company-provided retiree benefits, they did file a lawsuit on behalf of the retirees, but to no avail. While this certainly was a financial blow to me personally, I cannot even fathom what it meant to regularly retired Ameren employees who were now on fixed incomes with little opportunity to find jobs to help supplement this outrageous increase. At a minimum, the Company should have grandfathered all that were currently retired and begin the increases for those that were retiring later. This was just another example, in a long line of examples, of the greed

Life Between Innings

and despicable behavior of big business that I had experienced or had seen in my years in Labor Relations. When the massive company, Enron, finally fell apart and their employees lost their pensions as a result of criminal management tactics and greed, it became further cemented in my mind that I had chosen the right team to work for back in 1984 when I had options to work for management or for labor.

Attending a strongly conservative, predominately Republican church, as was Twin Oaks, my good Christian friends found it hard to understand my loyalty to the Organized Labor Movement. One key Ruling Elder in the church, Arne Molbach, affectionately called me their *bastard child*, but he, as did others, continued their encouragement of me to become involved in the church in various leadership roles. Speaking in very general terms, most of my Christian friends have no idea of the sickening underbelly of management and the constant lies that spew from their lips in the name of profits. How Christianity got tied in with the Republican Party and their support of Big Business has baffled me for most of my adult life. Obviously, the Democratic Party support for liberal issues such as gay rights and pro-abortion agendas are the central reasons for standing behind the Republican flag but, my goodness, I wish my fellow Christians could get just a glimpse of their self-righteousness when they start pointing their bony little fingers at other Christians who just can't stomach the bias that the Republican Party has toward ethnic groups of all races and the poor and middle class in particular.

I do have to admit that I voted for George W. in 2004, as I could not stomach the immoral issues that John Kerry was pushing forward, but I regretted almost immediately my vote for Bush; howbeit, neither vote would have been a good one. It was certainly a no win situation. While I tend to vote across party lines in most elections, I had not voted for a Republican

The Retirement Years 2002-beyond

president since voting for Ronald Reagan in 1980 while running for his first term. I quickly repented of that vote as well as Reagan began to destroy the fabric of the middle class with his anti-labor stances (i.e. breaking of the Air Traffic Controller's Union and the institution of using permanent replacement workers for those on lawful strikes), his trickle down economics and the deregulation of everything from the airline industry to the milk industry. His failed policies only enhanced big business even further creating a larger gap between the rich and the middle class and prices began to skyrocket from airfares to a loaf of bread. Republicans love to point their finger at Democrats as "those big spenders," yet Reagan pushed forward budgets that led to the highest deficient spending in our nation's history at that time. President Clinton began to bring the United States out of deficit spending, in fact, remarkably so, as the budget was balanced under his leadership with a surplus established over each of his final four years in office. However, President George W. Bush, Jr. took us right back into deficit spending with his war on Iraq, establishing a new record for such spending in the process. Unfortunately, Democratic President Obama continued our pattern of historical record spending to help fund our latest war in Afghanistan and attempts to bailout our failing banks and lenders, the housing market and the automobile industry. The reality is that I am happy that our hope is not in the Presidents that we elect but in the God, Jehovah, which we serve!

As with most retirements the lure of sleeping in and working in the yard soon lost its luster. I am not one that likes to piddle around the house or with cars or to spend my time fishing or on the golf course. The fact is that I played more golf when I was working than I ever have since retiring. After nine months, I was ready to do more than just coach basketball and be Tina's yardman. While I never regretted retiring early, even

Life Between Innings

on retirement's worst days, I did miss the give and take of the bargaining table.

For those who know me, but have never seen me at the bargaining table or on the sidelines coaching basketball, I am sure that they must wonder how I could ever have been successful in those endeavors considering that I am laid back, have an easy-going demeanor, am non-confrontational to a fault, a person long on patience and not easily flustered; what a fish out of water I must look to many! I am not sure what it is but every time I cross the end line of a basketball court to coach my kids or step into the arena known as collective bargaining, my whole personality changes. I loved the competitiveness and I loved that the end results benefited the kids or families if I did my job well.

In the spring of 2003, I received a call from the Business Manager of Service Employees International Union (SEIU), Local 2000, Grant Williams, headquartered in the Central West End in midtown, just off the DeBalievere Strip. This is where I use to ride my cousin's bicycle back in 1959 following our move from Salem to St. Louis. Mr. Williams had been referred by Sherry Schroeder, one of the attorneys from the Diekemper, Hammond, Shinners, Turcotte & Larrew, PC Law Firm that had handled so many of our arbitrations, Unfair Labor Practices (ULP) and other Labor matters when I was working for I.U.O.E. Local 148. Mr. Williams stated that I had come highly recommended and was wondering if I would meet him for breakfast and discuss the possibility of contracting myself to do some negotiations for SEIU. SEIU was very good at organizing employees; in fact, they are the largest union in the nation, but they had a poor reputation of servicing their contracts after obtaining (organizing) them. Since they were organizing units rapidly, they did not have many "gray hairs" on their staff who were available or experienced enough to negotiate

The Retirement Years 2002-beyond

Labor Agreements, and that is where I came in. I agreed to meet.

Grant Williams and I hit it off instantly, although it was apparent from the start that our way of doing union business was night and day. Grant was an impatient man, ready to fight first and deal with the results later. I had learned from Giljum the art of patience when it comes to negotiations and that some matters just can't be hurried along if it is a good product or result that is wanted. We were not long into the conversation when he offered me the job. He asked what I thought would be a fair price? I stammered only briefly and he threw the figure of $3,000 a month on the table if I would be willing to give them 20 hours a week. He agreed to pay my expenses and mileage when negotiating required that I be out of town. I accepted.

My first contract was with a group of nurses working at Georgian Gardens Nursing Home in Potosi, Missouri, who were trying to hold their Union together. The bargaining unit's contract was up but one of the members had started a de-cert petition trying to get the Union ousted. The group was fairly split between the union's hard-liners and the younger ladies who had become disenchanted over paying dues and getting little service or attention in return from SEIU.

With the help of one of the Organizers working with SEIU we were able to beat back the de-cert petition and proceed with negotiations. My first chore was to try to gain the trust of the Committee and ultimately the Bargaining Unit members. It was obvious that this would not be an easy chore, especially since many of them had become disenchanted with the SEIU leadership back in St. Louis. I felt that once I could get the Committee into negotiations and they could see my style and my tactics, I would eventually win their trust and ultimately a contract for them.

Life Between Innings

I had several prep meetings with the Committee developing our contract demands, which we took back to the full membership for any final thoughts prior to issuing them as *Demands* to the Home's representatives. With the exception of a few minor issues, the membership liked what we were trying to accomplish, especially with heath care.

I contacted the Director of the Home to attempt to get some dates for bargaining. Finally, after some needless delays, we established a date to meet at the Holiday Inn in Crystal City, Missouri. To my astonishment, Mike Lowenbaum, an attorney that we had dealt with on a number of Fairview Heights Municipal Workers issues, had been hired as the chief spokesman for management. Mike and I had not worked together across the table before, but we knew of each other's reputation and we hit it off well. Not long into negotiations Mike met me in a sidebar and blasted the principal members of his own committee as being insane, out of touch and incompetent . . . and those were the nice words that he used. I knew, however, regardless of his distaste for his "employer," he would still do them right, which he attempted to do. However, I also knew that his anger with and distrust of his own committee could play well into my hands if I handled the situation correctly.

The negotiations were extended long past what Grant Williams deemed necessary and he became a little impatient. It wasn't long before he wanted to start firing ULPs (Unfair Labor Practices) at the Company; in fact, it was practically from day one. This would have been a monumental mistake, as we would have lost each one that we filed and would have served only to have set the negotiation process back even further. However, it was this type of inexperience that I had to deal with from my side while Mike had to deal with a committee that he hated. It took as about five months from start to finish, but in the end we were able to get a fairly decent contract, one the Union Leaders at the Home were pleased with and that the membership accepted. I also gained tremendous respect for the ladies on the committee, and especially the Chief Steward, who had to try to hold it all together back at the Home with the young dissidents while we simultaneously worked to secure the contract at the bargaining table.

My next assignment was to negotiate a contract with Technicolor, SEIU Local 2000's largest client, located in Pinckneyville, Illinois. The company produces the DVDs of all the major movies that we rent or purchase after they finish their run in the local theaters. Tight security was always in place at the plant to ensure that no one was able to pirate the product. Again, I was given a group that was strongly union but very upset with SEIU for what they perceived as a lack of attention to their issues and grievances. Because the need for representation was so great, I actually took on the role of their Business Agent, conducting their grievance meetings and handling their arbitration cases, as well as negotiating their contract. I should have known better but my heart was bigger than my capacity to say "No." So, what started out as a really good job at 20 hours a week for $3000 a month, very quickly turned into a drastically underpaid job working upwards of 50-60 hours a week. I had signed the contract with SEIU and I would see it through, but I knew if I continued with them past this contract we would have to dramatically change the terms of our agreement with a significant raise in pay.

At Technicolor, things quickly turned in my favor as I connected with their Chief Steward, Bill Rheinecker. Bill was country through and through but he appreciated the honest conversations that we had and my forthright approach to doing business. He also detected that I was not too fond of management in general, which made him feel comfortable knowing that it was doubtful that I would get in bed with them at some

Life Between Innings

point, as the bargaining unit suspected past representatives had done.

I was also fortunate to have a very good committee, although it had several women on it, which usually spells trouble. In this case, the only trouble we had was with one of the inexperienced young guys whose girlfriend was in his ear all the time. I think he was afraid to ever agree to anything that I proposed for fear that she would rake him over the coals about it when he got home. I in fact hope she did, as payment for all the aggravation he caused the committee and me.

But, again, after a very lengthy process, a process that SEIU was not accustomed to, we crafted out one of the best contracts in their history with pay raises, a new holiday, vacation benefits, cheap but lucrative medical benefits and job protections. The membership, working for any company at any location, never feels that the committee got enough. Consequently, we had a few detractors, but the contract passed overwhelmingly and my job with Technicolor was over. I had really come to appreciate Bill and his wife and the committee during our struggle. These were good people that deserved better, and I left feeling like we had made some headway in accomplishing that for them and the people that they represented.

After putting the Technicolor contract to bed it was time to take off for Florida and our annual vacation on Sanibel Island. We were now up to taking a full month away, renting a nice home just a 3-minute walk to the beach. Sanibel had become our home away from home as this summer of 2003 represented some 15 years or so of enjoying this beautiful island paradise. Some of our greatest family memories are located here as we enjoyed years of having Whitney's friends join us and a few of our own.

After coaching girls' basketball at Westminster the past four seasons, two at the seventh and eighth grade level and

The Retirement Years 2002-beyond

two more as the Junior Varsity coach at the high school level, I was asked in April of 2002 to step in as interim Head Coach for the 2002/2003 season, filling the vacated spot of Doug Butte. Doug had been unceremoniously pushed out after mishandling several player/parent issues. The school believed that they had worked out a deal whereby Steve Stipanovich, former All-American at Mizzou and an NBA player with the Indiana Pacers, would come in the following year as the head coach. I readily agreed to the interim tag and looked forward to getting the pieces in place so that Steve would have a good foundation to build on. That summer I put into place a basketball camp, an in-house league for the girls at the school and placed them in a very competitive high school summer league at Meramec Junior College. Each of these endeavors was successful.

When the 2002/2003 season got underway, I once again found myself coaching many of the same girls that I had been coaching since the fourth grade. For me, it was a dream come true, as I had not considered in my wildest dreams I would ever be able to coach at this level. As we approached the season I knew that I had to address our point guard situation, as it had become the Achilles heel of the team over the past two seasons. Our ability to beat even a nominal press left us trapped in the backcourt over and over again, proving to be rather embarrassing. Our point guard, Amanda Beard, had held this position since her freshman year and now, in her senior season, it would take some head butting to move her to the off-guard position, especially to allow an underclassmen to take the position. However, I was quite determined and installed Cory Falb, a young athletic lady with great court sense, vision and competitiveness to the point, a move that proved successful. We were rarely trapped in the backcourt that season; however, our record only improved slightly from the previous campaign.

Life Between Innings

As it turned out this was the last season that Whitney would play. Whitney, now a junior, had been a starter since her freshman year as she had developed and maintained a nice touch on her shot from about 15 feet out. She was also just a tough cookie that threw herself relentlessly into the game's action. However, since her shoulder surgery following the previous season, she could no longer raise her left arm to full capacity. This impacted her ability to get loft on her shot, leaving her ball flat and not as effective. As she saw her time on the court diminishing and her starting role gradually being taken from her, it appeared that she began to lose interest and experienced some burnout. This is not an uncommon thing for young players, especially girls, who have played a competitive sport for a long time. While it hurt my own heart to see her pass up her senior season, I supported her in making that decision.

It was never made clear why, but Stipanovich decided not to take the job as planned for the 2003/2004 season; however, he agreed to assist his friend, Barry Mauer, who he had played with while a student at Mizzou. Mauer had a daughter that would be a freshman and it was obvious that she was going to be a very special player. Mauer and I finally met at the school to discuss my role and some of the personnel that we had coming back. Barry and I hit it off OK and he offered me my old position as Junior Varsity Coach. However, we could not agree on anything. I like to run and play pressure defense. Barry likes the half court game and did not like to press. I like to bring the parents in and get them involved; Barry wanted parents as far away from him as possible. I like to hold devotions as part of our school's mission; it did not seem evident that Barry had much interest in that. Knowing that I had a large contingent of parents who trusted me and liked the way I ran the program, I decided, in all fairness to Barry and to myself, it

The Retirement Years 2002-beyond

was best that I resign my post as Junior Varsity Coach. I knew that as soon as any controversy would start, and Barry had a reputation as being controversial, I would have parents in my ear all the time, and I did not want that.

It was tough sitting out the season and becoming a spectator again. However, my good friend Dave Hoefakker, the Assistant Superintendent of Schools of the Ritenour School District, told me that there was a girls' Head Coaching position opening at the Ritenour High School for the 2004/2005 season. I put my resume together and scheduled a meeting with Jerry Nolan, the Athletic Director (AD) of the school. Jerry and I meshed well; however, after some deliberations, it was decided that they would offer the job to a Black schoolteacher at the school, Ms. April Warren-Grice. April had been a terrific high school basketball player and had coached overseas in a military unit. She had also served as the JV Girls Head Coach the previous two seasons. Another meeting was called for me to meet with Coach Grice to see if there might be a fit. Coach was a little standoffish at first, and I think understandably so, as she had to wonder if this retired guy wanting to coach would try to help her succeed or undermine her efforts for his own personal gain. Soon, we discovered that we were both born-again believers and a good friendship began to develop between us. I was asked if I would like to assist Coach Grice or if I would prefer taking on the Junior Varsity coaching position. There was no hesitation on my part in that I wanted to coach, not assist, so I took the JV position. Ms. Jody Fowler, a white teacher at the school and a former high school standout in basketball, became the assistant. The three of us became great friends and remain so today.

I remained the girls JV Head Coach for four great years. I enjoyed coaching at Westminster but I really enjoyed my time at Ritenour. When I left Westminster and took on the Ritenour

Life Between Innings

job, a number of folks thought I had lost my mind, giving up the chance to coach at a Christian school for a position at a public high school in a tough conference working in some tough neighborhoods. In reality, the girls at Westminster were mostly white, came primarily from two parent, well-to-do homes; they really did not need me as the players would and did at Ritenour. At Ritenour, most of my girls were from single-parent homes or living with a grandparent. I became a father figure to many of my girls, and my parents and the school administration could not have been more helpful or supportive. In four years I had only two meetings with disgruntled parents, both which were white mothers representing two-parent homes. In one case the mom was upset over her daughter's lack of playing time. The other case involved a mother who was upset that I had cut her daughter at the conclusion of tryouts. To the first mom I explained that playing time is earned in practice and is a reward for the effort and abilities that are honed therein. However, neither mom ever got it or understood my reasoning or philosophy, but both the girls remained loyal to me despite their parents, as they both understood the realities of high school basketball.

My roster, except for my last season, generally consisted of seven black, four white and one Hispanic. My last season I had an all-black team and they became my all time favorite team. They bought into what I was trying to do about a third of the way into the season, especially defensively. We started the season 1-6 but ended up going 8-6 the remainder of the season, primarily because of our stellar trapping defense. I loved the cross-cultural aspect of this opportunity and threw myself into it with great enthusiasm. I appreciated the opportunities I had been given at Twin Oaks and at Westminster because it was there I learned the art of coaching. It was, however, at Ritenour that I was able to put that art form into

The Retirement Years 2002-beyond

practice. Our girls were woefully lacking in skills. Ritenour sits between Wellston, Normandy and Berkeley, renowned black schools in depressed areas, but with excellent women's basketball programs. For whatever reason, the Ritenour district was just unable to produce good female athletic basketball players, although our academics were tops in the area.

Consequently, here at the high school level, I was teaching basic basketball skills, skills that most players learn in the fourth and fifth grades. I never had a good shooting team at Ritenour so I always stressed defense. The girls soon discovered that if they played great defense two things would happen. One; they got on the court. Two; as a team we became competitive. Over the years we had some really good victories over tough schools like Hazelwood East, Hazelwood Central, Ladue, Clayton and Wentzville. The bus ride home was always much more pleasant when we were bringing home a victory.

Every coach has favorite players, and if they say otherwise, they are lying. Kayla Gischer, a white girl from a broken home and without much direction in life, tried out as a freshman. Kayla had some skills but she had temper and lifestyle issues that had to be dealt with, as well as a not-so-good academic record. But, she loved basketball. About two weeks into that first season Kayla began to get it and she began to get me. From there we simply clicked and she become one of the best players that I coached at Ritenour. She was a terrific three-point shooter and a better-than-average defender, learning how to "cheat" to make up for average speed and jumping ability. I also connected with her parents and was invited to her graduation party following her senior year. As she improved as a basketball player she also improved as a person and academically. Later, she took some pride in the fact that her new nickname became *Backpack Girl*, as she began to lug her books from school to home and back. This was a new experience for her.

There were others that also stood out such as Racquelle Givens and Crystal Campbell. Both these girls were black, had set for themselves high goals, were honor students, had strong moral fiber and were Christians. They both were captains, natural team leaders and tough as nails. Racquelle was my leading scorer and Crystal was my leading rebounder. It seemed every year God gave me a few Christians on the team, which I really enjoyed.

Just prior to my first game at Ritenour I had gathered all my team together outside the gymnasium door, but next to the lobby, waiting for the freshman game to conclude. A moment or two passed by and I realized that several of my girls had suddenly disappeared. I looked through the door window leading to the lobby and to my great surprise, but obvious delight, were four to five players kneeling at a bench in private prayer oblivious to the fans and their peers that were passing through. After the girls had finished praying I pulled Yarelis Soto aside, my Hispanic player, as she seemed to be the one leading the prayer time. I told her that I did not know if it was she who was the one who led her teammates to do this, but I just wanted her to know, and those that had joined her, how proud I was of them! My eyes welled up with tears, but this was really neat. I also added that they had my blessing to do that as often as they liked. What a great way to start my career at Ritenour!

The administration had made it clear that I could have team prayers before our games as long as I did not lead them. It was great to see individual girls, some with little Christian background, at least attempt to pray in public. We also had team meetings twice a week and it was not unusual for us to get into some good discussions regarding moral issues, such

The Retirement Years 2002-beyond

as abortion. There was an instance when three basketball players from nearby Pattonville High School became pregnant. At the same time a movie entitled, *Coach Carter*, came out and I was able to take the girls for a screening. In the movie, a player's girlfriend became pregnant and later obtained an abortion, which appeared to resolve all of her problems. I used this opportunity to discuss with the girls the issues of abortion and whether they thought the portrayal in the movie was accurate regarding the issue and the resolution of her problem. Again, I was so proud of my girls, especially the Christians that spoke up boldly and denounced abortion as a solution to a young girl's problem. Although I could not talk at length about my faith and my pro-life stance, I did take each opportunity afforded me to share with them my Christian faith and discuss the opportunities that I had working in the church with regard to world missions. And, I took the opportunity to lead the prayer before the last game of each season as my way of asking God to protect each of them throughout the summer months and throughout their lives; no one ever complained.

As much as I enjoyed the girls, the parents and the support of the administration, there came a point where the victories did not taste as sweet and the losses continued to hurt long after the girls had forgotten them and gone on with life. But, the most disturbing issue in coaching is dealing with incompetent referees on a consistent basis and having to just "take it." Now, from the causal fan, I can immediately hear a groan and see a sly wink. But the fact is most casual fans have no clue as to what goes on out on the court, game after game, week after week, season after season. Here is the reality: Our girls practice six days a week, two and a half hours a day from the end of October to the middle of February. I push my girls hard to take them beyond their own expectations so that they can achieve things that they never dreamed they could do.

Life Between Innings

Yet, after all that work and commitment to detail, when the game starts and the referees get involved, you wonder if it is truly worth it for yourself or for the kids. Many of the officials are out of shape, many do not hustle to get into position to make the correct call, many get caught up in the game and call the game with their hearts and not with their head (eyes); they just plain do not work hard at calling the game correctly. More often than not, especially in girls' games, the officiating is an absolute farce. If I get a well-called game one in five times, I consider that a victory. And, under the guise of "good sportsmanship," we coaches are expected to sit on our benches, take it and not complain. Then, unfortunately, the ugly head of racial prejudice pops its head up continuously, and that is an issue in which neither I nor the players can win.

As a white guy in a white world, it would be easy to duck my head and say that most Blacks use racism as an excuse for failure; however, I know better. As a Business Representative I saw it rear its ugly head time and again, and I would try to address it as best I could, but for the most part white companies like Ameren, CIPS and EEI simply ignore it unless it is just outright blatant. Because I was willing to work on Black issues, one of my fondest moments was being made an "Honorary Black" by the Black employees in Operations at the Labadie Power Plant. Of course they were speaking somewhat facetiously, but still there was an element of truth or appreciation that they were trying to convey. Several times I heard comments following that pronouncement much like this, *Mooney, you are white and you cannot think like a Black man, but at least you try!"*

On the basketball court racism comes at you in a variety of forms. As the white coach of a predominately black team, when I would take my team to neighboring black schools to play, the referees were "always" black, the crowd was black,

466

The Retirement Years 2002-beyond

our opponent was black, and the white coach, even though he had a black team, was not going to get a break in those circumstances. I learned early on that I had to conduct myself much differently in those situations than I otherwise would and to recognize the situation for what is was. I cannot ever recall winning a game in that environment; it was what it was and my girls paid the price for playing for me.

When we visited neighboring white schools such as Rockwood Summit in Fenton, Wentzville Holt in Wentzville or Fort Zumwalt North in St. Charles County, the scenario was reversed. As a white coach with a black team playing with white referees, white fans and against a white opponent, despite the fact that I was white, my girls were penalized because they were black. Ask me to prove it; I can't. But when you work in that environment as long as I have you know, and the kids know, exactly what is going on. At these particular schools I did not watch my Ps and Qs as well as I did at the black schools and this is where I invariably got in trouble. We did, however, win some games in this environment, including two games in a tournament at Fort Zumwalt North, despite some horrible injustices.

Incidents of racial bias at all three of those schools (Rockwood, Wentzville, Fort Zumwalt North) left indelible imprints on my brain that are as fresh in my memory today as they were the day they happened. However, the worst, the most blatant incident, came in my final season at a game at Wentzville Holt. Because we were not highly skilled we had to do several things well in a game to be successful. We must out rebound our opponent, we must shoot more free throws than our opponent, we must commit less fouls than our opponent and we must play outstanding defense. The facts support the case that the team who gets the most rebounds and the most free throws wins the game 90 plus per cent of the time. And,

Life Between Innings

we had to drive the basket hard picking up fouls or getting lay-ups to increase our percentage of winning. With our poor shooting ability we had to get the high percentage shot which is, of course, the lay-up. If we failed to do this we might as well have mailed in our score because we were going to lose.

At Wentzville we were driving the basket hard and getting the fouls, in fact six of them in the first six minutes of the first quarter. Suddenly, it was like the referees put their whistles in their pockets as they refused to call another foul the remainder of the first quarter and all of the second quarter against our opponent. We were getting hacked, pushed, shoved and manhandled, but no calls; my girls were getting pretty frustrated and they, like me, understood what was going on. The half ended with Wentzville up 13-11. I felt lucky at this stage to still be in the game, as we just were not getting any calls. As I headed toward the locker room with my team in tow I passed by the scorer's table and rather glibly told the hometown scorekeeper that the officiating was absolutely atrocious. Upon reaching the locker room my girls were livid, as was I. Now, while I understood these things were occurring throughout my coaching career, rarely, and I mean rarely, would I let the girls talk about it or use it as an excuse; to do so would serve no purpose and there was no recourse anyway. And, my girls, as well as I, were going to face these situations the rest of our lives in the "real world" and we needed to learn how to effectively deal with it. However, this time it was so obvious that I decided that we should talk about it and decide together how we best should handle it in the second half.

Upon our return to the floor I had to pass by the scorekeeper to get to our bench. He asked if I had settled down yet, to which I responded, *No I haven't, that whole second quarter was a farce.* Moments later I saw the white scorekeeper talking with the two white officials at the table and looking with half

The Retirement Years 2002-beyond

glances at me; I knew then I was screwed, I was in trouble. Two minutes into the third quarter we still had not gotten a foul call or any out of bounds calls on balls tipped away. Then, right in front of our bench an offensive rebound went up with one of my players and two from Wentzville going after the ball; the ball went out of bounds and we did not get what I considered a somewhat obvious call. I was standing at the time in the box near my bench and muttered something under my breath (truly was to myself and not that audible). Simultaneously, someone on our bench moved a chair, which made a slight but obvious noise. With that, I saw the lead official start walking toward me. I just turned and sat down. However, he continued walking toward our bench and stopped right in front of me. I expected he would say something like, *Stay seated and don't get up. You have been warned.* Not that I deserved that instruction but that is what I thought he was going to say since nothing had happened and I had not said anything audible. Instead, he looks at me and gives me the Technical Foul sign. I stood up and the following dialogue went something like this:

Coach Mooney: *What was that for, I didn't do anything?*

Referee: *You just sit down and don't say another word!*

Coach Mooney: *If you are going to call a technical on me, at least tell me what I did!*

Referee: *I said sit down!*

Coach Mooney: *I'll sit down when you tell me why you gave me a technical. You can't give me a technical and not tell me what I did!*

Referee: "*You are out of here* (Gave second Technical Foul sign)," and waved his arms indicating that I had been thrown out of the game.

Coach Mooney: (only now starting to get a little bit animated) *So you are kicking me out of this game but you can't tell me why?*

Referee: *Leave the court!*

Life Between Innings

Coach Mooney: *I'll leave the court when you tell me why you called a technical foul on me. It's obvious that you can't tell me because I didn't do anything!*

Referee: (Stands at midcourt still glaring at me but not saying a word.)

With that our Athletic Director, Jason Green, who lived nearby and had coached at Wentzville in the past, came rushing out on the court from the stands to help calm me and lead me off the court. By this time I had gone from "a little animated" to "very animated." It was quite a scene but I got my money's worth. Everyone, and I mean everyone, who was in ear shot knew two things: (1) I did not know what I had done to deserve two technicals and an ejection (except coach a team of Black ladies) and (2) and that the offending official could not tell me, the fans, the bench or my Athletic Director what I had done to deserve his wrath. Later, on his report filed with the State Association and with the two schools, he stated that his actions were based on my use of a vulgarity. Never happened!!!

Jody Fowler, our assistant coach, was summoned from the stands to take over for me. At the time I left we were still trailing by four points with a little over four minutes remaining in the third quarter.

Seeing their coach treated in the manner that he was, my team pulled out all the stops, storming back and taking a commanding lead by the end of the third quarter. Of course I had been removed from the immediate gym area but I could still see half the court and a scoreboard from my distant vantage point. It was unbelievable; my kids were not going to be denied! In the fourth quarter they struggled a bit to maintain the lead but ended up securing the victory, winning by three points. I could not have been more proud of my kids, ever. If I could have, I would have kissed every one of them. What tenacity,

The Retirement Years 2002-beyond

what focus, what determination! I wish I could have bottled that enthusiasm for later games, but this was one that I will never forget for a lot of good reasons as well as some bad ones.

I resigned following the 2007/2008 season, the season in which the above game was played. It was a tearful goodbye as my girls really did love me and loved having me as their coach; who can explain it? I was tough, yet fair, I was consistent in my dealings with them, and I think they saw that. They saw that I cared for them way beyond the game of basketball; every coach should be so lucky as I was.

During the 2008/2009 season I thought it would be fun to go over to Ritenour and watch my former girls play against Affton High School. As I came into the gymnasium I tried to just sneak in and climb up high into the stands. However, before I could get seated, a number of players came running and began to hug me one by one. I was blown away. Then I noticed that several of the cheerleaders had also got in line and were waiting to give me a hug! I was a little embarrassed by all the attention and, of course, I started tearing up immediately. It was neat, really neat, and something that I had totally not expected. It will be on my mental highlight reel for the remainder of my life!

Although I resigned for all the reasons stated, I had also been encouraged by my doctor to reduce some of the stress in my life. As he stated, *Norman, your body doesn't handle stress well!* Part of the stress was obvious in that I was shuffling coaching duties along with duties associated with our missions' ministry at Twin Oaks Church. In 2005, I had accepted a position as the Director of World Missions at the church, a job that I totally loved, but was likewise time consuming. I would go to the church office at 8:30 AM and work till 1:00 PM and then go home for a lunch break. At 2:15 PM, I would take off for basketball practice and, depending if I was out scouting afterward or

Life Between Innings

if we had a game, it would be 9:00 or 10:00 PM before I would return home; then do it all over the next day.

I had taken on the job of Director of World Missions in June of 2005. Rev. Herb Ward, a former missionary in South Africa, had served as our Missions Pastor for about four-five years; however, he had resigned to take a professorship at Covenant College on Lookout Mountain near Chattanooga, Tennessee. Since I was Chairman of the World Missions Committee and held Elder oversight as well, I manned the position while we awaited his replacement, Rev. Craig Sheppard, who was wrapping up his duties as a missionary in Bulgaria and Eastern Europe. However, Craig had second thoughts about leaving the field and decided that he should not come. Suddenly, we had few immediate prospects to fill the position. I was not anxious to continue doing the work gratis, as I wanted to get back to negotiating contracts for SEIU. Grant Williams had assured me that he wanted me back and that he was willing to re-negotiate a new and better compensation package. It soon became clear, however, that the church administration did not want to go through another nationwide search to replace Herb, and now Craig, so they had decided to assign one of the men already on staff to do the work. This concerned me greatly, as I was quite confident that the individual they had in mind did not have a heart or the energy for the work. His track record, while certainly a nice man, strongly indicated that he did not have the passion necessary to keep this vibrant ministry alive. I was simply afraid that this vital ministry, a ministry that Tina and I had given much of ourselves to since first coming to Twin Oaks in '91, might just simply die due to a lack of commitment and attention. And, should that happen, some 50 missionaries that we supported would be greatly affected. Twin Oaks itself had 11 homegrown member missionaries on the field that we were supporting at a very high level. Therefore, I

The Retirement Years 2002–beyond

was confident that if I did not act quickly, it would not be long before the financial support could or would dry up and this dynamic World Missions ministry would simply die a slow, but sure death.

The long and short of it was that in one of my "weaker" moments I mentioned to Duncan Highmark, the Executive Director at the church, that perhaps they should consider me for the job. I am not sure I was "really" serious but Duncan began to court me heavily for it and set up the proper interviews for me with him and Sr. Pastor Ron Steel. Following the interviews I was offered the job. Here my negotiating skills were a benefit, as I was able to carve out the World Missions portion of the job for me to lead. The Session (Church Board) then would have to determine who they wanted to lead the U.S. Missions ministry, a job that required a lot less attention, but one that I had little interest in administering. With that resolved we agreed that basically my job was to "get the job done," whether it took 10 hours a week or 30 hours a week. Therefore, I would not be considered full time or part time, just employed. We began to talk salary and Duncan offered me much more than I thought I should take at this juncture; but I suggested a reasonable figure upon which we agreed with the understanding that in a year we would take a fresh look at the job and see what kind of hours it really did take to run the ministry, and then adjust the pay upward accordingly. I had little reason to expect that when the year was up, Duncan would no longer be employed at Twin Oaks and there would be no one left to recall this commitment. Although I had been doing the job since June of 2005, effective January 1, 2006, I came on paid staff at Twin Oaks Church.

My taking the reigns of the ministry actually went rather well, in fact, almost seamlessly. Since I had been on the Committee for some 13 years at that time, had served as

Chairman for a number of years, had been mentored in that role by Herb Ward, was leading short-term missions teams and already directing our efforts for the past 7 months, about the only change was simply drawing a salary. I had an excellent Committee in place that supported my appointment so the future looked good.

Shortly after taking the position I approached Duncan Highmark and requested that I be relieved of my duties as an active (setting) Ruling Elder. I did not feel that it was appropriate for me to report to myself, but no decision was forthcoming. The Session had made it clear that they would like for me to stay on and at least complete my term, which still had another two years to go. However, I felt strongly about the issue so I gave the Session notice and resigned as an active Ruling Elder in the church as of April 1, 2006. This turned out to be a blessing in disguise for me as rumblings began to occur within the Session and the congregation regarding Pastor Steel's leadership.

Our previous Pastor, Rodney Stortz, was a strong, micro-manager with his hand in everything. And, Rodney loved to preach and it was hard to get him out of the pulpit, even during those months leading up to his death when he was obviously sick and in pain. Ron on the other hand was a macro-manager who provided little guidance to the staff and pretty much allowed everyone to run and develop their own ministries. This was not "necessarily" a weakness; it was just his management style. His style worked well for me, at least at first, as this was the management style that Giljum had employed in the Union and I thrived under that philosophy; however, this was not necessarily good for most of the men and women on staff. Ron also loved to preach on Sunday morning but was less than enthusiastic about preaching on Sunday night. Rodney was a strong proponent of EE (Evangelism Explosion)

The Retirement Years 2002-beyond

evangelism, Ron was not. Rodney preached sermons with three or four distinct points, Ron's sermon were more like a long essay with a central subject, making it sometimes hard to follow. Rodney used a limited amount of "high church" liturgy and written prayers, Ron loved the use of liturgy and written prayers. These stark differences in leadership styles between Rodney and Ron should not have been a surprise to anyone who met with Ron prior to his accepting the Senior Pastorate, as everything that Ron did was consistent with what he had told us he would do when he was interviewing for the job. Nevertheless, and unfortunately, a huge chasm soon developed between the pro-Ron camp and the anti-Ron camp, both in the congregation and on the Session.

Late in the fall of 2006 the rift between the factions was becoming so severe that Pastor Steel decided that he should resign. The Session decided to hold a special Wednesday meeting with the congregation, later to be known as the *Wednesday Night Massacre*, to discuss the issues; bad idea! In what I would classify as the worst moment in my entire Christian experience, words were spoken that night that shattered our fellowship from both sides of the "aisle." About 300, maybe 400 or more people, by the time all was said and done, ended up leaving Twin Oaks. At our lowest, I think the congregation numbers fell to about 450-475 from an average of about 900 or so each Sunday morning. My heart ached as I saw friend after friend leaving to go to other churches. Many of them felt that they had been told to leave in one way or the other, so they left. Some of those that left had hopes of starting a new work and eventually they did, creating the new Trinity Presbyterian Church. Our former youth pastor, Chris Polski, who had been serving as the Sr. Pastor at a church in the Deep South, would eventually resign that position and come to head up the new Trinity work.

Life Between Innings

In the end, probably 80% of the people who Tina and I would have considered as our closest friends ended up leaving, including about a third of the World Mission Committee. The Session members that I normally sided with on issues and the guys with whom I had the best relationship, were the guys that were ultimately "pushed" out the door. That point would be argued by some to say that they simply left, but the truth is that it was made very clear by a vocal segment of the church that they needed to "get out." I must admit that as they left my heart left with them. For a while, in fact it seemed daily, folks were coming by my office saying that they were leaving, but acknowledging that they understood why I needed to stay. I was glad they understood, because I didn't, except that the Holy Spirit just would not let us go. Tina and I wrote down all the pros and cons as to why we should stay and why we should go and the list for going far outnumbered the list for staying, yet the Holy Spirit would not let us go! As Christmas approached, the church seemed to be more of a morgue than a house of worship, yet the Holy Spirit still would not let us go!

Somehow we continued to make it through 2006 up until December when my Administrative Assistant, Pam Mehlhouse, with whom I had developed a very good working relationship and who was simply an excellent assistant, resigned to take a better paying job at Covenant Seminary. She had also lost heart in living through this nightmare and the new job provided the perfect escape for her. She went with my blessing; however, losing her just eight weeks prior to our annual World Missions Conference was just about the last straw, as I knew that there was no way that I could handle this responsibility by myself; yet the Holy Spirit would not let us go!

Early in January of 2007, I approached Donna Middendorf, a friend of ours in the church who served on the Missions Committee and was the wife of our small group leader, Bob

The Retirement Years 2002-beyond

Middendorf, to see if she might be interested in becoming my Administrative Assistant. I had worked with Donna on several short-term trips and had always been impressed with her organizational abilities and drive. The fact that she was on the Committee also made her employment advantageous as she already knew the landscape and had some familiarity as to how I was to work with. Surprisingly, I found that she was interested, so I petitioned the Session to move quickly and let me work out a salary for her and hire her ASAP. The Session responded favorably so in expeditious fashion Donna came on staff as my Administrative Assistant. What Donna did in the next few weeks in pulling the many loose ends of the conference together was remarkable, if not amazing. With her energy and drive we were not only able to get though the conference, but enjoy a remarkable conference. Our Faith Promise goal of $325,000 was easily surpassed, topping out at $353,000. One of the other remarkable tidbits that occurred was that during the church split we received $435,000 in actual offerings against our previous year's goal of $410,000 that was pledged. There is no simple explanation as to how that could have occurred; we just call it our *Loaves and Fishes* experience. From that tumultuous time early in 2007, Donna has continued to work in the World Missions ministry. To say that she is exceptional would be an understatement. She quickly connected with the staff and our missionaries; in fact I think the missionaries knew her better at times than they did me. How I was blessed to find her so quickly, and then to add her remarkable skills to the Missions Office, is just another example of the blessings of God in the most unexpected places and at the most unexpected times throughout my life.

Because I could understand why many left, and would have been one of them if it had not been for the restraints of the Holy Spirit, Tina and I had to walk carefully, keep our mouths

Life Between Innings

closed and stay as low under the radar as we could for the sake of the World Missions Ministry. And, as noted above, God seemed to bless our efforts as the ministry hardly skipped a beat in the midst of this huge storm.

Sometime in March 2007, shortly after the conference, I received a letter from one of the daughters of one of the key Ruling Elders that had left the church asking for support for her mission that summer in the Dominican Republic. The letter was meant just for me, as we had remained friends with the family; however, I felt led to take it to the Committee and seek a scholarship for her since she had not left on her own free will and she had been raised on our own pews. As far as I was concerned, she was still one of our "kids." The Committee at this time was a microcosm of the church that still remained. There was me, who was not mad at anyone who left, there were others who still harbored hard feeling towards the ones who left, and there were some who were kind of ambivalent. Consequently, I had no idea how my motion would fly. First came some very open and honest debate. I appreciated the struggle that some were having as they fought their feelings in the face of Holy Scripture. Finally, one of the men for which this was truly a heart stopper, raised his hand and said, *You know what, it's the right thing to do. And not only should we approve a regular scholarship, we should approve up to half of what she needs so that they (those who left) will understand that we are not in competition with them; they will be able to see that we love them!* The power of the Holy Spirit was so evident as one by one each voted to approve the motion. Goose bumps went up and down my arms and shoulders; while it was the right answer, I was stunned.

The following month I received another request from a daughter of a family that left asking for regular monthly support as she was going into a career in missions. In this case the

The Retirement Years 2002-beyond

family had not only left but had been very outspoken about the issues prior to their leaving. I took the same tact and brought the letter to the Committee. My first thought was that they would tell me to shove it and ask me how many more of these I intended to bring to them. Instead, without debate, one of the gentlemen on the committee stepped right up and made the motion that we approve, saying emphatically that it was simply the right thing to do. At that point I decided to go for broke and told the Committee that I intended to invite a number of those that had left to join us on our medical mission to Kenya that was upcoming that summer. Again, not one word in opposition was raised as it was "the right thing to do."

While things were peaceful on the Committee, it was not necessarily so for some in the congregation regarding the approval of these various motions. It was not long before I was approached by one of the former Ruling Elders, one of the ones caught in the middle of our mess and one of the ones who had obviously stayed. He asked if we could talk; of course I agreed. It didn't take long to get through the pleasantries and down to the business at hand, which was his disappointment over what he had heard regarding Twin Oaks' Faith Promise dollars being used to support the children of members who had left our church in their missions' endeavors. I let him talk and when he was through I began to lead him step by step through the thought process that the Committee had gone through in making their decision. Obviously, the thought process was based on love and forgiveness, and was biblical in all respects. As I was concluding, with tears welling up in his eyes, he said, *You were right; I was wrong! You will never hear from me on this matter again.* And, I didn't.

I shared with Pastor Steel what had been going on within the Committee and the decisions that they had made over the past two months. Consequently, at the following All-Staff

Life Between Innings

Meeting, Pastor Steel asked me to share what the World Missions Committee had done as he was impressed and pleased how they had thought the issue through and had come to the right decision. After sharing, I headed back to my office and was followed by one of the ladies on staff who asked if she could talk with me. Again, I agreed. She jumped immediately into addressing her point telling me how her husband was absolutely furious with what the Committee and I had done. In closing, she stated simply but firmly; *If you think you have had to go through a storm before, you have no clue how big this storm is going to be before this is finished.* I very patiently walked her though the Committee's thought process and when I concluded she said, *You know, you're right. But you cannot talk to every member in this church. Would you be willing to speak to the congregation if Pastor Steel will approve?* I stated that, *I would be somewhat fearful, but would certainly do it if Pastor Steel asked me too.* She left my office and headed directly to Pastor Steel's office.

About two hours later I received a call from Pastor Steel asking if I would be willing to stand before the congregation and tell them what actions the World Missions Committee had taken with regard to the issues. I agreed and we immediately went to seeking a date and the right place in a service to make such a pronouncement. With Calvinistic luck (loosely interpreted as God's sovereignty at work), the new Trinity Church was being officially recognized by the Missouri Presbytery as a mission church the following Sunday, an event that would not sit well with a good many in the congregation. Pastor's text that day, again by "coincidence," was, *Blessed are they that mourn,* the perfect subject to address the congregation on such a day.

Pastor preached an outstanding message on the subject and as he was about to close, asked me to come forward. He gave a brief intro regarding what I was to be speaking about

The Retirement Years 2002-beyond

and why it was germane to the subject at hand. As I told our story, Pastor Steel stood right next to me in the pulpit as a show of support for what the Committee had done; it was a powerful statement! At the end of my talk I received a nice ovation. At the end of the second service there was not an ovation but there did seem to be a kind of holy hush that came across the sanctuary. From that day to now I have only received one call from a disgruntled parishioner who did not like the fact that we were inviting folks from Trinity Church to go on mission trips with us. The Pastor addressed his issue personally and I never heard any other complaints. Praise God! It is hard to argue with His Word!

It gradually became very clear to me why the Holy Spirit would not let us go. While there is still much work to be done, many sins still to be confessed, reconciliation that needs to occur, God was using me and the World Missions Committee to begin the process of healing this deep wound. I say this as humbly as I know how to say it but, had there been any other person directing the World Missions ministry but me during this time, it is doubtful that any of this could have happened. But, due to a lack of animosity on my part toward those that left and the continuation of my friendship with them, it was easy for me to push the Committee forward in their processing of the issues and the right decisions that they made. Again, to God be the glory!!

One of the most significant things that occurred following these events was the development of an honest relationship and dialogue with Pastor Steel. While I still had huge questions regarding his leadership abilities, he did provide significant support for the World Missions ministry and me. In fact, there was a time, especially from 2007 up through 2009 that I was able to say with sincere honesty that not only was I glad that we stayed, I was thrilled that we had stayed, as God was

Life Between Innings

obviously blessing the efforts. There was one interesting and very poignant moment that Pastor Ron shared with me during this time. We were sitting in his office one day discussing the events of the past. He paused for a moment, and then laughed and said, *Well, Brother, while you were praying that I would leave, I was praying the same thing; but the same Holy Spirit that wouldn't let you leave was the same Holy Spirit that wouldn't let me leave.* We both laughed again.

I loved this ministry that God led me into here late in life. I have had such a great and wonderful opportunity to worship with the saints in Peru, Russia, Kenya, Bulgaria, Malta, South Africa and Mexico since becoming Director, and it was glorious. My favorite place to worship was with the saints in Pazardzhik, Bulgaria, in a church pastored by a wonderful man named Rongel. Their church building somehow survived the years of communism and seats about 125 people; it is usually packed when I am there. Each time I am there I feel so welcomed by these gristled old saints and feel such a wonderful presence of the Holy Spirit in their worship.

However, as one battle at Twin Oaks Church would begin to ebb, another one seemed to come rushing in. But, I would think it strange if we weren't in battle, since we are engaged on the frontlines of spiritual warfare, each day of our lives. And, when it comes to foreign missions, we are engaged in spiritual warfare on satan's turf; we should only expect to be embattled. During the last 2008 Presidential election, I faced a new and unexpected conflict. A team of far right, radical prolifers in the church decided to "out" me and have me removed from my position as Director on morals charges. Ellen, the key lady orchestrating this drive, called me one Saturday afternoon just prior to the national elections. She stated that she had heard that a Democrat was on staff at Twin Oaks and had found that it was "me." She asked me how I intended to vote

The Retirement Years 2002-beyond

in the election; however, I refused to tell her. I told her that I had been worshipping at Twin Oaks since the early '90s and had never become embroiled in the political talk, as it was evident that these discussions would not be productive. Many of the church leaders, including Pastor Stortz who had recruited me to come on Session, knew of my political leanings and none had ever made it an issue. She stated, however, that she intended to make it an issue and continued to insist to know how I planned to vote; would I be voting for John McCain or for Barack Obama. Since I would not tell her, and subsequently the others that she recruited to confront me, they took that as meaning that I had, or intended to, vote for Obama. Since Obama was outspoken in his support of "choice," anyone voting for Obama was, in their minds, immoral.

Twin Oaks has one of the strongest pro-life ministries, if not the strongest, I have ever seen in a local church. I have a great appreciation for their work and support their mission wholeheartedly. I am distinctly Pro-life! However, there are some extremists, like Ellen, that believe that if you are a Democrat, or even an Independent, you cannot be a Christian, but at the very least a Democrat (or Independent) should not be in any leadership position within the church. This issue caused quite a stir and took our Session's involvement to bring some civility to the issue. The Session wrote a strong letter of support on my behalf, which I appreciated. I am still not sure, however, that the issue has truly been resolved. I would imagine that in 2012 the issue will rear its ugly head once again. I will admit that folks who vote one-issue ballots scare me. Whether the issue is abortion, worker's rights, gay rights or gun control, the hatred exhibited by these single-issue proponents toward anyone who dares think differently is stifling. Some of the most hateful, despicable, self-righteous individuals that I have ever encountered, unfortunately, come from the

Life Between Innings

Pro-Life camp. They are correct on the issue; they do, however, need to work on their theology, attitude and image.

In the winter of 2007, I received a call from a Gerald Morgan representing Mission to the World (MTW). MTW is the sending agency for the foreign missionaries sent out by the PCA, our denomination. He had been summoned to call me and talk with me about the possibility of letting my name be put in nomination for a seat on the Committee to Mission to the World (CMTW). The CMTW is responsible for the oversight of all activities associated with MTW. The Coordinator for Mission to the World, Dr. Paul Kooistra, also reports to the Committee for accountability purposes. They were looking for a strong MTW guy to fill a vacated seat and the word had come to him that I was that guy. Obviously, I was greatly honored to have even been thought of. I discussed the matter with Pastor Steel, who was very supportive and thought it would be good for our own ministry to have someone in such a position. The nomination process went forward and I was elected at the General Assembly meeting in Dallas, Texas, in June of 2008. I attended my first meeting in September of 2008 and was greatly impressed with the staff and the overall operation of our missions' sending agency. I was placed on the Human Resources Committee where, along with my general duties, am privileged to interview and ultimately approve, as the last gatekeeper, all career missions' candidates prior to sending them onto the field. What a blessing to meet these committed visionaries and hear them share their hearts as they move forward in serving our Lord!

On July 24, 2007, Tina and I enjoyed our 25th wedding anniversary. And, it was during this time that Tina was on the last leg of fulfilling her Masters' Degree requirements at Maryville University, working toward her Nurse Practitioner's License.

The Retirement Years 2002-beyond

Because of her studies we were not able to celebrate our anniversary with a special trip as we had intended.

Before Tina had graduated, a nationally renowned Heart Surgeon, working out of the St. Joseph Hospital in Kirkwood, Missouri, asked her to come on staff and begin work with his team as a Nurse Practitioner under his oversight. Tina accepted the promotion which created a major time crunch for her as she now had new duties to learn while working a five-day week, versus her former three days a week with 12-hour shifts, and maintain her studies. With much dedication and considerable tenacity, she stayed with it. Finally, in May of 2008, she graduated and passed her licensure exam on her first attempt. With that we were free to make plans for our long-awaited "25th anniversary" trip to Greece and, in particular, the Island of Crete, sitting among the pure, clear, turquoise colored waters of the Mediterranean Sea.

Through the help of a travel agent we made our plans, and in late August of 2008, boarded our Delta flight from St. Louis to Atlanta to Athens. We were met by a travel agent at the airport and escorted to the Athens Gate Hotel located next door to the Athens Gate memorials and within view of the impressive Acropolis. The hotel had a roof top restaurant with a great panoramic view overlooking Athens where we ate breakfast a couple mornings; such an impressive sight.

For the first four days we had made plans to join a tour and take in the sights of classical Greece. Some of the sights I had visited on a previous trip when I lived in Crete while serving with the U.S. Air Force. On our tour we visited many great sites. The first day we crossed over the Corinth Canal on our way to Mycenae to visit the Lion Gate and the Tomb of Agamemnon. From there we proceeded to Epidauras and its famous theatre. This theatre, made of solid stone, was so

Life Between Innings

acoustically built that when standing at the top of this impressive structure, it was easy to hear someone talking standing at center stage way below. From here we headed out to Olympia, where the first modern Olympics had been held.

On the second day, on the grounds of the first Olympic stadium, our tour guide devised a race between us guys on the exact spot where previous runners had competed for the prize centuries ago. I was one of the oldest in the race, but no problem; our instructions were to run in slow motion reminiscent of a scene from the movie, *Chariots of Fire*. The guide gave the signal and we started, only everyone was running at a speed far beyond what we had been instructed, leaving me to eat their dust. Being quite a distance behind, but not wanting to be embarrassed, my competitive instincts kicked in and off I ran, my little 61 year old Freddy Flintstone legs taking me as fast as I could motor. Just as we reached the finish line I overtook the last "competitor" for a photo-finish win. Tina claims that the race was fixed and that I was allowed to win. I know that it wasn't and that I am the legitimate Olympic winner in the 50-meter sprint. I was called to the front of the group for the presentation ceremony where our guide placed the traditional olive branch crown on my head signifying my great Olympic victory!!

Immediately our new friends began to "demand" that I provide a urine sample and be drug tested on the spot, certain in their minds that I had used performance-enhancing drugs to win. I feigned indignation and outrage over such a claim and refused to meet their demands, instead holding up my new crown in jest as the trash talking continued. Oh sweet victory!! Tina's claim has not diminished nor tainted this great victory.

Following our Olympic competition we headed out to Delphi, perhaps our favorite spot on this four-day trip. Situated

The Retirement Years 2002-beyond

high in the mountains plastered against the side of these mammoth hills, this little ancient village of Delphi sat. Down below lay miles and miles of olive tree orchards as far as the eye could see. A walk into the little town from our hotel to one of the local pubs with our new friends, Dennis and Kitty Gee from Australia and Ross and Lynda Graham from New Zealand, that evening became one of the many highlights of our vacation.

On day three, after a visit to a wonderful museum and some local areas that were once used as part of the ancient Olympic games, we took a scenic (every moment of every day was scenic) drive through the picturesque towns of central Greece, arriving early evening at our final stop in Kalambaka.

The following morning (day four) we drove up into the nearby mountains to visit the ancient monasteries of Meteora, amid striking scenery perched atop soaring stone formations, seemingly suspended in mid-air. In fact, the word Meteora literally means "hovering in the air," bringing to mind the word "meteor." What created this rare geological phenomenon is one of the mysteries of nature. But, as amazing a marvel of nature as these giant rocks are, the monasteries built on the top of these are a marvel of man and seem just as miraculous, making Meteora one of the most spectacular places we visited. How these monasteries were built atop these huge mountains with smooth faces and no apparent, visible access to the top is still hard to comprehend. One thing for certain, if those living in these monasteries were looking for peace and tranquility, a place where they would not be disturbed, they found it here at Meteora. In the thrilling climactic scenes of the James Bond movie, *For Your Eyes Only*, one of the monasteries of Meteora was used.

After returning to Athens for a night we boarded our plane to Herakleon, Crete, for the final 10 days of our stay.

Life Between Innings

Herakleon is where I had lived while serving on Crete (U.S. Air Force) in the early '70s and I was anxious to see how much things had changed in 38 years. Our first assignment was to pick up our car rental. (As an aside, am I the only one who hates dealing with car rental agencies, regardless of city or country? Why is it that most of those with whom we deal in our travels, such as airline and hotel workers, seem, as a rule, to be professional and above board? But, when dealing with car rental folks, it is like suddenly being thrust into a carnival and you're dealing with every sleazy person imaginable, trying as best they can to scam you for every nickel you have!) Upon securing the car, we headed down the new modern highway to the small village of Ag (St.) Nicholas, about 70 kilometers away, sitting in a beautiful cove surrounded by mountains on all three sides with the Mediterranean Sea and harbor stretched out before us. What an unbelievable site!

Crete is nothing but a large rock with little vegetation, except in isolated places. The drive took about an hour or so as we drove through one mountain pass after another. The hillsides were barren, except for the small mesquite-like bushes and the endless rows of olive trees. Once there we began the arduous task of finding our apartment. Our rental agreement did not have an address on it and, and even if it did, it would not have helped as we couldn't read the street signs or speak the language. We stopped at various locations trying to find someone who could speak English and give us directions. Tina did most of the inquires in various shops with folks that knew where we wanted to go but, could not tell us how to get there. Little by little we kept getting close, but would find ourselves back at the starting point and just a little bit more frustrated. After about a 2-hour search, we finally located the apartment just one block from the place that we were using as our starting point. However, to get up the hill and over that one block to

The Retirement Years 2002-beyond

where the apartment was located was not an easy thing to do and it became clear to us why it had been so hard for anyone to help us.

Our fourth floor (top) apartment was definitely European with two small double beds, a small kitchen and living area with TV and air conditioning for which we had to pay extra. However, walking directly out from our front door was a huge patio/balcony that overlooked the whole bay and the harbor. Again, what an awesome site!! Night after night we would sit on the patio eating our various cheeses and drinking good wine, playing Scrabble, all the while enjoying the night air and the sights and sounds from the harbor and the streets. Sometimes when the moon would be coming up over the horizon and shining down on the village and harbor below us, the beauty of it all was almost too much to take in.

We lived on the economy for the 10 days that we were there, shopping at the local markets and trying to figure out what we were buying. It was great fun. And Tina, ever the exotic chef, prepared a delicious Greek breakfast every morning and a number of equally good suppers.

Down in the harbor we located a vessel that took daily fishing cruises out beyond the cove for some deep-sea adventure. Twenty-six years earlier I had agreed to go deep-sea fishing with Tina along the southern coast of Nova Scotia while on our honeymoon. Nothing much changed for me in those 26 years as I still caught only one fish that could be used for bait and nothing else. Tina did not do much better, although she caught a very poisonous fish about the size of her thumb that the captain ran over to take off her hook. He commented that had she tried to remove it from her hook, it would have very likely meant a trip to the medical room. With this fishing excursion behind me, I figure I am now good until 2034 (26 years hence) before I have to do it again.

Life Between Innings

We did take a non-fishing cruise several days later to visit the leper colony at Spinaloga. While the last leper had left long ago, this isolated but beautiful spot out several miles from the harbor located on a small island, but just a few yards from the mainland, provided an interesting visit for us. The isolation of these families living here must have been horrible, although they say this was one of the better leper colonies in its time. The guide for our little cruise ship loved to say the word "Spinaloga," to the point that we can hardly say the word out loud without cracking a smile or a laugh.

With each passing day I think we enjoyed ourselves even more. This was the first vacation that we had taken in years where Tina did not have a number of books to read and studies to do in pursuit of her Bachelors and Masters degrees. With all the extra time that we had to be with each other, we actually found that we still enjoyed each other immensely. I think I fell in love with her all over again, which has its obvious rewards!!

Among our excursions was a trip back up into the mountains near the interior of Crete to a place that had been called the *Valley of the Windmills* when I lived here another lifetime ago. The roads wound round and round as we passed though the hillside to reach the apex that overlooked a huge valley below. When I had been there some 38 years earlier, I remember standing looking down into the valley where the landscape was literally covered with white windmills used for irrigating the fertile fields. Now, only a few skeletons of these huge windmills remained; it was kind of sad to see.

On our way back down the hills we passed several small stands where the Cretans were selling olive oil, homemade wine and tikevo, a very, very strong local drink. We were offered the drink free of charge, which struck us as funny, considering that this is all that these Greek drivers need on

The Retirement Years 2002-beyond

these tightly wound roads to make their journey even more perilous. Obviously, there was not a MADD Chapter anywhere in this region of the world.

Of course we are beach people and therefore it was necessary that we spend considerable time enjoying the water, sand and sun. The sand on the beaches of Crete for the most part is made up of really small pebbles and they are not easy on the feet. However, the uniqueness of the beach here at St. Nicholas is the nude bathing. I knew that nude bathing occurred here but there was not much of it when I lived on the island previously; but, not so now. We got to the beach and rented our little beach cots and laid out to read and soak in the sun. I had brought along a really good book/study on 1 Corinthians that I had been reading and got into a good comfortable position. I was only a few pages into my book when I noticed the well-endowed lady in front of me was sitting there topless reading her book. So, as to stay in favor with my good wife and not go blind, I turned so as to be looking in a different direction only to find that there were several ladies enjoying the sun, sans their tops. I turned 180 degrees from where I had been looking, but no relief there either as the scenery was much the same. I then turned to Tina and said, *Hey look, I am really trying here, but there just is no way for me to turn.* She smiled knowingly and I went back to reading my book on 1 Corinthians. I must say it was hard feeling spiritual that day while on the beach.

On about our fourth or fifth morning on Crete, Tina was playing on her computer when up popped a little green face (evidence of a new facial) via skype; it was our daughter Whitney calling us from Santa Barbara, California, where she was working on her Masters Degree at Antioch University. In the course of the conversation she abruptly stated, *I think I have a boyfriend!* Up till this point Whitney had never allowed us to use the word "boyfriend," nor would she use the word to

491

Life Between Innings

describe any of the boys that she might have been dating at any point in her young life. This signaled to us, obviously, that this must be serious. The young man's name was Chris Allen and they had met at a Bible Study. This was exciting news and we were anxious to soon meet Mr. Allen and to see what all the fuss was about!

As we began our departure from Crete I wanted to drive past the air base where I had spent those 18 wonderful months back in the early '70s. The base was back near Herakleon where I had lived. As we entered into the base proper it was as if I was returning in some dream sequence with shadows and distorted pictures. Whereas this had been such a beautiful spot some 36 years ago it was now a ghost town, torn and tattered, weathered by the years and left in horrible shape by the Greeks. The beautiful beach looked cluttered, the gymnasium where I had become embroiled in an international incident with the Greek basketball team, was standing, but barely. The theatre was simply a shell waiting to fall, the communications center building where I had worked was covered with weeds and abandoned, and the bowling alley was hardly identifiable. The only building that seemed to survive the years was the chapel where I had attended and had preached via Armed Forces Radio one Sunday morning. The beautiful stained glass windows were still in place in the foyer and reminded me of God's blessing while serving here. But in many ways I wish we had not gone by as my memories of this wonderful place were now tarnished; it was sad!

We left the base, drove into town and found my old neighborhood; however, the area had grown so much and the identifying marks had changed in dramatic ways and I was unable to clearly identify my old home. Tina found for me a corner restaurant that was selling the old gyro sandwiches stuffed

The Retirement Years 2002-beyond

with broiled lamb that I use to love and even it did not taste the same. Maybe it is true that you can never truly go back home!

Later that day we flew back to Athens and stayed at a very nice hotel on the airport property and enjoyed a delightful end to our unbelievable vacation. The next morning we again boarded our Delta flight to Atlanta and on to St. Louis, signaling an end to a wonderful 25th anniversary (one year late.) God had been good and we had been blessed to enjoy some of His wonders in this magnificent country. We returned home happy with our experience and ready to return to the routine of our lives.

As 2009 rolled around it was time to face another new challenge. Early in January my doctor had informed me that my last PSA test had just clicked over the base line number of four. While he did not think it to be of any concern, he did say that he thought I should go to a specialist and get things checked out, just to be sure. The arrangements were made and I saw the specialist just a few days later.

The specialist voiced the same lack of concern as did my regular doctor. He left it up to me if I wanted to get a biopsy done. He reiterated that he thought there was little chance that I had cancer. He noted that it would probably not be unreasonable to recheck back in a year to see if there had been any significant changes, that was how confident he was that all was well. I decided this was a good option and that I would have another check up with my regular doctor later in the year or next.

As I drew near the appointment desk heading out the door I had a sudden change of mind. I was scheduled to be in Malta in just a few weeks, in South Africa a few weeks later and in Atlanta for a series of meetings in between, plus the upcoming missions conference at Twin Oaks later that month of February. However, I decided to stop and see what she had; fortunately they had an opening that fit that schedule perfectly, so I took it. Within a few days of the biopsy, Dr. Stillman, the specialist, called to say that surprisingly three of the 12 biopsies on my prostate were cancerous. The good news was that it was a low-grade cancer, non-aggressive and very early in its stage of growth. This was not the news I had expected, but nevertheless I had to deal with. Meetings were set up for me and Tina to discuss my options and a date was set for the procedure. I chose a very non-evasive procedure, commonly called a seeding procedure, where small seed-like bits of radiation are placed into the prostate. It was their prediction that within six months I should be cancer free.

A network of prayer warriors began to form. At one point I noted that if only one-fourth of those who said they were praying for me actually were, I had a tremendous group petitioning God on my behalf. I received a number of emails from literally around the world saying, *Count me in the one-quarter that is praying*. What a blessing! I must say that during this period I have never felt the power of corporate prayer in my life as I did in this instance. Do not ask me to explain, as I cannot; but I am convinced that God truly worked on my behalf, and prayer was a key instrument in making that so.

Late in December of 2010, my doctor gave me the all clear. Praise God! As most cancer patients, I now report for periodic check-ups twice a year for the next 5 years. Even if things had not turned out as good as they did, God remains good and remains sovereign; he will always be God. This experience gave me just a little taste of what Daniel experienced in Chapter 3:17-18 when he and his two friends were to be tossed in the fiery furnace because they refused to bow to King Nebuchadnezzar's idol. Daniel said, (17) *If we are thrown into the blazing furnace, the God we serve is able to save us from it, and he will rescue us from your hand, O king. (18) But even if he does not, we*

The Retirement Years 2002-beyond

want you to know, O king, that we will not serve your gods or worship the image of gold you have set up. In other words, Daniel was convinced that God Jehovah was the true God, regardless of whether he was to be delivered or not. Amen!

In May of 2009, Whitney was preparing to graduate from Antioch University. She had graduated from Missouri University with a Bachelors Degree in Business and was now adding her Master's to her resume in Sports Management. She had enjoyed quite an excellent experience over the past 18 months pursuing her education in California and enjoying the final months of college life. During her time in California she had endured record rains, major fires that threatened her residence on more than one occasion, a minor earthquake, mudslides, plus more positive things like an excellent internship with the athletic department of the University of California at Santa Barbara. How she ever managed to swing that, and not even be a student at that college, I still do not know, but it provided her a rather significant experience in a number of sports-related activities and venues associated with her chosen field.

Chris Allen, the young man we were briefed of by Whitney while we were vacationing in Greece, was a graduate of Westmont College in Santa Barbara, who like her, was a strong Christian, committed to his faith. As it was coming closer to Whit's time to leave, the relationship had grown such that both wanted to pursue it further. Timing is everything and in this case, the timing was perfect in that Chris had just taken a new position back in his hometown of Dallas and Whitney was keen on moving to Dallas as it afforded a number of job opportunities in line with her interests and education. Also, Anne Baxter, one of her former roommates at Mizzou, lived and worked in Dallas and it seemed good for them to move in together. With the pieces coming together nicely, Tina and I joined Whitney in Santa Barbara for her final days in the area,

Life Between Innings

packed up her Jeep and moved her back to St. Louis, then on to Dallas several weeks later.

About four months into the job search, she came across an internship with the Texas Rangers American League baseball club that looked promising. The Rangers were going through Chapter 13 reorganization, so while Whitney was coming on, many former employees were being let go. While negative in one sense, it also meant new opportunities for her, ultimately ending in a nice position in the front office working with the owners, Hank Greenberg and Nolan Ryan. While the hours have been long and the job has tremendous pressures, she continued to impress both her bosses and her clients. They were saddened when Whit came across a new job with many more benefits and pay as she had endeared herself to the Rangers' staff.

However, the bigger news came late in the fall of 2009 when Chris surprised her with a proposal of marriage. It was not so much that the proposal was a surprise as it was the circumstances in which the proposal occurred. For several years, Whitney and her old college room(house)mates from Missouri University would gather in a city in the Midwest for a reunion. This year the reunion was to occur in Tulsa, Oklahoma. With the permission of all the girls, but unknown to Whitney, Chris made arrangements to come to Tulsa and surprise her with the proposal and ring. With the help of the girls, the plan came off seamlessly, and Whitney happily and tearfully accepted his offer.

This significant event began an 11-month planning process of putting the wedding together. Tina traveled to Dallas on a couple occasions to help with the planning and we both came in for some pre-wedding activities. On October 16, 2010, Whitney and Chris were married in a beautiful ceremony, officiated by our good friend, Dr. Craig Sheppard, in downtown

The Retirement Years 2002-beyond

Dallas at the historic First Baptist Church, followed by an unbelievable wedding reception at the magnificent downtown Marriott Anatole Hotel. We were blessed to have many friends and family come in from St. Louis and other near and far reaches of the country to enjoy this great weekend with us; it truly was an affair to remember!! Whitney, taking time between the American League Divisional Playoffs and the World Series, enjoyed a wonderful honeymoon at a resort in Mexico, rushing back to fulfill her duties for the Rangers in San Francisco at games one and two of the World Series. Oh, what a life!

The issues with Pastor Ron Steel's leadership that had begun to develop in 2005 leading to the church split at Twin Oaks in October, 2006 began to slowly resurface again in 2009 and 2010 with almost identical consequences. Attendance was dropping off noticeably and of course this began to impact the World Missions' budget and our ability to do ministry. For the 2010/2011 fiscal year budget, it was necessary to trim $100,000 from our previous working budget of $430,000. It was becoming painfully obvious that we would probably need to cut another $100,000 in 2011, if not more. In fact, it seemed certain to me that if not in 2011, certainly by 2012, the Committee would have to reinvent the World Missions ministry as we would not have the finances to continue the ministry as we had known it over the last 15 years or so if our current leadership issues continued. While the financial issues weighed heavy on my mind, the continuing downward spiral of the church on all fronts was even more disturbing.

In July of 2010 I met with the Session of Twin Oaks Church for a full two hours explaining to them that I needed to resign, as I could no longer support privately or publicly the Senior Pastor. I had, by this point, lost all confidence in his leadership and all hope in his ability to lead us in turning our downward

Life Between Innings

spiral around. I never discounted the fact that the Holy Spirit could step in and resolve these ongoing issues at any moment, but absent that, my confidence had completely eroded. I noted for them that under Pastor Steel's leadership these past six-plus years, we had not added one successful ministry or outreach but, had in fact, suffered the following:

- ... loss in regular Sunday attendance from approximately 900 to slightly over 500 and still falling.
- ... we had cancelled our Sunday PM worship service due to a lack of attendance.
- ... we had cancelled one of our two Sunday morning worship services due to a lack of attendance.
- ... we had cancelled our once-vibrant outreach ministry, called Evangelism Explosion, and had not substantially replaced it with anything viable.
- ... our youth ministry was absolutely in shambles under the current Pastor of Families with Youth, and was getting worse.
- ... our children's ministry was likewise in trouble and we were losing young families at a frightening rate.
- ... we had no local outreach ministries of any ilk and the ones that had been attempted in recent years had either failed or were on life-support.
- ... the only viable ministries left standing were the Women's Ministry and World Missions.

At this point I asked them if they had a plan to right this wayward ship and they admitted they did not. Despite the fact that I had honestly told them I could no longer support the Senior Pastor and work under submission to him, they urged me to stay on as, in their opinion, it would be good for me, good for our missionaries and good for our church. They also stated that henceforth I would report to them and not to the Senior Pastor. Quite frankly, being a *good* Presbyterian, I did

The Retirement Years 2002-beyond

not understand their rationale. At this point they made several commitments to which I made clear I did not think they could achieve in the time necessary to save the church. After much urging, I agreed to stay on, but would not give them a commitment as to how long. I made it clear that I truly wanted to stay, in fact, it would be my dream to continue in this work for the next eight to ten years, the Lord willing, as my passion for world missions was stronger today than it was when I took on this ministry in 2005. However, I committed to continue to work hard with the Committee to move the ministry forward, but if a time came that I was convinced that they could not, or would not, make the changes needed to alter the direction of the church, I would resign.

In December of 2010 I was having lunch with Pastor Steel and we were talking about the missions ministry and the continuing issues at the church. For some reason he was compelled to tell me that he, himself, had tried to resign back in July, just prior to my meeting with the Session, but they would not accept his resignation. I was flabbergasted by this bit of information.

In January of 2011, we were having a serious discussion at our Ministry Staff meeting when Pastor Steel confessed to the entire team that he had *implored* the Session to release him back in July, but they had refused. Coupled with this announcement, it was also leaked that the Session was going to lay off two Assistant Pastors and at least one staff worker in nine days so as to meet budget. Without the cuts, the general fund would be broke on May 1.

By now my concerns over the leadership and the direction of the church had escalated even further since July of the previous year. No longer was it an issue that I had lost all confidence and trust in my Sr. Pastor, I had now lost all confidence and trust in my Session. I could, and did, continue to work

499

Life Between Innings

at Twin Oaks since 2006 to the present having serious question regarding the leadership and pastoral ability of the Senior Pastor; however, having now lost all confidence in the leadership of the Session, I knew I was finished at Twin Oaks. With a couple exceptions, it was this Session now in place that had overseen the total destruction of our youth ministry, not lifting a finger to resolve the issue until every single senior high student had left the church or was no longer participating. This group that once numbered in access of 100 kids was gone. And, the group had not "merely" shrunk to 10 or 15, but to zero, and had done so in full view of the Session and the congregation. This complete collapse had occurred despite families with youth and the youth themselves leaving the church and/or ceasing their active participation, with most of this occurring after voicing their concerns to the Session multiple times. The Session had also heard loud protests from volunteer youth workers, other interested parties within the church that did not have a child involved, but could obviously see what was happening, including me; they simply and inexplicably let it die. Sometime in November, and after the last senior high students had disassociated themselves from the ministry, the Session severed its relationship with the Pastor of Families With Youth who had played the primary role in the demise of the ministry. It was obvious that somehow these godly men of the Session had become blinded by the peripheral issues, although important, such as budgets, job cuts, and other miscellaneous issues, but were refusing, for some reason, to deal with the critical issues of the church, and certainly the core issue, by which these other issues were resulting, that being the continued employment of the Sr. Pastor. It appeared clear to me that they had set a course to oversee the total destruction of the church and they were incapable of stopping it.

The Retirement Years 2002-beyond

Representatives of the Session met with the Ministry Staff in late January 2011 to announce that they were laying off the two Assistant Pastors and the staff person as I had previously heard, plus they announced that they were putting Sr. Pastor Ron Steel on a three-month sabbatical, effective immediately, with a planned return to the pulpit of May 1. Several staff members strongly questioned the Session representatives if there was any indication that Pastor Steel would or would not return from the sabbatical. We were told that there was every indication that he would be returning and in fact they were planning in that direction. Over the past few weeks and months I had put things into place knowing that my resignation was probably at hand, sooner if not later. With these announcements and my clear understanding that the Session had no intentions of asking Pastor Steel to step down, my confidence in the Session's ability to lead was now fully and effectively crushed. It was at this point that I knew it was time for me to go and not remain to be a disruption or negative influence on the further direction of the church. While I truly loved these men individually, as several had been mentors for me through the years, collectively they had become dysfunctional to a fault. Having lost all confidence and hope in their collective leadership as well as the leadership of the Senior Pastor, it was time to go. What I did not know was that the Pastor of Music and Worship would also be announcing his resignation in a mere week or two followed by the Sr. Pastor's resignation two months hence on April 1. Of course there was no indication that this was going to happen at the time of my decision; in fact, all indicators were that he was coming back. Therefore, based on what information I had available to me, and having prayerfully sought guidance on how to proceed over many, many months, I drafted my Letter of Resignation and put into place the final things needed in order to resign. While I had

Life Between Innings

struggled with this decision going back to October of 2006, I finally felt at peace in leaving.

On Sunday afternoon, January 30, 2011, I met with the Committee and told them of my decision, effective immediately. To a person they understood. With tears flowing, I stood to leave. With our tears mingled together, they each gave me and Tina a strong embrace and words of thanks and encouragement. This was truly a unique group of committed saints, dedicated to the Great Commission, a group that will not soon be duplicated. I had been wondrously blessed to have worked alongside this team of men and women and I will not soon forget their love and their undying support:

THE TEAM:

Donna Middendorf	Tina Mooney
Don Jacobs	Patt Tiemeier
Dean Kappel	Jan Watson
Charlie Troxell	Don Newkirk
Darren DeGroot	Carol Nichols
Cheryl Nichols	

While not on the Committee at the time of my resignation, I owe much gratitude and thanks to several others who served alongside me so graciously for many years:

Doris Brown	Gwen Pollex
Coby McGinty	David Hoefakker
Stephanie Glass	Susan Newkirk

McGinty (South Africa), Hoefakker (Bulgaria), Glass (Bulgaria) and Newkirk (South Africa) had all served until forced to step-off of the Committee per our by-laws as they each had accepted full-time missions work with Mission to the World. Obviously, they were missed, but it was our great joy to send them into God's harvest field (*Matthew 9:38*).

Immediately following my meeting with the Committee I sent out my Letter of Resignation to the Session, key members

The Retirement Years 2002-beyond

of the staff and the full World Missions Committee. Over the next few days I received an outpouring of email, cards, letters and telephone calls from around the world, likewise providing words of thanks for our service, but most importantly to give us words of encouragement. This was so greatly appreciated. Only two negative emails came in; both from missionaries that we not only supported, but with whom I was very close friends. I appreciated their candor and questions as well as their willingness to listen and to understand; and we remain very close friends to this day.

It was true that my leaving seemed abrupt, especially to many of the congregation and staff, as I had not gone public with my issues with the Session or the Sr. Pastor's leadership. Certainly the Session, while perhaps surprised at the timing, could not be surprised at my actions as I had kept them abreast of my ongoing issues and struggles maintaining my vow as a Ruling Elder to work in submission to those over me since the previous July. With this being January 31, and just mere weeks before our annual Missions Conference in late February, I truly felt that I was between a rock and a hard place. If I stayed on through the conference and remained the chief cheerleader in raising Faith Promise support, only to resign shortly thereafter, to me seemed hypocritical. If I resigned effective immediately, as I did, there would be many who would see my actions as vindictive and detrimental to the missions' ministry that I so unabashedly had expressed my love and concern for over the years. However, I also knew that if I stayed on, but notified the staff and the congregation that I was planning to resign soon after the conference, there would be many, many questions from congregants as to why I planned to resign, since most knew of my passion for this work. Confronted with questions such as would be forthcoming, providing honest answers would not be beneficial to the "peace and purity" of

503

the church, something I was sworn to uphold as a Ruling Elder. Consequently, in trying hard to do the right thing, I decided it was best I resign effective immediately and remove myself from public worship at Twin Oaks for the foreseeable future.

Due to the outpouring of positive support that I received following my resignation, I truly believed that I had made the right decision and had left "doing it right." I did not receive any telephone calls from anyone in leadership at Twin Oaks; I did, however, receive three emails, all from Ruling Elders. One email came asking for forgiveness for "letting me down," another wishing me well wherever God may take us and the last was a very cordial note stating that he considered me a friend and hoped that we could maintain our friendship in the days ahead. Of course Charlie Troxell, the Ruling Elder who had oversight of the World Missions ministry and worked closely with me on the World Missions Committee, remains in contact with me to this day. We remain great friends and try hard to see each other each time I return to St. Louis for a visit. Consequently, not hearing one negative comment from anyone at Twin Oaks, I was confident that I had in fact did the right thing and that my exit strategy had been done the right way. Several months later I would find that I was wrong in that assumption; very wrong!!

Spring and summer of 2011 swiftly passed and fall was quickly upon us with gold and red leaves adorning the trees surrounding our home and neighborhood. In September, Twin Oaks had brought in Dr. Robert Stuart as an interim PCA (Presbyterian Church in America) pastor, a pastor who excelled in helping wounded churches bind up their wounds and return to health, even if ever so slowly. Early in October Tina and I had prayerfully made the decision to move to the Dallas area with a planned departure of October 14. Tina had received a very nice offer as a Nurse Practitioner at Baylor

The Retirement Years 2002–beyond

University Heart Hospital in Plano (suburb of Dallas) and the offer seemed too good to pass up.

At the urging of my former Administrative Assistant, Donna Middendorf, who was now serving as the new Director of Twin Oaks World Missions, Dr. Stuart contacted me a week prior to our departure to Dallas to see if he and I could meet for coffee. Dr. Stuart was interested in hearing my story, as well as the story of many others who had left Twin Oaks Church, to see if he could get a handle on the issues he was facing. We met for well over two hours at the local Starbucks and I found Dr. Stuart to be very engaging and insightful, a real delight to talk with. At the close of our meeting he asked if I might be interested in coming back to Twin Oaks that upcoming Sunday and say a few words from my heart to the congregation, and if I desired, even ask for forgiveness if I felt it appropriate. I told him I would welcome the opportunity, especially since it was to be our last Sunday in St. Louis prior to the move. I told him that I was not aware of any issues wherein I needed to ask for forgiveness, nor did I feel there were any out there who were in need of being reconciled to me. However, I did add that he might want to run this idea by a couple members of his staff and the Ruling Elders as there might be one or two who would not be in favor of me doing so. In reality, I really had no basis for my concerns other than knowing the personalities of two particular staff members who, in my opinion, were susceptible to seeing "ghosts behind every tree."

On Saturday morning prior to the service I received a call from Dr. Stuart saying that my concerns had materialized and that there was a Ruling Elder who was gravely concerned about me standing in front of the congregation to say a few words. Although Dr. Stuart had reminded him that I had offered by letter to come to the last Session meeting to answer any lingering questions prior to our leaving for Dallas, and none at

Life Between Innings

that meeting had felt it necessary, still the concerns of this Elder persisted. At the request of Dr. Stuart I called the gentlemen and we had a great conversation. I answered to his satisfaction his concerns and forgiveness was offered by us both for any misunderstanding that I may have caused and for any ill will that he might have been holding on to regarding my leaving. I called Dr. Stuart back to relay the success and fruitfulness of the conversation.

Late Saturday night prior to the Sunday service I found on my voice mail another call from Dr. Stuart suggesting I call a particular member of the ministry staff who had belatedly voiced concerns. Though it was 9:45 PM and not a good hour to engage in such a conversation, I contacted the gentlemen and told him why I was calling. As positive as was the first call, this call was negative. While the person later gave me "his reasons" for not wanting to talk with me at that hour of the night, I was on that night, and still remain, somewhat flabbergasted at how I was received in light of the seriousness of the issue coupled with the position he held on the ministry staff. At the end of our brief conversation he told me he did not intend to oppose Dr. Stuart regarding my coming; however, he made it clear he was not in favor of it. I then contacted Dr. Stuart again and recited to him the outcome of this latest call. I then told him that Tina and I would still be at the service and I would leave it up to him if he felt it good that we come before the congregation as planned.

It was now Sunday, October 9, 2011, some eight months or more since I had resigned. Tina and I arrived at the church a little apprehensive, but also very excited about being back for a worship service. Except for Easter Sunday, we had not been back for a worship service since my resignation. I still did not know if Pastor Stuart planned to use me or not, and as he later explained, he wasn't sure himself, until just moments before

The Retirement Years 2002-beyond

he asked us to come forward. In a meeting with the Session and several staff members just prior to the service, they had agreed to leave it entirely up to him and stated that despite some concerns they would support his decision. When called forward, he stepped down from the pulpit and met Tina and me at the front of the church. He opened by welcoming us and explaining to the congregation that he had invited us to say a few words prior to our leaving for Dallas. He asked a few questions regarding my involvement in world missions and the ministry at Twin Oaks and also my relationship with the former pastor, Ron Steel. I gave very honest answers to his questions and noted that while Ron and I had privately disagreed from time to time on leadership issues, our love for each other was genuine and that we expressed it to each other often. I also noted that we had actually sat together for lunch at the last Missouri Presbytery meeting when his resignation from Twin Oaks was affirmed. I also reaffirmed that with regard to me and to my ministry at Twin Oaks, Pastor Steel had been very supportive in all phases. I then offered up this heartfelt statement, which I paraphrase, *"I know that for some of you in the congregation my leaving [this past January] may have seemed abrupt, especially if you were not in the loop, leaving many of you confused or even hurt wondering what had happened and why we were gone. I never meant to hurt anyone, but it is obvious to me now that I did. To you I ask for your forgiveness as Twin Oaks remains our home church and we cherish you, and appreciate you, for all the support and love you have given us for some 20 years.* With that I handed the microphone back to Dr. Stuart and we headed back to our pews as a number of congregants from all over the sanctuary stood and applauded; this gesture was so unexpected but greatly appreciated.

When the service ended we were inundated with well-wishers shaking our hands, hugging us and making us feel

Life Between Innings

so loved, so welcome. In fact, we hardly were able to move from our seat area due to the throng of people. One of the staff people came by to ask me for forgiveness because he had harbored ill-will toward me since my resignation. Of course we embraced and things were made right between us in accordance with Matthew 18:15-17. Finally, as the last well-wisher departed, we looked around to find that we were the last people remaining in the sanctuary. What a great day of refreshment and reconciliation; what a great joy for us both to have been so loved on in such a genuine manner and to know we had been missed, even forgiven, by those that we had served alongside of for so many years.

Following the service, the staff person who had not taken my call very well the night before called and asked if we could meet for breakfast prior to our leaving for Dallas five days hence. We did meet and we discussed our issues openly. While it was evident that we would never agree on the validity of the issues leading me to resign, or the appropriateness or timing of my resignation, forgiveness was extended and reconciliation was reached. You might call it a Paul and Barnabas experience (Acts 15:39) which was later described in I Corinthians 9:6 as ending well.

That was October, 2011 and now it is February, 2012. Ironically, the Cardinals have just opened spring training in Jupiter, Florida. And, as we know, hope springs eternal in spring training. There are no losses at this point, only dreams and a renewed hope for the future. I am not sure what the future holds, which I guess is true for us all. But, as I look back over these 64 years of my life, I understand distinctly that I have been a blessed man, blessed way beyond anything I deserve. The ballgame is not yet over; it looks like there may be a few more innings to play. And, as such, I am hopeful for many more blessed days and fruitful years living out life between the innings. With some resolve I will take my life verse and continue to hold to it until that fateful day, that blessed day, when God summons me back from the on-deck circle and instructs me to put the bat back in the rack and to take a seat. Amen!

Trust in the Lord with all your heart and lean not on your own understanding; in all your ways acknowledge him, and he will make your paths straight." Proverbs 3:5-6 (NIV).

The 9ᵗʰ Inning
THE EPILOGUE

What would I do over? That is one of the favorite questions that people love to ask people of my age. I guess this is a popular question because it doesn't take a "rocket surgeon," as our infamous President George W. Bush, Jr. once was quoted as saying, to figure out that you can't live this long without making a few mistakes along the way. Certainly, if you have read this memoir you know I made my share of mistakes, and then some.

Like most old codgers (*not sure I have ever called myself that*) we dare to dream a little about some woman we wished we had chased a little harder, job opportunities that we regret not pursuing, some investments that should have been made, words that we wish we would have said or not said. Certainly I wish I had taken care of my health a little better. But, in reality, I was a pretty healthy guy without many sick days until at age 50 diabetes got me. Even then I have not suffered too many of the difficulties and side effects that most diabetics endure, so I continue to count my blessings. The bout with prostate cancer seems short-lived, so again I have been blessed. But, all in all, I am not sure I would want to start over again. Yes, there are innumerable things I would do differently; I would be an idiot not to, given the chance. However, I truly have had a wonderful life, being blessed abundantly each step of the way, God's grace always being sufficient.

Life Between Innings

In writing my memoir I think there was, at times, a penchant to accentuate the negatives that have occurred over the course of my life. I am actually "the-glass-is-half-full" kind of guy, but in order to demonstrate that I am in no way a perfect man, but a very flawed man and in need of God's eternal grace and forgiveness, it was necessary to dwell on the negative issues to reveal the importance of God's workings in my life. It's kind of like watching the evening news where the news is not about the good things going on around us, but the bad. The fact is that day-by-day I have had one heck of a good life, filled with much laughter and sprinkled with considerable joy! It would be easy to sit back and moan over my regrets, I guess, but in reality this has been a good ride. And, I have been very blessed to have shared the past 29 years of this life with a special friend, my wife, Tina!

I reminded Tina that most of the book is about certain small segments of my life that were not so positive. As such, the 29 great years of life I have shared with her did not take up much print as these have been the best years. To write of them, while interesting to us, would, by comparison, be less interesting to the reader. However, for us, these years are cherished! These 29 years have simply flown by!

I do regret the many detours in life that Dionne and Marc have made, seeing their struggles year after year. But, I no longer blame Shirley or me for their difficulties as they have had numerous opportunities to turn things around over the past 25 years or more. And, there is still time for them to do more with their lives if they desire by making a strong commitment to change, developing a clear focus on positive goals while maintaining the willingness to put it all together with a well-thought-out plan. While having a personal relationship with Jesus Christ does not guarantee that all will go well in life, Christ does promise that His grace will be sufficient (II

The Epilogue

Corinthians 12:9) for all that they face if they make Him Lord over their lives. Certainly developing a personal relationship with Christ does trump all the other elements in seeking a "successful" life, especially in light of eternity. I love them both and I pray that they do develop life-plans at some point with positive elements listed up and down the "page." It is often said that for change to occur, one must stop repeating the same things over and over again and expecting a different outcome.

As I put the finishing touches on this book, it is a joy to write that Dionne has been sober for well over six years, has regained her wonderful sense of humor, has a heart as big as Texas, has recommitted herself to God and is involved in her local church on a regular basis. This has been our consistent prayer for many years and we are gaining confidence each day that God is truly making her paths straight as she makes better decisions on a consistent basis. She lives in St. Louis County so we were able to stay in frequent contact until our recent move to Texas.

I cannot give a similar report on Marc as he continues to face hardships brought on by a life devoid of responsible living and decision-making. But, we maintain hope that at some point in the future the light will come on and changes will be made such that his children and family can emphatically call him "blessed;" it would be nice for this to occur while I am still amongst the living.

Whitney has taken full advantage of the opportunities that she has had put before her and it has been a joy to watch her mature in her Christian faith and to grow as a young lady. She has continuously and intentionally gathered together positive influences around her, pushing aside those that weren't, even when it was painful to do so. I remember one of the more poignant moments for Tina and me was the day she broke off a relationship with a young man that she had enjoyed for three or four years. As she stated it to us, *I want a man who will walk with me or lead me in my faith walk; not a man that I have to lead or drag along.* That is a powerful conviction, one that any dad worth his salt would stand up and give a shout of thanksgiving and a thundering cheer! Because of her commitment to Christ and responsible living, she has developed great relationships with folks all across the country who will be supportive of her for life; like me, she has been greatly and richly blessed, but she had a "life-plan" and has stayed focused on it. In October of 2010, she married Mr. Chris Allen, a godly man that she met at a Bible Study while attending college in California; we absolutely love and respect Chris who is truly an answer to years of prayer.

My childhood was unbelievably blessed, as was my teen and Bible School years. Obviously the first marriage would be a do over, but that is about it. Accepting the fact that I had not been called into Pastoral Ministry was probably the first big step in finding a direction for my life; I was fortunate to make that discovery when I did.

Serving in the Air Force was both an honor and a privilege and I loved each day, except the first, of that experience. I had great bosses and great assignments and found some incredibly neat people along the way to worship with who were strong, committed believers, rooted deeply in their faith from all denominations. Experiencing Christians of deep faith from varied denominations, especially from the ones that I had been taught for years housed "dead and Christless" parishioners, may have been one of the greatest lessons, life changing lessons, that I had to unlearn from my up-bringing.

Working with Union Electric was a tremendous financial blessing. While I am not a wealthy man, I cannot believe the money and the opportunities that this company provided me.

The Epilogue

Again, for the most part, it was here that I found really good people who worked hard and who took pride in their work. We also had some fun along the way. Had it not been for the way we retirees were screwed over by Gary Rainwater, the CEO of Ameren (formerly Union Electric), with our health benefits AFTER we were retired, I would say that working with them and for them was an unspeakable blessing.

My years as a Business Representative probably changed and impacted my life more than anything else that I did in the secular world. I went from a pretty happy-go-lucky guy, laid back, non-confrontational (except on the softball field or basketball court), often the life or center of the party, to a guy that my peers thought was a very serious man. I do know that somewhere in there I lost my health and lost a good deal of my sense of humor. Certainly my appreciation of the workingman and my distrust of management and big corporations were birthed in me during those 18 years of service. One of the distinctives that I noted in my relationship with management was that Protestant (professing Christians) managers were much harder to work with than Catholics and non-believers. The Protestants (professing Christians) pretty much saw things as black and white and would not be a party to compromise, the cornerstone of Collective Bargaining. Catholics and non-believers on the other hand were more ready to work things out in a fashion that is called win – win bargaining. I'll let you draw your own conclusions as to how those two management philosophies impacted people (workers); the Catholics and unbelievers seemed to get it right. That is a hard one to explain.

Another issue that I ponder from time to time is why that I so often find myself siding with those that my Christian friends and colleagues hold with such distain in the political arena. I just confessed that I found Christians much harder

Life Between Innings

to work with in labor/management situations. When looking at my voting record, my ultra conservative Christian friends have got to wonder *what in the world is Leo smoking when his favorite presidents are Bill Clinton and Richard Nixon and he strongly dislikes Ronald Reagan and George Bush, Jr.?* I guess I see too much hypocrisy and self-righteousness in the political "right," coupled with little compassion for the workingman and the poor, and I am completely turned off by it. I also like my world-leaders (from the U.S.) to be men and women whose lives have had some ups and downs, some hard times, some sins that need to be forgiven; they seem to have a more realistic view of the real world. I think King David of the Old Testament would have made a great president, as a man-after-God's-own-heart (Acts 13:22), but certainly he would not get the vote of the conservative right here in the U.S. in today's political arena. And, quite frankly, single issue Christians just scare the living daylights out of me...and YES, I am pro-life to the core.

Not that I take any great pleasure in this, but in 2008 my old nemesis at the Bargaining Table, Mr. Bob Powers, was unceremoniously let go by Ameren (formerly Union Electric) for alleged financial improprieties involving kick-backs with contractors. After I retired, Bob had received several promotions based on his ability to "get things done." At some point, it had to catch up with him and eventually it did. His boss at EEI, Alan Kelly, who approved of Bob's tactics because of the financial rewards it created for the company and himself, also received some nice promotions within Ameren (Ameren owned about 80% of EEI), but he too was unceremoniously pushed out the door a few months after Bob for similar alleged reasons. In both cases the record will show that they retired, it's just that the choice was not voluntary.

I do miss coaching basketball and I especially miss the girls. These kids, especially the ones at Ritenour, gave me such

The Epilogue

great respect and such great effort; they gave me much more than I was ever able to give them. Coaching Whitney, especially in her grade school years, was an unbelievable delight for me and helped create a bond between us unlike that of most fathers and daughters.

My experiences associated with being the Missions Director at Twin Oaks were awesome, to say the least. I have often said to the Committee, however, that I would rather stand in front of a crowd of Union guys than in front of them because I could just tell the Union guys what I was going to do and they got on board or missed the train. True, they could have voted us out, but they didn't. In church work I have had to fall back on my mediating skills, trying to massage gently those I needed to move in the direction that I felt God wanted us to go. However, these are volunteers who don't have to follow my lead if they do not want to. The truth is, my Committee was unbelievable to work with and equally supportive; I love those guys with all my heart and will always greatly admire them for their commitment and focus to the great cause of global missions.

I have likewise been blessed to have been able to work and worship in great churches throughout my adult life where the power of God has been very evident. I received my fundamentals of the faith as a child at a small church in Salem, Missouri, named Revival Tabernacle. However, my faith really began to mature and grow at Carsonville Full Gospel Tabernacle, where as a teenager God provided a great place to grow along with other godly teens among other godly men and women that nurtured and cared for us.

At Bible College, I was able to get in on the ground floor of Trinity Assembly (now Cornerstone), a dynamic church in San Antonio, Texas with a solid vision for the community and the world, led by Rev. John Hagee. Time spent here represented many hours of great preaching and a living example of what can be done when the Holy Spirit is allowed to move and operate freely. Full Gospel Tabernacle in East St. Louis, and later in Fairview Heights, Illinois, likewise offered solid preaching, leadership and a worldwide vision under Rev. Henry Redman and gave me a place to exercise my gifts and watch God grow them. Even during my time in the Air Force, God seemed to always provide a solid church with good pastoral preaching and the fellowship of other saints that we needed, even in the base chapel on the island of Crete. God gave me Hope Congregational Church in north St. Louis County at probably the most critical hour of my life, as it was here that God met me and restored me into His fellowship following my divorce.

And lastly, Twin Oaks Presbyterian Church just may have been the most dynamic of them all when I weigh the overall impact that it had on my life and the life of my family. The history of Twin Oaks Church is that of a community of reformed believers jointly working together reaching into the local community and across the world engaging men and women for Christ, and it was wondrous. Consequently, until just these past few years, I was so blessed to have mostly been in a growing church with a solid, active vision for the local community and the world. To be a Christian most of my life and to be able to say that is simply a quick study of God's grace in action.

Lastly, I have walked the reader through some of the dregs of church life as it affected me. I am sure that the uninitiated would wonder why, with all that I have shared regarding church issues such as, but not limited to, the church split at Twin Oaks and all its ugliness, the problems I encountered with my Pro-life friends who set out to destroy my missions ministry, the total dysfunction of the Session (our board) leading to my resignation from my dream job as Director of World Missions, etc., why in the world would Tina and I remain at Twin Oaks Church as long as we did, or for that matter, in any

The Epilogue

church. Take an hour or two and read the books of I Corinthians and II Corinthians, just as a starter. Realize as you read that the Apostle Paul is writing these books (letters) to Christians in the church, not the sinners living on the outside. Those early churches, like ours today, were filled with Christians doing sinful acts. But, it is in the church that we build upon our maturing relationship with God. It's not always easy, but where else would you turn – to the world? Bob Mumford, a very charismatic preacher of the '70s and '80s, used to say that God, as a Father, and like most fathers, has some good kids and some bad kids. And, boy don't we know it. Despite all the troubles I have faced within the church, I love the church! I strongly believe in the local and universal church. I just need to keep reminding myself to keep my eyes clearly and intently focused on our Lord and Savior, Jesus Christ, and not the failures of men. And, if I do, God will make my paths straight because He has promised (Proverbs 3:5-6).

So there it is. There is my life played out between innings and summed up in a few hundred pages. It's been a good game with more than my fair share of good bounces. To God be the glory!

And now, may the God of all grace be your comfort and guide! Amen!

Star of the Game
POST GAME SHOW

It is only appropriate that my wife of almost thirty years, **Tina Lynn**, appear here as the Star of the Game on the Post Game Show. I owe her many thanks for the encouragement given me in persevering with this project and seeing it through to completion. It started out as something I would work on each summer while vacationing on Sanibel Island, Florida and then I would not touch it again until the following year. When I began to have doubts as to whether it was a good idea to even put my thoughts, my sins, my failures and my few successes on paper for anyone and everyone to read, she continued to encourage me until at last I have this finished manuscript. As in most of my personal endeavors, be they the pursuit of my college education, my labor activities, coaching or missions work, she has been my biggest fan, cheering me on at every juncture. She also, more than anyone, knows the struggles I have had in trying to be the kind of dad to Dionne and Marc that I wanted to be and the joy I have had in being dad to Whitney. So, to Tina, I express my love and appreciation, as she has been my greatest blessing! Her patience and joy in watching me bring this book to fruition has furthered my love and appreciation for this exceptional woman!

The Scoreboard Show

LISTS

EDUCATION
1. William H. Lynch: Grade School (1-6 grades)
2. Fremont: Grade School: Diploma (7-8 grades)
3. O'Fallon Technical High School: Diploma (9-12 grades)
4. International Bible College: Ministerial Diploma
5. Air Force Communication Specialist: Diploma w/ Honors
6. Air Force Air Traffic Control School: Diploma
7. St. Louis Community College at Belleville
8. Jefferson Junior College
9. St. Louis Community College at Meramec: Associates of Arts - Business
10. St. Louis Community College at Meramec: Associates of Arts - Communications
11. St. Louis University: Bachelor of Arts in Organizational Management; Magna Cum Laude

JOBS I WORKED FOR PAY
1. Newsboy (1959): Selling the *Post-Dispatch* newspapers on the corner of Arsenal Street and Lemp Street - St. Louis, MO.
2. Housekeeper (1960-1961): Keeping the house straightened-up (paid weekly by my sister, Bonnie) - St. Louis, MO.

Life Between Innings

3. Receptionist/Activities Director (1963-1965 and 1967): Junior Staff at the *Boys' Club of* St. Louis on South 11th Street.
   a. Receptionist
   b. Directing general club activities and janitorial work
4. Stock Boy/Bagger/Cashier (1965): *Piggly Wiggly Supermarkets* – San Antonio, TX.
5. School Bus Driver (1966-1968): *Northside Independent School District* – San Antonio, TX.
6. Camp Counselor (1966): *Teamster Camp Local #688* – Pevely, MO.
7. Athletic Director (1966-1968): Boys' Club #4 – San Antonio, TX.
8. Route Salesman (1968-1969): *Cardinal Chip Company* (St. Louis County, MO)
9. Airman (1969-1973): *United States Air Force (E=Enlisted Personnel; Number= Pay Grade)*
   03/04/69: (E-1) Airman Basic (Slick Sleeve)
   04/15/69: (E-2) Airman (1 Stripe)
   10/01/69: (E-3) Airman First Class (2 Stripes)
   01/01/71: (E-4) Sergeant (3 Stripes)
   10/01/72: (E-5) Staff Sergeant (4 Stripes)
   . 1969-1972: Communication Center Specialist - Wichita Falls, TX, San Angelo,
   TX and Iraklion Air Station, Crete, Greece.
   . 1972-1973: Air Traffic Controller - Biloxi, MS and Laredo, TX
10. Linesman (1969): *YMCA Little League Football* - San Angelo, TX
11. Umpire (1969-1970 & 1972-1973): *Baseball/Softball: USBAA* – San Angelo and Laredo, TX.
12. Referee (1969-1973): *Southwest Texas Officials Association* – San Angelo, TX; Crete, Greece; Laredo, TX.

Lists

13. Snack Shop Attendant (1971-72): Iraklion Air Station Communication Center – Crete, Greece.
14. Package Delivery Driver (1973): *United Parcel Service* – St. Louis, MO.
15. Union Electric (1974 – 1984):
    a. 1974 & 1975: Janitor – Union Electric General Office Building
    b. 1974 & 1975: Laborer: Venice Power Plant (General labor duties of shoveling, cleaning, repairing railroad tracks and ties, training for operational jobs within the power plants.)
    c. 1975: Turbine Auxiliary Operator: Venice Power Plant
    d. 1975: Mill Tender: Venice Power Plant
    e. 1975-1976: Assistant Boiler Operator: Venice Power Plant
    f. 1976 – 1978: Stationman: Rush Island Power Plant (Same as Laborer duties).
    g. 1978-1984: Control Attendant Operator: Labadie Power Plant
16. Sr. Pastor (1974): *First Assembly of God Church*: Laredo, TX.
17. Christian Bookstore Manager (1975-1976): *Christian Missionary Bookstore*, an arm of the Full Gospel Tabernacle World Missions Ministry/Christian Missionary Association - Fairview Heights, IL.
18. Business Representative (1984-2002): The *International Union of Operating Engineers, Local 148 - Stationary.*
    a. 1984-1987: Union Electric Operations Jurisdiction; Fossil Fuel Plants.
    b. 1988-1991: Local 148 EAP Representative, PAC Representative & Union Organizer.
    c. 1991-2001: Electric Energy, Inc. Jurisdiction.
    d. 1991-2001: Central Illinois Public Service Jurisdiction.
    e. 2001: Local 148 Organizer

Life Between Innings

  f. 2001-2002: Local 148 Grievance & Arbitration Facilitator.

19. Girls Basketball Coach (2000-2003): *Westminster Christian Academy* - Ladue, MO.

  a. 2000-2002: Junior Varsity Girls' Head Basketball Coach.

  b. 2002-2003: Varsity Girls' Head Basketball Coach.

20. Labor Consultant (2003-2004): *Service Employees International Union, Local 2000* – St. Louis Metro Area.

21. Girls Junior Varsity Head Basketball Coach (2004-2008): *Ritenour High School* – St. Louis, MO.

22. Director of World Missions (2005-2011): *Twin Oaks Presbyterian Church (PCA)* – St. Louis, MO.

<u>COUNTRIES I HAVE VISITED</u>

1. Bulgaria
2. Canada
3. Ecuador
4. England
5. Greece & Crete
6. Kenya
7. Malta
8. Mexico
9. Nicaragua
10. Peru
11. Russia
12. South Africa

<u>ALL TIME WOMEN OF RENOWN</u>

1. Julie London
2. Kate Winslet
3. Catherine Zeta-Jones

4. Ava Gardner
5. Rhonda Fleming
6. Cheryl Ladd
7. Milla Jovovich
8. Maureen O'Sullivan
9. Kim Novak
10. Rita Hayworth

FAVORITE MALE ENTERTAINERS (Non-Musical)
1. Steve Allen (although he is also a talented musician)
2. Fred Allen
3. Johnny Carson
4. John Candy
5. Groucho Marx
6. Henry Fonda
7. Spencer Tracy
8. George Burns
9. Humphrey Bogart
10. Jerry Seinfeld

FAVORITE MUSICAL ARTISTS
1. Frank Sinatra
2. Jerry Rafferty
3. Al Green
4. Elton John
5. Billy Joel
6. Carol King
7. Carly Simon
8. James Taylor
9. Nat King Cole
10. Bing Crosby

Life Between Innings

FAVORITE MUSICAL GROUPS
1. Steely Dan
2. Bee Gees
3. Bill Gaither (Homecoming Singers)
4. Chicago
5. Oak Ridge Boys
6. Beach Boys
7. Andrew Sisters w. Glen Miller Orchestra
8. Beatles, pre Abby Road
9. Little River Band
10. ABBA

FAVORITE SECULAR SONGS
1. Baker Street – Jerry Rafferty
2. Anything Steely Dan
3. Just the Way You Are – Billy Joel
4. Benny and the Jets – Elton John
5. Theme From a Summer Place – Percy Faith & Orchestra
6. Reminiscing – Little River Band
7. Emotion – Samantha Sang
8. Last Dance – Donna Summers
9. Don't It Make My Brown Eyes Blue – Crystal Gayle
10. Right Down the Line – Jerry Rafferty

FAVORITE HYMNS & INSPIRATIONAL SONGS
All Hail the Power of Jesus Name
om at the Cross
rength is Perfect
God Alone
h My Soul

's Love

Lists

9. A Mighty Fortress
10. Just As I Am

CONCERTS ATTENDED
1. Steely Dan at the Fox Theatre in St. Louis
2. Many Gospel Quartet "Singins" at the Kingsland Theatre in St. Louis
3. Bill Gaither Homecoming at the Savvis Center in St. Louis (2X)
4. Bill Gaither Homecoming at the Family Center in St. Charles
5. Bill Gaither Homecoming at the Fort Worth Convention Center, Texas
6. Elton John/Billy Joel (The Piano Men) at Busch Stadium in St. Louis
7. Billy Joel at the Arena in St. Louis (2X)
8. Village People w/ Gloria Gaynor at the Checkerdome in St. Louis
9. John Denver at Kiel Auditorium in St. Louis
10. Elvis Presley at Kiel Auditorium in St. Louis
11. Bee Gees at the Arena in St. Louis
12. Christmas Concert with Contemporary Gospel Singers at the Savvis Center in St. Louis
13. Barry Manilow at the Arena in St. Louis
14. Moody Blues at the Arena in St. Louis
15. Gloria Estefan at Riverport in Earth City – St. Louis
16. Kingston Trio at the Barn in Pond, Missouri
17. The Little River Band at the Arena in St. Louis

FAVORITE OLD-TIME RADIO SHOWS
1. Yours Truly, Johnny Dollar
2. Dragnet
3. Fred Allen Show

Life Between Innings

4. Gunsmoke
5. Amos and Andy
6. This is Your FBI
7. Gang Busters
8. Lum & Abner
9. The Shadow
10. Fibber McGee and Molly

TV FAVORITES: SHOWS '50s THROUGH THE '60s
1. Steve Allen Show
2. Dragnet (Original Shows)
3. Jackie Gleason Show
4. Perry Mason (Original Shows)
5. The Untouchables
6. The Roaring 20s
7. The Deputy
8. Highway Patrol
9. What's My Line
10. Flip Wilson Show
11. Leave It To Beaver
12. Doby Gillis
13. Twilight Zone
14. The Line-up
15. Adventures in Paradise
16. Superman
17. Lone Ranger
18. Death Valley Days
19. Sonny & Cher Hour
20. Dean Martin Variety Hour

TV FAVORITES: '70s TO THE PRESENT
1. Seinfeld
2. That 70s Show

530

Lists

3. Fawlty Towers
4. M*A*S*H
5. Gilmore Girls (Shameful, I know!)
6. Cheers
7. Johnny Carson Show
8. Barney Miller
9. Survivor
10. Big Brother

FAVORITE MOVIES
1. Planes, Trains and Automobiles
2. Home Alone #1
3. Blues Brothers
4. Field of Dreams
5. The Shining
6. Breaking Away
7. Casablanca
8. Shawshank Redemption
9. Grease
10. Rear Window.

FAVORITE BASEBALL PLAYERS
1. Lou Brock
2. Dick Groat
3. Don Blasingame
4. Wally Moon
5. Jim Edmonds
6. Willie McGee
7. Ernie Banks
8. Pete Rose
9. Bob Gibson
10. Vinegar Bend Mizell

Life Between Innings

FAVORITE BASKETBALL PLAYERS
1. Cliff Hagen
2. Pete Maravich
3. Bob Pettit
4. John Havlichek
5. Jerry West
6. Larry Byrd

FAVORITE BASKETBALL COACHES
1. Bob Knight
2. Rich Grawer

FAVORITE BROADCASTERS
1. Harry Caray
2. Jack Buck
3. Joe Buck
4. Buddy Blattner
5. Vin Scully

TRUE-LIFE HEROES
1. Ken Wild

FAVORITE PREACHERS
1. Rodney Stortz
2. Dan Betzer
3. Billy Graham
4. Chuck Swindoll
5. Bob Mumford
6. C.M. Ward
7. John Hagee
8. Dr. Richard Pratt
9. Henry Redman
10. David Coote

Lists

DEAD PEOPLE I WOULD HAVE LIKED TO HAVE MET
1. Jewell Lee Mooney
2. Walter Cronkite
3. Martin Luther
4. Steve Allen
5. John Calvin
6. Julie London
7. Chuck Colson
8. Franklin D. Roosevelt
9. Harry Truman
10. Marilyn Monroe

LIVING PERSONS I WOULD LIKE TO MEET
1. Billy Graham
2. Bill Gaither
3. Lou Brock
4. Bob Knight
5. Bill Clinton

BEST PRESIDENTS IN MY LIFETIME
1. Bill Clinton (D)
2. Harry Truman (D)
3. Richard Nixon (R)
4. John Kennedy (D)
5. Dwight Eisenhower (R)

WORST PRESIDENTS IN MY LIFETIME
1. George W. Bush, Jr. (R)
2. Ronald Reagan (R)
3. Jimmy Carter (D)
4. Lyndon Johnson (D)
5. George H. Bush, Sr. (R)

*Barack Obama (D) is in his first term but seems headed for this list.

Life Between Innings

MY PRESIDENTIAL VOTING RECORD
1. 1968: voted for former VP <u>Richard Nixon</u> (R) over VP Hubert Humphrey (D) and Gov. George Wallace (I)
2. 1972: voted for Pres. <u>Richard Nixon</u> (R) over Sen. George McGovern (D)
3. 1976: voted for Pres. Gerald Ford (R) over former Gov. <u>Jimmy Carter</u> (D)
4. 1980: voted for former Gov. <u>Ronald Reagan</u> (R) over Pres. Jimmy Carter (D)
5. 1984: voted for former Gov. Walter Mondale (D) over Pres. <u>Ronald Reagan</u> (R)
6. 1988: voted for Gov. Michael Dukakis (D) over VP <u>George Bush, Sr.</u> (R)
7. 1992: voted for Gov. <u>Bill Clinton</u> (D) over Pres. George Bush, Sr. (R)
8. 1996: voted for Pres. <u>Bill Clinton</u> (D) over former Sen. Bob Dole (R) and Businessman Ross Perot (I)
9. 2000: voted for VP Al Gore (D) over <u>George Bush, Jr.</u> (R)
10. 2004: voted for Pres. <u>George Bush, Jr.</u> (R) over Sen. John Kerry (D)
11. 2008: voted for <u>Barack Obama</u> (D) over John McCain (R).

*winner of election is underlined.

FAVORITE RESTAURANTS
1. Chop House (Chicago)
2. Kemolls
3. Nantucket's Cove
4. Dierdorf's and Hart's
5. Ruths' Chris
6. Olympia Tavern
7. Shannon's
8. Uncle Bills (Breakfast)

Lists

PET PEEVES
1. Cluttered, messy house
2. Older children asking for money
3. Being asked a question the second time.
4. Restaurant seating near a child, near the restroom, near the door to the kitchen, near the clean-up area, the first table inside the restaurant, a table in the middle of the room and a chair at the bar. Otherwise, I am happy.
5. Being late or people who consistently run late
6. Referees & poor (sports) officiating in general (All basketball referees are going to Hell . . . count on it).
7. Racism (and reverse racism)
8. Complaining/Excuses
9. People who gossip
10. Do-gooders
11. Guys who wear their ball cap crooked. It may be "styling," but it looks like Gomer Pyle, who we all used to laugh at as being kind of "stupid," because he was. And, you can throw in wearing pants that sag down on the hips as well. There use to be a country comedian named High Pockets who did that and we laughed at him as well because he looked stupid. Enough said.
12. My forgetfulness
13. Handed a phone that I did not answer
14. People who talk without a period at the end of their sentences.
15. Political emails from my conservative-right friends and family.
16. The "Prevent Defense" in football
17. A younger person telling an older person (me) what is good for them or what they will like.
18. Drivers turning left off of a cross street in front of me and having the right-of-way, but not aggressively

Life Between Innings

making their turn, leaving me coming from the side street indecisive as what to do (a wreck waiting to happen) ... *for goodness sake, stop trying to be a do-gooder; just block me off, make your turn in front of me like you are suppose to and then I will know exactly what to do without all the confusion!*

19. Smokers anywhere but especially in my house or car. If they ask nicely first, the answer will always and still be NO!
20. Attempts to pressure me into fishing or camping on the pretense that *I just don't know what I am missing!*
21. Dealing with car rental agents; there like dealing with carnival workers or worse.

REGRETS

In my memoir I say that I have only two regrets, which is true. I truly regret that my divorce led to both (1) Dionne and (2) Marc being victims of a broken home. While I regret it, I no longer live in guilt, as both children have had multiple opportunities to chose better friends and make better decisions that would have resulted in more positive opportunities for life and for work. Here are a few other regrets:

1. Never knowing my father
2. Not pursuing, and not being encouraged to pursue, a profession in the world of athletics such as:
   a. Broadcaster
   b. Sports Journalist
   c. College Basketball Coach
   d. Major League Baseball Umpire
2. Not taking more risks in life
3. Not living a stronger, more committed Christian life.
4. Getting married at age 20.
5. Getting diabetes.
6. Dionne and Marc never ever being able to share in one of our 20-years of great summer beach vacations.

About the author:

Leo Mooney was born in St. Louis, Missouri in 1947, but spent the first 12 years of his life growing up in rural Missouri in the small town of Salem (pop: 3000). As small boys do everywhere, he spent most of his waking hours playing baseball on sandlot fields and basketball on his backyard court.

His father, Jewell, was accidentally killed on the job when he was four months old. However, growing up without a father did not seem to negatively hold him back as his circle of influences were constructive helping to forge his mind and attitude in a positive direction.

Leo states that moving back to St. Louis at age 12 was like "going to heaven," as his beloved St. Louis Cardinals of the National Baseball League and the St. Louis Hawks of the National Basketball Association were located there. He also could buy baseball cards on almost every street corner and play on a variety of baseball fields and basketball courts scattered throughout the neighborhood. More importantly it was here that school actually became a meaningful challenge and Christianity began to have a genuine impact on his life. Perhaps the greatest influence outside of Christianity, however, was discovering and participating in the Boys' Club of St. Louis, an unbelievable place for a boy to grow and learn. It was here that his true hero in life, Mr. Ken Wild, the Director, served as his

Life Between Innings

coach and mentor in both baseball and basketball as well as in life and work.

From such humble beginnings he went on to graduate from O'Fallon Technical High School in St. Louis as a Machinist, graduated from International Bible College in San Antonio, Texas with a Ministerial Diploma, from Meramec Community College of St. Louis with Associate Degrees in Business and Communications, and a Bachelors Degree in Organizational Management from St. Louis University, graduating Magna Cum Laude.

Upon completion of Bible College, he served for over four years in the U.S. Air Force, both as a Communications Specialist and as an Air Traffic Controller. Upon being honorably discharged, he worked for an electrical utility in various power plants prior to his active involvement in Organized Labor as a Business Representative for the International Union of Operating Engineers (Stationary), Local 148. Upon taking early retirement from the Union at age 55, he was fortunate to be able to enjoy two other of his passions serving as a basketball coach at Twin Oaks Christian School, Westminster Christian Academy and Ritenour High School, plus serving as the Director of World Missions at Twin Oaks Presbyterian Church (PCA), all located in St. Louis County.

Leo has been married to his beautiful wife Tina for almost 30 years and has three children: Dionne Reshea, Marcus Vaughn and Whitney Renea.

Made in the USA
Charleston, SC
10 November 2012